In this collection of essays ten anthropologists and two historians develop new cultural and political approaches to human reproduction. Fertility has commonly been treated from a specialized demographic perspective, but today there is widespread dissatisfaction with conventional demographic approaches, which neglect the roles of culture, history and politics in reproductive life. For their part, anthropologists have only recently begun to apply their characteristic approaches to the study of reproduction. Drawing on new ethnographic and historical research and informed by contemporary anthropological theory, this book elaborates a culture and political economy of fertility that incorporates the place of culture and history, gender and power in reproductive life.

Situating fertility

Situating fertility

Anthropology and demographic inquiry

EDITED BY
SUSAN GREENHALGH
University of California, Irvine

Published by the Press Syndicate of the University of Cambridge
The Pitt Building, Trumpington Street, Cambridge CB2 1RP
40 West 20th Street, New York, NY 10011-4211, USA
10 Stamford Road, Oakleigh, Melbourne 3166, Australia

First published 1995

Printed in Great Britain at the University Press, Cambridge

A catalogue record for this book is available from the British Library

Library of Congress cataloguing in publication data
Situating fertility: Anthropology and demographic inquiry
    reproduction / edited by Susan Greenhalgh.
        p.   cm.
    Includes bibliographical references and index.
    ISBN 0 521 47044 7 (hardback) – ISBN 0 521 46999 6 (paperback)
    1. Fertility, Human – Cross-cultural studies.   2. Human
    reproduction – Cross-cultural studies.   3. Demographic anthropology.
    I. Greenhalgh, Susan.
GN241.C85   1995
304.6′32 – dc20   94–28528   CIP

ISBN 0 521 47044 7 hardback
ISBN 0 521 46999 6 paperback

To three people whose resistance to disciplinary hegemonies provided crucial inspiration: Paul, Geoff and Ed.

Contents

Figures

Tables

Contributors

CAROLINE BLEDSOE: Department of Anthropology, Northwestern University

CANDICE BRADLEY: Department of Anthropology, Lawrence University

ANTHONY T. CARTER: Department of Anthropology, University of Rochester

TOM FRICKE: Department of Anthropology and Institute for Social Research, University of Michigan

RACHEL G. FUCHS: Department of History, Arizona State University

SUSAN GREENHALGH: Department of Anthropology, University of California, Irvine

EUGENE A. HAMMEL: Department of Demography, University of California, Berkeley

DAVID I. KERTZER: Departments of Anthropology and History, Brown University

ROBERT LAUNAY: Department of Anthropology, Northwestern University

LESLIE PAGE MOCH: Department of History, University of Michigan, Flint

JANE SCHNEIDER: Program in Anthropology, Graduate School, City University of New York

PETER SCHNEIDER: Division of the Social Sciences, Fordham University, College at Lincoln Center

Preface

Long neglected by cultural anthropology, the subject of human reproduction is now being retrieved and made the focus of scholarly inquiry. Inspired by developments in feminism, political economy, and practice theory, growing numbers of anthropologists are probing the culture and political economy of reproduction. This book seeks to coax form out of this diverse body of studies, thereby making it accessible to colleagues in other branches of the discipline. Our hope is that, by bringing out the intellectual roots and intellectual promise of this new work, we might move this fundamental feature of human life closer to the center of anthropological inquiry.

Because demographers are the main group of scholars who have studied fertility, building an anthropology of reproduction entails critical reflection on and assessment of their work. Demography has developed impressive techniques for analyzing population data, but theoretical work on the sources of fertility change has lapsed. In seeking to improve the understanding of fertility dynamics, we aim not to reinvent the field of demography, but to create a different kind of demography, one better suited to the anthropological enterprise.

This book originated in a session called Rethinking Reproduction: Toward a Political Economy of Fertility, held at the 1990 annual meeting of the American Anthropological Association in New Orleans. Three chapters (those of Anthony Carter, David Kertzer, and Peter and Jane Schneider) were presented at that session and later revised for publication here. The other chapters were solicited from the authors with the aim of getting cutting-edge work in the small but growing field of demographic anthropology. All chapters are original contributions that have not been published elsewhere. The volume originally included two other chapters by the editor, an intellectual, political, and institutional history of demographic theorizing about fertility, and an ethnographic piece on the gender politics of birth planning in China. Due to space limitations those essays had to be omitted.

xiv

Many people have helped in the construction of this volume. Special thanks go to Jessica Kuper, Marigold Acland and Sandy Anthony, at the Press, for their editorial and other assistance, and to Doreen Totaram of the Population Council for creating the consolidated bibliography and helping in a myriad other ways to bring the volume to completion.

Susan Greenhalgh
Dwaarkill, New York
July 1994

Conceiving reproduction:
Trans-disciplinary views

1   Anthropology theorizes reproduction: Integrating practice, political economic, and feminist perspectives

Susan Greenhalgh

Since the end of World War II changing birth rates have had far-reaching consequences for social life. In every region of the world couples have been having fewer children, shrinking the basic unit of social life. Issues surrounding reproduction, once considered the most private and taboo of subjects, have become matters of intense public concern, as neo-Malthusians and environmentalists claim third-world overpopulation as a threat to the future of mankind. Cultural understandings of reproduction have also been transformed, as new technological and biomedical breakthroughs have forced us to rethink our notions of personhood and gender, family and kinship.

As students of human societies and cultures, anthropologists ought to be curious about the causes and effects of these remarkable demographic changes. Yet, until recently, matters relating to human reproduction engaged the attention of a surprisingly small number of cultural anthropologists.[1] (This discussion excludes work in biological anthropology and paleodemography;[2] henceforth "anthropology" is used as shorthand for the cultural branch of the field.) In the 1960s and 1970s the issue of fertility remained the province of the subfields of demographic anthropology, cultural ecology, and cultural materialism.[3] While interest in reproduction was keen in these specialized fields, anthropology at large continued to view social life through the lens of kinship and other traditional theories of the discipline, neglecting the impact of changing human numbers on social and cultural life.

In the last ten years or so, however, things have begun to change. Reflecting the growing salience of reproductive issues at home, where increasing numbers of anthropologists are doing their fieldwork, anthropological interest in matters demographic has picked up.[4] Anthropological demography has also been gradually institutionalized, albeit as a branch of demography rather than anthropology.[5]

Reflecting their diverse intellectual origins – in demography, political

3

economy, and feminism – several anthropologies of reproduction have been developing.[6] Demographic variants such as Penn Handwerker's (1986b, 1986c, 1989) explain fertility outcomes in terms of quantified social and economic variables. Political-economic demographies such as those of Jane and Peter Schneider (1984, 1992) and David Kertzer (1993; also Kertzer and Hogan 1989) stress the links between macro political and economic processes such as the development of capitalism and the modern state, and micro reproductive behavior. Feminist projects such as those of Emily Martin (1987, 1991) and Faye Ginsburg and Rayna Rapp (1991) focus on the politics of the reproductive process, and its implications for gender and cultural constructions of the body, sexuality, and procreation.

This volume, which was inspired by work in all three areas, outlines a broad, synthetic agenda encompassing reproductive dynamics and results. The authors include ten anthropologists, some with strong links to history, and two historians. Drawing on work in several areas of contemporary anthropological theory – practice approaches, political economy, and feminism – the volume situates fertility both theoretically and empirically, placing it in the context of historically developed cultures and political economies. Its larger aim is to draw anthropological attention to this neglected arena of social life in the hope of making reproductive research more central to the anthropological project.

This volume also has contributions to make to demography. Since the late 1970s demographers, led by John Caldwell, have shown growing interest in anthropological approaches to demographic research. Through the use of "quasi-anthropological methods," Caldwell and his collaborators have developed intensive, participant-observation methods into a bona fide (if still rarely employed) style of demographic research (e.g., Caldwell and Caldwell 1987; Caldwell, Reddy, and Caldwell 1982). Since the turn to anthropology a decade or so ago, however, demographers have displayed considerably more interest in anthropological methods and field data than in anthropological theories or even concepts (e.g., Caldwell, Hill, and Hull 1988). With the benefit of ten-plus years of hindsight, one might submit that the demographic appetite for anthropology has been whetted by a somewhat romantic vision of the anthropologist-as-ethnographer (or even modern-day explorer), who lives in remote villages in distant places to discover how the demographic "other" really lives. Such a vision may have fostered the notion, still current today, that the anthropological contribution to demography lies in its ethnographic descriptions and the field methods that elicit them, not in the more fundamental area of theory. Yet it is here, in the area of theory, that anthropology can make its greatest contribution. This is so not only because demography finds itself relatively weak on theory today, but also because anthropology has developed analytic frameworks that provide insight into precisely the forces omitted from conventional demographic theories of fertility. This volume seeks to spell out what that theoretical contribution might be. It offers a reconceptualization of the subject of interest, fertility or reproduction, terms we use synonymously, and new thinking on four aspects of reproductive dynamics: culture, history, gender, and power.

This introductory chapter locates this project in the context of intellectual developments of the post-World War II period. The first section reviews the development of demographic theories of fertility, noting their limitations. The following section outlines an alternative, anthropologically informed culture and political-economy approach to fertility, while the final section highlights the contributions of this volume to its development.

Demographic theories of fertility: A brief overview and critique

Since the mid-1940s, when the understanding of fertility change became a central preoccupation of the field, demography has developed five major theories or groups of theories of fertility dynamics: demographic transition theory, the leading approach until roughly the mid-1970s, and four other sets of explanations developed since then, three "post-classic" transition theories, which dominate fertility research today, and a fourth, much smaller class of institutional approaches to reproductive change.

Classic transition theory

Classic demographic transition theory (or simply transition theory) posited a tripartite transition composed of a pre-transitional phase of high fertility, high mortality, and thus slow population growth; a transitional phase of falling mortality causing rapid population growth before fertility too begins to descend; and a third phase of low vital rates bringing a return to slow or no growth (Davis 1945; Notestein 1945). In this account the transition in fertility was ushered in by broad forces of modernization such as urbanization and industrialization, which altered the economics of childrearing, lowering desired family size.

Classic transition theory was a version of modernization theory, the paradigm of third-world development that dominated social-scientific research on Asia, Africa, and Latin America from the early post-World War II years until roughly the late 1960s. The modernization school, which embraced many disciplines and diverse points of view, created universal theories that were beyond time and place, and that focused on social and economic forces for change, to the exclusion of political and cultural ones (traditional culture was seen as an obstacle to modernizing change).

This class of explanations for third-world development was rooted in nineteenth-century evolutionary theory.[7] Born in the aftermath of the

Table 1.1 *Demographic transition theory as modernization theory: Shared assumptions rooted in evolutionary theory*

1. Fertility transition is a *phased* process. Societies begin with the primitive or traditional state and end with the advanced or modern stage.
2. Fertility transition is a *homogenizing* process that produces tendencies toward convergence among societies.
3. Fertility transition is a *Europeanization* (or Americanization) process.
4. Fertility transition is an *irreversible* process. Once started, it cannot be stopped.
5. Fertility transition is a *progressive* process – in the long run it is desirable.
6. Fertility transition is a *lengthy* process.

Source: Adapted from So 1990:33–34

industrial revolution, evolutionary theory viewed social change as unidirectional and progressive, irreversibly moving societies from a primitive to an advanced stage, making them more alike in the process. Thus, Tonnies spoke of the shift from *Gemeinschaft* to *Gesellschaft*, Durkheim of mechanical and organic solidarity, Spencer of military and industrial society, and so on.

Demographic transition theory shared with other classic modernization theories a set of characteristic assumptions. In his broad review of theories of economic development, sociologist Alvin So provides a useful list of traits that characterized all classic modernization theories (1990:33–36). By substituting "fertility transition" for "modernization" in So's original text, we can see just how closely transition theory conformed to the standard assumptions of the day (see Table 1.1). Although there is not space to document these points of similarity, readers familiar with the mid-1940s work of Frank Notestein (1945) or Kingsley Davis (1945) will readily see how apt these characterizations are.

Post-classic fertility transition theories

Faith in classic transition theory was gradually undermined by the Princeton University-based European Fertility Project (for details see Kertzer, this volume). Launched in 1963, this massive two-decade-long endeavor was designed to test transition theory with historical data from roughly 700 provincial-level units throughout Europe. The results were disappointing: no consistent relation existed between the timing of the onset of fertility decline and measures of social and economic development (Knodel and van de Walle 1979).

While providing little support for the economic and social hypotheses of transition theory, the project did produce one tantalizing lead: fertility was significantly related to "culture," defined operationally as language, ethnicity, or geographical region (Knodel and van de Walle 1979; Watkins

1986). Thus were sown the seeds of the cultural or diffusion interpretation of fertility decline, arguably the trendiest approach in fertility research today. In this interpretation, changes in the economics of childrearing, and thus parental demand for children, do not explain when and why fertility falls. Rather, it is ideational change – more specifically, change in ideas about the acceptability of birth control – that explains when fertility falls (Knodel and van de Walle 1979:239; Cleland and Wilson 1987; Cleland 1985; Watkins 1987, 1990, 1991).

The slow, empirically driven shift from classic transition theory, with its broad emphasis on social and economic modernization, to diffusion theory, with its narrow focus on attitudes toward birth control, divorced from their social and economic context, has been one main strand of theoretical work in social demography over the past twenty years. A second strand, also driven by dissatisfaction with classic transition theory, has emphasized microlevel changes in family organization and the status of women. The best known of these approaches is the wealth-flows theory of John Caldwell. Developed in the late 1970s, this theory tied fertility decline to a reversal in the net intergenerational flow of goods and services (from the older to the younger generation), which followed the emergence of Western ideas regarding the benefits of the non-patriarchal child-centered nuclear family (Caldwell 1976, 1978, 1982). For a number of reasons, however, including difficulties in operationalizing the theory (Thadani 1978; Cain 1982; Schultz 1983), remarkably little research has been done to test Caldwell's ideas. Caldwell himself is no longer actively pursuing the wealth-flows research program.

While classic transition theory and wealth-flows theory included small arrows running from (improved) women's status to (reduced) fertility, in the 1980s women's roles and status moved center stage in a number of part-theories of fertility. Among the most influential of these is that of Karen Mason. Following a broad review of the demographic literature on women and fertility, Mason (1986, 1987) proposed a set of hypotheses connecting "female status" and fertility. Among the most important aspects of women's position for fertility, in her view, are women's education and their position in the family and household. These affect women's autonomy from male control, economic dependency, and social status, which in turn influence child supply, child demand, and child costs. While these and other family-level approaches have considerable merit, so far they have produced little empirical research and even less cumulative theory.

While sociological theories such as those just reviewed have provided the theoretical staple for demographers working in population research centers, microeconomic theories of fertility have preoccupied the smaller number of demographers based in economics departments. In the 1960s the

Chicago School associated with Gary Becker developed a theory of fertility as a branch of the theory of consumer choice (Becker 1960). Children were treated like other consumer durables, costing time and money and providing psychic benefits. Households decided on the optimal number of offspring given their costs, household income, and the household's relative preferences for children and other goods. Less doctrinal and hence more influential have been the theories of Harvey Leibenstein and Richard Easterlin, which take into account the social and biological constraints on the economic process of fertility decision making (Leibenstein 1975; Easterlin 1978; Easterlin and Crimmins 1985).[8] While broader than the consumer-choice models, these later approaches still focus on the economic calculus of fertility decision-making, neglecting contextual and historical forces impinging on those cost–benefit deliberations.

Institutional approaches

A final and very different strand of theorizing is that advanced primarily by Geoffrey McNicoll under the term "institutional determinants of fertility change" (1975, 1980, 1984, 1994; other institutional approaches have been developed by Cain 1981, 1986; Lesthaeghe 1980; Potter 1983). In a recent essay, McNicoll (1994) draws on institutional theory in economics and other fields to explain why fertility transitions, although similar at a distance, appear highly idiosyncratic when viewed at close range. He argues that the pattern of reproductive change is shaped by the institutional endowments each society has inherited from its past – the community structures, family systems, sex roles, and so forth – and by the continuing process of institutionalization of individual behavior as it adjusts to realities, hopes, and expectations. Reviewing five broad patterns of fertility transition or incipient transition that have unfolded in different regions of the world, McNicoll argues that some combinations of institutional endowments permit a smooth path to low fertility, while other combinations impede and delay that process.

Contemporary fertility transition theories: Some puzzling features

From the vantage point of anthropology, much of the recent theorizing about reproduction in demography exhibits two puzzling features: a narrowness of scope and a lingering influence of the Eurocentric theory of modernization developed at mid-century, or, put another way, the absence of any critical – that is, politically oriented – perspectives in the field. The institutional work represents a striking exception to these generalizations. Indeed, as we shall see, it has much in common with the anthropological approaches developed in this book. But first, the critique of the sociological and microeconomic theories, which are the dominant approaches in demography today.

First, the analytic domain of these theories is very narrow. The microeconomic theories are resolutely microlevel, focusing on the individual couple. The sociological approaches broaden the conceptual terrain to include families, kin groups, and personal networks, but the connections between these things and the macro-structures of social life remain *terra incognita.*

Ironically, among the narrowest of approaches is the cultural or diffusion perspective, adopted in reaction to the poor empirical showing of the extremely broad transition theory. While some of the earlier proponents of diffusion theory created places for both development and diffusion mechanisms in their schemes (Retherford and Palmore 1983), more recently the issue has been framed by some in either/or terms, with cultural forces explaining everything, and socioeconomic factors virtually nothing (Cleland and Wilson 1987). The human drama of fertility decline is now reduced to a technological issue, one of the adoption of a modern innovation – contraception – through diffusion.

This formulation has a number of obvious advantages, not the least of which is its stark simplicity. Another strength of the diffusion approach is its ability to model the social structure of contraceptive diffusion, a topic neglected in the past. Yet while the turn to cultural theories after forty years of domination by economic theories would appear to be promising, this particular approach to culture is worryingly reductionistic. It places tremendous analytic weight on communication about contraception, neglecting the distinct possibility that when women get together they chat not only about bedtime inconveniences, but also about their children's schooling, work, and other matters bearing on the socioeconomics of reproduction. Also, by treating culture as something separate from the rest of social life – something that facilitates or obstructs contraceptive communication – it reproduces the functionalist myth that culture can be taken out of social, economic, and political organization. In fact, it is *in* those dimensions of life, shaping the form they assume. The diffusion approach is also problematic in its silence regarding the dynamic of change and its omission of the context of contraceptive communication. Instead of separating culture from context, contraception from socioeconomics, the real challenge is to construct whole demographies that illuminate the mutually constitutive relations between culture and political economy, and the implications of these relations for reproductive actors.

A second perplexing feature of much recent work in demographic theory is the lingering influence of modernization theory or, conversely, the absence of critical perspectives such as those of political economy or feminism – to say nothing of any of the postmodernisms – which entered the other social sciences in the late 1960s, the 1970s, and the 1980s. Even as they abandoned the main hypotheses of classical transition theory, demographers seeking new approaches managed to retain many of the implicit assumptions that underlay it. Indeed, many features of contemporary fertility theory bear the clear stamp of the demographic version of mid-century modernization theory.

For example, the central problematique of most demographic theories of fertility change – how "traditional" fertility regimes become "modern" ones – is clearly formulated in terms of modernization theory's evolutionary and Eurocentric view of societal development. (The institutional approaches are less colored by such presumptions.) In embracing this modernist preoccupation, demographic theories take on a whole series of unstated assumptions that are part and parcel of it: that history moves in a unilinear, predetermined fashion; that History can be collapsed into traditional and modern phases, but histories (small h), including the unique histories of individual societies, play trivial roles in reproductive change; that women's status, a key determinant of fertility, improves with modernization; that fertility transition is caused by and in turn causes further Westernization; and that reproductive Westernization – becoming more like us – is good for everyone.

In social science at large assumptions of this sort have been called into question by successive waves of critical thought, none of which have had much perceptible impact in demography. In the late 1960s and 1970s global political economic perspectives such as dependency and world-systems theories challenged the central tenets of modernization theory, arguing that Western involvement in Asia, Africa, and Latin America produced not development but underdevelopment and permanent inequalities between different parts of the globe. In the 1980s and 1990s the critical edge has shifted to cultural studies, where a variety of broadly postmodernist perspectives have contested Eurocentric presumptions and representations of the world.

Within this new wave of scholarship, the work of the critical geographer James Blaut bears particular relevance to the demography of fertility. In an important new book, *The Colonizer's Model of the World*, Blaut (1993) argues that scholarly work in history, geography, and many other fields is informed by a deep-rooted, often implicit belief in the historical superiority or priority of Europe over the rest of the world (for related critiques see Said 1978; Amin 1988; and the work of postcolonial scholars such as Prakash 1990). This belief forms the core of an overarching worldview, or supertheory, of Eurocentric diffusionism. According to this complex of beliefs, the world has a permanent inside (Europe and its overseas offshoots) and a permanent outside (non-Europe); Europe naturally progresses or modernizes while non-Europe naturally is stagnant or traditional; and cultural change in non-Europe normally occurs through the diffusion of European ideas, technologies, or other influences. While Eurocentric diffusionism was nurtured by colonialism and the European elite's need for scholarly validation of the colonial project, it did not die with the death of formal colonialism after World War II. Rather, it was carried forward in the form of modernization theory, which, as we have seen, postulates that non-Europeans are transformed from "traditional" into "modern" people by the diffusion of European ideas and technologies, a process predicated on the persistence of neocolonial control. Blaut argues that both classical (colonial-era) and modern (post-World War II) diffusionism present fundamentally erroneous views of the world: they are rooted in unsubstantiated beliefs about the superiority of European culture, they emphasize the good things being diffused to the neglect of the bad, and they see non-Europeans as passive recipients of European diffusion, denying their role in the transformation of their own cultures and those of Europe.

While this is not the place to elaborate a lengthy critique of the demographic assumptions – an abbreviated critique similar in key respects to that of Blaut is offered below – it is the place to express wonderment that such a critique was not systematically developed in the field in the past. Demographers' own assessments of their field suggest that such a critique is urgently needed. Over the last decade or so a long line of eminent demographers has bemoaned the disappointing state of the field. By these accounts, demography is theoretically thin, substantively shrinking, and neglectful of global political and economic changes that are transforming its object of study. In 1980 Geoffrey McNicoll wrote: "It is widely agreed that we do not have an adequate *theory* of fertility, if by theory we mean a coherent body of analysis linking a characterization of society and economy, aggregate or local, to individual fertility decisions and outcomes, able to withstand scrutiny against the empirical record" (1980:441). Although classic transition theory has virtually ceased to be an area of theory building (van de Walle 1992:488), nothing of similar scope has taken its place, leaving, in Samuel Preston's judgment, a field lacking in ideas (in Holden 1984).

With loss of theoretical vigor, the field finds it cannot even hold onto its substantive turf. Nathan Keyfitz has observed that: "Far from being imperialistic, [demography] has withdrawn from its borders and left a no man's land which other disciplines have infiltrated" (1984:1). As the field has contracted, it has become inattentive to major political and economic developments of the day that may bear fundamentally on demographic change. In a plea for a "demography for a more turbulent world," McNicoll (1992) has argued that profound changes in the post-Cold-War world – altered North–South relations, renewed ethnic polarizations, environmental changes that respect no borders, among others – are turning what are now treated as background variables, safely assumed away, into active forces for demographic change. Yet, with very few exceptions, demographers have shown little interest in such matters. In a familiar disciplinary trajectory, demographers are now preoccupied with technical issues, "bankclerkly and backroom activities that . . . are increasingly divorced from any larger, cumulative social scientific enterprise" (1992:400).

Despite their dismay over the current state of affairs, none of these writers has proposed abandoning the demographic project. Their hope, rather, is that something might be done to reinvigorate the field. The authors of this book hope to contribute to this process of disciplinary critique and reconstruction by illuminating the constricting effects of the modernization and other assumptions on reproductive theorizing, and by proposing new, anthropological and historical approaches to fertility analysis that might complement the work done by more quantitative researchers.

Situating fertility: Toward a culture and political economy of reproduction

What should the agenda of an anthropology of reproduction be? The hallmark of anthropology is its holism, its attempt to achieve broad, multi-angled understandings of the phenomena of interest. In fertility research, the aim would be the creation of "whole demographies" that contextualize reproductive behavior not only in the social and economic terms of conventional demographic theory, but in political and cultural terms as well.

Though rooted in contemporary anthropological theory, these whole demographies have much in common with the institutional demography of Geoffrey McNicoll (esp. 1994). In contrast to the universalizing and quantifying thrusts of most demographies, McNicoll's institutional demography recognizes historical contingency and societal specificity, and embraces narrative modes of explanation that can accommodate such forces as gender and power that are difficult to incorporate into standard empirical models of demographic behavior. Where the two differ is perhaps in emphasis. While both attend to societal structure and individual agency, by definition the institutional approach gives greater weight to structures, while the anthropological work pays more attention to agency.

Political economy, feminism, and practice approaches: Analytic tools

In constructing such whole demographies, this volume draws on three areas of contemporary anthropological theorizing: political economy, feminism, and social constructionism or, more generally, practice approaches to social life.

The anthropological political economy that emerged in the 1970s and 1980s drew attention to history and power writ large. Neither world-systems nor dependency theory, anthropological political economy reached back to an earlier version of culture history to focus on the construction of anthropological subjects at the intersection of local and global histories (Roseberry 1988, 1989; also Wolf 1982). Clearly, such macro-processes as the extension of capitalist relations of production, the rise of states interested in counting, surveilling, and policing their families, and the spread of family planning institutions and ideologies to the most remote corners of the third world have profound effects on childbearing behavior. By bringing these forces into the picture we can greatly widen the scope of reproductive theory.

In an earlier essay I argued that anthropological political economy provides the broadest possible rubric for the construction of whole demographies (Greenhalgh 1990). That essay charted the contours of a political economy of fertility that took as its object the location of demographic subjects at the conjuncture of historically developed local, regional, national, and global processes. Political-economic demography is a form of institutional demography that directs attention to the embeddedness of community institutions shaping fertility in structures and processes operating at regional, national, and global levels, and to the historical roots of those macro–micro linkages. In contrast to most demographic approaches, which tend to stress the individual level, to neglect history and politics, and to rely heavily on quantitative data and methods, a political economy of fertility is a multi-leveled field of inquiry that is explicitly historical and attentive to political and economic as well as social and cultural forces. It combines societal structure and individual agency, both of which generally escape the demographer's attention, and draws on both quantitative and qualitative research methods and materials. Although it incorporates action on multiple levels and in many domains of social life, demographic political economy sees reproductive life as, in Sherry Ortner's words, "a relatively seamless whole" (1984:148). The aim is not to decide which level is primary, or to "break the system into artificial chunks" – society, culture, polity, economy; or, as in demographic practice, fertility, mortality, nuptiality, migration. The objective, rather, is to understand how a particular set of reproductive institutions and behaviors evolved and how its constitutive elements relate to each other. The chapters in this book, which all engage political economy at some ethnographic level, demonstrate the ability of a demographic political economy to illuminate reproductive dynamics in a wide range of spatial and temporal settings.

This book also broadens the earlier agenda by incorporating more fully into the analysis two features of social life with special import to the reproductive process: culture and gender. Given fertility's place in the creation and perpetuation of families and kin groups, communities and nation-states, it has come to be surrounded by a thicket of confusing, conflicting, contested, and vitally consequential moral values. Untangling these broadly cultural processes must be a central task of reproductive research. Hence, our approach might be called a "culture and political economy of fertility" in recognition of the special role of culture in shaping reproductive outcomes.[9]

Reproduction is a deeply gendered process. Physiologically, only women can give birth, but men are required to produce the life force. Socially, women are usually assigned the "reproductive work" of raising the next generation. As a result of these biological and social facts, reproduction has come to be enwrapped in gender relations, relations of difference and inequality in beliefs, resources, and power. Gender analysis is central to reproductive research, and feminist approaches, which take gender as their organizing concept, occupy a special place in our analytic repertoire. By stressing women's agency in constructing their own reproductive outcomes, the complex and contradictory character of change in gender relations, and the pervasiveness of gender in all of social life, feminist approaches allow us to broaden the intellectual agenda beyond that offered by the conventional women's-status approach to gender and fertility.

Social constructionism – the view that social organization is not given by broad societal norms, but is a human product, actively constructed by human agents – suggests ways to think about social relations and group formation in dynamic, politically informed ways. This shift from societal norm to individual agency was part of a larger development in the 1970s and 1980s of "practice" approaches that sought to clarify the complex and mutually constitutive relations between structure and action (Berger and Luckmann 1967; Bourdieu 1977; Giddens 1979). Because marriage and kinship were prime arenas for theorizing in this area, it was perhaps natural that anthropologists interested in the family would extend this perspective downward to the family and fertility. Doing so has allowed us to reconceptualize reproduction, transforming it from a biological event, the demographic view, into a socially constructed process.

In demography fertility is a biological term: what matters is the number of live births, regardless of whether the children live or die, are raised by their biological parents or someone else. In a popular model of fertility causation, social and cultural factors affect fertility only as they work through a small number of biological and behavioral "proximate determinants" (Bongaarts 1978). Similarly, in "natural fertility" populations, biological, or "supply" factors are held to explain virtually all variation in the age pattern of fertility (Knodel 1983:69–70). This is maintained despite considerable evidence, especially in the anthropological literature, of deliberate tampering with the spacing of births (e.g., Ohadike 1977; Cashdan 1985; Bledsoe et al. 1994). Research on the demand for children also reflects the biological assumption that parents raise, and thus pay the costs and enjoy the benefits of, only the children they bear (Bledsoe 1990b).

While biological factors are of obvious importance, for cultural anthropologists the biological view must be supplemented with a social one that takes account of the myriad means people use to transform their biological fertility into their social families. Over the years, anthropologists working in many parts of the world have documented the abundant cultural means people have devised to regulate their fertility, both prenatally and postnatally (on prenatal methods see Devereux 1955; on postnatal methods Scrimshaw 1983; a useful review of this work is Nardi 1981). It is only very recently, however, that this ethnographic insight – that people without access to modern contraception take steps to limit their family size – has been theorized in terms of contemporary notions of social constructionism. Drawing on the practice and processual approaches of Bourdieu (1977), Comaroff and Roberts (1981), and others, Caroline Bledsoe has argued that not only social reality (Berger and Luckmann 1967), but also demographic reality is a social construction. This approach:

> stresses the fundamental ambiguity of biological . . . relations, highlighting people's active efforts to achieve demographic outcomes by restructuring household compositions and influencing children's obligations, rather than acting strictly within the biological bounds or cultural norms that seem to be imposed on them. Individuals constantly tinker with family structures in ways that cumbersome biological acts of fertility cannot. (1990b:97–98)

In this book the social construction of the family is seen as a political process that unfolds over time. It is political in that relations of power within society both shape reproductive practices and in turn are shaped by them. It is dynamic in that the social management of the family begins prenatally, with the manipulation of marriage and birth control practices such as contraception and abortion, and continues long into the postnatal period, through infanticide, fosterage, adoption, and a myriad other means. Thus, micro-power and micro-history become crucial dimensions of reproductive process.

Undoing the Eurocentric and evolutionary assumptions of demographic transition theories

A culture and political-economy perspective stands in sharp contrast to most demographic approaches to fertility. Virtually all the non-institutional theories of the demographic transition, both classical and post-classical, make four key assumptions: first, there is but one pattern of change that all societies undergo, that of moving from "tradition" to "modernity"; second, this pattern of change is one of movement toward Western-type lifestyles which include, among other things, low fertility; third, change of this sort is irreversible, once set in train; and, fourth, it is progressive and ultimately good.

A culture and political-economy approach is based on a different set of assumptions. Adherents of this approach read global reproductive history (to the extent that it has been written, which is not great) as saying that there are more than two kinds of reproductive arrangements (or three, if one includes the transitional one). That is, there may be more, and more intriguing, variations between high-fertility societies, or between low-fertility societies, than there are between high- and low-fertility societies. There are, in short, many kinds of reproductive institutions and outcomes, each worthy of investigation in its own right. The espousal of a culture and political-economy approach entails the rejection of one of the central assumptions of demographic research: that the shift from high to low fertility (in which, of course, Europe *was* historically prior) is the most interesting and important object of demographic study.

Second, students of the culture and political economy of fertility challenge the assumption that demographic change invariably follows Western patterns. Like institutional demographers, they argue that demographic dynamics follow distinct cultural logics. While some demographers have noted culture's effect on the pattern of demographic change (for example, how it "diffuses" from one place to another), many anthropologists would broaden the influence of culture to embrace the direction of reproductive change. They would thus harbor strong doubts about the third assumption spelled out above, that low fertility is the end point of demographic history. This depends not only on the culture, but also on the political economy in which reproduction is embedded. Finally, proponents of a cultural political-economy perspective would question the notion that low fertility is necessarily good or "progressive." What is good is culturally conditioned. Low fertility may be best for Western societies, but bad for sub-Saharan African ones. What is good is also group-specific. Having few children may benefit the upper classes but hurt the lower ones. Something that is good in some respects may be bad in others. Thus, rapid fertility reduction may increase per capita income but destroy the social and cultural fabric of people's lives.

In general, the labels "traditional" and "modern" might be considered objectionable on grounds of their ethnocentricity and their innocence of (or blindness to) the power differentials between those who are studying and trying to change the fertility of others, and the objects of these study and change efforts, whose fertility behavior is labeled "traditional" and "natural" (and, by extension, less civilized). Like the dualisms of modernization theory, the traditional/modern and natural/controlled labels in demography may serve to mystify more than to clarify a complex reality. They mystify demographic behavior by embedding and thereby perpetuating implicit assumptions about rationality and progressiveness that are both ethnocentric and scientifically suspect. Anthony Carter, for example, elucidates the human controls exerted over childbearing in "natural" fertility populations, and the limited control achieved by many women in "controlled" fertility groups. Peter and Jane Schneider look behind the apparent irrationality of early twentieth-century Sicilian laborers, whose huge families were impoverishing them. They show that reproductive "irrationality" is produced not by ignorance and backwardness, but by power differentials that constrain people to have many children at the expense of their own well-being. Their work and that of others in this book makes clear that power is fundamental to reproduction; when it is assumed away we lose our ability to understand how the world really works, especially for the powerless.

An anthropology of reproduction eschews these ideologically tinged labels and concerns itself with all types of reproductive arrangements, regardless of the degree and direction of change. A working assumption is that there are many kinds of fertility patterns, all of interest, and each shaped by a combination of forces that is to some degree spatially, temporally, and culturally specific. Given our limited understanding of the diversity of reproductive behaviors throughout history, and of the forces that shape them, a central aim of current research is to *situate fertility*, that is, to show how it makes sense given the sociocultural and political economic context in which it is embedded. The eight ethnographic chapters in this book elucidate the dynamics of specific cases. Once enough cases are collected and understood, they might serve as the building blocks of more general understandings of reproductive dynamics.

Other anthropologies of fertility: Historical precedents and alternative visions

While a culture and political economy of fertility grows out of the dissatisfaction of anthropologists with demographic theories of fertility decline, the research of today can be seen as building on work in demographic anthropology that was done in the 1960s and 1970s. One can discern two relatively distinct streams of research in those decades, a first methodological, a second more theoretical.[10] The methodological work, in particular that of Nancy Howell (e.g., 1974, 1976, 1979), formulated data collection techniques suitable to the rigorous measurement of population processes in non-literate, especially hunting and gathering societies, and provided solid empirical evidence for demographic processes in those types of societies, which had been little studied by population specialists. The substantive work, as well as the reviews of the small sub-field of demographic anthropology in widely read publications such as the *Annual Review of Anthropology*, paved the way for today's research by providing measurement tools for those studying non-literate societies, fostering appreciation of the value of demographic methods, and legitimizing demography as an area of anthropological inquiry.

The more broadly theoretical work, in areas as diverse as ecological anthropology (Polgar 1975; Macfarlane 1976; Netting 1981), social anthropology (Lorimer 1954; Nag 1962, 1975) and family planning research (Polgar 1971; Mamdani 1972; Marshall and Polgar 1976), explored population processes within their social and environmental contexts. Although these scholars were primarily concerned with social organization at the community level, their work can be seen as a precursor to today's more cultural and political-economic investigations of reproduction. The critiques of family planning programs, though not theoretically oriented, are certainly consistent with current themes in political economy. And some of the insights into the social factors affecting fertility inform today's thinking. In general, one might say that this earlier work has been enveloped by today's broader, more theoretically explicit approaches that treat community-level social factors as one set of a much wider array of factors impinging on reproductive life.

Before proceeding, a note on inter- and intra-disciplinary dialogue. Because demographers are the primary group of social scientists who study human fertility, in this volume we direct our attention largely to the work in demography. However, much of what we have to say applies with equal force to a number of anthropological approaches to fertility. For example, recent evolutionary, cultural ecological, and cultural materialist approaches to fertility, while having the advantages of providing the "long view," and of highlighting important relationships between population and resources, nevertheless afford little opportunity to explore the sorts of nuanced political, historical, and gendered processes that we argue are fundamental to the understanding of fertility process and outcome. Nor do all anthropologists share our concerns about the assumptions underlying modernization theories. Some anthropologists (e.g., Handwerker 1986c, 1989) have advanced complex, evolutionary approaches embodying features of the modernization approach that is the particular target here. Developing a dialogue within anthropology – especially between the increasingly popular evolutionary and culture and political-economy perspectives – is an important project for the future.

Culture and history, gender and power in reproductive life

I argued above that demographic theories of fertility omit or misspecify the role of a number of reproductive forces considered important by anthropologists. In this section I elaborate the critique, highlighting the contributions of this book to alternative understandings of how those forces operate.

Culture and agency

Of all the concepts employed by demographers, it is the treatment of culture that has left anthropologists most dissatisfied. In an illuminating essay on culture in demography, Eugene Hammel (1990b) reviewed the history of anthropological notions of culture, and showed how demographic research has invariably drawn on older definitions, neglecting newer meanings that may have special relevance to demographic behavior. As he put it, "the use of 'culture' in demography seems mired in structural-functional concepts that are about 40 years old, hardening rapidly, and showing every sign of fossilization" (1990b:456).

In his contribution to this volume, Carter argues that, until recently, two concepts of culture and human agency have dominated thinking in demographic research on fertility. Caricaturing slightly for analytic emphasis, he calls these the passive concept, which envisions people as mindlessly adhering to cultural rules, and the active concept, which portrays them as conscious decision makers who deliberately choose their fertility levels through abstract rationality. However, the passive notion of culture, which denies people agency, or the ability to shape their own lives, breaks down before ethnographic fact. The active notion of people as rational utility maximizers is equally unsatisfactory, for real maximization is too time-consuming and complex to be a workable cognitive modus operandi.

The chapters in this volume propose two solutions to Carter's problem of giving demographic actors agency without endowing them with a utility-maximizing rationality. The first is developed by Carter himself. Drawing on the work of Anthony Giddens and Jean Lave, he interprets human agency not as a sequence of discrete acts of choice and planning, the standard view, but as a reflexive monitoring and rationalization of a continuous flow of conduct, in which practice is constituted in dialectical relation between persons acting and the settings of their activities. In this way, both cultural concepts – the values assigned to different behaviors – and political economy – the forces creating the setting – become ingredients to, rather than external to, action, and the human agent is placed center stage.

Carter's solution to the problem of agency requires a micro-micro research program. A second, more macrolevel solution is proposed by the Schneiders. They are concerned with why people caught in the demographic trap of high fertility and low mortality sometimes are unable to escape. Rejecting both culturalist (passive) models which see such people as fatalistic, and "demand for labor" (active) models which hold that they have a conscious preference for many offspring, the Schneiders argue that in such circumstances the exercise of "rationality" is likely to be constrained by relations of power. In the Sicilian case studied, they argue that the landless laborers were prevented from lowering their fertility by interclass relations of dominance/subordination that robbed them of the abilities to imagine and to achieve smaller families.

The recent elaboration of a diffusion approach to fertility change has added a third sense of culture, which some contributors to this volume see as equally problematic.[11] In this approach culture is used in two senses: first, as a facilitator or inhibitor of the spread (diffusion) of knowledge about contraception measurable by common language, ethnicity, and/or region; and second, as an evaluative mechanism by which people, generally pictured as women, evaluate their contraceptive options (Watkins 1990). Reviewing this work in Chapter 2, David Kertzer complains that what these demographers mean by culture is often unclear; that some authors conflate culture and social structure; and that features selected as "cultural" are chosen on the basis not of theory, but of their availability in the data file. Eugene Hammel's chapter on historical fertility change in the northwest Balkans casts doubt on the usefulness of ethnicity (and language) as variables in explaining reproductive change. Despite its embrace by the people of the Balkans themselves, Hammel finds that ethnicity disappears as a reproductive force when larger political forces are brought into the picture. On a microlevel, he shows that economic factors are more salient than ethnic ones in explaining reproductive outcomes. Hammel sees ethnicity and local culture as important only because positions in the socioeconomic structure have been allocated to distinct ethnic groups by imperial political elites.

History

In most demographic theories of the fertility transition, reproductive behavior is extracted from its real historical context and fitted into abstract, metaphorical histories that all societies are said to undergo. In these models neither historical phase, tradition or modernity, itself has a history: in the former vital rates are portrayed as stable and high; in the latter they are stable and low. Within these two phases time stands still. It is only during the transitional phase – when first mortality and then fertility rates fall – that change takes place. In this way, history is flattened and removed from demographic inquiry.

While "real history" is increasingly entering demographic discourse (see for example Lesthaeghe and Surkyn 1988; van de Walle 1992), a good deal of demographic research on fertility continues to be ahistorical. Descriptions and analyses of fertility at the microlevel invariably exist in historical vacuums. Similarly, cross-national empirical research is built on the assumption that the specific histories of the countries included have little relevance to their fertility levels.

Reflecting anthropology's rapprochement with history in the 1980s, anthropological political economy takes it as axiomatic that an analysis of the historically developed political economy at local and supralocal levels is essential to the understanding of all aspects of local life. This history, however, is not the old-fashioned one of "something that happens to people." Rather, history is seen as something people make, within the powerful constraints imposed by the political and economic structures of their societies (Thompson 1963, 1978; Roseberry 1989). Following Eric Wolf (1982), the history of anthropological political economy is history of global scale, one that resists a view of the world as a congeries of bounded societies, cultures, or populations, seeing it instead as an interconnected totality in which developed and underdeveloped, we and they, are participants in the same historical trajectory.

The chapters in this book suggest how real history can be made an ingredient of demographic practice, and actors an ingredient of history. Robert Launay places macro-political history at the center of his story of demographic change. In his chapter on the Dyula of Côte d'Ivoire, he ties the increase in public illegitimacy to changes in the wider political economy – the politics of local factionalism and the economics of weaving and the cloth trade – that undermined the political and the economic rationality behind the formation of large, solidary kinship groups. With control over group members no longer a strategic resource, clan heads lost interest in claiming excess members, and children with dubious origins were cast aside as illegitimate.

Other chapters write different elements of this new, non-oppositional, history-as-history-making into their accounts of reproductive life. In the essay by historians Rachel Fuchs and Leslie Moch, Parisian women during the Third Republic (1871–1914) are shown making their own history by constructing networks of kin and friends through which they can pursue their reproductive agendas.[12] In Tom Fricke's chapter, the Himalayan Tamang, a pre-transitional population, is treated not as a stable society, a baseline against which change can be measured. Rather, in his account this population itself has a history, and it is one of state intervention in local life to create social hierarchies that in turn produce demographic inequalities. The Schneiders' contribution illustrates well the interconnections between traditional and modern, them and us. In their portrayal the "traditional" reproductive behavior of Sicily's landless laborers is a modern construction, formed by interclass relations of inequality. And the demographic fate of "them" – here, the Sicilian peasantry – becomes intimately bound up with that of "us," when emigration to the US is blocked by economic depression and anti-immigration laws in the US These chapters convey a vision not of isolated populations – traditional and modern, them and us – but of reproductively interconnected groups, classes, and parts of the world economy, in which people shape history and history shapes them.

Time is also important at the microlevel of the individual life course. Demographic students of reproduction tend to imagine that fertility decisions are made once-and-for-all, generally at the beginning of the reproductive lifespan, with at most small adjustments after that. In this way they make people into timeless strategizers who never change their minds. In doing so they neglect the ambiguity, spontaneity, and improvisation, the bungling, changing-of-mind, and full-scale about-faces that characterize most peoples' lives, reproductive and otherwise (cf. Rosaldo 1989:91–108).

The practice and other processual approaches that emerged in anthropology in the 1980s made the temporal organization of individual action a central concern. Instead of accounting for practices in terms of fixed cultural rules, researchers see the practices themselves as having a developmental structure that works itself out over time (Bourdieu 1977:9). In these views time is not merely lived, but is "constructed" in the living. In new research on "modes of temporalization," descriptions of activities take account of the irreversible, ongoing time of activities, agents' strategic manipulation of time, and the form imparted to action by time (Munn 1992:105–109).

This new anthropology of microtime has obvious relevance to the practices of childbearing. Real demographic actors constantly monitor their reproductive activities, fine-tuning and micro-modifying them as the need arises. Bledsoe's previous research documents these temporalizations for the Mende, showing how reproductive actors ongoingly tinker with their biology, and how that tinkering has a definite, reconstructible temporal sequence and structure that follows Mende cultural logic (Bledsoe 1980, 1990b, 1993; Bledsoe and Isiugo-Abanihe 1989; see also Renne 1993).

Bledsoe and Carter elaborate on these points, showing how microhistory, or individual time, might be made more central to the anthropological analysis of reproduction. Working again with the Mende, Bledsoe questions the notion, common in demographic research, that children have comparatively stable values that aggregate into a single, relatively fixed desired family size. In Mende society, she shows, the value placed on specific children can change from one time to another as their mothers' relations with the children's fathers and other males undergo change. Children who are initially valued, because they are offspring of current unions, can be just as easily de-valued and deprived of resources when the union goes sour. Bledsoe brings time into the analysis by seeing children not as ends in themselves, but as symbols of the ongoing ebb and flow of adult relationships.

Carter's notion of flows-in-conduct provides another kind of tool for exploring the microhistory of reproductive decision making. In this view decisions are distributed along the whole reproductive life cycle. People intervene only at certain decision points that may occur at various times during the course of family formation. In North India, for example, cultural constructions of the body and of pregnancy help to define decision points at which women may intercede in the flow of reproductive events. Missed menstrual periods, for example, may provide an opportunity to "regulate" menstruation through the use of abortifacients. Carter's work points the way to a temporalized account of reproductive practice that analyzes the temporal structure of reproductive activities, the strategic manipulation of timing by actors, and the fertility consequences of these manipulations.

Gender

Although women's activities and lives have played increasingly prominent roles in demographic explanations of fertility, demography has remained curiously resistant to the sorts of feminist interrogation and transformation that fields such as anthropology, history, and sociology have undergone. In anthropology, for example, the understanding of sex-linked differences has moved from a prefeminist state in which women were neglected or misrepresented, to an "anthropology of women" in the 1970s, in which androcentric biases were corrected and women's experiences retrieved for scholarly analysis, to an "anthropology of gender" in the 1980s and 1990s, in which fundamental assumptions, concepts, and theories are being critically examined and reformulated.

In the mid-1990s, demography remains lodged somewhere between a prefeminist stage and a "demography of women." Women's social and economic characteristics appear increasingly often as variables in demographic models, suggesting the emergence of a demography of women. At the same time, however, the field seems almost prefeminist in the implicit assumptions and biases that inform its work (for example, that only women aged 15-49 are reproductively "dynamic" and thus worth studying, that women and men occupy separate spheres, the former private, the latter public) and in the narrow range of women's characteristics considered demographically important (Watkins 1993:559). The second step in the feminist transformation of knowledge, the rethinking of basic analytic categories, remains not only undone, but largely unrecognized as a task worth doing.

The intellectual gulf between demography and these other fields can be seen in the choice of concepts guiding research on women. The demographic literature on fertility relies on two concepts about women that have been widely critiqued and have increasingly fallen into disuse in feminist studies at large: women's roles (e.g., Anker et al. 1982; Oppong 1983) and, more commonly, women's status (Mason 1986, 1987). (A third, less frequently used concept, female autonomy [e.g., Dyson and Moore 1983], is subject to the same sorts of criticisms.) While the status concept has obvious appeal to a quantitative discipline like demography, the continued use of women's roles and status in demographic research is worrying. Use of these notions not only neglects problems highlighted by scholars in other fields, but also allows demographers to think they have "done women" – and often rejected "the variable" as unimportant – when in fact they have hardly scratched the surface (for elaboration see Riley 1993).

During the 1970s and 1980s these concepts were called sharply into question by feminist scholars in many disciplines (Connell 1985; Stacey and Thorne 1985; Moore 1988; Mukhopadhyay and Higgins 1988; Scott 1988a; Ferree 1990). Both notions treat sex-linked differences as individual- or family-level attributes, ignoring inequalities in larger societal institutions. They assume that "women" or "sex roles" are universal constructs, neglecting differences across culture, class, ethnic group, and nationality. Both terms are profoundly ethnocentric, based on Western values that may have little meaning in other contexts. Both are objectifying, seeing women as passive objects acted upon by others, rather than agents of their own lives. Finally, both constructs are radically depoliticizing, "strip[ping] experience from its historical and political context and neglect[ing] questions of power and conflict" (Stacey and Thorne 1985:307).

In feminist research in anthropology and history (as well as sociology), notions of women's roles and status have given way to notions of gender. Gender differs from these constructs in several crucial respects: it entails the study of men as well as women; it is a cultural construction rather than culture-free; it denotes power differentials and sex-related ideologies as well as material inequalities; and it is a structuring principle of social life rather than simply an attribute of individuals. The gender construct thus provides a powerful tool for exploring the influence of male–female differences and disparities on fertility. The implied research agenda is staggeringly broad.

Although we are nowhere near a comprehensive understanding of how gender shapes reproduction in different times and places, the chapters in this book suggest some elements of a truly gendered understanding of fertility dynamics and outcomes.[13] We make three points. First, gender is a pervasive force that structures all aspects of life. Reproductive life is no exception. In their chapter on the reproductive strategies of poor Parisian women in the last century, for example, Fuchs and Moch describe the gendered character of the networks through which migrant women sought marriage partners, abortions, and aid with childcare. Not only did women make much more use of networks of kin and friendship than did men, but their networks took on a distinctly female quality: they were activated in female spaces, and were tied together by women in female occupations.

Second, gender connotes agency. Some demographers, seeking to emphasize the subordination of third-world women and its profound impact on their childbearing options, have portrayed them as passive victims of patriarchal institutions who have little choice but to surround themselves with many children (Caldwell 1978; Cain et al. 1979). While there is a large element of truth in these portrayals, they paint too passive a picture of women in patriarchal societies. Even in North India, where women are subject to their husband's authority in all matters reproductive, women secretly defy their husbands and in-laws, going behind their backs to arrange for contraception and abortions (see Carter, this volume). Even in China, where women are subject to some of the harshest fertility controls in the world today, they manage to resist the state's one-child-per-family policy, and to negotiate a new, informal version of that policy that is more consistent with their fundamental reproductive needs (Greenhalgh 1994; at times, however, their resistance is no match for the power of the state [Greenhalgh and Li 1995]).

Following research in history and anthropology, the contributors to this book maintain that women are not just victims of oppressive systems, but are also social actors who use the resources at their disposal to devise strategies that challenge – and sometimes alter – the systems that oppress them. They are thus active agents of their own reproductive destinies (see also Martin 1987; Fuchs and Moch 1990; Rapp 1990, 1991). Fuchs and Moch stress the agency of Parisian women whose social constructions – networks of information sharing and mutual support – helped them solve critical reproductive problems. Though invisible, these networks were strategic resources in a world that offered few protections.

Third, theories of gender are less optimistic and more agnostic about the direction of change in gender relations and thus in women's lives. Demographic theories of fertility predict that women's status will improve with social and economic modernization, prompting fertility decline. Perhaps because demographers have relied almost exclusively on measures of women's status, defined in social and economic terms, the notion that women's lives have gotten, or will eventually get better has persisted in the field despite twenty-five years of research in the field of women and development showing at best mixed gains and contradictory changes. Candice Bradley's chapter challenges the views that women's lives are steadily improving and that increases in socioeconomic status lead to fertility decline. In her study of western Kenya, she shows that socioeconomic development may empower women through improvements in education, employment, and political voice. But at the same time women may lose ground in other areas. In a context of shrinking job opportunities, the redistribution of resources toward women is strongly resisted by men, resulting in rising levels of domestic violence in which women are, indeed, victims. Bradley's chapter suggests that the pattern of change is complex and multidirectional, and that it is scarcity in the wider economy, not the empowerment of women, that has underlain Kenya's fertility decline.

Power and politics

As noted above, demographic theories of fertility tend to be consensus theories that neglect the role of power and politics, conflict and inequality in the reproductive process. The diffusion approach illustrates this idyllic, conflict-free view of the world particularly well (see esp. Retherford and Palmore 1983). At the community and societal levels, the pace of diffusion is affected by "social integration," which depends on such "good things" as good communication, shared values, cultural homogeneity, and common political authority (1983:767). Contrary to accumulated anthropological and historical wisdoms, small village populations are thought to have a high degree of social integration, and thus to foster the diffusion of contraceptive knowledge (1983:771). In the rare case that the sources of the contraceptive technology – in the contemporary period, international agencies and state bureaucracies – are brought into the picture, they are seen as benign forces, "catalytic" agents of diffusion that have "provided the critical spark to get things moving" (1983:778).

The small body of work on the politics of fertility by political scientists, political sociologists, and social historians challenges such consensus accounts, suggesting that power and politics are central to reproductive process. This literature illuminates the activities of states in regulating family life, both directly and indirectly (e.g., Gillis et al. 1992:Section IV), and the contests that have developed over such issues as the definition of the population problem in the international population community (Finkle and Crane 1975, 1976, 1985) and the direction of national population policies and programs (Warwick 1982, 1986; Ness and Ando 1984; Finkle and McIntosh 1994). Even the numbers demographers use turn out, on inspection, to be political artifacts (Alonso and Starr 1987).

Such work tends to focus on the politics of formal organizations. By contrast, the distinctive contribution of this book (as well as other anthropological studies cited above) is to tease out the informal politics of reproduction by extending recent anthropological concern with relations of power to the demographic domain. We probe reproductive politics at the microlevel of individuals, households, networks, and communities; at the "meso" level of clan, class, and gender groupings; and at the macrolevel of the state.

At the micro-political level, Launay illumines the role of power in the production of illegitimacy. Among the Dyula, which children are declared illegitimate is determined less by the cultural rules than by the distribution of power to apply them by labeling someone a bastard. Reproductive outcomes are also shaped at the meso level by conflicts and inequalities between groups within society. Among the Tamang of Nepal, Fricke shows, members of hierarchically ranked clan groupings manipulate culturally given possibilities of marriage in an intergroup competition for advantages in the flow of obligations and labor. Adopted to enhance status and resources, marriage strategies also affect fertility outcomes. In Kenya, Bradley argues, the recent decline in fertility is due less to the empowerment of women than to the deterioration of the economy and the struggle between men and women for pieces of the shrinking pie. At the macrolevel, states are important reproductive actors with their own interests in surveilling and controlling the population. The Hapsburg state emerges as a major demographic actor in Hammel's historical account of fertility change in the Balkans. In the military border area of the region studied, fertility was heavily conditioned by Austrian policies that controlled household division, buffered the population from economic shocks, and required service in an unending series of military campaigns.

Overview of the volume

This book contains three parts, each elaborating a different facet of the culture and political economy of fertility. This first part suggests new ways to conceive reproduction. Moving back and forth between anthropology and demography, it shows how concepts and analytic approaches from anthropology (and, to a lesser extent, history) can illuminate reproductive behavior, and why they are needed at this point in the history of demographic theorizing.

The second part explores the social management of fertility, illuminating the agency of individual reproductive actors and the political processes at individual, family, and community levels that shape the social construction of reproduction. The third part probes the reproductive consequences of inequality and conflict among groups and categories of individuals within society – in particular, gender, class, and clan – and highlights the impact of historical changes in the macro political economy on these contests.

A brief afterword by the editor draws together the main theoretical contributions of the volume, suggests directions for future research, and highlights the importance of reproductive research for social and cultural anthropology as a whole.

Notes

I am grateful to Anthony Carter, Tom Fricke, Eugene Hammel, David Kertzer, Geoffrey McNicoll, Jane Schneider, Peter Schneider, and Arland Thornton for their critical comments on an earlier version of this chapter.
  1 The diverse meanings of reproduction are sorted out by Rapp (1993). Today

scholars of quite different persuasions are increasingly using it to refer to human reproduction (see for example Robertson 1991; Ginsburg and Rapp 1991).

2 Biological anthropologists and archeologists are less guilty of neglecting demographic matters. For introductions to that work see Hassan 1979; Schacht 1981; Howell 1986; Wood 1990, 1994. This introductory chapter deals primarily, although not exclusively, with the work of social and cultural anthropologists in the US. Outside the US some very original work on fertility has been done by Philip Kreager (1982, 1986, 1993), among others. Many more have worked on family demography more generally (see for example Goody 1990; Macfarlane 1976, 1979).

3 For reviews of this earlier work see Nag 1973; Nardi 1981. Recent work in cultural ecology and cultural materialism includes Netting 1981; Hammel and Howell 1987; Harris and Ross 1987; Betzig et al. 1988; Abernethy 1993; Chisholm 1993; Fricke 1994. Earlier work in this tradition is reviewed in Swedlund 1978.

4 Recent reviews are Greenhalgh 1990; Ginsburg and Rapp 1991; a short list of recent monographs and edited collections includes Handwerker 1986a, 1988, 1989; Levine 1988; Simonelli 1986; Harris and Ross 1987; Martin 1987; Ginsburg 1989; Kertzer and Hogan 1989; Robertson 1991; Ginsburg and Rapp 1994. A growing body of research in medical anthropology also deals with reproduction, broadly defined. Ginsburg and Rapp (1991) provide a useful introduction to this work.

5 In the mid-1980s the International Union for the Scientific Study of Population (IUSSP) established a Committee on Anthropological Demography. Its forerunner, the Working Group on Micro-Approaches to Demographic Research, was formed in 1982 to promote the use of anthropological and other intensive field-research methods in demographic research. One of the more impressive accomplishments of this group is the conference volume edited by Caldwell et al. (1988). For most of its existence the IUSSP group has been headed by a demographer.

6 Less abundant but no less interesting are studies employing ecological and evolutionary approaches (cited in note 3).

7 Modernization theories were also rooted in the mid-twentieth-century functionalist theory of Talcott Parsons. The implications of functionalism for demographic theories of fertility must be left for another time.

8 Easterlin's "synthesis approach" served as the analytic framework for the massive two-volume National Academy of Sciences study of the determinants of fertility in developing countries (Bulatao and Lee 1983).

9 The "culture and political economy" formulation was first advanced by Jane and Peter Schneider in their 1976 book, *Culture and Political Economy in Western Sicily*. Students of gender have also found it a useful rubric (e.g., di Leonardo 1991).

10 I am indebted to Tom Fricke for his generous input into this section.

11 For other critiques of the diffusion approach see Mason 1992 and Kreager 1993.

12 Readers interested in the historian's perspective might consult the exemplary collection of essays on European fertility edited by Gillis et al. (1992).

13 For other elements see Gillis et al. 1992:Section II.

2 Political-economic and cultural explanations of demographic behavior

David I. Kertzer

The last decade has been a stormy time for demographic theory. Long-held theories and paradigms for explaining demographic behavior have come under relentless fire, and even the methods employed by demographers to explain such behavior have come in for sharp criticism. What is most notable about this development from an anthropologist's viewpoint is how much the criticisms being voiced by demographers reflect perspectives, methods, and concepts traditionally identified with anthropology. Curiously, this rethinking has not primarily come as a result of demographic work done by anthropologists, nor is it due to anthropologists' criticisms of the work done by demographers. Rather, it has largely sprung from within the ranks of demographers who have had little if any anthropological training.

There are many facets to this movement, including, for example, the call for intensive village studies to supplement demography's typical survey methods (Leibenstein 1981:397; Caldwell, Reddy, and Caldwell 1988). However, I here focus on one of the central theoretical issues that emerges from this confrontation: the role of culture in demographic explanation. In doing this, I examine the attempts to replace more traditional economic perspectives with cultural explanation in demographic studies. This movement actually has two different (though not always clearly distinguishable) threads. In the one most commonly articulated by demographers, culture is treated as a grab-bag of non-demographic, non-economic characteristics that influence behavior without themselves being susceptible to economic or demographic explanation. In its other form, emerging largely from the ranks of anthropology (Schneider and Schneider 1984; Kertzer and Hogan 1989; Greenhalgh 1990), a political economic approach has been championed that places economic forces in a broader context that includes both political and cultural factors. In this latter approach culture is not opposed to economic factors in explanation, but rather is part of a model of the interaction of political, economic, and cultural processes which is designed to produce a better understanding of the determinants of demographic behavior.

In reviewing these theoretical debates, my focus is principally on the implications of work done in European historical demography, though some contemporary African studies are cited as well. I look, in turn, at attempts to explain three different – though related – patterns of demographic behavior: (1) fertility decline; (2) marital timing; and (3) household formation and composition. In each case I first examine some of the work by other scholars in the field, and then provide some data of my own to shed light on the competing theoretical approaches.

My data come from a continuing study of the town of Casalecchio di Reno, near Bologna, in northern Italy for the period 1861–1921. This study is of particular interest because it deals with a period of major demographic, economic, political, and social change, and because the availability of population registers and a wealth of other microlevel documentation has made possible the reconstruction of the life course of the people who lived in this community during this six-decade period. Thus, before turning to the major questions before us, it is useful to pause to provide a brief description of Casalecchio.

Casalecchio di Reno

The commune of Casalecchio lies just outside what, for centuries, had been the rural belt surrounding the walled city of Bologna, in Emilia-Romagna, located in north central Italy. It had long been part of the classic sharecropping area that extended south through Tuscany, the Marches, and Umbria. Landowners lived in the cities and let their land out in small parcels to sharecropping households, either directly or through middlemen. The produce was split (often evenly) between landowner and sharecropper.

A contract bound the entire sharecropping family, and landowners exerted extensive control over sharecropper family life. Emblematic was the fact that landowner consent was required before a family member could marry. Since landowners stood to gain by maximizing the number of adults on each farm, hence maximizing the overall amount (and thus their share) of produce, households composed of more than one kin-related family were the rule. Indeed, the sharecroppers followed the cultural norm of patrilocal postmarital residence quite closely, with sons (not just a single son) bringing their brides into their natal household, and daughters joining their husband's household at marriage (Kertzer 1984; Kertzer and Hogan 1988).

A sharp rise in the rural population in the Bologna area that began in the late eighteenth century, combined with the move by landowners to place more land on a wage labor basis, resulted during the nineteenth century in a surplus rural population that could not be absorbed into the sharecropping sector (Bellettini 1978). This population was funneled into both agricultural and nonagricultural wage labor. Thus the late nineteenth and early twentieth centuries were a watershed period, when wage labor began to replace sharecropping as the backbone of the rural economy (Sereni 1968; Masulli 1980).

Casalecchio reflects these patterns; its population swelled from 2,400 to almost 6,000 in the six decades from 1861 to 1921. At the beginning of this period, when Bologna had just been liberated from papal state rule and made part of the unified Italy, a majority of the Casalecchio population worked directly in agriculture, and 70 percent of these were sharecroppers. But changes were already evident, for the largest textile factory in the province had just been established in Casalecchio, employing large numbers of women, children, and men. By the end of the sixty-year span, slightly over a quarter of the workforce was in agriculture, with another half composed of nonagricultural wage laborers, alongside a growing number of small merchants and artisans.

This also was a time of major political changes. A powerful socialist movement was sweeping across the Bologna area in these years, at the same time as the expansion of suffrage extended voting rights dramatically. The advent of universal public elementary education in this period also produced dramatic changes. In 1861, just one-quarter of all of Casalecchio's children aged 10–19 were literate, while sixty years later 97 percent were. Moreover, the scourge of infant and child death was being defeated as well, so that the nearly universal family experience of losing a small child became less and less common (Hogan and Kertzer 1986).

In short, over the period 1861–1921 Casalecchio witnessed many of the dramatic social, economic, demographic, and political changes associated with the nineteenth-century transformation of western Europe: the movement away from agriculture; the spread of proletarianization, socialism, and literacy; the decline of infant mortality; population growth; and the growth of nearby cities.

Explaining fertility decline

One of the ironies of anthropological demography arises from the fact that the most influential demonstration of the need for anthropological contributions to demographic research came from a research group whose most notable characteristic was a complete absence of anthropologists from its ranks. The Princeton European Fertility Project, under the guidance of economic demographer Ansley Coale, brought together a talented group of economic and sociological demographers whose goal was to generate a provincial-level data base which would allow them to explain the reasons for the decline of fertility in Europe. The expectation was that the various socioeconomic and demographic variables they would be able to measure would permit them to specify the conditions under which fertility began to fall.

As is by now well known (see Chapter 1), what they found was that none of their socioeconomic or demographic variables correlated very well with the timing of the fertility decline. The clasic predictor variables under Demographic Transition Theory – urbanization, literacy, infant and child mortality, industrialization – all failed to account for the transition. In Bulgaria, for example, marital fertility began its fall while almost the entire population was rural, agrarian, and illiterate.

These findings have occasioned some serious rethinking of the theory of fertility decline and, by implication, of demographic behavior more generally. A number of prominent demographers associated with the Princeton group, as well as others influenced by them, called attention to the need to identify "cultural" factors to explain fertility behavior. Knodel and van de Walle (1986:412) summarized their findings in the following terms: "Cultural setting influenced the onset and spread of fertility decline independently of socioeconomic conditions. Proximate areas with similar socioeconomic conditions but dissimilar cultures entered the transition period at different times, whereas areas differing in the level of socioeconomic development but with similar cultures entered the transition at similar times." Chapter after chapter in the Princeton project's summary volume (Coale and Watkins 1986) chronicle the failure of socioeconomic and demographic variables to explain the fertility decline. For example, Sharlin (1986:258) finds that urban–rural differentials are of minor significance within countries in comparison with differences among "discrete cultural areas (regions)."

Of all the scholars involved in the Princeton project, Ron Lesthaeghe has subsequently become the most active in championing "cultural" variables in demographic explanation. In work both on historical European and contemporary African societies, Lesthaeghe has called for combining demographic and anthropological methods, data, and conceptual tools. The lesson he draws from the European fertility transition is that:

> over and beyond the effects of changes in the mode of production and its ramifications with respect to the terms of household economic calculations, diversifications emerged in the timing and format of the marital fertility decline that were closely associated with the development of differential and sometimes compartmentalized ideological codes. This diversification of the moral code was a necessary permissive agent and the lack of it a suppressant of marital ferility control. (1980:539)

Lesthaeghe offers similar perspectives in interpreting the lack of fertility decline in sub-Saharan Africa. As in Europe, he places great emphasis on religious belief which he sees as supporting a culture in which both the belief system and social organization support high fertility (Lesthaeghe and Surkyn 1988; Lesthaeghe 1989).

Closely related to Lesthaeghe's work is that of Cleland and Wilson

(1987), who also utilize both the results of the European fertility history studies and the World Fertility Survey to argue that economic theories cannot explain fertility decline. Instead, they claim, "the most striking feature of the onset of transition is its relationship to broad cultural groupings...The spread of knowledge and ideas seems to offer a better explanation for the observed pattern than structural determinism" (1987:20).

Similar conclusions are reached by Dyson and Moore (1983) in their study of demographic behavior in India. Their point of departure is the divergence between northern and southern India, with the former characterized by significantly higher fertility and mortality rates. They attribute this demographic disparity to two different "sociocultural systems" which differ in both kinship system and extent of female autonomy. Not finding any clear link between these sociocultural differences and any differences in material (agrarian ecological) conditions, they argue that "it seems safer and more realistic to take culture as the primary determining factor for purposes of the present analysis" (Dyson and Moore 1983:48).

In providing this capsule outline of the rush by demographers to embrace cultural explanation of fertility decline, mention must be made of the work of Jack Caldwell. The similarities between his recent statements on the importance of religion and belief systems, and the work of Lesthaeghe and others is striking. For example, Caldwell and Caldwell (1987:409) recently explained the greater resistance to birth control in sub-Saharan Africa by saying that the "reasons are cultural." Note that, like Lesthaeghe, they see religious belief systems as molding social organization, with the two acting together to inhibit fertility decline.

The conclusion that fertility decline in Europe could not have been caused by economic forces is primarily based on the results of various aggregate-level studies, most notably those of the Princeton project. These have been reinforced by the single microlevel study connected with the Princeton project, conducted by John Knodel (1988). Only Knodel was actually able to compare people from different occupational groups, and thus escape problems associated with the ecological fallacy. That Knodel essentially failed to find any significant occupational differences in the timing of fertility decline in his population from fourteen German villages has thus assumed considerable importance in bolstering the provincial-level-based findings of other demographers.

Knodel's is just a single study, however, and, though it has many merits, it cannot bear the weight that has been placed on it. First of all, many of the villages studied by Knodel failed to experience a fertility decline in the period of his study (eighteenth to nineteenth centuries). Indeed, in only three of his fourteen villages did the value of I_g actually fall from the beginning of the eighteenth century to the end of the nineteenth (1986:356). Although there is evidence that women were beginning to stop childbearing slightly earlier by the last half of the nineteenth century, there is little evidence that they bore fewer children than had earlier cohorts. In such a situation, finding little occupational differentials in fertility can hardly be used as evidence against the role of economic forces in fertility decline. More importantly, the almost complete lack of historical economic, political, and social analysis of these communities in Knodel's work means that comparisons among the three occupational categories he provides (artisans, farmers, laborers) are not interpretable. Neither economic nor political economic analysis has been attempted here, so they can hardly be said to have failed.

More richly textured microlevel analyses of the fertility decline are available from Italy. Schneider and Schneider (1984, 1992; see also their chapter in this volume) combine ethnographic, oral historical, and archival sources to reconstruct the path of fertility decline in a Sicilian village in the late nineteenth and twentieth centuries. In contrast with Knodel, they find sharp differences among different socioeconomic groups in the timing of the fertility decline, with elite and artisans experiencing the decline decades ahead of the poor peasantry. They attribute these differences to changing macroeconomic and political factors, as well as to social-cultural mechanisms that facilitated the adoption of birth control. Their close attention to the way historical events and changing state action impinge on various segments of a local population takes them well beyond either a mechanistic economic approach to demographic explanation or a reified cultural approach. I will return to this point later.

The other microlevel study of occupational differentials in the Italian fertility decline is the analysis of Casalecchio carried out by Dennis Hogan and myself, which also seeks to combine political and economic analysis in examining people's behavior at the local level.[1] Examination of the population of Casalecchio over the period 1865–1921 reveals a clear relationship between type of household economy and the timing of the fertility decline. As in the Schneiders' Sicilian case, the fertility of the elite declined first, with the fertility of the artisans, merchants, and wage earners declining later in the nineteenth century. Most striking, however, is the finding that, long after the other groups in the community had begun their fertility decline, the sharecroppers in Casalecchio continued to maintain high fertility levels, with no sign of decline (see Figures 2.1 and 2.2). This finding is particularly provocative because the continued high fertility came during a period of soaring literacy rates, declining infant mortality, and great cultural change, including the spread of socialist ideology and organization among all sectors of the non-elite population, including the sharecroppers.

I will not rehearse here all the reasons Dennis Hogan and I have given to explain this pattern, but some of the more important factors in accounting for the fertility decline among the wage workers, artisans, and (small)

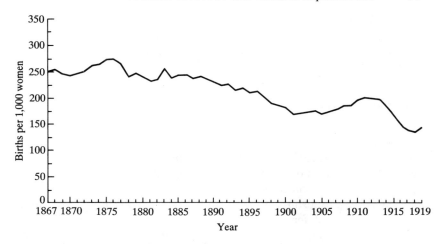

Figure 2.1 Annual number of births per 1,000 married women (five-year moving average), Casalecchio, 1867–1919

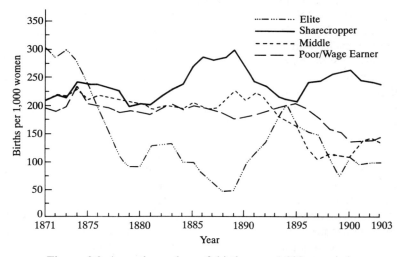

Figure 2.2 Annual number of births per 1,000 married women by occupation of household head (five-year moving average), Casalecchio, 1871–1903

merchants include the effects of compulsory school attendance, the advent of child labor laws, and the demise of the child service market on the economic value of children to parents. By contrast, for sharecroppers the economic value of having many children (especially sons) continued to be great, for the economic pressures confronting the sharecroppers were largely unchanged in these years. Moreover, the large, multiple-family household in which sharecroppers predominantly lived diminished the cost to individual women of bearing children, for childcare responsibilities were shared by women within the household.

The timing of marriage

In assessing the power of economic, cultural, and political economic approaches in explaining demographic behavior, the question of marital timing looms large. (Fricke's chapter in this volume illustrates this point well.) Not only is marital age crucial to the organization of the life course, and intimately associated with many aspects of the social system; it is also closely related to fertility. Indeed, in the classic Malthusian view, under a system of natural fertility (to use a post-Malthusian term; for further discussion see Chapter 1), levels of fertility are in good part a function of female age at marriage. This mechanism has received special attention in European historical demography, for traditional western Europe was notable for unusually high female age at marriage. Updating the Malthusian view, Wrigley and Schofield (1981) use three centuries of English evidence to argue that it was secular changes in the age at marriage in response to economic cycles that regulated the size of the English population.

A corollary of the proposition that age at marriage varies over time in response to changing economic conditions is that, at any given time, different segments of the population marry at different ages depending on their economic positions. In the traditional view, European peasants, insofar as they were dependent on the family farm, did not marry until they could take over that farm or accumulate the resources to acquire one of their own. This led to a relatively late age at marriage. On the other hand, according to many scholars, those who worked for a wage – the proletarianized sector of the population – knew no such constraint and tended to marry earlier. Such a synchronic difference would have implications for long-term trends, for as a peasant population became increasingly proletarianized, marriage age would be reduced and total fertility – and with it the rate of population growth – increased (Anderson 1971:132–134; Levine 1977:146). These arguments, however, have recently been called into question.

But before evaluating these claims for an economic explanation of marriage age, let us look at some evidence from Italy. By the 1870s, Italy's pattern of female age at marriage differed little from that found in France and England, with 61 percent of the Italian women married by age 25, compared to 60 percent of the French and 64 percent of the English. By the turn of the twentieth century, the mean female age at first marriage in Italy stabilized at 24, with a male age of 27.

Based on all civil marriages

Figure 2.3 Mean age at civil marriage, Casalecchio, by period

Marital age patterns in Casalecchio are typical of those found in Emilia-Romagna and Italy as a whole. Throughout the nineteenth century, age at first marriage for men hovered around 28, with women marrying, on the average, at age 24–25. What is striking is how little this pattern changed through a period of dramatic social and economic changes, as can be seen in Figure 2.3. No historical trend is detectable in either men's or women's age at first marriage from 1861 to 1921, despite the fact that the community had been transformed from an agricultural, largely sharecropping community, to one dominated by wage labor.

By utilizing the occupational information provided in the Casalecchio marriage records, we next ask whether any significant differentials in marital age are masked at the commune level. In particular, we would like to see whether the Casalecchio data tend to support any of the previously mentioned generalizations relating marriage age to economic position and security. Local folklore, in fact, provides some basis for believing that such a link may have existed. The Bolognese saying, "better to say 'poor me' than 'poor we'," explicitly makes just such a link between economic resources and marriage.

Yet, despite both the folk and the scholarly wisdom, the Casalecchio data provide little support for these generalizations. As can be seen in Figures 2.4 and 2.5, there is little difference among occupational groups in either male or female age at marriage, and some of the differences are not in the predicted direction. Of the principal male occupational groups, only the

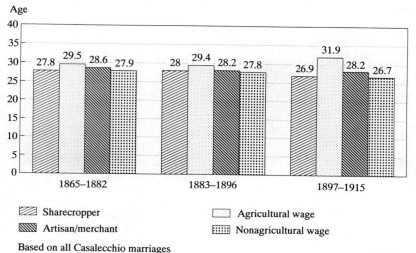

Figure 2.4 Mean age at first marriage, men, by occupation and period

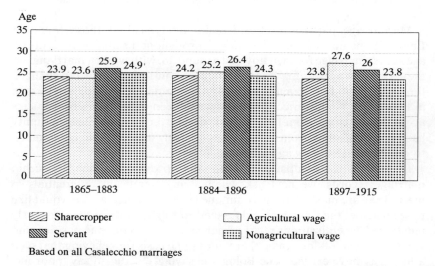

Figure 2.5 Mean age at first marriage, women, by occupation and period

braccianti (agricultural wage workers) had first marriage ages consistently above the mean. This mirrors McQuillan's (1989:342) finding for the Alsace region of France in this period that the *journaliers* (agricultural day laborers) married later than the rest of the population. Such a finding is in keeping with the argument that poverty acts as a brake on marriage, but goes against the view that rural wage labor leads to earlier marriage.

To look at the impact of industrialization on the timing of marriage in this once predominantly sharecropping community, it is instructive to compare the sharecroppers with the nonagricultural wage laborers (as can be seen in Figures 2.4 and 2.5). The similarity in the marital timing of these two groups, whose family economy could hardly be more dissimilar, is almost uncanny.

The data examined to this point come from Casalecchio's marriage records. A different look at occupational differentials in marriage rates is available in the case of men through use of the conscription register. All men were required to register for the draft at age 19, at which time they listed their occupation. Of the 1,646 men who registered in Casalecchio in the period 1865–1921, 403 were sharecroppers, 192 were *braccianti*, 259 were artisans or merchants, and 485 were nonagricultural wage laborers. A survival analysis was conducted to compare the rates at which men in these various groups married in subsequent years. The results showed no significant differences ($p < 0.05$) among the four groups.

These results mirror Knodel's findings in his study of German villages in the nineteenth century, for Knodel too was struck by the "similarity in age at first marriage across occupational categories." Indeed, insofar as any difference was found in these German villages, it was the wage laborers rather than the farmers who were marrying later (1988:130–131). Likewise, Lehning (1988:320), in his aggregate-level study of marriage in thirty-three rural French villages of the Loire, is struck by "the weak influence of most socioeconomic factors on either the timing or prevalence of marriage." He goes on to observe: "especially noteworthy is the absence of any significant correlation between the proportion of textile workers and any measure of nuptiality."

Although the Princeton European Fertility Project focused primarily on fertility, the vast provincial-level data base generated by the Princeton project was also employed to address the issue of marriage age. Paralleling their findings regarding the lack of close relationship between economic variables and the decline in fertility, scholars found no clear relationship between economic development and marriage age. Indeed, through a period of tremendous economic and demographic change from the late nineteenth century to the first third of the twentieth century, no clear trend in marriage age was evident.

Susan Watkins (1986), in her review of this evidence, attributes differences in marriage age to cultural differences. But neither Watkins nor any of the other scholars involved in the Princeton project went on to identify just what these crucial cultural differences were, or where they come from.[2]

The Casalecchio case, in short, reflects what is becoming evident in an increasing number of historical European studies: previous generalizations regarding the predominant role played by family economy in determining marriage age cannot be supported. Studies elsewhere in Europe have certainly revealed cases where different occupational groups do have distinctive patterns of age at marriage. However, the impact of family economy is conditioned by other forces, especially by locally-based cultural norms regarding the appropriate age of marriage and related social organizational structures. But I am here running ahead of my argument.

Household composition

As has been recognized in the emergence of the sub-field of family demography, household formation processes are themselves closely linked to the more traditional demographic topics of fertility, marriage, migration, and mortality. Just as fertility cannot be analyzed without an analysis of marital age, both fertility and marital age can be better understood when the rules and practices regarding domestic group-formation are known. The link between household systems and age at marriage has often been made. Hajnal (1983), for example, argued that it was northwestern Europe's neolocal system that underlay its distinctive pattern of late age at marriage. This thesis holds that in this neolocal system people had to delay marriage until they were in a position to establish themselves as a separate economic unit. Richard Smith (1981:614) has argued that this household system cannot itself be explained by economic forces; rather, it was a "highly distinctive cultural situation which demanded economic independence for the newly married that underpinned this pattern." With marital age, in turn, exercising a significant impact on fertility, coresidential systems can be seen to play a noteworthy indirect role in regulating fertility. More controversial is the direct role played by household composition in influencing fertility, with a woman's reproductive behavior presumably affected by whether she is sharing her home with other kin (e.g., her mother-in-law).

Historical demographers have expended a great deal of energy over the past two decades in seeking to shed light on the kinds of households in which Europeans lived in the past, and on what impact urbanization, industrialization, and the other forces generally associated with "modernization" have had on household organization. In considering the relationship between political economy and culture in demographic explanation, the case of household composition is instructive.

Modern historical demography of the household is founded on the rejection of previous theory that linked industrialization (or modernization) with household nuclearization. In rejecting this evolutionary view, the work of Laslett (1972) and colleagues brought about a reaction against economic explanation in historical household study. If, for example, English people had lived in nuclear-family households for 600 years or more, including eras marked by monumental political and economic changes, it would seem that there was little point in seeking an economic explanation for household form.

More recent recognition of the diversity that characterized household patterns in Europe, however, has led to renewed interest in political economic forces, and a rejection of the purely empiricist, descriptive studies that have characterized some of the work of the Cambridge Group.[3] Eastern Europe has provided fertile ground for such political economic perspectives, for not so long ago serfdom was widespread there and manorial lords controlled the land on which people depended. In this setting, the rules governing household composition were largely determined by the lords, based on their calculation of what would best serve their political and economic interests. The complex nature of the Russian serf household, Czap (1982, 1983) tells us, was due to the fact that the lords who controlled the estates discouraged the serfs from dividing their households. Plakans (1983, 1984) finds a similar pattern in the Baltic, where the serf estate system imposed the rules governing coresidence. With the demise of serfdom in the nineteenth century, the incidence of complex family households began to decline.

In Poland (Kochanowicz 1983), where labor was scarce, lords forbade their serfs from leaving the village in which they lived, and tried to encourage marriages within the estate. Because the serfs' labor obligations to the lord were based on household units, the Polish lords encouraged neolocality, often against the wishes of the peasants who saw advantages in larger, complex family households which would have proportionately less of their productivity siphoned off by the lords.

As this case shows, peasants often struggled against the pressures of landowning and political elites, and peasant household forms must be understood not simply as outcomes of elite interests, but also as the product of attempts to circumvent such pressures. Thus, for example, in parts of what are now the Czech Republic and Slovakia, the conscription of unmarried men led serf families to encourage the early marriage of their sons, which led, in turn, to a higher proportion of complex family households (Gaunt 1983).

Studies which have distinguished within individual communities between landed peasants and landless workers (agricultural or not) have consistently found the latter to be characterized by much lower levels of complex family coresidence (Comas d'Argemir 1988; Shaffer 1982; Darrow 1989; Sella 1987; Angeli and Bellettini 1979; Andorka and Balazs-Kovacs 1986). Landless workers typically lived in tiny, cramped quarters that they had to rent. Because adults sold their labor on the market as individuals, they did not face the kinds of pressures favoring complex family coresidence faced by those for whom the household was the unit of production.

The evidence from Casalecchio, and from Italy more generally, shows not only the importance of political economic perspectives, but also the necessity of integrating culture into the political economic model. The sharecropping belt that cut through central and adjacent portions of northern Italy gave rise to perhaps the highest rates of large, complex family households in western Europe. It was not uncommon for three-quarters of those living in sharecropping communities to be residing in households containing two or more patrilaterally linked nuclear family units. The land was owned by an elite and given out to sharecropper families on a lease that had to be renewed every year. The owners sought to maximize their half of the farm's produce, and this they could do by maximizing (within limits) the number of adults in the household, with all household members bound by the sharecropping contract. In times, such as the nineteenth century, when a growing population meant that there was more labor supply than demand, a process of selection took place in which those who failed to form complex family households were often evicted from the land.[4]

Returning to Casalecchio, we find, in 1871, that 71 percent of all those living in sharecropper households lived in households containing two or more kin-related simple family units, and another 11 percent lived in households containing kin beyond the simple family. Fewer than one in eight lived in simple family households. By contrast, only 20 percent of the nonagricultural wage laborers lived in multiple-family households, with another 16 percent living in households having some kin beyond the nuclear family. Over half (58 percent) lived in simple family households.[5]

Such data provide clear support for a political economic interpretation of household composition, but they also raise an interesting question. In the areas of Italy that had long been dominated by sharecropping, we find that while non-sharecroppers lived much less often in complex family households than did neighboring sharecroppers, their propensity to live in such households was much greater than people with similar occupational niches elsewhere in western Europe. Evidence of this sort has been taken to mean that in any given area, cultural norms regarding appropriate postmarital residence guide people's behavior, and that such norms are to a large extent shared by people in a community regardless of their particular economic situation.

This is essentially Peter Laslett's view. He argues that "A cultural element in the shaping of the domestic group organization both as to production and reproduction seems inescapable" (1983:558). Similarly, Laslett's Cambridge Group colleague Richard Wall (1983:63) concludes that "when it came to interpreting the pattern of household composition across Europe, it has not been easy to find convincing 'economic' explanations. Hence we have argued above for cultural factors." In another recent influential study, the historian Steven Ruggles takes this argument further, arguing that classical economic explanations of family behavior are flawed by the untenable assumption "that people always behave rationally in order to maximize their own economic interest." He claims that such an assumption is invalid and, moreover, that "Decisions about the family are probably less often rationally calculated than virtually any of the other major decisions people make" (1987:24). In Ruggles' view, the guiding force here is not so much economics as culture, which he equates in somewhat murky terms with psychological predispositions, values, and norms.

Reher (1988), analyzing household patterns in Cuenca, Spain, offers a more nuanced perspective. He argues that understanding the household system requires examining the demographic and economic forces that, over a period of centuries "made up a good part of what could be called the cultural substructure of the people of Cuenca. In this sense, the concrete cultural form can be explained to a considerable degree by social and economic variables." He goes on to argue that "Once this cultural substratum was created . . . it ended up becoming an essential part of people's life expectations. Within this context, relatively early and universal marriage, neolocal household formation, property transfers via inheritance, etc., ceased being simple demographic, social or legal acts, and became normative cultural behavior patterns" (1988:71). In this view, cultural norms come about as a result of political, economic, and demographic forces, but once formed they take on a life of their own. Though far from impervious to changing political and economic conditions, cultural values "were embedded enough in the fabric of society to persist, even in the face of social and economic changes which might counsel other forms of behavior" (ibid.). He thus concludes that "More than any other, the cultural variable comes close to explaining the almost unchanging permanence of a family and household system for more than two centuries" (1988:72).

Specifying culture

"If economic models are strong on theory and weak on evidence," writes Kevin McQuillan (1989:333), "approaches which emphasize the role of culture suffer the opposite problem." Indeed, while many demographers have proclaimed the need to study the impact of culture on demographic behavior, just what they mean by culture is often unclear. The economist Gregory Clark (1988:161), for example, tells us that the challenge is to find a way to treat culture as something "other than a residual to be resorted to when all other explanations fail." "As far as most contemporary economists are concerned," he writes, "the game with culture is to try to explain it away."

Writing of demographers, Lesthaeghe (1989:3–4) likewise argues that "'cultural' explanations are frequently residual explanations, or a messy bag into which everything is relegated that is not properly understood." This is essentially the way the culture concept was used by most participants in the Princeton European Fertility Project. For example, when Barbara Anderson (1986:293) discovered that the standard economic and demographic variables did little to explain variation in the province-level timing of fertility decline, she advocated employing "culture factors," by which she meant religion, ethnicity, language, and region. The features thus selected to measure the "cultural" were chosen not on the basis of any theory linking culture and demographic behavior, but simply because they were variables that happened to have been coded in the Princeton project.

Anthropologists have long debated how culture is to be defined most usefully, with some limiting the concept to the ethereal realm of "an historically transmitted pattern of meanings embodied in symbols" (Geertz 1973:89) or "an organized system of shared meanings" (LeVine and Scrimshaw 1983:667). In somewhat more tangible form, we have such definitions as Marvin Harris' (1979:47) "a learned repertory of thoughts and actions exhibited by members of social groups," or Kreager's (1986:136) "the sense people make of their material environment," emphasizing the "application of criteria of right and wrong." As Kreager also notes, if defined in this way, we can view demographic behavior as not simply one kind of cultural behavior, but as a central focus of cultural activity, for "vital processes are the true playground of moral systems" (ibid.). Such issues as the importance of virginity and what kind of marriage a person should make are at the heart of the cultural process.

A review of the demographic literature points to a lack of conceptual clarity about just what is being referred to when culture is invoked. Economists often do not differentiate among variables that are noneconomic and nondemographic, lumping them all together in one hodge-podge which some label "culture." Indeed, Lesthaeghe (1989:2) makes this point, arguing that for those involved in comparative demographic analysis, the assumption typically made is "that everything that is not 'economic' must be 'cultural'." Leibenstein (1981:388–389), for example, refers to decisions made outside of an economic cost-benefit framework as "passive decision-making." These, he argues, are based on "routines" or "well-established conventions to which most of the population adheres." He concludes that "to explain most behavior we have to understand routines and why routines are established" (for more on Leibenstein and passive decision-making see Carter, this volume). To an anthropologist, this has an antiquarian ring, reminiscent of mid-nineteenth-century proto-anthropologists, still groping toward a culture concept.

Lesthaeghe's recent attempts, in his African research, to get away from generic references to cultural differences to a specification of cultural variables is instructive here. He argues against the common tendency of demographers to identify such units as ethnic, regional, or language groups as cultural entities and to use them in demographic explanation without further examination of just what it is about them that is supposed to influence demographic behavior. Yet, he is hesitant to make direct use of what he calls the "narrow" meaning of culture, which he defines as "pertaining to normative systems." Instead, he takes ethnic groups and identifies them in terms of "selected characteristics of social organization," such as type of lineage organization and the productive roles of women (1989:3). It is worth noting that his broad-scale comparative African research is based on the use of Murdock's world ethnographic classification scheme and the Human Relations Area Files.

What this and other attempts to specify "cultural" variables in recent demographic explanation reveal is the conflation of that which anthropologists typically treat as two different phenomena: culture and social organization. For the economic demographer, and for most sociological demographers, both of these are subsumed under the single residual category of what is left over after economic and demographic variables have been used. Greater conceptual clarity about just what is being referred to when "culture" is invoked would be useful, though, if progress is to be made in identifying just what role noneconomic, nondemographic forces have in explaining demographic behavior. In particular, it should be recognized that leaving demographic and economic variables behind need not entail entering into an ethereal arena of "meaning-worlds," accessible only through an interpretive anthropology.[6] Much of what affects demographic behavior may lie, as Lesthaeghe suggests, in the realm of social organization and social institutions.

Although there is undoubtedly a close relationship between culture (in the limited symbolic sense) and social organization, the nature of causality between the two is far from clear.[7] I am a bit uncomfortable, for example, about the recent explanation by Caldwell and Caldwell (1987) for continued high fertility in sub-Saharan Africa. "The reasons," they claim, "are cultural and have much to do with a religious belief system that operates directly to sustain high fertility but that also has molded a society in such a way as to bring rewards for high fertility" (1987:409). They continue: "Such beliefs have important demographic consequences. The fact that one's living ancestors will one day become powerful shades strongly reinforces the earthly power of the old" (1987:416). This link between high fertility on the one hand and certain forms of kinship organization and religious beliefs on the other is provocative and probably on the right track, but the assumption that the religious beliefs are primary and the forms of social organization (e.g., power of the elders) derivative is questionable and probably unnecessary to the argument.

While Europe does not have ancestor cults, it does of course have well-developed religious institutions, practices, and beliefs, all of which would fall under the omnibus definition of culture often employed by demographers. It is striking how little attention has been given to religion in attempts to explain differences and historical changes in demographic behavior, with the notable exception of Lesthaeghe. Indeed, Lesthaeghe and Wilson (1986) argue that the onset of the fertility transition required the conjunction of two separate forces: economic and cultural. The cultural force that they highlight is religion. Indeed, they begin their essay by identifying two primary determinants: economics and religion (1986:261).

Inquiry into the role played by religion helps us recognize the difficulties of sorting out causal relations between what is considered to be part of culture as narrowly defined and that which is linked to social organization. Churches throughout modern (and premodern) European history played a major role in shaping people's reproductive behavior. They taught what was appropriate sexual activity, they specified which marriages could be contracted and with what timing, and they regulated the breaking off of marriages and the appropriateness of remarriage. They also played a crucial role in defining the meaning and demographic result of illegitimacy. For example, due to changes in Church policy linked to the sixteenth-century Council of Trent, unwed mothers became increasingly stigmatized in Italy, reaching the point where the Church was active in ensuring the abandonment to foundling homes of illegitimate children, a practice which had major consequences for infant mortality.[8]

Understanding the evolution of infant abandonment in Europe, a major chapter in the history of both illegitimate fertility and infant mortality, requires not simply an analysis of economic factors, but also an analysis of these religious institutions. The relationship between these, in turn, and people's own "commonality of perception," or "evaluative discourse," terms Hammel (1990b:469) uses to help define culture, is problematic. Social institutions such as the Church have coercive powers even aside from their power to mold people's thoughts. Yet the same could be said of other social institutions, leading us to two conclusions: (1) the impact of social institutions on demographic behavior need not be mediated through culture at all, if culture is defined in its more limited sense of views of right and wrong, of attitudes and norms; (2) culture itself is not some primordial product of the masses, but is itself molded by various powerful institutions in society. In short, the relationship of culture and social organization must be examined carefully rather than assuming either an identity or an autonomy of the two.

Before leaving the question of how culture is to be defined, it is worth mentioning Hammel's (1990b) recent proposal of "A theory of culture for demography." While approving of the attempts of many demographers to turn their attention to culture, Hammel takes them to task for embracing an outdated culture concept "mired in structural-functional concepts that are about 40 years old, hardening rapidly, and showing every sign of fossilization" (1990b:456). Sharing in the broad anthropological movement against a reified use of the culture concept, and in the concomitant move to view culture as a process of negotiation of individuals in interaction, Hammel argues that "culture does not exist in some autonomous sense, but rather it is constituted." He thus defines culture in terms of "the commonality of perception that emerges between actors as they establish and conduct their social relations" (1990b:465–466).

The difficulty this perspective presents can be expressed by considering what Hammel himself artfully refers to as the contradiction between a view of "culture for the people" and one of "culture by the people." The traditional notion of culture as existing independently of any individuals (i.e., what Durkheim described as its "superindividual" property) – that of culture for the people – can lead to a view of individuals as automatons or "cultural morons." This is a view that Hammel and most other contemporary anthropologists reject. However, as Hammel implicitly recognizes, the contrary view of culture as a matter of individual creativity leads to the dissolution of the culture concept altogether. Although individuals may manipulate symbols for their own perceived benefit, just what benefit they seek, and what symbols they can manipulate, are very much determined by a larger cultural universe in which they live. Thus, to argue for an "anarchic view of culture" as Hammel (1990b:469) does, identifying culture with people's "commentary on behavior," does not really escape the superindividual concept of culture, for it presupposes a community of evaluation, a set of ideas about what is to be evaluated, by whom, and with what criteria. This of course does not mean that all individuals share the same set of ideas or identical stock of symbols, but it should not be any surprise if a social encounter between two Dani goes more smoothly than one between a Dani and a Nuer.

The question of communication takes us to the last perspective on culture in demographic explanation I want to consider here, that offered by Susan Watkins (1990, 1991). As one of the participants of the Princeton European Fertility Project who has attempted to cope with the failure of economic variables to explain demographic behavior, Watkins has called for work which goes beyond economic models of individual calculation to examine cultural differences. Watkins' model, similar in certain basic respects to Hammel's, focuses on the social process whereby individuals come to define what constitutes appropriate behavior. In the past, she argues, this process has taken place in the context of networks of kin and neighbors, whose ideas about such important questions as how many children it is best to have play a major role in determining individuals' demographic behavior. Watkins thus advocates an approach that focuses on following such networks. The story she tells of the past century in western Europe is one where these networks progressively extend out from local to national boundaries, resulting in greater national homogeneity in demographic behavior.

While this conceptualization has the merit of raising the question of the social context in which people actually make behavioral decisions, it is not one which helps much in answering questions of why some populations act differently than others, or what accounts for change other than alterations in boundaries of communication. From an anthropological perspective, it also seems to place undue emphasis on language, an emphasis that is rather suspect in that language happens to be a variable available in the Princeton provincial-level historical fertility data base. The use of geographical units, moreover, only roughly corresponds to a gossip-network model, since there is no simple coincidence between social networks and geographical entities. This was nicely illustrated in the Schneiders' (1984, 1992, this volume) analysis of the differential timing of the fertility decline in a Sicilian village, where different class groups constituted distinguishable moral and interactive communities.

Watkins' difficulty in operationalizing a view of cultural forces in historical demographic research reflects a larger problem that all those working with historical materials face. The unfortunate fact is that classic economic models are easier to examine in historical work than are the more complex cultural or political economic models. It is, for example, easier to trace the link between sharecropping and fertility than it is to say anything about the cultural values of sharecroppers vs. agricultural wage laborers in past centuries. However, we can do more than we have in historical demography to get at the cultural dimension. Here I envision work ranging from oral history for the more recent past (Schneider and Schneider 1984) to a much broader search of archival materials than has typified most historical demographic research to date.[9] For example, to continue with the case of illegitimacy in Italy, examination of trial records for infanticide cases, along with various records associated with foundling homes, provides a great deal of insight into the attitudes of the illiterate masses to marriage and illegitimacy (Kertzer 1993).

Culture and political economy in demographic explanation

Susan Greenhalgh (1990; see also Chapter 1) recently identified an emerging demographic approach which she refers to as the political economy of fertility, a multidisciplinary effort that makes use of some of the conceptual and methodological tools of cultural anthropology. I would like here to review some of the evidence discussed above in light of this perspective, broadening it in this way beyond the original focus on fertility to demographic behavior in general.

According to Greenhalgh (1990:87), a political economy of fertility "directs attention to the embeddedness of community institutions in structures and processes, especially political and economic ones, operating at regional, national, and global levels, and to the historical roots of those macro-micro linkages." Explanation embraces "not only the social and economic, but also the political and cultural aspects of demographic change" (1990:88). Analysis must be multileveled, and because the effects of the various processes at work take time to show their effects, "a political economy of fertility must be an explicitly historical field of inquiry" (1990:94). Special emphasis is placed on the political economic sphere, which Greenhalgh identifies not only with "the links between political and economic processes," but also with the "political-economic dimensions of social and cultural organization" (1990:95).

Looking back at the evidence from Casalecchio, we can see how some of these principles may be employed. To understand the fertility decline in Casalecchio, it was necessary to differentiate the local population according to their relations to the means of production. It was also necessary to examine changes in the regional economy (proletarianization) – itself linked to national and international forces – broad developments in regional demography (population increase leading to a larger rural population than could be sustained in the sharecropping system), and political developments (such as the impact of Italian Unification, various social legislation, and the rise of the socialist movement). The fact that such changes had a different impact on different segments of the Casalecchio population argues for the primacy of political and economic factors in this case, although undoubtedly these changes occurred through cultural mechanisms which remain largely unspecified in the work done so far.[10]

Results from our analysis of marital timing in Casalecchio, combined with results from other microlevel historical studies of marriage age in Europe, appear to accord less well with some of the central tenets of an approach that focuses solely on political and economic factors. We have shown, for example, that there was little difference between the marriage age for the most traditional (some would say archaic) agricultural segment of the population – the sharecroppers – and that of the most modern segment – the nonagricultural wage laborers. Moreover, during a period of great political and economic change, the community as a whole showed rather little change in age at marriage. The lesson here is not that political and economic forces have no impact on marital age, but that cultural norms and associated aspects of social organization heavily condition marital timing, and that these have a momentum of their own. Looked at another way, political and economic changes have their impact on people insofar as they are filtered through the social organizational arrangements that people have adopted as means of adaptation to their environment. Unless under great pressure, such cultural and social features change only slowly. Moreover, preexisting cultural and social features may condition the way in which people react to these political and economic forces, so that the behavioral endstate cannot simply be predicted from the political and economic forces at work, but only from a more complex analysis of the impact of those forces given the preexisting social and cultural arrangements.

This is nicely illustrated in Susan Rogers' (1991) recent book on Ste Foy, a village in the *département* of Aveyron, in southwestern France. Part of a traditionally stem-family household system, Ste Foy has been economically and politically transformed over the past two centuries, and especially as a result of economic changes since World War I. Yet, rather than undermine the stem-family system, the increase in wealth, along with such demographic changes as an increase in longevity, have led to a proliferation of three-generational, stem-family households. People adapted to changes in the agricultural system, as well as to political alterations in various benefit programs, by utilizing their preexisting cultural norms and forms of social organization linked to the ostal system. Increase in wealth and increase in communication with the national society did not (*contra* Watkins) in this case result in homogenization with the nationally predominant household system.

The case of household composition in Casalecchio provides another view of the relationship between culture (broadly defined) and political and economic factors in demographic explanation. If we review the pattern of household formation rules and practices across Europe over the past several hundred years, we can see that there is a link between economic forces and household formation systems. Large, complex family households are common only under certain political economic conditions. Yet, to argue for the crucial historical influence of such conditions is not to argue that cultural norms are simply produced by them out of whole cloth. Nor can we argue that the rules followed by individuals simply reflect their placement in a particular family economy.

Part of the problem here is identifying the mechanism through which political and economic forces are thought to operate. The simplistic notion, sometimes embodied in demographic and economic models, that such forces act essentially directly on behavior must be abandoned. Rather, part of the way these forces operate is through nurturing particular norms of behavior and particular conceptions of what is appropriate, desirable, or even inevitable. Once such systems of norms are established, they are influential in guiding people's behavior. Moreover, they tend to act on communities of people.

Here we get onto complex ground. As we saw in the Casalecchio case, there are dramatic differences between the household behavior of share-croppers and proletarians who live practically side by side. These may be attributed to the different economic constraints they face. However, the fact that both agricultural and nonagricultural wage workers in Casalecchio were much more apt to spend part of their lives in complex family households than were proletarians in northwestern Europe demonstrates not only a possible "cultural lag" of the kind which is implicit in Greenhalgh's discussion of the necessity for a longer historical view, but also the possibility that earlier forms of social organization and cultural norms will shape people's experience in confronting new political economic pressures, resulting in long-lasting adaptations.[11]

What is needed if we are to make progress in understanding demographic behavior, and the changes that have taken place in demographic behavior over time, is an analytical framework that pays attention both to political and economic forces and to social organizational structures and cultural norms. Research which ignores some of these factors – whether based on provincial-level historical European data bases or World Fertility Survey (WFS)-type contemporary surveys – is unlikely to yield satisfactory explanations of demographic behavior.

Notes

1 Details on this study are available in Kertzer and Hogan (1989:148–173).
2 Watkins must be given credit, however, for subsequently trying to develop cultural perspectives on the provincial-level Princeton fertility data, a point which will be discussed later in this chapter.
3 A review of some of this work is found in Kertzer (1985, 1991a).
4 For more on the political economy and demography of Italian sharecropping, see Kertzer (1984, 1989).
5 For further detail on Casalecchio household patterns, see Kertzer and Hogan (1989, 1991).
6 This is not to say that analysis of symbolism is unimportant to cultural analysis of demographic behavior, but only that it does not exhaust the important kinds of research to be done in the arena demographers have come to label 'cultural.'
7 For a somewhat different view of the relationship between culture and other aspects of society, see Handwerker (1986:10–11).
8 For more on this subject, see Kertzer (1991b; 1993). Church regulation of sexuality is by no means limited to the Roman Catholic Church. For a northern European example, see Mitchison and Leneman (1989).
9 For attempts to move in this direction, see Seccombe (1993) and the essays in Gillis et al. (1992).
10 Contrast this with the work of Schneider and Schneider (1984), who have done

much to shed light on what such cultural mechanisms look like in a Sicilian community.

11 For a much longer historical horizon in conceptualizing the link between culture and demographic behavior, see Hammel and Howell (1987).

The social management of fertility

3   Agency and fertility: For an ethnography of practice

Anthony T. Carter

Two concepts of agency, one active and one passive, have dominated attempts to account for fertility change in Western social science since the emergence, toward the end of World War II, of concern with explosive population growth. The passive concept of agency sees people as adhering to conventions or following rules. Human conduct is thus narrowly channeled by norms and institutions. The active concept of agency sees people as deliberately choosing the level of their fertility through some form of abstract rationality. Though the balance between these two forms of agency has shifted, social science accounts of fertility change remain caught between the two poles they define.

In the first versions of demographic transition theory (Notestein 1945, Davis 1945), it was assumed that wherever people exercise deliberate choice or active decision-making with regard to family size they invariably impose sharp limits on their fertility. However, this was thought to occur only in modern societies in which the forces of industrialization, urbanization and education have reduced mortality and freed individuals from the weight of tradition. In premodern and transitional societies, according to this version of transition theory, decision-making remains passive and social and cultural constraints continue to produce high fertility. Most contemporary economic and sociological accounts of fertility change assume that human beings are free to behave rationally in both traditional and modern societies. Economists work with more formal models of decision-making, but economic and sociological accounts of fertility differ primarily in the indirect determinant that they emphasize rather than in their conceptions of rational agency. Most take for granted that fertility conduct turns on some form of active decision-making involving utility maximization.

In an important though relatively little noticed paper, Harvey Leibenstein (1981) has called into question the general assumption of instrumental rationality and maximization in contemporary accounts of fertility change. Arguing in part that maximization involves decision-making processes that are impossibly complex, time-consuming and costly, Leibenstein urges an approach built around what he calls "passive decision-making" or "non-decision decisions." He thus returns us to a position somewhat like that of the original transition theorists. Under the impact of sufficiently strong stimuli, the choices involved in fertility may be made on the basis of partial or even full calculation. However, in all but the most unusual circumstances, they are made passively or routinely on the basis of an ethic or cultural convention. Where classical transition theory equated modern societies with active decision-making and traditional societies with passive decision-making, Leibenstein sees both forms of decision-making as occurring in both kinds of societies. Nevertheless, the nature of the distinction between the two forms of decision process remains essentially the same. And, though Leibenstein holds that the dominant form of agency is everywhere passive, he preserves the distinction between traditional and modern societies.

> Those living in a village in a developing country are likely to exhibit a considerable amount of routine behavior, and hence this would appear to be a desirable context within which to study passive decision-making. In other words, the general hypothesis is that so-called traditional behavior is likely to involve a great many passive decisions. (1981:397)

This chapter has two aims. The first is to show that the concepts of agency that have been employed in theories of fertility change are unworkable. The second is to propose an alternative view of agency designed to free us from the sterile opposition between passive and active decision-making. The first section uses Leibenstein's argument to review a variety of recent demographic studies. I take seriously Leibenstein's concerns with realistic assumptions about decision-making processes and with the fit between theory and statistical tests, but argue that his concerns lead to precisely opposite conclusions. Instead of macro-theories of agency stressing passive adherence to cultural conventions and macro-statistical tests, we need to search out micro-theories of agency and appropriate micro-statistical tests. The second section of the paper turns to recent theoretical and ethnographic work on practice for clues to a more satisfactory approach to agency. This work suggests that a more realistic conception of active decision-making requires us to escape from the separation, deeply embedded in Western social thought, of agency and culture, and that one way to effect this escape is to attend to what Anthony Giddens calls "flows of conduct." Subsequent sections of the paper apply this approach to material from North India and California.

The separation of agency and culture: A theoretical dead end

As noted above, Leibenstein's case for "the passive decision dogma" (1981:388) rests on several arguments. In microeconomic accounts of fertility, decision-making is assumed to be active and to be based on maximization. As Leibenstein observes, however, "maximization is frequently an incompletely stated postulate" (1981:383). In many cases, what is being maximized is unknown, left unstated or cannot be specified in a manner that permits of empirical tests (see also McNicoll 1980:442). In addition, while most maximization theories of fertility operate on a microlevel, specifying how representative persons or families would behave under varying circumstances, they generally are tested on a macrolevel with statistical data on the average behavior of population aggregates. Such tests may give misleading results. Using only aggregate statistics, two populations may appear to differ in the way or ways predicted by some micro theory while substantial components of one or both populations in fact act in ways that are inconsistent with the theory (Leibenstein 1981:384–385). For my purposes, Leibenstein's most important objection to maximization is that it is complex and time-consuming (1981:383). It is doubtful that such procedures are routinely employed in the absence of the kinds of institutional resources available to departments of economics, schools of management and the public and private bureaucracies with which they are associated. If they are within the reach, in the conduct of our everyday lives, of those of us who are what Jean Lave (1988:4) calls "just plain folks," we surely avoid them much of the time.

Leibenstein constructs his theory of passive decision-making to avoid the weaknesses of maximization and to bring theory in line with statistical aggregation. In developing an alternative approach I do not intend to defend maximization. Quite the contrary. It can be argued, however, that recent empirical studies of fertility are inconsistent with passive decision-making procedures. Nor do statistical techniques in and of themselves require macro models of decision-making.

A good deal of effort has been invested, particularly among anthropologists interested in demography, in the design of techniques that can be used to obtain accurate measures of macrolevel aggregate demographic rates or of social rules amid the welter of potentially misleading microlevel observations available for small populations.[1] At the same time, however, some of the most interesting work on demography in anthropology and social history achieves its results precisely by carefully preserving and exploiting the microlevel character of its data. An early example of the efficacy of this approach is Thomas Smith's (1977) elegant study of marital fertility in eighteenth-century Nakahara, a village in Japan. Here a remarkably complete run of annual population registers, listing village residents on a household by household basis with information on gender, age, and relation to household head, provides the basis for a study of demographic processes at the level of individual couples. Other examples of disaggregation and microlevel comparison include Burton Pasternak's (1978) study of the seasonality of birth in Taiwan, Caroline Bledsoe's (Bledsoe and Isiugo-Abanihe 1989, Bledsoe 1990b) work on fosterage and the social management of family formation among the Mende of Sierra Leone and Nancy Levine's (1987) study of childcare in Tibetan communities in northwest Nepal.

Economists, too, have taken advantage of this kind of approach, sometimes in the process recasting seemingly intractable materials. One suggestive example is the study by Paul David and his colleagues of birth-spacing strategies among northern French peasants in the latter half of the eighteenth century (David et al. 1985; David and Mroz 1986). The heart of the David study is a method of analysis designed to enable the investigator to break up a large, aggregated data set in order to obtain estimates of the effects of antecedent conditions on the length of subsequent birth intervals at the level of individual couples. This method revolves around the use of statistical modeling procedures to estimate how much of the variance in the length of the intervals between live births may be explained by selected characteristics of couples and their environments. These estimates in turn are used to simulate the monthly probabilities of a live birth for various sorts of women and couples. When the results of these simulations are compared, statistically significant relationships between family composition and the length of subsequent birth intervals are treated as indications of deliberate fertility control just as, in Smith's (1977) work on infanticide in Tokugawa Japan, statistically significant relationships between family composition and the sex of subsequent children entered in the population registers are treated as indications of active intervention in child survival.

If it turns out that we need or can attain a satisfactory concept of active decision-making, the problem of developing appropriate statistical tests no longer stands in the way. The results obtained by Smith, the David study, and other microlevel investigations suggest that some sort of concept of active decision-making is, in fact, precisely what we need. Contrary to the standard representations of transition theory, a small body of evidence has accumulated in the last decade or so suggesting that couples in pre-transition populations sometimes deliberately intervene in processes of family formation to shape their course and outcome. These are populations, in other words, in which fertility and mortality remain high and in which neither age-specific fertility rates nor parity progression ratios indicate the use of contraception. Nevertheless, and depending on the institutional framework, a rough balance between household personnel and resources may be achieved by the selective use of apprenticeship and of heirship strategies such as fosterage and adoption (Wrigley 1978; Bledsoe and Isiugo-Abanihe 1989, Bledsoe 1990b). Immediate or deferred infanticide also may be used to limit family size and/or to control the gender composition of the "stock" of offspring (Smith 1977; Scrimshaw 1978; Chen et al. 1981; David et al. 1985; David and Mroz 1986; Das Gupta 1987; Levine 1987).

Nor is active interference in the course of family formation limited to shifting children from one family to another and/or to mortality, spheres of activity in which the possibility of control is not in doubt. Though the conduct at issue has been masked by conventional definitions of contraception, the deliberate control of family formation also extends to fertility. Couples in "non-contracepting" populations in Taiwan (Pasternak 1978) and India (Carter 1985) schedule conceptions so that births will occur during periods of low infant mortality or other favorable times in the cycle of seasons. There is evidence from the same Indian population and from rural eighteenth-century France that, at least during some phases of family formation, some couples delay or accelerate further conceptions in response to the gender of their previous children, in part by controlling the duration of breast feeding but also by abstaining or not abstaining from intercourse (Carter 1984; David et al. 1985; David and Mroz 1986).

The paucity of studies attesting to active intervention in family formation is due, I suspect, not to the infrequent occurrence of the phenomenon but to methods of data collection and analysis that focus on characteristics of large aggregates or on so-called representative couples. Most of the evidence referred to above comes from small, intensive anthropological or historical studies or, in the case of Paul David and his associates, rests upon sophisticated statistical techniques designed to disaggregate a large data base. It is probable that more such evidence will emerge if demographers heed Caldwell, Reddy, and Caldwell's (1988) call for micro-demographic investigations, but that is another story. Here I want to concentrate on more theoretical issues. Or, more precisely, I want to suggest some of the ways in which anthropology might best contribute to such micro-demographic studies.

Central to demographic transition theory is the notion that the demographic transition – the shift from high, though fluctuating, mortality and high fertility to low mortality and low, though varying, fertility – is accomplished in part by a shift from natural fertility to controlled fertility (Henry 1961; see also Knodel 1983). This somewhat misleading pair of terms does not juxtapose any or all forms of fertility control with its complete absence. It is based, instead, on the notion that human populations fall into two groups, those that practice deliberate control of fertility and those that do not. Deliberate control, in turn, is defined as practices designed to terminate childbearing when some target family size has been reached. Such practices are dependent, in other words, on a married woman's parity, the number of children she has born to date (Bongaarts 1978:107). In controlled fertility populations, low fertility is achieved by the practice of contraception so defined and by the parity-dependent use of abortion. Fertility also may be held to levels well below the biological maximum in natural fertility populations, but there the mechanisms are customs that restrict marriage and that regulate nonparity-specific practices such as breastfeeding.[2]

The distinction between natural and controlled fertility rests in turn upon the separation of culture and agency. In Frank Notestein's (1945) classic macro-sociological account of the demographic transition, individual conduct in premodern societies is narrowly channeled by social institutions and cultural norms, especially those centered on the family. The high levels of aggregate fertility required by such societies to balance their high mortality may be directly linked, therefore, to enduring cultural constraints. Fertility declines when modernization, especially industrialization and education, both reduces mortality and produces a more rational social life, one in which deliberate individual decision-making is freed from cultural constraints. Microlevel models of decision-making are not required at any stage of this process for it is assumed that people who exercise deliberate choice with regard to family size invariably impose sharp limits on their fertility while people who have large families do so only as the result of social and cultural constraints.

True to their strengths, economists interested in fertility transitions argue that they are best explained using microlevel models of individual decision-making cast within one or another version of "the new home economics" (e.g. Nerlove 1974, Easterlin 1978). In these models, the unit of analysis is the representative or average couple without regard to the institutional setting within which couples act and in which they may be differently situated. High as well as low fertility is explained as the result of deliberate choices made in response to quantifiable socioeconomic circumstances. Though economic theories of the demographic transition emphasize individual decision-making, they resemble the earlier theories derived from Notestein in treating culture as an external constraint, the significance of which declines with modernization. Culture thus consists of "norms" or "shared expectations about how those in particular statuses should behave, usually reinforced by sanctions imposed for deviations" (Bulatao et al. 1983:13). In premodern societies, when the demand for children exceeds the supply and couples do not choose to limit their fertility, norms specifying family size, the duration of postpartum abstinence, breastfeeding and so on may modify the biology of reproduction and therefore affect the aggregate level of natural fertility. But when, during modernization, the supply of children exceeds demand and couples increasingly choose to intervene in family formation, these norms become peripheral, for individual choice is "strongly influenced by economic and social conditions" (Bulatao et al. 1983:2).

The importance of deliberate interventions in family formation in pre-transition populations does not consist in their effects on overall levels on population growth. These effects may well be small. Rather, the significance of such conduct lies in the challenges it poses to central features of demographic theory and practice. Indications of active decision-making in these circumstances directly undermine the distinction between natural and controlled fertility. They also threaten the separation of agency and culture. Leibenstein has argued persuasively that a theory of active decision-making involving maximization procedures is at the very least implausible. Yet evidence of deliberate and systematic intervention in family formation in what have been regarded as natural fertility populations suggests that the usual alternative, a theory of passive decision-making channeled by external cultural norms, is equally unsatisfactory. We are stuck on the horns of a dilemma.

Flows of conduct: An alternative view of agency and culture[3]

As Sherry Ortner (1984:134) has observed, the separation of culture and agency is deeply embedded in the presuppositions of modern social science. This certainly suggests that we should not be too sanguine about the possibilities of escaping from the dilemma in which, as I have argued, demographic theory and practice is caught. Since demography is not alone in its difficulties, however, demographers are not forced to rely on their own efforts to find a solution. Others have been there before us and we may hope to profit from their attempts to resolve similar problems.

Anthony Giddens' (1979) theory of structuration is a good place to start.[4] Two features of Giddens' work are of particular interest. First, he argues that human agency is correctly understood not as a sequence of discrete acts of choice and planning, but rather as the reflexive monitoring and rationalization of a continuous flow of conduct. Second, he suggests that cultural principles and social institutions have a virtual rather than a substantial existence, taking shape as they enter into activity. The first of these concepts enables us to detach ourselves from abstract, universal rationality. The second allows us to put aside the concept of culture, shifting our attention from enduring principles of social action to the practices in which rules that are never more than provisional are produced and reproduced.[5]

Giddens has relatively little to say about the details of ongoing human conduct. However, two additional sets of concepts help bridge the gap between the broad framework of his theory of structuration and the requirements of detailed descriptive analyses of the conduct involved in fertility. One set of concepts comes from *Uncertainties in Peasant Farming*, Sutti Ortiz' (1973) study of production decisions among Páez Indian farmers in Columbia. The other set comes from *Cognition in Practice*, Jean Lave's (1988) work on the uses of arithmetic among grocery shoppers and participants in the Weight Watchers diet program in California.

Ortiz (1973:7–20 and 247) argues that previous work on decision-making has been handicapped by its inability to distinguish more than two types of behavior. One is what Herbert Simon (1958) called "programmed decisions" in which individuals decide on courses of action in advance of undertaking them. The other is habitual behavior in which people follow routines or employ conventional rules of thumb. This is the familiar opposition between agency and culture. Ortiz replaces this well-worn binary opposition with a three-part scheme. It is important, she shows, to pay attention to where in the flow of activity "decision-making points" are located. From this perspective, habitual behavior is much reduced in scope while two new varieties of decisions are introduced.

What Ortiz calls "planning decisions" are made well in advance of the activity with which they are concerned. Planning decisions involve active information-gathering and some attempt at maximization (1973:269). Such decisions are more likely to be undertaken when the level of perceived uncertainty is limited, economic activities are interdependent, and decision-makers are relatively independent of other agents. They also are more likely to be undertaken with regard to activities that are evaluated in terms of relatively few goals (1973:254–264).

Planning decisions are the equivalent of Simon's programmed decisions, but they are no longer the only alternative to routine. A second class of decisions is made in the midst of action. Satisfaction and security rather than maximization are the primary concerns in decisions made during the course of action and the attention devoted to information acquisition may be safely reduced (Ortiz 1973:247 and 269). Finally, "on-the-spot decisions" or gambles are made just before action is undertaken. These decisions predominate in situations in which the actor has little information and "can only estimate outcomes in terms of a particular probable loss and an expected but undefined high gain" (1973:248, 269 and 276–277).

Ortiz locates decision-making in the flow of conduct but continues to treat it as an intramental process. Lave, however, argues that our focus should be on "activity-in-setting."

> The point is not so much that arrangements of knowledge in the head correspond in a complicated way to the social world outside the head, but that they are socially organized in such a fashion as to be indivisible. "Cognition" observed in everyday practice is distributed – stretched over, not divided among – mind, body, activity and culturally organized settings (which include other actors). (1988:1)

Practice is neither activity nor setting nor yet a combination of the two, but something entirely different.[6]

Concerned from the start with activity-in-setting, Lave and her fellow investigators in the Adult Math Project began by following study participants through their everyday activities for a week. When this proved to be infeasible, it was arranged that investigators would join participants on their shopping expeditions. No matter the time of day, "[w]e arrived at the house in time to observe preparations for shopping, went to the store together, shopped, and returned home to follow the process of storing groceries as the expedition ended in their kitchens" (1988:49).

From the perspective of participants in the Adult Math Project, the supermarket is the arena in which one of their activities, grocery shopping, takes place. The product of the business activities of its owners, operating in a particular political economy, the supermarket is a relatively durable construction. However, different sorts of shoppers traverse the supermarket in quite different ways, depending upon their age and gender, their dietary preferences, their budgets and many other factors. In Lave's terms, by following different paths through the market on different days and at different hours these shoppers construct different settings for their shopping activity. The setting also changes when shoppers note new displays, search for new items, stop to talk to acquaintances and so on (1988:150–151).

These settings in turn shape the activity of shopping. Consider, for example, a shopper approaching the case of frozen enchiladas.

SHOPPER: [speaking hesitantly, eyes searching the shelves to find the enchiladas] Now these enchiladas, they're around 55 cents. They were the last time I bought them, but now every time I come . . . a high price.

OBSERVER: Is there a particular kind of enchilada you like?

SHOPPER: Well, they come in a, I don't know, I don't remember who puts them out. They move things around too. I don't know.

OBSERVER: What is the kind you're looking for?

SHOPPER: Well, I don't know what brand it is. They're just enchiladas. They're put out by, I don't know. [Discovers the display of frozen Mexican dinners.] Here they are! [Speaking vigorously and firmly.] They were 65 the last time I bought them. Now they're 69. Isn't that awful. (1988:153)

The shopper's knowledge of enchiladas, particular varieties as well as prices, is distributed over persons-acting and setting. The quality and specifics of her knowledge alter as she physically places herself in front of the display.

Similarly, Lave observes that "conventional assumptions treat calculation as a cognitive function and its context merely as a stage on which action occurs. But activity-in-setting, seamlessly stretched across persons-acting and setting often turns the latter into a calculating device" (1988:154). Thus one shopper used the fact that packages of chicken thighs all contain six pieces to get the portion size she desired without going to the trouble of dividing weight by number of pieces. A more expensive package, she explained, would give her larger portions and a less expensive package smaller portions (1988:154).

The dialectical relation between persons-acting and setting extends to the definition of "problems" and the procedures used to "solve" them. Not surprisingly, none of Lave's grocery shoppers traversed their supermarkets methodically calculating unit prices or determining best-buy purchases by comparing price ratios with quantity ratios for pairs of items. Most choices are made in terms unrelated to such calculations:

> OBSERVER: This seems like a big package of elbow noodles, and you add these to the macaroni?
> SHOPPER: I add some, I just take a handful and add it to the rest, to the other packaged macaroni, 'cause I add macaroni to it. Plus I use that for my goulash.
> OBSERVER: For the goulash. O.K. And you like this particular kind? Are there other alternatives here?
> SHOPPER: Yeah. There's large elbow. This is really the too-large economy bag. I don't know if I, probably take me about six months to use this one. And I just, I don't have the storage room for that kind of stuff. I guess if I rearranged my cupboards, maybe I could, but it's a hassle . . . I don't know, I just never bought that huge size like that. I never checked the price, though, on it. But being American Beauty it probably costs more even in that large size. (1988:161–162)

Though the items for sale are labeled with price and quantity, neither these features of the arena nor their own budgets force arithmetic problems on consumers. Arithmetic is drawn upon when other decision-making procedures are blocked or come to an end without producing a choice and then only when "the problem" has been reduced to a manageable scope. It is used only occasionally when three alternatives are being considered and never when the number of alternatives is greater than three (1988:157).

This use of math in shopping illustrates a final aspect of Lave's analysis that I wish to emphasize. Lave argues that an activity may be structured in different ways.

> Suppose you are asked to solve a math problem like 75×114. A school taught scenario is one possibility: Get out paper and pencil, use a place holding algorithm, write 114, below it $\times$ 75, draw a line beneath, multiply from right to left, 5×4, carry 2, 5×1 is 5 plus 2 is 7, 5×1 is 5, move to the left, 7×4, carry 2, 7×1 plus 2, 7×1, writing down the answers all along. Then add down the answer columns. Or, use a calculator, punch in 7, then 5, the multiply button, then 1, 1, 4, the total button and read the answer on the display. Or, ask a friend, "how much is 75 times 114?" "Well, let's see . . . 75 hundred is 7 thousand 5 hundred and 750 is 8,250. Remember that. Okay.

And 4 × 70 is 280 and 4 × 5 is 20. So that's 300. What have you got?" "850." 'So its 8550." The product may very well be the same in each case, but the process has been given structure – ordered, divided into units and relations, in action – differently in each case. (1988:98)

That which gives structure to an activity in this sense Lave terms structuring resources (1988:97, 122, 124). As her example indicates, these may include social relations and material objects such as paper and pencil or calculators. One activity also may serve as a structuring resource for another carried out concurrently, as when arithmetic practices are differently structured by school, shopping and various research strategies (1988:97–122). Finally, activity may be structured by ideas about what constitutes proper conduct. The use of arithmetic by supermarket shoppers when other decision procedures are stalled is an example of a structuring resource in this last sense as well as the previous one. The use of math associates shoppers with the paradigmatic practices of rationality in our society. It also is "a move outside the qualitative characteristics of a product to its characterization in terms of a standard of value, money" (1988:157). By such means "just plain folks" can experience themselves as, and demonstrate to others that they are, rational agents who know the value of money.

The examples I have given tend to push the notion of reflexively monitored flows of conduct in the direction of calculation in the broad utilitarian sense of balancing means and ends. However, as Charles Taylor argues,

to be a full human agent, to be a person or a self in the ordinary meaning, is to exist in a space defined by distinctions of worth. A self is a being for whom certain questions of categoric value have arisen and received at least partial answers. (1985:3)

We do not simply choose among alternative courses of action, which crops to plant or how many children to have, in order to best achieve our desires. We also evaluate the worth of various possible desires, rejecting abortion, for example, as inconsistent with our concept of life or endorsing choice as inherent in gender equality.

The body resourceful: Embodiment and fertility in India

I begin to explore some of these questions using material from *Labour Pains and Labour Power*, a study by Patricia and Roger Jeffrey and their associate Andrew Lyon (1988) of women and childbearing in two villages, one Hindu and one Muslim, in Bijnor District in western Uttar Pradesh, India, between 1982 and 1986. The Jeffreys' work is an attempt to demonstrate the centrality of women's roles in a sharply stratified agrarian society by placing the experience of childbearing in its social and economic context. The Jeffreys' study is not linked to a systematic treatment of the region's demography, providing only occasional references to and a few longer discussions of abortion and contraception. Nevertheless, their work may be used to make several points concerning fertility. First, though the villages in which the Jeffreys worked are located in a region where fertility remains rather high, there do appear to be opportunities for women to make deliberate interventions in family formation. In this limited sense, fertility is not "natural." Second, these occasions can be discerned more easily if we look for a variety of decision-points spread over the course of family formation. Third, and not very surprisingly, concepts of the body and what Mauss (1979) called "body techniques" are important ingredients of fertility practices.

It is around this last point that my use of the Jeffreys' ethnography links up with the structuration or practice theoretic approaches to agency sketched in the previous section. Following Lave, I suggest that the culturally constructed body is among the elements of activity-in-setting.[7] As such, the body helps to shape decision points that have an impact upon fertility and serves as an information-gathering or calculative device. It also is among the signs that may be deployed to assert claims to agency or personhood and to a position in what Taylor (1985:3) calls "a space defined by distinctions of worth."

On the face of it, Bijnor District is not a promising place to look for relationships between conceptions of the body and deliberate interventions in family formation. In general, the district would fit the North Indian pattern delineated by Dyson and Moore (1983; see also Miller 1981) and described in greater detail, for the Khanna District in nearby Punjab State, by Wyon and Gordon (1971).[8] In the north, infant and child mortality are relatively high. The age of women at first marriage is relatively low and fertility is high. Both the sex ratio (males per 100 females) and the ratio of male to female infant and child mortality also are high. Uttar Pradesh exceeds other northern states on many of these measures.

Many of the Jeffreys' observations confirm Dyson and Moore's (1983) contention that contraception is relatively infrequently used and fertility is high in North India because the status of women is low. In general, the Jeffreys' informants were "offended" by questions concerning sexual relations and so "reticent" on the subject that the Jeffreys could obtain little or no information on the incidence of sexual relations (1988:250, n70; 261, n12). When newly married and still sharing a joint household with his parents, a man's mother may "regulate" when he and his wife "sleep together (at least at home at night)" (1988:29). In general, however,

> the husband has the right of sexual access to his wife at times when he decrees: she should neither take the initiative nor refuse him. Many men in Dharmnagiri and Jhakri were explicit that sexual intercourse involves the exercise of power over a woman who is degraded in the process. (1988:29)

As regards contraception, a term that in this population has come to mean sterilization or the use of intrauterine devices, the distribution of power was precisely captured by the woman who said, "[w]hatever my husband's opinion is, I have to make that my opinion too" (1988:195). Nevertheless, women do seem to have some room for maneuver.

How many children, how fast?

Among Muslims in particular, many men state that they will accept as many children as God gives. This is a somewhat ambiguous position. On the one hand, it may convey a moral stance on family planning. As one man put it, "[i]t's not what I want, it's what God decides. We Muslims don't think about things like family planning" (1988:197). On the other hand, as the following conversation between Andrew Lyon and a Muslim man indicates, it acknowledges that Bijnor villagers, not unlike the rest of us, have limited control over their ultimate family size and composition.

ANDREW: How many more children do you want?
FAROOQ: Do you have some in your pocket to give away?
ANDREW: No, I just want to know what you want. You had three children when I went away.
FAROOQ: If you know so much, tell me how many I've got now!
ANDREW: How could I know? You could have had no more or one or two and they could be boys or girls.
FAROOQ: Or some might have died also.
ANDREW: Yes, that's right.
FAROOQ: Ah, now you are beginning to understand how God's will might work. (1988:177)

Some women make similar statements (1988:196), but for them the bodily experience of family formation provides an altogether different calculus. As one woman put it, "[e]nough. I endure the trouble, my husband doesn't" (1988:197). Another spelled out the "trouble" in more detail, emphasizing the spacing between births.

You see how we must deal with babies' pee and shit. Babies cause a lot of worries. Last night my new baby was sleeping on my bed but my two-year-old refused to sleep with anyone else, so he was on my bed too. My sleep is always broken, never complete. My head aches. Having too many children has brought weakness to my body. With every child I lose a bit more of my spirit. Bearing a child every two years does not let us remain young for long. We are not as old as we look: women here become old quickly. (1988:167)

And a local midwife observed, calling attention to the consequences of prolonged breastfeeding,

[w]hen a woman breast-feeds while she is pregnant the new baby may not grow strong. But it is more likely that the woman will become weakened from

two directions: the baby in her belly and the child sucking at her breasts. (1988:173)

"Going behind the husband:" Menstrual regulation and abortion

Where delayed menstruation may be a sign either of illness, menstrual irregularity, or pregnancy, a decision point is created in which what might otherwise be an illegitimate use of abortifacients may become the legitimate regulation of menstruation. According to Ngin (1985), Malaysian Chinese women apply a hot–cold medical theory to the womb and to menstrual regularity.

> When the womb is "warm," it is susceptible to conception. A "cold" womb, on the other hand, is the cause of infertility. The sign of a warm and healthy womb is regular menses, whereas irregular menses indicate a cold womb. Since warmness of the womb cannot be detected, a woman is thought to be in poor health when her menses are irregular. Therefore, great efforts are made to ensure menstrual regularity . . . (Ngin 1985:37)

Chinese indigenous fertility regulating preparations are thought to be both emmenagogues and abortifacients. As a result, a preparation taken to induce menstruation and test for a pregnancy may also terminate an unwanted pregnancy (see also Browner 1985). Something similar apparently occurs in North India.

Though Hindu and Muslim women in Bijnor routinely affirm that their husbands are their masters and that they should do nothing "behind" their husbands, not a few do precisely that. Though the Jeffreys "cannot gauge how often such secret defiance occurs," they did obtain anecdotal evidence that

> a woman's visits to her natal village may provide some space for action independent of her husband. Her mother is more likely to be concerned about her well-being, and to arrange for an abortion or contraception to protect her health. Several women married out of Dharmnagiri, for instance, had abortions performed or IUDs inserted while staying in their parents' house . . . (1988:197)

Clearly, women's surreptitious resort to abortion or contraception in western Uttar Pradesh revolves in part around the differential constraints they experience in their marital and natal villages. Concepts and practices connected with the body also are a crucial resource.

To begin with, women distinguish between contraception and menstrual regulation. The principal method of contraception offered by the government family planning program is sterilization. This is understood to "put a stop to children." It does not "extend the gap" or "avert a baby" (Jeffreys

1988:204). Condoms, intrauterine devices and oral contraceptives also are available through the family planning system and are "locally . . . regarded as means of extending the gaps between pregnancies" (1988:208). Of particular interest is the Hindi term "*safai*" or "cleansing." Included under this term is a variety of products and procedures which result in abortions: oral and injected abortifacients, dilatation and curettage, and surgical abortion per se. These fall into two groups. Those which may be used early in pregnancy are thought to "avert a baby" that, in the local view, is not yet there. "Surgical procedures," on the other hand, "are likely to be recommended only after the spirit has entered the baby and involve 'causing a baby to fall'" (1988:206).

In the North Indian view, menstrual regulation has to do with the accumulation and dissipation in the body of heat. All forms of blood are hot. A body in good health maintains a balance between heat and cold. An excess of heat may be of particular concern, because heat accumulates in the head where it may cause madness. In men, blood is transformed into semen and the heat that it carries is dissipated during intercourse. In women, heat accumulates between periods but is dissipated by the menstrual flow. "Thus, women are particularly anxious if menstruation is delayed or light, although an excessively heavy menstrual flow is considered weakening" (1988:24). A woman "whose period is late may consume very [hot] items 'to avert a baby'" or, and here is that word again, "to cause 'cleansing' (safai, that is an induced abortion)" (1988:200). What, in the one case, a woman's husband expects to be the master of and may forbid, is, in the other case, none of his concern.

Critical to the ambiguous relation between contraception and menstrual regulation is the cultural construction of pregnancy. The critical transition occurs with the "completion" of three months. At this point,

> life (jan) enters the baby, its body parts begin developing and its sex is settled
> . . . When three months are completed women talk of pregnancy and say that
> the baby has adhered or flourished . . . Thereafter, vaginal bleeding would be
> called a baby or the belly falling . . . (Jeffreys 1988:76)

Before the completion of three months, vaginal bleeding would merely be a later period. Women say that "'there was no pregnancy,' merely a 'blob of flesh'" (1988:76.).

The opportunity provided by concepts of pregnancy to maneuver between menstrual regulation and abortion is preserved by bodily practices that may maintain the privacy and autonomy of pregnancy diagnosis in a woman's marital household. Central to these practices is the concept of shame (*sharm*). By so covering her body that only her hands and feet are visible and by other bodily practices, an in-married woman expresses the shame appropriate to her sexuality. In so doing she also conveys to observers that she is properly under the control of her husband, for whose honor she has respect and concern (1988:29–30). At the same time, however, she effectively conceals changes in her body from others whose intentions may not coincide with her own. Indeed, it is thought proper for her to do so. Some women "regularly interrogate their [daughters-in-law] to check if they are menstruating normally," but an in-married woman's mother-in-law usually "may guess she is pregnant only by noting when she last had a purifying bath signifying the end of menstruation." "A pregnant woman practices more than usually rigorous bodily concealment" and this may, no doubt, disclose her condition to watchful eyes, but shame prevents her from making an explicit announcement (1988:72).

I suspect that it is at least in part as a result of these practices that women generally diagnose their own pregnancies.

> the cessation of menstruation is a key factor. Additionally, the retention of blood . . . is evidenced in symptoms of [heat], such as nausea, vomiting, and rashes. Most women note the start of their menstruation according to a lunar calendar and, if their next period does not begin [on schedule], they say that one month is completed. (1988:75)

Given the cultural construction of pregnancy, they have roughly two months in which to "avert a baby" rather than to "cause a baby to fall." In this part of India, shame prevents women from giving birth in their parents' households, but they apparently do not feel it is shameful to visit their natal households before they are visibly pregnant, the cutting point being "six complete months" for one of the Jeffreys' informants (1988:82). All of this is hardly perfect freedom of choice, but it does provide a space in which to intervene actively to "extend the gap" between births and to obtain the help of one's natal kin in so doing.[9]

"Overturning the pattern"

North India also is known as an area of strong son preference. This is best documented in studies of infant and child mortality (Miller 1981). As I noted above, there also is evidence that some of the couples observed by the Khanna study during the 1950s sought to delay or accelerate further concentrations in response to the gender of their previous children, at least in part by abstaining from or engaging in intercourse. More recently, the use of amniocentesis and abortion to control the gender of children in North India has attracted widespread attention (e.g. Jeffrey et al. 1984).

Here, too, the body is an important resource. Though all this may change with resort to amniocentesis, in this part of North India the nature of pregnancy would appear to vary with the gender of the fetus. The most general view seems to be that a child's sex is not determined until the completion of three months of pregnancy, when "life (jan) enters" the fetus and it becomes a baby instead of a mere "blob of flesh" (Jeffreys 1988:76). Some people think that from that point on a baby's gender can be read from signs in the mother's body,

> though several [midwives] (in particular) were very sceptical: craving for bitter foods or dust signifies a boy, sweet foods or ashes a girl; a female foetus moves earlier than a male; male babies lodge on the woman's right side, female on the left; with girls, women become languid and develop ruddy complexions, with boys, their buttocks do not enlarge much and late in pregnancy they sit with their right leg forward; . . . or (among Hindus) the woman's palm can be read or her birth horoscope consulted. (1988:76)

According to what appears to be a different line of thinking, "women have two uteri, one on the left for girls and one on the right for boys" (1988:255, n9). Still another view suggests that the ability of a fetus of one gender or the other to become established in the womb is influenced by the balance of heat and cold in the mother's body. Thus it may be said that "women who persistently bear girls are not garm [hot] enough for the baby's sex to be fixed as male" (1988:192). Whether it is a matter of the balance of hot and cold or of a woman's destiny (1988:192), some people think that the gender of a next baby can be read in the birth of its predecessor:

> the previous baby's placenta may have indicated a boy would follow (if it was round) or a girl (if it was thin and flat). (1988:76)

Together, these several cultural constructions of pregnancy and gender create decision points when women may attempt to intervene to determine the gender of their next child. Thus the Jeffreys report that

> [w]omen who have had a succession of girls can resort to treatments called seh palat medicines for overturning the pattern (seh) of their deliveries. Tablets are generally obtained direct from local [indigenous medical practitioners] or a few renowned expert [midwives] and taken at the end of the second or third month of pregnancy. (1988:192)

Some fraction of the Jeffreys' informants did not believe that these medicines worked as their purveyors claimed (1988:192). Nevertheless, even though the Jeffreys' work does not lend itself to statistical measures, it is reasonably clear that the use of such medicines is not uncommon. Regardless of whether or not they work or how often they are tried, their well-known existence indicates an aspect of information-gathering by actors that is still too often ignored in demographic theory. While most demographic models focus on completed family size and imagine that couples set family size goals at the beginning of their marriage, *seh palat* medicines suggest that couples may, and sometimes do, monitor the pattern of successive births of boys and girls in order to alter it as it transpires.

Contraceptive risk-taking and abortion in the United States

A more nuanced sense of what an account of fertility informed by practice theory might entail may be obtained by looking at the literature on contraception and abortion in the United States. One of the most richly documented and widely cited studies in this area is Kristin Luker's (1975) *Taking Chances*, an investigation of contraceptive risk-taking in California. Luker's work is based on interviews with sixty women undergoing therapeutic abortions in Northern California, fifty at a Planned Parenthood clinic and ten from a private practitioner, plus examination of the records of the clinic's first five hundred clients. Her research was carried out in 1971–72 during a period of large and rapid change in the legal regulation and use of abortion. Though *Roe* v. *Wade*, the decision of the United States Supreme Court establishing the right to abortion on demand, was not handed down until 1973, the California abortion law was liberalized in 1967. Under the revised law, a woman seeking an abortion, or her doctor, had to apply for permission from the therapeutic abortion board of an accredited hospital. Grounds for abortion included rape, incest, and a threat to the woman's physical or mental health. Statewide, the vast majority of women gave a threat to mental health as their reason for seeking an abortion. They were required to undergo a psychiatric interview with a therapist to validate that claim, but "this was largely a formality because virtually all petitions were approved" (Luker 1975:9). From 1968 to 1971, the number of induced therapeutic abortions recorded by the California Department of Public Health rose from 5,018 to 116,749 (Luker 1975:175).

Luker's account of contraceptive risk-taking

Luker's account of contraceptive risk-taking has three components. The first, the skeleton of her argument, is that risk-taking behavior, even though it may lead, perhaps repeatedly, to a painful abortion, is the product

> of a "rational" decision-making chain produced by a person who is acting in what he or she perceives to be his or her best interests, although often in the presence of faulty data. (1975:138)

In other words, the decisions of sexually active women to use or to refrain from using contraception result from "a series of decision junctures at which women must assign values to certain variables and plan their behavior on the basis of these assigned values" (1975:78–79). To begin with, women must assess the relative costs and benefits of contraception and of pregnancy. In addition, they must weigh the chances of actually becoming pregnant and of terminating a pregnancy. Only those women who regard contraception as relatively costly and pregnancy as potentially beneficial arrive at an initial favorable "cost benefit 'set'" toward risk-taking. They are likely to go ahead with risk-taking only if they judge they are unlikely to become pregnant and that the chances of reversing a pregnancy that proves to be unwanted are relatively high. Since this process must be repeated on each occasion of sexual intercourse, the decision-making process is continually modified in the light of previous experience. Both successful risk-taking, i.e., unprotected intercourse not leading to pregnancy, and unsuccessful risk-taking lead to the reassessment of the costs and benefits of contraception and pregnancy and of the probability of becoming pregnant.

The second component of Luker's argument concerns the mental processes by means of which the women she studied might negotiate this series of decision junctures. The decision-making processes of the women Luker interviewed often were "inarticulate and less-than-fully conscious" (1975:79). They could be reconstructed in retrospect, but were not explicitly articulated at the time. Thus,

> I: You said that you had a strong maternal urge. So you think that could have been a factor in getting pregnant?
> R: I think so, yeah. I don't know how exactly, but taking a wild stab, I think it would be that getting pregnant means having someone who will take my love and care, 'cause lots of times I think no one else wants it. (1975:68)

Or,

> R: I think I realized I needed help with professional people. So I went this drastic way to get it. I got myself into real trouble so I would have to go for help. (1975:75)

In spite of the apparent muddle, Luker argues, these women can be conceived of as employing rational decision-making processes. To make this point, she borrows Thomas Schelling's concept of "tacit coordination." Schelling (1963) uses the term "tacit" for bargaining or coordination among two or more persons that is unspoken. In tacit bargaining, in other words, adversaries or partners try to anticipate one another's expectations, but do not discuss them. Luker (1975:80) suggests that tacit coordination can take a "purely individual" form as well.

> Thus a hypothetical tacit argument carried on intrapsychically could run: "Well, it's really a bother to get out of bed and put more jelly in the diaphragm and it's right before my period, so I probably won't get pregnant and if I do get pregnant maybe we can get married." (1975:85)

The third, and largest, component of Luker's account consists of an analysis of the costs, benefits, and probabilities that her informants assigned to contraception, pregnancy, and abortion. To summarize briefly, the costs of an abortion are social as well as financial. Once one assumes that women seeking abortions are no more and no less rational than the rest of us, the fact that they are prepared to take contraceptive risks in the face of the substantial costs of abortion serves to draw attention to other aspects of the process. Abortion is costly, but so is contraception. The contraceptive costs mentioned by the women Luker interviewed go far beyond biological side effects and the strictly economic expenditure of time and money. Luker classifies the factors considered by the women in her study under the following heads: (1) "structural problems and prices" involved in obtaining "clinical" or "drugstore" supplies and services; (2) biological and medical side effects; (3) "social and cultural costs," including "acknowledging" and "planning" sexual activity, "continuing" contraception over time from one relationship to another and the loss of "spontaneity" in sexual relations; and (4) "maintaining costs," including the difficulties posed by persisting in the use of contraception in the face of difficult or unsupportive attitudes on the part of male partners and the changing character of ongoing relationships (Luker 1975:41–64). Finally, pregnancy may be seen as having a number of potential benefits. If these benefits turn out to be unobtainable and the pregnancy ultimately proves unwanted, it can be terminated with relative ease.

A critique and an alternative approach

Luker's analysis of contraceptive risk-taking achieves many striking successes, marking a very considerable advance over previous studies. I would not quarrel with the overall thrust of her argument nor with the great majority of substantive points on which it is based. I would, however, recast the argument in the theoretical terms I outlined above.

According to Luker, one advantage of a "'decision-making theory' of unwanted pregnancy" is that "it sees contraceptive risk-taking as an orderly social process that is open to analysis, rather than an intrapsychic enigma that must be dealt with on the same terms as other 'irrational actions'" (1975:34). Nevertheless, this "orderly social process" turns out to be composed of two parts that, unsurprisingly, repeat the separation of agency and culture. Decision-making remains intrapsychic. "[T]he social situation sets up the background for who will and will not become a risk-taker, by providing the elements to be interwoven into a cost accounting" (1975:90), but rational individuals carry out their own cost–benefit analyses.

The separation of agency and culture embodied in the distinction between individual cost–benefit analysis and social situation underlies a narrative device that is common in studies of this sort. Though Luker had relatively extended conversations with a small number of women, the data that her informants provided is chopped up into small, anonymous pieces. The presentation of these pieces is organized around Luker's own analytical scheme rather than the narrative devices of her informants.[10] Nowhere in Luker's text are we offered a sustained account of the experiences of a single woman subject as she narrated them to Luker, together with an attempt to provide a complete and coherent account of that woman's circumstances. Nor can the reader piece together such a narrative from a collection of fragments from the same person since informants are identified only by a generic "R" for "Respondent." For all that this mode of presentation fits the separation of agency and culture and is a standard feature of sociological writing, it obscures a number of Luker's most interesting observations.[11]

Luker is well aware that fertility, contraception and abortion cannot be isolated from other aspects of women's lives. What is, in Luker's theoretical analysis, parceled out among a variety of costs and benefits is a complex whole in the lives of individual women. The use of contraception is deeply embedded in our notions of gender, sexuality, and courtship. The whole process of contraceptive risk-taking goes forward in the context of the relationship between a woman and her sexual partner or partners, other important relationships and the changing social and economic statuses of men and women.

One axis of these relationships is the life course of particular persons. One of Luker's informants spoke of this in the following exchange.

I: Did you ever think you might get pregnant [as a result of risk-taking behavior]?
R: Sure, yeah, I thought I might get pregnant because it's there all the time, no matter what. There's such a discrepancy in what people do and say. I don't really think I want to be pregnant. I was miserable at the time. But at that moment I didn't make the decision to protect myself. This time I got pregnant on my diaphragm. As I look back, my husband had gone to the National Guard. He was gone for two weeks. I went to see my mother. I just packed everything, but I didn't take my diaphragm, I didn't think I would be able to see my husband. He had said there was a chance but a small one. Four days later I found out I was going to be able to see him. I tried to get a diaphragm. A doctor I knew ordered me one. So I went to pick it up, but they said I should have come sooner, it was too late. The next day I went to see my husband and for two days we didn't use anything. When I'm pregnant, I don't like it. But my husband's been married before and he has a child. His ex-wife has a lot of hold over him because of that and maybe I wanted to get knocked up for that. (1975:55–56)

Luker discusses this exchange in a section of her argument detailing the costs of carrying through on the use of contraception from one situation to another, noting "how the cost of maintaining motivation and action all the time can often make risk-taking the 'line of least resistance'" (1975:56).

More broadly, however, this woman's narrative locates the activities in which she engages around fertility, contraception, and abortion in the continuously shifting contexts of relations with her husband, places of permanent or current residence, a doctor with whom she has an established relationship and so on.

As Luker recognizes, it is, in part, life-course experiences of these sorts that make sense of the fact that the great majority of the women in her sample, all of whom were currently terminating an unwanted pregnancy, had previously used contraception effectively (1975:20). As one of her informants put it

> R: At the time I broke up, I had no reason to continue [with the pill] and then, well, my first guy, I was engaged with, Larry, when we broke up, there was no logical reason to continue, so I didn't. (1975:49)

Other brief narratives provide contrasting perspectives on flows of conduct. Several of these concern the details of sexual encounters. Thus,

> I: Did you ever think about getting pregnant?
> R: Sometimes I thought about it, but I didn't really pay too much attention, because we weren't really into . . . we were goofing around . . . in an intimate . . .
> I: Could you clarify that?
> R: We started in on one thing and then we would go on to another thing and finally we would have intercourse. We never said, "Well, we're going to do it today." It just happened. (1975:47)

Or again,

> I: Whose decision was it not to use contraception?
> R: (Male) I would've wanted her to and talked to her, but I didn't take a firm hand. Thinking of myself, I didn't want to use condoms, I couldn't ask her. We just went from one time to the other without thinking of the whole thing. (1975:59)

Others concern encounters between women and their (male) doctors.

> R: I was on the pills for eight months. I came out to California and I ran out of pills and I went to a gynecologist I knew out here and I didn't tell him I had a previous abortion, and I was just embarrassed. I told him I was out of pills and I needed a prescription and he said, "If you're having a relatively inactive sex life I'd like to take you off the pills for three months to see if you ovulate." I didn't like the idea, but I said to myself, he's the doctor. He told me to use foam. (1975:62)[12]

Here the short time frame both increases the detail of interaction, though much detail is still missing, and highlights the generic relations between men and women. Among the important aspects of these relations are characteristic ways of speaking, including patterns of silence.

All of this lends credence to Giddens' (1979) argument that human agency involves the reflexive monitoring and rationalization of continuous flows of conduct rather than discrete acts of choice and planning. Luker's material also confirms Ortiz' emphasis on the role of time in the differentiation of decision points. Here it should be emphasized that Luker's decision junctures are not equivalent to Ortiz' decision points. The former refers to alternatives to be evaluated. The latter refers to occasions when this takes place. Though this is not one of Luker's concerns, clearly different kinds of decisions are made about different sorts of things at distinct points in the flow of activity.

For many women in Luker's sample, the decision to obtain an abortion in the event of an unwanted pregnancy appears to have been what Ortiz calls a planning decision undertaken well in advance of action. These women knew precisely what they would do if they became pregnant in their current circumstances.

> I: How did you decide to get an abortion?
> R: I decided long before I ever found out I was pregnant. I decided that if I ever did get pregnant, I would get an abortion. (1975:96)

For some, learning about the availability of abortion leads to a change in contraceptive risk-taking.

> R: I was really careful before, I guess because I thought I would end up in a home for unwed mothers.
> I: Did anything change your mind about that?
> R: Well, my sister had an abortion. (1975:97)

Nine women said they became pregnant right after writing a school research paper on abortion (1975:97). In accordance with Ortiz' suggestions concerning the location of decision points in the flow of activity, these are occasions when the women concerned have little uncertainty about possible outcomes, are relatively independent of other agents and are responding to a limited set of goals.

Where a woman is using a diaphragm or she or her partner are using one or another drugstore contraceptive, decisions to use or not to use contraception appear to be what Ortiz calls decisions made in the course of action or on-the-spot decisions, that is, appropriately enough, gambles. The woman who unexpectedly met her husband while he was on duty with the National Guard is, perhaps, an example of the first class of unplanned decisions. Not unlike the peasant farmer who plants manioc "until other commitments become pressing" (Ortiz 1973:247), she sought a new diaphragm until her search became more trouble than it was worth. The woman who reported that

> [w]e started in on one thing and then we would go on to another thing and finally we would have intercourse. We never said, "Well, we're going to do it

today." It just happened. (1975:47)

was, with her acquiescent partner, engaged in a series of gambles.

These are instances in which the agents involved are dependent on others and are juggling a variety of interdependent concerns. As they repeatedly make clear, they are acting under conditions of considerable perceived uncertainty and in response to multiple goals. According to Luker, many women apparently are given reason to believe that they are infertile by their doctors.

> [D]octors will often tell women whose reproductive organs vary from the norm that they may have trouble conceiving. In fact, what the gynecologist usually means is that if, at the appropriate time, women find they have trouble conceiving, they should investigate medically the possibility that their physical idiosyncrasies are the cause. Women, however, tend to hear this pronouncement as meaning that they are sterile or at best infertile. Thus an incredible two-thirds of the women interviewed said that they had been told by a doctor that they couldn't get pregnant or would have trouble doing so. (1975:63)

Pregnancy also may have many potential benefits. A sign of "fertility, femininity, adulthood, independence, and a wide variety of other meanings" (Luker 1975:65) including vitally important caring relationships, a pregnancy may be put to many uses even if it ends in an abortion. For one thing, it proves that one is a woman. Luker argues that in a time when gender roles are increasingly contested this is of considerable importance in and of itself. Pregnancy also may be used to define or redefine relationships, though these effects, too, are fraught with uncertainty. Parents may be punished or mobilized to help, a partner's commitment tested, or a marriage propped up. As one of Luker's informants put it,

> [y]ou always wonder how well a fiancé or a boy friend will react to what society says is a responsibility of his. Will he freak out, say "get away," or will he be loving? He became more loving and so I think for us a pregnancy makes you work out a lot of things with each other. (1975:70)

Luker's work also supports Taylor's concern with the role of "questions of categoric value" in decision-making. This appears in a number of contexts. For one thing, according to Luker, it helps account for the fact that aspects of contraceptive decision-making and family planning are not discussed but instead remain tacit. As Luker puts it,

> The intuitive nature of most of the decision making that goes on in everyday life is sustained by the fact that the social milieu dictates exactly how explicit such decision making can be. It is one thing, for example, to study stock prospectuses, or the performance rating of different brands of cars. It is an entirely different thing to evaluate explicitly the health, education, and future

earning power of a potential mate, although there is ample sociological evidence that most people weigh those factors implicitly. (1975:78.)

We may plan our families, but sexual intercourse itself is felt to be more "natural" if it is unplanned and spontaneous (see Cassell 1984). This conflicts with the premeditated use of contraception. Except for the pill or the IUD, inserting a contraceptive into this process may destroy the illusion of romance. "I bought the foam and never used it. It's hard to jump out of bed, it just ruins the whole mood" (1975:49). In spite of the sexual revolution, moreover, women still are made to feel that they are not supposed to be sexually active outside of marriage or a stable relationship. "I have nothing against sex," one woman said, "but I feel that there has to be a mutual feeling, that you have to be very much in love. It's my way of giving everything I have to someone" (1975:49). "Innocent" women do not use or need to use contraception. To obtain and use contraceptive pills or an intrauterine device after a relationship is ended, is to be defined as a woman who, in the face of the precept that "sex is to be expected only within a relationship of some duration and commitment," anticipates intercourse with a new and as yet unknown partner (Luker 1975:46–48). It is to acknowledge to oneself and to others that one is "looking to have sex" with the implication that one is a "woman who's been around," perhaps even a "rabbit" or "a sexual service station" (1975:46–49).

It is not my intention in all of this merely to add to the already impressive list of fertility determinants, this time emphasizing *very* close factors. By the social and cultural embeddedness of fertility, I mean to point to the ways in which practice is "constituted in a dialectical relation between persons acting and the setting of their activities" and to the manner in which "'cognition'... is ... stretched over ... mind, body, activity and culturally organized settings (which include other actors)" (Lave 1988:145 and 1). This emerges most clearly in the ways in which women describe how the dimensions of the problems they face and the values of various outcomes emerge not before but *during* risking-taking behavior and the ensuing events. Once again, perhaps the best example of this in Luker's material is the narrative fragment, quoted above, of the woman who unexpectedly saw her husband while he was serving with the National Guard and she had gone to visit her mother.

Talk is another means by which agency is socially distributed. Pierre Bourdieu (1977:59), for example, stresses the importance of talk in collecting and evaluating information on and choosing among alternative marriage arrangements and notes that this talk is structured by gender roles and household organization. Anthropologists generally have not documented such talk in detail, but Maclachlan (1983:10–11) notes that agricultural tasks in South India "involve symbolic interaction, mostly talk. The countless hours of human effort used in constructing the agricultural system I observed and the many thousands of hours employed in its operation and ongoing construction during my stay were organized with talk; people told themselves and one another what to do" (1983:10–11). In another field, the brief transcripts reported by the constructivist sociologist of science, Karin Knorr-Cetina (1983:127–128), suggest that scientific facts and arguments are socially constructed out of ambiguous materials in the course of laboratory talk. There are only the briefest hints of this sort of talk in Luker. In part, this is because of Luker's strategy of data presentation, but it also reflects the fact that, especially with the advent of the pill, contraception seems to be less and less a topic of explicit discussion (see below). Nevertheless, the imaginative reader will have little trouble elaborating the scenes suggested by the following exchange.

> I: Did you or he think you might get pregnant?
>
> R: He worried about it terribly, but I would just shrug and say, "It can't happen to us." I did say to him all this time, "We've lived on luck and I don't think one of us is fertile," and he said, "Don't take your chances." But I did. (Luker 1975:87)

Little of the foregoing, finally, is timeless or universal. On the contrary, as Luker notes, much of it is dependent upon a particular array of contingent cultural circumstances. It responds to changes in the surrounding political economy. In the absence of contraception, the probability of pregnancy following sexual intercourse is largely a function of biology, but the cost of contraception, the benefits of pregnancy and the availability of abortion are all shaped by the social setting. In particular, recent changes in the status of women and in the *mores* of courtship and sexual intercourse have shifted the balance between the costs of contraception and the benefits of pregnancy. "In the open market of contemporary courtship," Luker argues, "women as a class are bargaining with a deflated currency" (1975:121). Women remain dependent upon marriage even if it increasingly has become a bad bargain. Economic discrimination constrains women to exchange domestic services for men's larger income and provides them with few alternatives to the traditional roles of childbearing and motherhood, both still closely connected with marriage. However, the importance of marriage is falling for men. Sexual intercourse and domestic services are increasingly available outside of marriage, while the value to men of childrearing and parenthood is declining. In such a situation, there has been a substantial rise for many women in the potential value of pregnancy as a stepping stone to marriage "and thus the pool of potential risk-takers has increased astronomically." The availability of abortion has only compounded the effect.

[W]hereas in the past women were faced with the options of either marriage or an illegitimate pregnancy should the gambit fail, today the easy availability of therapeutic abortion [and, now, abortion on demand] means that risk-taking which ends in pregnancy can be fairly easily reversed, should the hoped-for marriage not occur. In brief, contraceptive risk-taking as a gamble for marriage is not a high-risk gamble. Should it fail, the costs are relatively low. (1975:122)

The calculus of contraceptive risk-taking also rests upon a particular contraceptive technology. Luker quite properly insists that many of the considerations she discusses pertain to men as well as women. "Biologically both men and women become pregnant – immaculate conceptions are virtually unknown in the literature" (1975:125). Given that both men and women take contraceptive chances, it is remarkable that much of her analysis is concerned with women only. The explanation, she argues, lies in the fact that changes in contraceptive technology have reallocated both the responsibility and the accountability for contraceptive choices. Older contraceptive techniques and devices, withdrawal, the condom and the diaphragm, were all intercourse related and involved both partners to a greater or lesser degree. Newer devices, the pill and IUDs, however, are female contraceptives. The newer devices also are regarded as more effective as well, so that women may feel that to rely on "drugstore" methods is to brand themselves as risk-takers (1975:53, 126). The effect of these changes, Luker argues, has been to transfer responsibility for contraception from couples to women. She cites

> an unpublished study by a local contraceptive clinic, which reports that fewer than one out of ten high-school and college age men asks a woman at first intercourse whether she is contraceptively protected. (1975:134)

This transfer of responsibility fits in with the ideology that women should control their own bodies, but it is not an unmixed blessing. Contributing to the perception that women may be treated as "sexual service stations," it helps to raise the costs of contraception. As one woman said,

> I had thought about getting birth control pills with the boy friend before, but that worked to where it was a one-way street for his benefit, not for mine. It would be mine because I wouldn't get pregnant, but safe for him, too, because I wouldn't put him on the spot. So I get sick of being used. I'm tired of this same old crap, forget it. I'm not getting pills for his benefit. (1975:128)

Men become "passive spectators."

> Although virtually every man in the study was reported either by himself or by a woman to be aware of the contraceptive risk-taking that was going on, no man in this study was able to effectively take action to stop the risk-taking. (1975:131)

And women are made accountable. More than 90 percent of the women in Luker's study paid all of the costs of their abortions themselves. Married couples tended to regard an unwanted pregnancy as a joint problem, but even here "the bulk of the decision" generally was left to the wives.

One of the virtues of a practice-theoretic approach to the flows of conduct involved in fertility is that these political-economic factors are not left outside the action as indirect or even more remote determinants, but are made ingredient to action.

Conclusion

Science, we are told, achieves its remarkable results by making simplifying assumptions. Sometimes the assumptions on which a given body of theory is based seem quite unrealistic, but this is justified if the theory works. The several theories of fertility change embedded in demographic transition theory do not work particularly well, however, and this only serves to highlight the impoverished character of their underlying assumptions. Among these assumptions are the notions that culture consists of a set of constraining norms separable from action and that we in the modern West are progressively freeing ourselves from its influence. Theories of fertility change are vitiated, in other words, by economism,

> the view that the moving forces in individual behavior (and thus in society, which is taken to be an aggregate of individual behaviors or some stratificational arrangement of them) are those of a need-driven utility seeker manoeuvring for advantage within the context of material possibilities and normative constraints: "the home-bred economizing of the market place . . . transposed to the explication of human society" (1976:86). Man (and, in her own place, Woman) the strategiser, manipulating "mean–ends relations [within] an eternal teleology of human satisfactions" (1976:85), takes the centre and most of the rest of the social stage. Custom, convention, belief, and institution are but *mise-en-scène*, the particular setting within which the universal drama of boundless desires and scarce fulfilments or, in the Marxist version, productive forces and class interests, is played out. (Geertz 1984:516, citing Salhins 1976)

Determinants, whether proximate or remote, remain external to agency. Agency collapses under the demands of abstract rationality and is reduced to a mechanical implementation of cultural prescriptions that ill-accords with observed outcomes.

A theory of fertility able to account for the remarkable variations within demographic regimes as well as for secular changes requires new concepts of agency and culture. Here I suggest that a more productive theory may be built on Giddens' notion of reflexively monitored flows of conduct, Ortiz' work on decision points and Lave's concept of activity-in-setting. I have tried to provide an illustration of this contention using material on concepts and practices of the body in North India and contraceptive risk-taking in California. It is through such exercises as this, I contend, that we will find ways to break out of the distinction between agency and culture, perceiving political economy as ingredient rather than external to action and agency as socially distributed.

At first sight, the analogies I have sketched between fertility, on the one hand, and agricultural decision-making and the everyday use of mathematics, on the other, might appear to block rather than foster further anthropological research on fertility. Regardless of how they might be brought into proximity by metaphor and advertising, sex is not the same as either shopping or agriculture. The canons of modesty and the Federal guidelines for protecting the privacy of human subjects set limits on what the anthropological investigator of fertility might attempt. The research practices of Lave's Adult Math Project cannot be transferred to the study of family formation without alteration. Investigators in such a study could not and should not arrange to join participants during incidents of their reproductive careers, arriving at their homes, for example, in time to observe preparations for sexual activity, going to the bedroom with them to discuss their thoughts on the use or nonuse of contraception as intercourse proceeds, and returning at regular intervals to follow the process of dealing with the outcome.

Nevertheless, concepts developed by Giddens, Ortiz, and Lave suggest a variety of questions that might inform anthropological research on the flows of conduct involved in fertility. To begin with we must pay attention to the diverse flows of conduct of which fertility is composed. Concerned with the "value" of children, students of demography have become accustomed to investigating the relations between fertility, on the one hand, and the management of the domestic economy, paid work outside the household, and education, on the other, though few, if any, investigations of these interrelations provide detailed accounts of ongoing activity. Fertility also needs to be located much more emphatically in relation to sexuality and the body. For all of these domains of activity, we need to ask questions such as the following. How do the interactions of persons-acting and arenas constitute activities-in-setting? How do the activities of which fertility is composed serve as structuring resources, one for the other? What ideas about proper conduct also serve as structuring resources?

We also need to know in much greater detail what sorts of "problems" connected with fertility people attend to and how these emerge during the course of action. As early as 1972, Steven Polgar observed that analyses in which the goals involved in family formation are characterized in terms of completed family size are seriously incomplete. Still using the terminology of norms, Polgar argued that the anthropological evidence . . . would rather lead us to look for norms concerning *who should have children, when childbearing should start, what is a desirable interval between children, and at what juncture in social aging childbearing should cease.* (1972:209, italics in the original)

Noting that strong son preferences can have a significant effect on fertility behavior, demographers long have been aware that gender composition concerns may influence family formation as well. These complications are likely to be little more than the tip of the iceberg. There is no reason to believe that the problems posed in demographic research – the determination of family size at the microlevel and the control of population growth at the macro level – are the same as the dilemmas that concern "just plain folks."

Further, where are decisions about how many children of each sex one wants, whether or not to have another child, whether or not to engage in sexual intercourse, whether or not to use what sort of contraception, whether or not to have an abortion, how long to breastfeed a child, and so on located in the flows of conduct involved in fertility? Does the location of decision points affect the decision-making process? Are solutions to these problems best understood as individual, intramental accomplishments or are they socially constructed, the result of "cognition" distributed over "mind, body, activity and culturally organized settings (which include other actors)" (Lave 1988:1)?

Notes

This is a revised and expanded version of a paper prepared for presentation to the American Anthropological Association Annual Meeting session, "Rethinking Reproduction: Toward a Political Economy of Fertility," New Orleans, 2 December 1990. I am grateful to Susan Greenhalgh for inviting me to participate in the panel and for her helpful comments on earlier drafts.

1 Examples include Dyke's (1974) work on St. Thomas, US Virgin Islands; Wachter et al.'s (1978) work on household composition and Howell's (1979) superb study of Dobe !Kung demography.

2 As I note above, it is not in fact clear that breastfeeding is entirely disconnected from parity.

3 The preceding analysis is intended to bring us to a point near the one from which Gene Hammel's recent essay, "A Theory of Culture for Demography" (1990b), began. Like Hammel I reject the notion of a "universal, decontextualized rationality." With Hammel I propose something like "an agenda for a culturally smart microeconomics." However, such an agenda requires that we abandon both terms of the relationship, culture as well as agency. Neither can account for observed patterns of fertility alone. Nor does it make sense to think of culture as the context of agency. If the idea that agency is mediated by culture is to be taken seriously, both concepts must be transformed.

4 Many anthropologists interested in practice theory begin instead with Pierre Bourdieu's concept of "habitus," a "durably installed generative principle of

regulated improvisations" (1977: 78). This seems to me a kind of *deus ex machina* cobbled together after the fact to do that which, as Bourdieu convincingly demonstrates, structure cannot do. Moreover, the habitus remains a determinative structure. As a result, the actor, in Bourdieu's theory, is what Giddens (1979: 52) calls a "structural dope."

5 Edward Levi's (1948) discussion of legal rules and legal reasoning is a valuable concrete illustration. Against the presumption that legal rules are clear and unambiguous, Levi argues that we never know what a legal rule means until we apply it to a case, and that the meaning of a rule changes every time we apply it. The effect of this is to shift our attention from legal rules to practices of legal reasoning.

6 On the notion of practice as socially distributed see Vološinov (1986) and Wertsch (1991).

7 Among the important contributions to and reviews of the burgeoning literature on the body are Gallagher and Laqueur (1983), Turner (1984) and Featherstone et al. (1991). In all of this literature the body is treated as a cultural construction. Following Foucault (e.g. 1979), much of this literature sees the body as among the important means through which discipline and power is exercised. It is less common to see the body treated as an element of individual agency (but see Johnson 1987).

8 Too much homogeneity should not, however, be assumed. Amongst the more prosperous Gujars in neighbouring Saharanpur District and to the southwest in Ajmer District, Rajasthan, but still within a distinctively North Indian demographic region, Raheja (1988) and Gold (1988) find rather different configurations of women's roles and practices.

9 For other instances of menstrual regulation as a form of fertility control see Akhter and Rider (1983) for Bangladesh and the Boston Women's Health Collective (1984) for the United States.

10 For a contrasting approach, see the use of narratives in Ginsburg (1989).

11 Nor does Luker comment on the effects on her study of carrying out her research in the facilities of an agency one of the purposes of which is to regulate sex. The 1973 Supreme Court decision striking down most state abortion regulation eliminated screening devices such as the therapeutic interview. However, counselling sessions continue to be an integral part of the process by means of which family planning agencies deliver contraceptive supplies and abortion services. These sessions often perpetuate the labeling process of the therapeutic interview. Concerned to prevent repeat abortions, counselors try to help their clients " 'understand' [their] 'self-destructive' behavior in becoming pregnant and then deciding upon an abortion" (Luker 1975: 146; see also Joffe 1986).

12 For more on the relations between women and their doctors, including transcripts of consultations, see Todd (1989).

4 Invisible cultures: Poor women's networks and reproductive strategies in nineteenth-century Paris

Rachel G. Fuchs and Leslie Page Moch

Twenty-eight-year-old Marie Madeleine Ditte worked as a cook, and in March 1873, when she first feared she might be pregnant, asked the *concièrge* of her building what she could take to restore her menstrual periods. A little later she also chatted with a pregnant neighbor whom she met on the stairway of her building, and from whom she obtained the name of a midwife. Ditte's employer, a doctor, soon thereafter dismissed her for "bad conduct," forcing her to look for a new job and new housing. Ditte moved across Paris to a furnished room and immediately found a job in a workshop making rugs. She now lived near Madame Clèmence Baronne, a compatriot from her home town in the Haute Marne about 150 miles to the east. In June she confided to Mme. Baronne that she had not had her periods for three months. She then sought help from a fresh-produce peddler who told her that she needed to drink a beverage including extracts of the plants rue or savin. When she asked her pharmacist for these herbs, or for something to bring on her periods, he replied that he did not know the right ingredients. Finally, Ditte went to the unlicensed midwife recommended by her former neighbor whom she had met on the stairway of the building where she had served as a cook. During the night after her fourth visit to the midwife, Ditte experienced intense cramping and stomach pains. The following day she announced that her periods had returned. Her talk of fearing pregnancy and her searching for help inspired gossip which led to her arrest and trial. The twelve-man jury acquitted her.[1] Ditte had sought aid from professionals, neighbors, and compatriots.

Women fearing pregnancy were not the only women seeking aid through networks of friends and relatives; mothers with young children did the same. For example, Marie-Thérèse Dubon needed help. Having lost her job, she had been unable to pay her infant daughter's wetnurse. The nurse's neighboring countrywomen had written that the infant was being left to starve, so Dubon had spent her last sou fetching her daughter. Because the wetnurse had refused to give up the baby's clothes until the debt was settled, Dubon returned to Paris on a hot summer's day in 1907 with the infant wrapped in her shawl. By the time she reached the sweltering city, Dubon concluded that her only recourse was to end her life in the River Seine. But Marie-Thérèse Dubon does not appear on police records of retrieved bodies, on the registers of shelters for homeless women, or in judicial records of abortion and infanticide trials. She is invisible to the public record because her sister took her in, despite the fact that Dubon's brother-in-law violently disliked her and she crowded their one-room home (Henrey 1951:29–30).

The poor women of Paris are most visible when they mount the well-illuminated stage of charitable organizations, public-welfare institutions, courtrooms, or hospitals. Nonetheless, it is well known that the primary source of information and aid is networks of kin and friendship through which rich and poor alike move, find jobs, engineer their social lives, and deal with crises (Granovetter 1974). This essay is an attempt to reconcile our institution-bound view of the poor with social theory and the realities of human connections; it does so by analyzing extant evidence of poor women's networks that informed, aided, and empowered them. We focus on the networks women relied upon in their reproductive strategies – especially to seek marriage partners, abortions, and aid with childcare – during the prewar years of the Third Republic (1871–1914).[2]

We write with an awareness that the poor women of Paris operated within a broader political context that shaped their reproductive choices and strategies (Ginsburg and Rapp 1991: 312–313; Martin 1987: 200–201). After 1871, as prominent French politicians became increasingly concerned with France's "depopulation," their rhetoric encouraged increasing fertility and decreasing infant mortality, especially after the census of 1891 revealed almost zero population growth. Abortion continued to be illegal, although rarely prosecuted, and with juries seldom convicting. Moreover, the French state adopted increasingly populationist policies to reduce infant mortality and protect the infant's "right to life."[3] These measures included well-baby clinics, free sterilized milk dispensaries, and programs of aid to single and married poor mothers with infants. By the turn of the century, protecting babies became a national patriotic duty; as a result the reproductive strategies of Parisian poor women developed within this extended nationalist and populationist culture (Fuchs 1992).

Most research on nineteenth-century Paris tells us a great deal about some aspects of working-class life, but very little about the social glue operating among women neighbors, co-workers, and kin. The lack of work on community or networks among poor women is partly due to the nature of documentation, and the dearth of direct evidence. Because legislators and reformers of France discussed the poor, and tried to enact legislation pertaining to them, much work is couched in terms of the state (Donzelot

1979; Stewart 1989). Contemporary reformers who observed Parisian housing, workplaces, and families were more concerned with the family, health, and work legislation than with helping networks among the poor (e.g. Simon 1861; Le Play 1877–79). For the most part, studies of working-class culture have focused on men, although the writings of working-class men were frequently concerned with women and the family (an excellent analysis of this is Scott 1988b). Our primary concern here is with ferreting out the active role and the culture of poor women themselves.

In thinking about ways to view poor women, we can see that within powerful structures and historical processes, "there is," as Joan Scott writes, "room for a concept of human agency," the attempt "to structure an identity, a life, a set of relationships, a society with certain limits and boundaries" (Scott 1986:1067). The bedrock of human agency is contacts among people and the powerful sharing of resources. Scott acutely observes that "to pursue meaning, we need to deal with the individual subject as well as social organization and to articulate the nature of their interrelationships, for both are crucial to understanding how gender works, how change occurs." This chapter is an investigation of networks that constituted the individual poor woman's most immediate society in the context of Parisian life and the French state. These networks upon which poor women drew were the fundamental tools with which "an identity, a life, a set of relationships" were constructed (Scott 1986:1067). The networks of poor women in Paris, like Marie-Thérèse Dubon and Marie Ditte whose stories open this chapter, provide the primary link between their self-perceived identity and the social identity visible on public records.

This perspective dovetails well with current approaches to reproduction in feminist anthropology (an excellent overview of this work is Ginsburg and Rapp 1991). The anthropological literature challenges the view of reproduction as a "natural" process, portraying it instead as a social construction involving negotiations and contests over the means and meanings of childbearing. This work highlights the role of women as agents of their own reproductive experiences (e.g. Martin 1987), illuminating both the strategies they deploy in constructing their reproductive lives and the networks of nurturance they create in the process of conceiving, bearing, and raising their children (see for example Bledsoe, this volume).

Networks and their operation are as gendered as the old school tie, yet much less visible. Unlike the relations among the powerful, the networks among the poor cannot be gleaned from historical records of dowry, notarized marriage contracts, shared ministry positions, school ties, charity affiliations, or legislative concerns. Rather, the networks among the poor are truly off the record. Those of women are particularly obscure because they are rarely manifested in the workplace and political solidarities that put men on police records or in workers' writings. They were less likely than those of men to appear in diaries, letters, or stories because poor women were more likely to be illiterate than any other group in pre-war France. Moreover, when networks could successfully help poor women in their reproductive strategies those women successfully stayed out of the written records and off the police, court, charity, hospital, and shelter registers of the city.

For women, "how gender works, how change occurs" is intimately related to their networks of contact and aid in both their objective position and their lived experience. More often than men, women moved and found work through private contacts because they were less likely to move and work as a team, unlike men in harvest, railroad, construction or road work (Moch 1992). Because there were so few occupations that allowed women to be self-supporting, it was in their best interests to marry. How they fared in urban marriage markets depended a good deal on social protection and sponsorship (Alter 1988; Elliot 1981). After in-depth interviews with those who moved to Paris in the 1920s, Isabelle Bertaux-Wiame observed that "while men move through the family network to find work, women move through jobs networks to find a family." Not only did women seek out a home, but they also perceived themselves in relational terms; Bertaux-Wiame concluded that "men consider the life they have lived as their own," yet "women do not insist on this . . . Instead they will talk at length about their *relationship* to such or such a person . . . They bring into view the people around them and their relations with these people" (Bertaux-Wiame 1979: 28–29). Perhaps because women were less socially and economically powerful than men, they were more dependent on personal networks that are less visible to the historical record. In any case, women's contacts not only inform us about their means of entering new places and new occupations, but they also inform us about an arena of particular importance to women's life experience.

Networks and urban life

Although networks elude the historian, they were evident to contemporaries and clearly were effective among the poor; the lively subcultures and occupational solidarities among migrants in the growing city were evidence of vital relations (Chevalier (1950) is the classic study of this topic). One person to whom Marie Ditte turned when she suspected pregnancy was a woman from her home town, even though she had not seen her for several months. When historians think of networks they think of the close net of ties formed by kin, compatriots, neighbors, and fellow workers – ties which often overlapped with one another to form dense subcultures like that of the famous masons from central France who lived and worked together in Paris, or the Sicilian artisans who shared their knowledge of birth control (Corbin 1975; Schneider and Schneider 1984).

We should also consider what sociologist Mark Granovetter labeled "weak ties," the link to outside one's quotidien network of contacts, connecting with other groups. "Weak ties" with the distant relative, vaguely-known compatriot, or friendly face on the block or stairwell, for example, enabled nineteenth-century people to find help in hard times. The "strength of weak ties" is that very effective aid could be offered not only by close kin and friends, but also by distant acquaintances or distant kin who may be better placed to help with information (Granovetter 1973; Wellman and Wortley 1990; for historical examples outside of France see Cressy 1986; Gribaudi 1987). It is important to note, then, that networks of contact could be quite fluid; the person with crucial information about birth control or abortion may not have been called upon again (Lee 1969). These "weak ties" bridging to other social groups became more accessible in the 1871–1914 period as French women traveled farther from home than ever before and as Paris attracted women from farther afield (Fuchs and Moch 1990). As Europeans sought aid for employment and social problems in the changing economies and society of the nineteenth century, they moved in networks of kin and neighbors, and reached out through more distant, mobile, and ephemeral contacts.

We analyze extant evidence of poor women's networks of contact as they resolved crises of pregnancy, childbirth, and childrearing. We look to the mechanics of contact and aid, distinguishing the arenas in which weak ties best served poor women. We scrutinize the kinds of connections that helped women, including those with men and middle-class people – kin, home-town compatriots, neighbors, friends, and charitable bourgeois women. Our evidence comes from the autobiographies of working-class women, a fresh reading of studies of women in nineteenth-century Paris, and court records of abortion and infanticide trials. Although staying out of institutional records indicates successful social support and protection, those records are useful; a careful analysis of women's stories and of witnesses' testimonies can reveal their networks prior to their appearance in court, hospital, or public shelter.

We consider networks within the spatial, occupational, and social considerations that structured opportunities for contact and information exchange in Paris. The most female spaces in the city, outside of their very cramped homes, were the landings and courtyards of apartment buildings – the locus of both privies or toilets and wells or spigots well into the first decades of the twentieth century. The women of the popular classes considered the street, market, and shop their domain where they both bought and sold wares and passed on information and gossip. The prototypical female space was perhaps the wash house, first the sixty-some wash-boats (*bateaux-lavoirs*) that dotted the Seine in the 1880s, then the dry-land wash houses (*lavoirs*) which offered a place to talk, protect, and instruct each other (Perrot, 1979, 1988; descriptions of housing in Le Play 1877–79; descriptions of the market in Zola 1979 [1872–73]).[4]

Some occupations offered many more occasions than others for making contacts and discussing problems and solutions. The homeworker in the garment trades (as well as those in flowermaking), among the most numerous of Parisian workers, and living on the top floors of apartment buildings, had relatively few occasions for contacts with those outside her family during her very long work day; on the other hand, she had the physical liberty to seek out a contact (Coons 1985; Henrey 1951; Boxer 1982; Coffin 1991). The most frequent daily contacts of the largest occupational group, domestic servants, aside perhaps from those with fellow servants, were those with their middle-class employers. By contrast, seamstresses who sewed together in sweatshops and fashion houses (*maisons de coûture*) had abundant occasions to talk, except when they were ordered to be silent or the noise of sewing machines interfered, as was sometimes the case (Bouvier 1983:88). As anthropologist Emily Martin notes, women workers used "backstage" areas, usually squalid places, for "solidarity and resistance" in discussion of reproductive matters (Martin 1987:95–97). Similarly, the saleswomen who worked for such department stores as the Louvre and Bon-Marché lived under the same roof and ate lunch together, as well as worked together; like servants they worked long hours and were closely supervised, but they had more opportunities for contact with their peers (McBride 1978). Laundresses, whose long-lived corporate structure reflected their strong collective organization, had the most opportunity for information exchange, since they hired on by the day in a public market and worked in groups (Perrot 1979; Scott 1988b:356; Simon 1861:22–27).

These spatial and occupational considerations gave privileged positions to some women, who, by the nature of their job or location, could easily act as nodes, or bridges, among networks of contact. They would come to the fore in addition to, or even in lieu of, kin and workmates, and were particularly important for women who sought to terminate a pregnancy or who needed help during or after childbirth.

Midwives played a pivotal role in the lives of poor women. Their vocation brought them into contact with women in their moments of greatest vulnerability; furthermore, midwives had access to information and expertise about both abortion and aid to poor mothers (McLaren 1978, 1983; Fuchs 1992). They directed poor women to charity and welfare services or to the public foundling home, informed needy postpartum women about available aid, and even told them how to apply for it. Mothers who did not deliver their babies in one of the public hospitals usually found out about public assistance from the midwives. Midwives often knew the pregnant woman through connections with a neighborhood herbalist if the pregnant woman had sought to abort.[5] Midwives were the link not only between the destitute mother and public assistance, but also between bourgeois women and their objects of charity. It was they who usually told charitable women about needy pregnant and postpartum women. Midwives were instrumental in directing the poor women's strategies of reproduction and motherhood. Most women delivered their babies with some assistance from a midwife, and strangers to Paris virtually depended on these women.

Of all the people in the neighborhood, *concierges* were second only to midwives in their importance in women's networks. The *concierge*, who was placed to greet and observe residents and visitors in her building, was in a position to possess a wealth of information and could either help or harm a woman with her information and reports to others. It is possible, for example, that the *concierge* caused Marie Ditte to lose her job by informing Ditte's employer of their exchange about her missed menstrual periods.[6] *Concierges* also responded to queries from welfare officials and the police.

Next in importance, the laundress garnered power by virtue of the fact that her workplace gave her access to local information and her work gave her access to intimate linens. Laundresses gave depositions in cases of suspected infanticide and abortion; they testified to quantities of blood they found on sheets that indicated an abortion or childbirth and to the absence of blood for several months, that indicated a pregnancy.[7] They could keep secrets and help, or gossip and hurt the poor women. A laundress was partly responsible for the investigation of Marie Merlin for infanticide in 1878 because, after washing Merlin's sheets bloodied by a recent childbirth, she notified the police of a suspected infanticide.[8]

Female networks did not always offer support. Because women had so much power over each other, they could use that power to punish each other – for stealing a lover, committing infanticide, or failure to participate in a neighborly exchange of goods and services – as well as to assist one another. Punishment could take the form of reporting bloody sheets to police investigating an alleged abortion, reporting an abortionist to the police because she violated neighborhood norms by charging high fees, or refusing to subcontract work to a poor and dependent young seamstress.[9]

Marriage partners

Much social life – including finding marriage partners – for women in Paris took place through family. For those without relations in the city, social contacts were also made and enjoyed within their apartment building. The top floors of the city buildings where workers or servants rented small rooms were notoriously unhealthy, uncomfortable, and sexually dangerous, but they also provided an important arena for working people's sociability. The gatherings in servants' rooms between 10 p.m. and midnight, although viewed as immoral and disruptive by employers, probably had an innocent element to them, and were doubtless informative. It may have been in such a setting that Yvonne Yven discussed an introduction to her future husband with the valet of the house – who had a friend who had worked with her future husband (Chabot 1977:154–161). The lively social life under the eaves is attested to by the repairman who reported that an entire street of Montparnasse had a single top floor that functioned as a street suspended in midair – because residents had removed the stones of the joint walls between the buildings (Guiral and Thuillier 1978:40–41). Although Jules Simon (1861:225) mournfully intoned, "God preserve the girl" who lives among servants on the sixth floor, Jeanne Bouvier's experience as a young woman worker in a sixth-floor rented room reflects a quite different experience: one of solidarity, friendship, and mutual support. For several years during the 1880s, the workers who rented rooms on the sixth floor in her building lived in harmony as a community, cooking over a little charcoal burner in the hallway to avoid asphyxiation, sewing for each other, and caring for each other when they were ill (Bouvier 1983:84–85). This was not a community of women, but rather a mixed-gender community.

The harmony and domesticity of this community was very different from the charged atmosphere of the public dances of prewar Paris, one of the few public places for men and women to meet. These offer perhaps the greatest contrast with the sponsored and contained social relations of the French village, for men and women utterly without previous social ties would meet, court, and conceive children from these occasions. Juliette Sauget met the father of her child – an electrical engineer from Uruguay – at the Elysée-Montmartre public dance in 1908; at about the same time, talented hatmaker and single mother Marie-Thérèse Dubon met her future husband, the chief butler for a wealthy family, at the Magic City dance hall (Mouillon 1970:6; Henrey 1951:39–42). But public dances were risky, and had offered the occasion at which Dubon became a single mother in the first place.

Working-class autobiographies and studies of marriage partners suggest, however, that Parisian women more often found their husbands through mutual friends, family, and neighborhood interchanges than at public dances. Domestic servants, the vast majority of whom were born outside the city, married shopkeepers often enough to suggest that their errands introduced them to neighborhood tradesmen (McBride 1976; Sewell 1985: chap.10). Many newcomers, like the thousands of women in Paris from the Auvergne in central France, met husbands from home through contacts among compatriots in Paris. Doubtless, in the marriage market more distant "weak ties" introduced many a future spouse. For example, the mother and father of Madeleine Gals met when he visited an old army friend whom he encountered by coincidence when he first arrived in Paris from the south. His wife was a home-seamstress, and when Emile Gals arrived at their apartment he was introduced to the beautiful young seamstress to whom his friend's wife subcontracted work. Courtship and marriage quickly followed (Henrey 1951:12–18; for similar marriage patterns in other cities see McBride 1976 and Sewell 1985: chap.8). Networks of support, particularly parental presence, were among the chief factors helping women in the urban marriage market. Recently-arrived Parisians whose parents were not in the city entered the marriage market without parental sponsorship (Elliot 1981; Fuchs and Moch 1990).

Single motherhood

Not every courtship ended in marriage. Paris, more than other cities, was the center for the nation's out-of-wedlock births. In many cases women were single mothers because they lacked parental support; they were older, had lower social origins, and were more likely to have been orphaned than women who married before childbirth. As George Alter (1988:131) found for Verviers, Belgium, each of these factors "made it more difficult to find a partner, more difficult to refuse his sexual advances without jeopardizing the relationship, and more difficult to apply social pressure to bring him to marriage." In Paris, single migrant women – especially those in recently formed migrant groups that had relatively few male compatriots – were disproportionately likely to bear a child out of wedlock (Fuchs and Moch 1990).

Yet family support often continued with a single woman's pregnancy. Court records reveal that a young woman from the provinces sometimes could engage her parents or a relative to raise her first out-of-wedlock child while she sought employment in Paris. Indeed, some women averred that one baby was acceptable, and affordable, but more would go unforgiven and unsupported. For example, Marie Beurette, a 19-year-old domestic servant, already had an out-of-wedlock daughter whom her family was raising at home in Brittany when she came to Paris to get work to help support that child.[10]

Entire families supported and aided poor women. Marie Forney's family not only helped her raise her first child, but provided information on the termination of an unwanted second pregnancy. Forney and Eugène Bouton, from families of "poor but honest cultivators" in northeastern France had intended to marry as soon as he fulfilled his compulsory military obligation. Their entire village seemed to know of their arrangements. In the meantime, they had one son. Her parents helped raise him for three years while she continued to live at home and earn her living as a seamstress. When Marie became pregnant for a second time, just before Eugène was scheduled to depart for his military service, his sister, Claire Bouton, advised her how to secure an abortion in Paris. Claire herself had been living with her parents when, at age 20, she had her first child, a boy who lived for about three weeks. At age 23 she became pregnant again but went to Paris to conceal this second pregnancy from her parents and to obtain an abortion. They had forgiven her first "mistake" but promised to show her the door if she became pregnant again. Claire Bouton referred Marie Forney to the same midwife/abortionist who had taken care of her.[11]

Young women raised in Paris differed little from their rural counterparts in the support they received from their mothers for their first out-of-wedlock pregnancy and their avowed fear that a second pregnancy would incur the wrath of their families. Marie Moran, living with her parents in Paris, first became pregnant at age 16; her parents kept and raised the infant despite having seven children of their own. Moran continued to live at home, sharing a bed with a sister, and working as an embroiderer. When she became pregnant again three years later she successfully hid this pregnancy, to spare her parents. She planned to give birth in a public hospital and then work far away from her family, so that she would not cause them further pain and financial burden.[12] When Louise Laffont, a sewing-machine operator, quarreled with her abusive husband, she left and went to live first with her mother, a daily maid, and then with a friend in the needle trades who shared in caring for her child.[13]

One mother who testified in court articulated a widely-shared sentiment when she declared that had she known her daughter was pregnant she would "have made all sacrifices to help her raise her infant."[14] Mothers could be more supportive of their sexually-active daughters than fathers. Louise Martin represents one unwed woman who had a sympathetic mother and hostile father. Pregnant at age 20, she left her village for Paris to avoid the reproaches of her father. Her mother knew she was pregnant and tried to facilitate Louise's stay in Paris by helping her find a place to live with a compatriot from her home town. Louise wanted to return home, but fear of her father's violence kept her in Paris.[15]

Working-class families readily acknowledged consensual unions and helped support the children of those unions. Living in a consensual union was not always a stigma. What the bourgeois family would not allow its daughters, the working-class family could not avoid.[16] Even if a couple did not marry, a mother could receive childcare help from those who would have been her in-laws. For example, Ernestine Pallet had the help of her lover's widowed mother who raised her baby for almost three months – for a fee. The unwed father's parents seemed more likely to support his child if he had been called to military service, because he could not marry until he fulfilled his military obligations. For example, 24-year-old Anastasie Siredey planned to marry a young man, Jobert, and they had a son together, whom he legally recognized and his mother helped support. When he went off to fulfill his military duty, Anastasie left her son with Jobert's mother, whom she paid a small sum, and went to Paris where she found work as a laundress, intending to marry Jobert later.[17]

Other relatives as well as parents offered support to women in Paris.

Cousins found jobs for one another and even testified that they would have cared for the out-of-wedlock infant of a relative.[18] Mélanie Briolet, orphaned at 14, supported her younger brothers with the help of her cousin, a laundress who gave her work for over ten years.[19] Relatives who helped a new mother with childcare received some payment, sometimes as much as 30 francs a month – what a good wetnurse charged.

For the domestic servant, who was usually a young migrant woman, the most consequential person was her employer, who could take advantage of the maid or protect and support her. Tales of employers or their sons seducing their servants are legion, but rarely were these seductions mentioned in court testimony. Far more commonplace were employers who fired their servants when they became pregnant as a result of relations with a person of the servant's own social standing.[20] Less well documented are the incidents when a sympathetic employer would retain her domestic throughout the pregnancy and even take her to the hospital when labor began, and promise to re-employ her after the baby's birth – provided the domestic gave her baby to a wetnurse.[21] The power of the purse and knowledge that some employers had could help the pregnant servant enormously. For example, Juliette Sauget's employer at the time of her pregnancy in 1909, the wife of a Jewish physician in the Opéra neighborhood, lightened her work load and hired an additional maid. The doctor saw that she delivered at the public hospital, and their physician son at that hospital did all that he could to support her at the time of the birth. After Sauget had a long convalescence and worked as a wetnurse, the family hired her on again, advised her on the legal status of her daughter, and eventually helped her leave domestic service for a more independent and stable occupation (Mouillon 1970).

Domestic servants also had contact with one another; if they were the only servant in the household they met others in the course of their duties. They performed tasks outside the house which brought them in contact with peddlers, laundresses, neighborhood merchants, and other domestics, some of whom probably liked to gossip and dispense advice. Cooks especially knew merchants on the street, and they were the people who frequently helped pregnant women find an herbalist, pharmacist, or midwife to perform an abortion.[22]

Abortion

Networks among poor women were especially important in an era in which contraceptive information and devices were virtually unavailable or non-existent. Furthermore, abortion was illegal and the pronatalist politics of the Third Republic encouraged women to have babies. In an attempt to increase the birth rate, doctors and politicians spoke out against "angel-making" midwives who performed abortions, and castigated women who had abortions. Nevertheless, untold numbers of women who desperately did not want a child sought a way "to bring on their periods" (Fuchs 1992; McLaren 1978, 1983). Many had abortions, relying on an informal information network to obtain information and support. Abortion served as a back-up form of birth control, a second line of defense against unwanted children if the male method (coitus interruptus) had failed. Economic constraints, as well as the cultural and legal position of women, established disproportionate burdens of childcare on the mother, leading her to desperate measures.

The search for abortifacients from a druggist or for an abortionist probably operated through discreet physicians for bourgeois women; but the poor, like the Boston, New York and California women studied by Nancy Howell Lee, looked to people of their own gender and social standing for information (Lee 1969). While herbalists and pharmacists kept their shops or open stands in the neighborhood where poor women would find them in their daily routines, finding a safe and inexpensive abortionist was more difficult. Some abortionists actually advertised in the Paris newspapers that they could resolve menstrual problems and bring on a woman's periods – discreetly and infallibly (Bertillon 1911:243–244; Pelletier 1913:8; McLaren 1983:143). Some abortionists clustered near the Paris train stations and large department stores to provide for women coming to Paris from the country. Yet it is likely that most women found an abortionist by word of mouth.

Women knew about abortifacients and abortionists not because midwives pushed them, but because women wanted to know; this information seems to have been transmitted horizontally from one working-class woman to another, rather than vertically from the elite to the masses. Sensitive reading of abortion- and infanticide-trial testimony allows us to eavesdrop on a host of confidential conversations. As recounted above, in the 1870s Marie Ditte first asked the *concièrge* in her building where to get something to bring on her periods. She then talked to the pregnant woman she met on the stairs of their building who provided the name of a midwife. Englantine Pelitte met another servant from her street; she confided that she had not had her periods for three months and received the name of a woman on the same street who would help. Seamstress Céline Gerbaud confided to her cook friend that she was pregnant and was sent to a neighborhood midwife.[23] The prominent feminist writer and physician, Madeleine Pelletier, witness to women's solidarity in the face of unwanted pregnancies, observed in 1913 that women "do not make a mystery of these [abortive] practices. On the landings of the working-class tenements, at the bakers, the butchers, the grocers, the housewives advise neighbors . . ." (Pelletier 1913:6–7; also in McLaren 1983:145).

In nineteenth-century France, as in America during the same era, securing an abortion *necessitated* women working together. Indeed, the search for an abortion constituted "a shared female experience" (Gordon 1977; Petchesky 1984:33). Women employed in a workshop with other women had access to an information network which often included women from their home villages. Residential networks sometimes overlapped with home-town ties, as for Marie Ditte. They also had networks among their merchants and neighbors. Some herbalists ran a regular referral system to their favorite midwife/abortionist. Domestic servants, who usually lived in isolation, had a more difficult time getting information; when possible, they consulted other domestic servants, usually the cook. Cooks knew the community because they gained access to information as they went about the neighborhood in the course of their daily grocery shopping. Together with the laundry workers, cooks were central to the working woman and domestic servant's network.[24] Yet, neighborhood networks could be problematic; the more people who knew that a woman was concerned about her missed periods, the more people who could point an incriminating finger at that woman. Abortion required an information network and support, but that very network could also lead to a woman's arrest. Women went to the police, when provoked, to protect themselves from suspicion as an accomplice, but women also helped one another, especially after the birth of a child.

Aid to new mothers

Raising children called for the help of family and more distant contacts. Considerable aid to new mothers, however, came from the state and from private charities, transmitted by "weak ties" among non-kin. Aid for new mothers, especially if single, was more likely to come from the neighborhood, some of which is visible in the bureaucratic record. In order to receive some charity or welfare, women needed a certificate of morality from the mayor's office, signed by two witnesses who would attest to their habits. Neighborhood shopkeepers and other tenants in the same building often testified for needy women.[25]

As mentioned earlier, the midwife who delivered the child was potentially the most helpful non-kin for a poor woman. The midwife was at the center of a web of networks that could direct poor women to charity and welfare services, inform needy postpartum women about available aid and even tell them how to apply. Midwives were the link not only between the destitute mother and public assistance, but also between bourgeois women and their objects of charity. It was they who usually told philanthropic women about needy pregnant and postpartum women or directed women to one of the few shelters for homeless new mothers that philanthropic women founded at the turn of the century.

Charitable middle-class women provided one of the chanciest and "weakest ties" between poor women and their sources of support. They were also one of the most important because they were among the best-equipped people to aid poor women in monetary or institutional ways; they founded shelters and organized philanthropies specially geared to women. Charitable women also knew one another, served in the same philanthropic institutions, and notified one another of their encounters with needy women in distress. Charities had constituted important support systems among poor women for centuries.

One of the oldest philanthropic foundations devoted to assisting poor women during childbirth and for several months thereafter was the Society for Maternal Charity, founded in 1784 and continuing throughout the nineteenth century. Like other religiously sponsored charities, it confined its assistance to married women and rested on connections between the poor and their economic betters. Religiously inspired bourgeois Ladies of Charity, volunteering for the Society, visited each aid recipient once a month; they would assess the mother's behavior, inspect her surroundings, instruct her in proper religious behavior, and advise her in hygienic care of her baby. Recipients had to request aid during the last two months of pregnancy and furnish a certificate of indigence and good morals from their mayor or clergyman; as mentioned earlier, they customarily had their neighbors and nearby shopkeepers testify to their "good morals."

Until the last decades of the century, connections between the poor and charitable women were sparse, and almost non-existent for single mothers. Starting in the 1870s, however, more to protect newborn infants and increase France's population than to assist poor mothers, philanthropic women founded additional charitable aid societies. In 1876, Marie Béquet de Vienne founded the Society for Maternal Breastfeeding to save infants by providing mothers with moral and material sustenance, without regard to their marital status or religion. As for the Society for Maternal Charity, midwives played a crucial role in alerting Béquet de Vienne and other members of this organization when a particularly needy woman had just given birth. A member of the Society then visited the unfortunate mothers to provide aid if they thought it justified. They brought used clothes for the family, food, a layette, a crib, and linens.

Some charitable bourgeois women did not depend on the midwife for references; indeed they recount finding poor destitute mothers and babies crying on the street, and bringing them to a shelter. A network of charitable women sought out and aided unfortunate new mothers. In one case a poor mother had been abandoned by her husband, who left her seven months pregnant and with two older children, aged 4 and 6. She worked as a cook but could not manage the crisis of childbirth. Overcome with despair she thought of abandoning her baby, but a chance encounter with a member of a bourgeois women's network of charities led her to a different path, one in which charitable volunteers assisted. After providing free childbirth, they took the mother and her newborn to a convalescent home until she regained her strength. When she left, the Society for Maternal Breastfeeding helped her find and pay for a wetnurse nearby. The Society provided her with clothes and a layette, and helped her find work. In many ways, this program differed little from traditional Catholic visitation of the poor. Throughout the nineteenth century, religious charitable women went to welfare bureaus to obtain the names of needy new mothers whom they could then aid – with food for the body and soul. Private charity was based on personal referrals and contacts (Fuchs 1992).

In 1901, the philanthropic French League of Mothers of a Family emerged to help poor women in childbirth, regardless of marital status, religious or political affiliation.[26] If women gave birth at home, the League provided nurses to assist the midwife and take care of the parturient women before the midwife arrived and after she had gone. If women gave birth in a hospital, members looked after the mother's home and family in her absence. To preserve ties between mother and child, League members helped women find work to do at home (usually sewing) in order that they could care for their children without having to leave their homes to work. Alternatively, they helped the single mother secure public assistance to enable her to send her infant to a wetnurse. Then, they found her a job and helped her maintain contact with her baby so that she eventually could reclaim her child. Other women donated used clothing and household goods to the League to distribute to the poor; its members discovered who was needy through a network including Parisian midwives.[27]

The League started slowly, providing assistance to only 100 women during its first year of operation. By 1909, however, it had given childbirth and postpartum assistance to 3,699 women, most of whom were widowed or were married but whose husbands were sick or disabled. Dozens of volunteer nurses and female inspectors visited women's homes to dispense advice on hygiene along with clean clothes, linens, and food. Volunteers came during the day, when the husband was at work, helped clean the house, make the dinner, and take care of the older children. They also notified other private charities and public-welfare authorities if the family needed further assistance from another agency. They viewed themselves as an institution of solidarity, without religious or political affiliation, to bring assistance in the form of jobs, money, linens, and cribs. Likewise, smaller organizations brought the poor in contact with helpers aiding women during and immediately after childbirth by supplying the linens for childbirth, the midwife herself, and people to look after mothers while they recovered from home deliveries.[28]

Private charity was not alone in helping poor mothers during the last decades of the nineteenth century. In the repopulationist mentality of the

Third Republic, prominent politicians believed that a child, once born, had a right to life, and it was the government's responsibility to help assure that life. In the mid-1870s, Paris's government therefore instituted a program of aid to mothers to prevent infant mortality. This aid came in the form of a barest minimum amount of money (the equivalent of one-month's wages for a domestic servant) for new mothers for the first few months after the birth of a child. To secure aid for their dependent babies, mothers had to have sufficient information to know where to go to apply for it and how to qualify for it. They usually obtained this information from the midwives, but there was also neighborhood information about the availability of public assistance (Fuchs 1992). The state and informal networks crossed paths.

Not only did mothers obtain information about aid through networks, but they also needed the help of others to receive it. After a mother made her written and oral request for welfare at the offices of the public agency, officials then interrogated her about her family, her morality, and her need. They also investigated her living quarters and place of employment, and sought evidence that despite her so-called error of having a baby even though single, she was essentially moral. This they did by asking questions of her *concièrge*, neighbors, and parents, and even shopkeepers in her neighborhood.[29]

The friendless mother could easily be thwarted in her search for state aid. On at least one occasion, it took a concerted effort on the part of several prominent philanthropic women for a poor mother to secure public assistance. In 1902, Jeanne Deau, an abandoned single mother, left a free public maternity hospital with a new baby but without resources. She applied for public assistance but after several days was refused. Each time she returned with her infant, whom she nursed, she was refused and sent away. After five weeks she could not pay her rent, and was out on the streets with no shelter or bread. A passerby took her to Jeanne Leroy, a well-known charitable woman, who contacted another philanthropist, Marie Béquet de Vienne, who admitted the young mother to a temporary shelter run by the Society for Maternal Breastfeeding. Leroy instructed the young mother on how to obtain immediate assistance, but bureaucratic officials put off the mother again. Finally, forty-nine days after the mother left the hospital, she received twenty francs.[30]

If a new mother received public welfare, a series of visits and inspections followed. A network of information rendered these visits rarely a surprise; news of the inspectors' visits spread through the neighborhoods and buildings in which the mothers lived. Since aid recipients lived in working-class quarters of the city, it is likely that a women's street culture and information network existed. Women living alone may have belonged to a network of kin and friends providing help to one another with food and childcare and forming a supportive family or neighborhood community.[31] By a web of information, people would learn when a mother received her welfare money and could repay money and services lent during leaner times. The network could also warn mothers of inspectors' arrivals or could spread the news that a certain mother had lost her welfare because she lived with a man. Such news might have inspired in some single mothers the fear that the same might happen to them, so many might have foregone marriage or overt cohabitation. Furthermore, inspectors contacted *concièrges* for information about aid recipients. Inspectors, reluctant to climb six flights of stairs to the mothers' rooms, would ask the *concièrge* for information. A kindly *concierge* could help ensure a mother's continued aid; a hostile one might cause it to be terminated.[32]

Childcare is another arena in which women used network resources to grapple with state requirements. Working for a wage was a condition of receiving aid, and unless mothers did piece work in their rooms, they had to secure some kind of childcare while they worked. Their choices were neighbors, relatives, or institutional infant care, a *crèche*. However, only 2 percent of mothers receiving welfare placed their babies in *crèches*; the vast majority relied on neighbors and kin. Some mothers may not have placed their babies in a *crèche* because it "'would be to take the bread out of the old peoples' mouths'" (Ross 1983:19). In a community, the older women helped the younger ones with childcare, and in turn childcare was their main source of income. Moreover, *crèches* were insufficient and inadequate. They were usually open from 7 a.m. to 7 p.m., but the women often worked longer or more irregular hours than these. Few *crèches* were located in the working-class districts where the poor single mothers lived. Since *crèches* charged 20 *centimes* a day, while a neighbor or relative often charged four times as much, mothers were not deterred from using the *crèches* on grounds of relative cost. In any case, many mothers did not use *crèches* because they thought the infants were poorly supervised, badly cared for, in danger of disease epidemics, or mistreated; they considered neighbors' care to be better.[33]

Reports from Lille and Mulhouse in the 1830s testify that women brought their infants to the mills with them and cooperated in hiring someone to watch the babies in a corner of their workplace (Reddy 1984). Such evidence has not been uncovered from Paris, but there is little reason to believe that women behaved differently in Paris than in other cities. When Parisian legislators at the turn of the century advocated the establishment of day-care facilities in industries employing numbers of women, they may have been acknowledging women's practice of bringing their babies with them to work. Reports from public-assistance inspectors indicate that women who worked outside the home often gave their babies to willing neighbors to watch.[34]

Government concern with infants provided important meeting places for poor mothers, although that was not the officials' intention. Around the turn of the century, doctors and politicians established well-baby clinics and milk dispensaries in the continued interest of preventing population decline and saving babies' lives. While waiting in the crowded well-baby clinics or milk dispensaries for the staff to weigh their babies and provide instruction, the mothers chatted with each other, comparing their experiences with their babies, doctors, and other public officials. Not only professionals, but also mothers provided each other with support and information. The well-baby clinics and the more numerous milk dispensaries served a dual role in women's lives: they functioned as places where they received instruction on childrearing, and they served as social centers. As historian Catherine Rollet-Echalier (1991:355) correctly asserts, the "milk dispensaries replaced the laundries and the fountains when running water in apartments led to the disappearance of these former social meeting places."

Since there was never sufficient assistance for all, there may have been competition for welfare and some women may have refused to share information. But that thread of evidence is missing. The emerging picture is one of mutual support among the women in securing what they could from the authorities, or from each other. If a midwife or hospital authority failed to inform a needy mother about public assistance for maternal nursing, the monthly rounds of the inspectors were hardly a neighborhood secret. A pregnant seamstress undoubtedly noticed when her neighbor received assistance and visits. She had only to ask for details. Women chatted about "giving the baby to Enfants Assistés for the ten months," by which they meant having public assistance pay the wetnurse for ten months.[35]

The father of the child is usually absent from the support networks of single mothers. Some men doubtless supported their out-of-wedlock child but are absent from the picture gleaned from private charity and government documents since the combined family income usually disqualified the women and children from charity or welfare. In any case, administrative records failed to note the unwed father's contribution. Ironically, fathers appear in the administrative records only when public assistance recorded that their support for their child disqualified that child from welfare. Florence LeLong's brief statement at the infanticide trial of her cousin is one of the few pieces of direct evidence of a father supporting his out-of-wedlock child. LeLong testified that "my cousin was pushed by despair because her lover abandoned her while mine surrounds me with care and helps me raise my child." Other considerable evidence of consensual unions in which the father provided support is derived from records of those couples who sent their babies to wetnurses.[36]

The stories of individuals reveal the wide range of family relations. Poor women were at the mercy of strangers, kin, neighbors, and institutions in their reproductive strategies. Furthermore, by the turn of the century, with increasing government and institutional involvement in women's lives, places of childcare, such as day-care centers and infant milk dispensaries, tended to replace the former centers of women's social networking – the laundries and the water spigots.

Conclusion

When we train our peripheral and our night vision to function, we see that the action in poor women's lives is off the brightly-lit stage of the institutional record. Here we have read extant studies, court cases, and autobiographies for evidence of poor women's networks as they operated in meeting men, and in pregnancy, childbirth, and securing childcare assistance. Even this preliminary investigation confirms that it is possible to do research on women's networks that will enrich our understanding of both gender and social organizations.

Although we are far from a nuanced understanding of the fabric of street and neighborhood life, we can draw some conclusions about poor women's networks of contact and aid from the situations we have investigated. First and most obviously, kin were absolutely central to Paris-born women and to migrant women who maintained contacts with their families in their places of birth; they were among the few resources of the poor and were called upon in the most desperate situations. Kin networks were among the few that included men. As Ellen Ross (1983:5) observes for the city of London, "ties of friendship and mutual aid among non-kin seldom crossed gender boundaries." On the other hand, female friends provided aid whenever possible and in some situations were more helpful than kin; almost invariably women consulted female friends about terminating a pregnancy, although men may have assisted in supplying information (Lee 1969:143–144). Poor women, however, did not procure information, aid, and support from other poor women alone; contacts with middle-class employers and neighbors – as well as with charitable *bourgeoises* who had the power of the purse and valuable information – played a role in crucial moments. Finally, the operative networks of contact and aid were not necessarily intimate or immutable; rather "weak ties" with distant cousins or an acquaintance on the street could, and did, introduce poor women to new adjoining networks – ones that could offer life in a new city, a different kind of occupation, a sympathetic abortionist, or help with childcare. "It was the very shifting nature of these contacts which ensured their effectiveness," concludes Bertaux-Wiame; "there was a constant adaption to the needs of a particular situation" (Bertaux-Wiame 1979:28).

These observations alert us to the fact that gaining information and aid from the people who were around her, for the long or short term, was a fundamental strategy for the poor woman in *fin-de-siècle* Paris. Networks among poor women were resilient resources in a world that offered no protection from either poverty or pregnancy. Indeed, the essential strategy of the urban female subculture was a sharing of information that enabled poor women to live by their collective wits because they knew that alone they could not resolve the difficulties of work and family life. Behind this knowledge lay their fundamental solidarity with one another.

Notes

The authors wish to thank Elinor Accampo, Alice Goldstein, Lynn Lees, and Susan Cotts Watkins for comments on an earlier version of this chapter.

1 Archives de Paris [hereafter AP], D2 U8 (23), Dossiers Cour d'Assises, Dossier 10 December 1873. Ditte and the midwife were acquitted. Given the absence of memoirs and autobiographies by single mothers, court testimony is one of the few sources that open even a small window on the lives of individual women. A careful reading of the interrogations, depositions, witness reports, character investigations, and letters that some of the women wrote to their parents or lovers should correct for possible distortions in the documents themselves. In this chapter, all surnames are pseudonyms.

2 Unfortunately information on networks for securing information on contraception is completely absent from the historical record. For a summary of contraception among the poor see Fuchs (1992: chap. 8). For the contrast between France and other states, see Sklar (1990: 1109–1114).

3 Politicians and other social reformers in the late nineteenth and early twentieth centuries used this exact phrase (*droit de vivre*) in their writings and in legislative debates.

4 Additional evidence in the Calepins des Cadastres (records of each building in Paris, their apartments and commercial enterprises, their owners and renters for Paris from 1852 to 1900) in AP, D1. P4.

5 For these reasons, the midwife became an increasingly embattled and regulated figure, a suspect abortionist. See AP, Dossiers Cour d'Assises, D2 U8 (51), Dossier 19 August 1876. Court cases are used here for their illustrative value.

6 For the narrative of one *concierge*'s life, see B. Smith (1985). The police dossiers on the women accused of giving or having abortions contain numerous pieces of testimony from *concièrges*. When the police first sought to contact either the accused or witnesses, they sought their initial information from the *concierges*. See, for example, AP, D2 U8 (23) Dossiers Cour d'Assises.

7 AP, Dossiers Cour d'Assises, D2 U8 (37), Dossier 13 April 1875.

8 AP, Dossiers Cour d'Assises, D2 U8 (75), Dossier 7 August 1878.

9 AP, Dossiers Cour d'Assises, D2 U8 (37), Dossier 13 April 1875, (75), Dossier 7 August 1878; Henrey 1951. A further discussion of ways in which women acted against one another is beyond the scope of this chapter.

10 AP, Dossiers Cour d'Assises, D2 U8 (21), Dossier 13 September 1873; (146), Dossier 22 May 1883; (169), Dossier 22 September 1884.

11 AP, Dossiers Cour d'Assises, D2 U8 (88), Dossier 22 August 1879.

12 AP, Dossiers Cour d'Assises, D2 U8 (114), Dossier 23 March 1881. For another example of maternal support see AP, D2 U8 (108), Dossier 8 December 1880.

13 AP, Dossiers Cour d'Assises, D2 U8 (122), Dossier 12 October 1881.

14 AP, Dossiers Cour d'Assises, D2 U8 (175), Dossier 29 January 1885.

15 AP, Dossiers Cour d'Assises, D2 U8 (88), Dossier 4 August 1879.

16 For an example of an upper-class family's attempt to conceal the out-of-wedlock pregnancy and birth see *Marthe* 1981.

17 AP, Dossiers Cour d'Assises, D2 U8 (109), Dossier 7 January 1881.

18 AP, Dossiers Cour d'Assises, D2 U8 (53), Dossier 29 September 1876; AP, D2 U8 (4), Dossier 29 May 1867; AP, D2 U8 (166), Dossier 26 July 1884.

19 AP, Dossiers Cour d'Assises, D2 U8 (128), Dossier 3 March 1882.

20 AP, Dossiers Cour d'Assises, D2 U8 (189), Dossier 4 September 1885 (case of employer seducing his domestic); (192), Dossier 17 October 1885 (sample case of a pregnant domestic servant who was fired, but whose employer promised to take her back after she had the baby and put it out to a wetnurse).

21 AP, Dossiers Cour d'Assises, D2 U8 (192), Dossier 17 November 1885; (146), Dossier 22 May 1883; (153), Dossier 23 October 1883; (139), Dossier 10 November 1882; (48), Dossier 9 June 1876; (83), Dossier 22 April 1879; Guiral and Thuillier 1978: 10–11.

22 See for example, AP, Dossiers Cour d'Assises, D2 U8 (47), Dossier 10 May 1876.

23 AP, Dossiers Cour d'Assises, D2 U8 (23), Dossier 10 December 1873 (Ditte); (47), Dossier 10 May 1876 (Englantine P.); (51), Dossier 19 August 1876 (Celine A.).

24 For examples see AP, D2 U8 Dossiers Cour d'Assises, especially (23), 29 December 1873; (47), 10 May 1876; (48), 29 May 1876; and (51), 19 August 1876; (162), 24 May 1884.

25 AP, Vbis 61³1, Certificates of morality, November 1846.

26 Bibliothèque Marguerite Durand (BMD) DOS 362 LIG.

27 "Ligue française des mères de famille," *Bulletin*, 1 (Paris, 1903), 15, 29.

28 "La Société de l'allaitement maternel et des refuges-ouvroirs. Compte rendu moral par Madame Béquet de Vienne, fondatrice," *La Revue philanthropique*, 26 (1909–10):472–473; "Ligue française des mères de famille," *Bulletin trimestrier* (Paris: Siège social, 1906) not paginated; BMD, DOS 362 LIG; "Ligue française des mères de famille," *Bulletin*, 1 (Paris, 1903), 15, 29; Mornet 1909: 124–126; Rollet 1958.

29 AP, "Rapports d'Inspection sur le Service des Enfants Assistés de Paris," Mss., M. Montravel, 1892 (hereafter cited as AP, "Rapports d'inspection," Mss., author and date).

30 Jeanne Leroy, "Lettre ouverte à M. Mesurer, Directeur de l'Assistance publique de Paris," *La Revue philanthropique*, 11 (1902):641–648; G. Mesurer, "Réponse à la lettre de Mme Jeanne Leroy," dated Paris, le 20 octobre 1902, *La Revue philanthropique*, 12 (1902–3):32–34.

31 Stack (1974:28) on networks among the poor in a midwestern city during the 1970s is suggestive.

32 AP, "Rapports d'inspection," Mss., Brindejont, 1892 and Forgeot, 1892.

33 Data on the French crèches from: AP, "Rapports d'inspection," Mss., Brindejont, 1893; Lucas-Dupin, 1893; *Rapp.* Cons. gén., Patenne (1898), p. 23; AP, D.1X⁴ (21), *Rapport de l'Inspecteur principal à M. le Préfet de la Seine* (Paris: 1894), 21.
34 AP, "Rapports d'inspection," Ms., Brindejont, 1893.
35 AP, Dossiers Cour d'Assises, D2 U8 (120), Dossier 27 September 1881.
36 Quote from AP, D2 U8 (166), Dossier 26 July 1884. AP, V bis 1Q7, 3Q7 and 10Q7 Registres de placement des enfants en nourrice, 1878–94.

5 The power of names: Illegitimacy in a Muslim community in Côte d'Ivoire

Robert Launay

Except indirectly, in their general study of kinship and paternity, anthropologists have not contributed greatly to the problems surrounding the topic of illegitimacy.

(Alan Macfarlane 1980:72)

An anthropology of bastardy?

Alan Macfarlane's reproach to his colleagues is not entirely unjustified. Notwithstanding several notable exceptions, anthropologists have been surprisingly silent on the subject, as compared to sociologists and, more recently, demographic historians. On the other hand, I wish to suggest that the relevance, both direct and indirect, of anthropology to the study of illegitimacy goes well beyond the "general study of kinship and paternity."

The approach which has prevailed since Kingsley Davis' (1939) seminal paper on illegitimacy has been a normative one. Illegitimacy was to be understood as one type of deviant behavior. The epitome of such an approach is Goode's (1964:23) elaborate typology of types of illegitimacy, each defined by the precise type of norm which has been breached. Laslett (1980a:1–2) has aptly criticized the somewhat naive functionalism of such writing. However, the problem is more deep-rooted. More recent attempts, by Laslett and others, to free themselves from this kind of functionalism have nevertheless, in important ways, retained the normative perspective. The problem lies with approaches which see illegitimacy as a *direct* function of sexual behavior. For example, Hartley (1975), in a book about the subject which consciously attempts to avoid both moralizing and psychologizing, nevertheless defines the problem, in the very first paragraph of the introduction, in terms of the discrepancy between "the ideal of legitimate reproduction, which is found everywhere" and "the reality of variations in human behavior, which are manifest in measures of illegitimacy" (1975:1). "Ideal" and "real" have been substituted for "normal" and "deviant."

108

Deviations from the "ideal" can then be explained as "the product of social forces that can be examined as potential causes of behavioral processes leading to the production of births out of wedlock" (1975:252). The image is that of the individual subjected to a variety of (sometimes conflicting) social "forces" affecting the probability of a specific behavioral outcome. The precise nature of these "forces" is left unspecified; they are invoked on a piecemeal basis. By and large, the essays in Laslett et al. (1980) adopt a similar perspective, looking at illegitimacy as an index of sexual *behavior* which deviates from the ideal *norm*. In an only slightly different vein, Laslett (1980b) raises the possibility that a "bastardy prone sub-society" might hold alternative norms. Even so, illegitimacy is seen as the result of the interplay between "norms," "behavior," and various "social forces."

Not surprisingly, such a normative approach runs into the most difficulties in situations where measures of illegitimacy are especially high, most notably the West Indies, where the space between "ideal norms" and "real behavior" can more aptly be described as a "gulf" than a "gap." Indeed, the anthropological literature on the West Indies is the one most glaring exception to Macfarlane's charge that the discipline has neglected the issue. Admittedly, these works are generally couched as discussions of the West Indian "family," but since it is virtually impossible to discuss the West Indian family without confronting the existence of widespread illegitimacy, the distinction is irrelevant for all intents and purposes.[1] More important, anthropologists writing about the West Indies tend to view illegitimacy as an integral feature of one or another family system, rather than primarily as an instance of individual "behavior."

Obviously, family "systems" do not exist outside the "real" behavior of specific individuals. However, a focus on the system rather than on individual behavior generates a different set of questions: what broader features of the social and cultural environment serve either to perpetuate or to change the "family system"? The difference between approaches focusing on individual behavior and those focusing on broader "systems" is apparent in discussion of the importance of factors such as "class." In the first kind of approach, "class" is one "social force" among others influencing behavior, as evidenced, say, in correlations between measures of illegitimacy and levels of income. The second kind of approach is concerned, rather, with demonstrating how specific kinds of social inequalities are created and perpetuated, and how this process of perpetuation affects the developmental cycles of different families.

More recently, O'Neill (1987) has applied this second kind of approach with particular thoroughness and elegance to the study of a Portuguese hamlet in a region with high rates of illegitimacy. He argues that this phenomenon is comprehensible in terms of an "Alpine" system of rural inequality, with close analogues in Central Europe,[2] characterized by a combination of partible inheritance and consistent efforts to the contrary, to keep holdings intact. In O'Neill's judicious phrase, "matrimony" takes a second place to "patrimony," though this devalorization of matrimony is experienced differently by women at the apex of the hierarchy, who tend to remain celibate, and by women at the bottom, who bear illegitimate children to "unknown" fathers.

I certainly do not wish to suggest that this kind of systemic approach is a disciplinary monopoly of anthropologists. Hajnal's (1965) classic paper on European marriage patterns, for instance, exemplifies just such a systemic approach, with rather obvious direct implications for the study of illegitimacy. Simply put, the same kinds of insights, in whatever discipline, which have been brought to the subjects of "marriage" or "the family" need to be applied to "illegitimacy." After all, has "celibacy" been treated as a form of "deviance" which needs to be explained in terms of individual sexual behavior?

The view from Africa

In parts of Africa, this last question is hardly absurd. Among the Dyula, where virtually all adults are expected to marry, older unmarried adults, especially men over forty, are definitely considered "deviants." It is no accident that those anthropologists who have most directly addressed the issue of illegitimacy have written about European and North American cases, specifically those with particularly high measures of illegitimacy. There is at least an implicit consensus about what these measures mean, about who is or is not "illegitimate" and indeed what constitutes "illegitimacy." This is not to say that there is neither variation nor ambiguity in basic definitions, but the range of such ambiguity is kept within a reasonable minimum. It is this very lack of ambiguity which lends credence to the optical illusion that illegitimacy is a direct function of "norms" and "behavior," that, for example, "cases of bastardy can . . . be used to test the outlook on sexual offenses as well as their incidence" (Macfarlane 1980:72).

This optical illusion melts in Africa, as well as in other parts of the world culturally as well as geographically removed from Western Europe. What, or who, is a "bastard" in Africa? Even so seemingly straightforward a definition as "an individual born out of wedlock" turns out to be of little help (for a Sierra Leonean demonstration, see Bledsoe, this volume). One answer merely begs a second question, a question about which (*pace* Macfarlane) anthropologists have had a great deal to say: what is "wedlock"? In Côte d'Ivoire, to cite only one example, there exist a plethora of (sometimes contradictory) definitions of marriage. Legally speaking, according to the Civil Code of 1965, only marriages which have been duly and properly registered in the appropriate administrative offices are recognized as such.[3] In the north of the country, only an infinitesimal fraction of unions are ever registered. Technically, most of the population is "'illegitimate." Of course, many more individuals consider themselves married according to one or another "customary" definition. Unfortunately, however one counts, there is a welter of such "customary" definitions in a country which, for its size, is bewilderingly heterogeneous, with approximately sixty "native" languages (Dérive and Dérive 1986:45). The criteria for what constitutes "marriage" may be markedly different from one culture to the next.

At first, it might seem as if there were an easy ad hoc solution: apply whatever cultural criteria are "relevant" to the couple in question to determine whether or not this union constitutes a "marriage." There are several reasons why such a solution is inadequate. In the first place, as more and more Africans move into large multi-ethnic urban communities, inter-ethnic unions are increasingly commonplace. What if the union is considered to be a "marriage" by one set of kin and rejected by the other? Is this a marriage? Are the children legitimate? These are issues which plague real people, and not simply a conceit of unruly anthropologists to confute demographers who try to measure empirical phenomena.

As if this were not enough, ambiguity is not by any means confined to inter-cultural unions. Even with a single culture, it may not be clear whether a particular couple is actually married. It has long been a commonplace in Africanist anthropology that, in the words of Radcliffe-Brown (1950:49), "To understand African marriage we must think of it not as an event or a condition but as a developing process." The problem, of course, is that some processes develop more smoothly than others. Assuming that something does go wrong, at what point, precisely, is it possible to assert with authority that the couple is – or was ever – "married"?

John Comaroff (1980:163) has taken this line of reasoning one step further, arguing that, among the Tshidi, such ambiguity is not simply at issue when unions break down:

> the ambiguities surrounding the creation and categorization of heterosexual relationships are not regarded as anomalous, unfortunate departures from [the happy opposition between the "ideal" and the "real"]. On the contrary, they are given explicit cultural recognition: the status of everyday unions is viewed, in the natural order of things, to be potentially equivocal and negotiable.

If ambiguity is in some way intrinsic to the "system," any clear-cut operational definition of "marriage" or "illegitimacy" will distort rather than uncover reality.

The issue is rendered all the more complex when we bear in mind that, in many cultures, "bastardy" is less an objective fact than an objective stigma. If the very categories of "marriage" and/or "bastardy" are under dispute, it should be clear that "illegitimacy" may have little or nothing to do with the sexual behavior of parents, but is *always* a matter of the social ascription of children. The only behavior which bastardy directly reflects is not sexual intercourse but rather labeling or, more simply, name-calling.

What's in a name? The Dyula answer

The contention that "'illegitimacy" is not directly a function of sexual behavior might seem to apply only in special cases. For example, one might contrast "African" systems of illegitimacy, where marriage is a process and where the status of offspring is consequently ambiguous and open to negotiation; and "Eurasian" systems where marriage is an event and the status of offspring depends uniquely on the occurrence or non-occurrence of this event.[4] Although such a distinction may well be cogent, I wish to discuss a specific African case where marriage is in fact an "event" and not a "process," but where, nonetheless, an approach based simply on "norms," "deviance," and "sexual behavior" is inadequate and misleading.

The Dyula of northern Côte d'Ivoire have for centuries been Muslim.[5] Islam strongly condemns all acts of sexual intercourse outside of marriage. For pious Muslims, it is consequently of importance to know precisely who is married to whom. Otherwise, how can one distinguish between licit and illicit sex? The Dyula solution is straightforward. The Dyula verb *furu* can be translated as "to marry"; as a noun, "*furu*" also refers to a specific ceremony, involving the untying of a bunch of specially wrapped kola nuts,[6] their distribution to everyone present as witnesses, and the presentation of a series of prestations, most notably from the groom's to the bride's family. Once and only once the *furu* has been "tied" has the marriage taken place. This is not to say that the notion of "process" is totally foreign to marriage among the Dyula. The negotiations may take several years, during which the groom's family regularly offers gifts to the bride and to her family. For the bride's family to accept such gifts and then to refuse to go through with the *furu* would constitute an act of extreme bad faith. Even so, such gifts are not returnable, and in no way constitute "marriage" as such, but rather a quasi-contractual "intent to marry." The extent of the prestations offered during the *furu* ceremony are, to an extent, negotiable. In exceptional circumstances, the bride's family may even insist, in the course of the ceremony itself, on more generous prestations than those offered. Such demands will delay the proceedings, as the two parties may bicker, neutrals may attempt to intervene, and, ultimately, the groom's family will scurry to satisfy whatever additional demands have eventually been agreed upon. I have been present on occasions when this has happened; every time, the *furu* has been eventually completed. Such last-minute public haggling occurs only in cases where the bride's family wants to signal publicly that, in one way or another, its hand has been forced, specifically in cases where the couple has effectively eloped. In the case of the *furu*, the groom's family may publicly promise additional prestations at some later date. Whether or not these prestations are ever made may well affect the future relations between the kin of the bride and of the groom, but not the status of the marriage itself. Once and only once the *furu* is over, has the marriage taken place.

Any act of sexual intercourse between individuals who are not married to one another constitutes *nyamogoya*, "fornication." The child, *den*, of any such union is – rather logically – a *nyamogoden*, a "bastard." It is a rather common term of abuse. However, the term can be taken literally to refer to specific individuals, not necessarily in order to insult them, but simply as a statement of "fact."

In 1984, when I returned, after thirteen years' absence, to the Dyula neighborhood of Koko in the town of Korhogo, I was struck by the visible prevalence of "bastards." What had, a decade before, amounted to a few, seemingly isolated cases had blossomed into a full-scale epidemic. This unfortunate state of affairs was publicly acknowledged and lamented, particularly by respectable members of older generations. Most Dyula explained this phenomenon in terms of the "deviance" of "real sexual behavior" from "ideal norms"; in other words, they complained that sexual morality was just not what it used to be. It may be that they are right. However, the rapidly growing incidence of "illegitimacy" was not simply, if at all, a result of immorality (or "deviant sexual behavior") per se.

The case of the missing manuscript: A digression

If we and the Dyula perceive a sharp difference in the incidence of illegitimacy between the "old" and the "new regimes," what can account for them except for changing patterns of sexual behavior? A story I was told in 1973 sheds some light on the matter.

I had been searching diligently and unsuccessfully for Arabic manuscripts, specifically clan histories, in a large village. The fact (unknown to me at the time) that much of the village had burned to the ground some years before no doubt accounted in large measure for my failure. Though I never discovered any manuscripts, I uncovered a very curious story. Even before the fire, some clans had deliberately destroyed their historical manuscripts. It turned out that these were not always ordinary manuscripts. Some of them had powers we would describe as "supernatural." If such manuscripts were deemed too dangerous to their possessors, they were buried. Such had been the fate, I was told, of a history of the village's largest clan ward. So powerful was this manuscript that anyone who beheld it and who was not a true-born member of the clan – anyone, notably, who was the child of an adulterous union between the wife of a clansman and an outsider – was condemned to a mystical death. Faced with such a choice, the clan preferred their bastards to their manuscript. There is a moral to this story. By "objective" criteria – and what criteria could be more objective, if by this one means "impersonal," than automatic mystical death? – there was a potentially large pool of "bastards" among the Dyula. However, the active collusion of groups and individuals worked to restrict the actual attribution of illegitimacy. In other words, the change from the old to the new regime was plausibly a question, not of sexual morality, but of how individuals were or were not labeled "bastards."

The old regime

Before it is possible to discuss changing patterns of bastardy among the Dyula, it is essential to provide background information about who they are and were. The Dyula in and around the town of Korhogo are, and have always been, a cultural, ethnic, linguistic, and religious minority. They speak a dialect of the Manding language, widely used as a *lingua franca* throughout much of West Africa. This language was associated with the medieval African empire of Mali, but also, after the empire's breakup, with a vast Muslim trading network of which the Dyula were a part: the very word "*dyula*" means "trader." The Dyula probably began arriving in the Korhogo region in the seventeenth century. The area was already settled at the time by a people now known as "Senufo," speaking a very different language. By the beginning of the twentieth century, the Dyula accounted for approximately one-tenth of the region's population. Their language, their culture, and their religion – Islam – linked them with other traders throughout the West African savanna. They had a vested interest in distinguishing themselves from their "pagan" and more provincial Senufo neighbors, as a means of monopolizing control over long-distance trade, and more importantly over the arts of weaving and the local trade in cloths.

The importance of trade and weaving for the Dyula had critical repercussions in the domain of social organization. Trade is a highly competitive enterprise, where achieved success counterbalances ascribed status. At every level of social organization, individual or sectarian interests constituted a recognized and culturally sanctioned force inhibiting or threatening the long-term stability of larger units. There was no question, however, of rampant individualism, for there were countervailing pressures in favor of larger-group solidarity, in the interests of pooling resources, mounting military campaigns for attack or defense, and ultimately maintaining strategic monopolies of any sort.[7]

The two units of social organization among the Dyula with the most relevance for the discussion of bastardy are the *kabila*, or clan ward, and the joint family. The core of a *kabila* consisted of a coresident group of related men sharing a common patronym (*dyamu*) and descended from a common ancestor. Around this core, along with their wives and children, were slaves as well as friends and clients – "strangers" or *lunan* – who chose to settle in the community and placed themselves more or less under their protection; the descendants of such strangers, if they became numerous enough, eventually constituted a *kabila* in their own right. Most of these groups were relatively small, on the order of 50–150 individuals; some were significantly larger, and were in turn subdivided into smaller named units. The relatively small size of these units was partly a function of the mobility of Dyula society, a necessity for traders. Individuals frequently left their home communities to establish themselves elsewhere where prospects seemed better. Large Dyula communities might contain as many as twenty such *kabila*. Some *kabila* owned or shared rights to specific offices, such as chief or *imam*. Some specialized in one activity or another, such as Islamic scholarship. A relatively large and unified *kabila* was in a strong position to play a leading role in local factional politics; the proliferation of small *kabila* ensured that factionalism was a perpetual feature of political life.

The joint family, rather than the clan ward, was the critical unit in the cloth trade, the economic mainstay of the Dyula communities of the region. It was clearly to the advantage of any unit to pool the labor of several weavers. Weaving was an exclusively male occupation, and so such pools typically took the form of a group of related males. Specifically, sons were expected to work for their fathers, at least until they were married and had children of their own. Many sons were unlikely to have achieved such independence before their father's death, and were expected to continue working for one senior male kinsman or another, usually a father's brother or an elder brother. However, it is important to stress that young orphaned men might work for any senior male kinsman they chose, matrilateral or patrilateral, close or even relatively distant.

Success in the cloth trade depended, among other things, on the ability of older men to control the labor of their younger relatives. The key to such control lay in the marriage system. In the first place, young men were obliged to wait a considerable time – sometimes until they were in their thirties – to marry. It was, of course, in the obvious interests of those for whom they worked, fathers or others, to delay their marriages as long as possible in order to prolong their dependence. On the other hand, the man for whom a younger kinsman worked was morally obligated to arrange and pay for his marriage. An elder with a reputation for delaying the marriages of his dependents beyond the bounds of decency would hardly attract orphaned kinsmen to work for him.

The control by elder men over the labor of their younger kinsmen was reinforced by the strong preference for in-marriage within the *kabila*. Considering the modest size of these groups, rates of in-marriage have been, until recently, spectacularly high, on the order of 50 percent of total marriages.[8] In the first place, one effect of such marriages is to concentrate the kin networks of individuals within the *kabila*. Close maternal relatives might simultaneously be distant paternal relatives. This way, even if young men were allowed to choose to work for any relative, they were nevertheless likely to work for someone within their own *kabila*. Indeed, young men were doubly dependent on elders of their own *kabila* for brides. Control over the marriages of the young women in the group was a direct means of controlling the labor of the young men.

In part because of the system of marriage, the *kabila* emerged as a focal unit in between the local community as a whole and small, competing units of production. The *kabila* was simultaneously an actor in factional politics, a cluster of kin related to one another in multifarious ways, a pool of eligible brides and of young male labor. Obviously, conflict within the group was a rather commonplace fact of life. However, pressures were very strong to keep such conflicts within the group, to resolve them through collective meetings where everyone was allowed to air grievances and where, ideally, some sort of consensus emerged. Either party to a dispute might attempt to bring in putatively "neutral" mediators from outside, but it was generally bad form to attempt to take the quarrel for adjudication to some higher authority out of the hands of the *kabila* as a whole.

Rules of ascription

The story of the *kabila* which buried its manuscript to save its bastards suggests that, at least during the old regime, the membership of alleged bastards in specific kin groups was a salient issue. The principles of ascription are quite clear. A *nyamogoden* born to an unwed mother belongs to the mother's father's family. The child assumes the mother's clan patronym, and is specifically under the authority of the mother's father or his successor. A *nyamogoden* born of an adulterous union belongs to the mother's husband. By virtue of the *furu* ceremony, he has rights over his wife's offspring until her death or until he chooses, through divorce, to renounce those rights. Aside from general stigma, a *nyamogoden* has no rights either to inherit property from whichever family – mother's father's or mother's husband's – can rightfully claim him or to succeed to any office.

The rules are straightforward. Their application is not. As the tale of the magical manuscript suggests, many individuals in the community are "really" bastards, but they are not necessarily treated as such. The following cases illustrate the ways in which "illegitimacy" can be acknowledged in principle and occulted in practice.

Case 1: The elopement of Siriki and Aminata

Siriki (this and all other names are pseudonyms) is now a prominent, prosperous middle-aged polygynist, well respected in the community.

However, in his youth, it may not have been apparent that he would turn out to be such an attractive son-in-law. The family of his first wife, Aminata, wanted nothing to do with him. Undeterred, he "ran off" with Aminata, bringing her home to his father's house. The elopement was ratified by the chief of Korhogo, as it would be nowadays by the *sous-préfet*. Elopers can now contract a civil marriage at the *sous-préfecture*, the only form legally recognized. This way, the bride's parents cannot compel her to return; on the contrary, her civil "husband" has all legal rights. This legal procedure was made possible by the Civil Code of 1965; before that, as in the case of Siriki and Aminata, the chief's court functioned more informally in the same manner.

Elopements among the Dyula were not uncommon in Korhogo town, strategically situated near the chief's court and the administrative headquarters of the civil authorities. I knew of relatively few cases where village men eloped with brides, but townsmen eloped often enough with village girls as well as with girls from town. Usually, the women had already been formally promised to someone else. The elopement not only thwarted the plans of the bride's family, but put them in the unenviable situation of not being able to fulfill their promises. On the other hand, elopements never took place without the active collusion of the man's family. If the man's kin had already arranged another match for him, plans for any elopement were generally vetoed; one marriage for a young man was enough. As long as the man's family was willing to take her in, the elopement was possible.

Elopement did not constitute marriage. No *furu* had been performed. A *furu* involves the active participation of both the husband's and the bride's families. Invariably, the bride had already been promised to a particular suitor, and her family could not decently participate in the *furu* immediately after the elopement, whatever their private sentiments. To do so would suggest that they connived at, or even staged, the elopement. One way or another, they would appear to be people who go back on their word. Such behavior is known as *nambaga*, and a reputation as a *nambagato* – a double dealer – is an unenviable one.[9]

The outcome of the case of Siriki and Aminata is typical. While Aminata was "living with" Siriki, a son, Ali, was born to the couple. It is generally at this stage that the woman's family publicly reconciles itself to the elopement by agreeing to perform the *furu*. It was on a similar occasion that I witnessed haggling during a *furu* ceremony, a public statement of the bride's family's reluctance. Almost always, the woman's family eventually gives in, agrees to hold the *furu*, and legitimates the marriage post hoc. However, I know of at least one case where the woman's family persisted in its opposition, even after the birth of several children.

The point is that Ali, Siriki and Aminata's first child, is technically a *nyamogoden*, a bastard. At the time of his birth, his mother and father were not married. His name, for those who know his family well, hints at his status. Typically, men name their first son after their father, their first daughter after their mother. Alternatively, children will be given the names of their mother's parents, or of other close relatives on one side or the other. Such naming creates a symbolic relationship of identity. A man who names his child after his own father will never address this child by name, any more than he would so address his father. Such sons may be called *gbema*, "grandfather"; *cekoroba*, "old man," "elder." One must never name a *nyamogoden* after one's own father or mother, thereby implying that one's parent is in fact a "bastard." A *nyamogoden* should bear a name from outside the family, and which will consequently give no offense. Ali, for example, was not named after anyone. The lengths to which people go to provide an "outside" name for a *nyamogoden* – or, for that matter, an "inside" name for a legitimate child – are variable. Nevertheless, "anomalous" names – but their abnormality is exclusively defined within the context of the pool of names of any particular family – suggest the "anomalous" status of *nyamogoden*.

Of course, the fact that Ali's mother is married to his father makes him a rather special, though by no means unusual, kind of *nyamogoden*. Quite often, a child is born to an eloping couple before the *furu* can be performed. In fact, the possibility, slim but real, remains that the woman's parents will never acknowledge the union, and that all their children will be "bastards." Nevertheless, Ali (and others like him) is certainly not treated as a "bastard." On the contrary, both inside and outside his circle of relatives, he is treated as if he were the fully legitimate eldest son of his father. His unambiguously legitimate younger siblings are expected to defer to his authority. Strictly speaking, as a *nyamogoden*, he has no right to exercise such authority. Indeed, he should not even bear his father's patronym, but instead belong to his mother's family. However, for all intents and purposes, Ali is never treated as a *nyamogoden*, by either his mother's or his father's kin.

In short, Ali is logically a "bastard" and sociologically "legitimate." However, no one, inside or outside his family, calls him a bastard to his face or treats him in any way as if he were one. Let me make it perfectly clear that I am not simply drawing my own inferences from the "rules" as explained to me. It never occurred to me that he might be considered a *nyamogoden* until it was pointed out to me, in strict confidence, by a senior kinsman of his. Nor was Ali being singled out on this occasion, the target of a backhanded slur. Rather, my friend was somewhat puckishly identifying to me all the "bastards" in his immediate family, on the occasion of the birth of a son to his as yet unmarried daughter, pointing out that, although the child's father had agreed to (and later did) marry his daughter, his grandson, too, was a *nyamogoden*.

While there were in actual "fact" a number of "bastards" in the family, this was in no wise to be publicly acknowledged in any way. The implications of this strategy were that such "bastards" were not to be treated as such in any sociologically relevant context, *including* the arena of internal relations between family members. Although I was present on frequent occasions when Ali quarreled with other members of his family, his "illegitimacy" was never an issue. There was, as it were, a conspiracy of silence on the part of Ali's kinsmen, a common commitment to concealing the origins of "bastards" within the group, even if it might appear to be in the private interests of certain members of the group to stress such origins. To stigmatize, publicly and in all seriousness, a member of one's own group as a *nyamogoden* is a flagrant violation of Dyula codes of honorable behavior, even if, perhaps especially if, the accusation is justified. For this very reason, individuals who might seem to have an interest in labeling kinsmen as *nyamogoden* in fact do not do so; such behavior would automatically place them in the wrong in any family or *kabila* council, and thus be entirely self-defeating.

Case 2: A pregnant virgin bride

It is readily understandable in cases like Ali's why, whatever the "technicalities" of the situation, no one would treat such individuals as *nyamogoden*. They are, after all, children of men of the group and of their wives; to insist on a mechanical application of the rule is either unreasonable or crassly manipulative. However, there are cases where people may hide the status of children who are not their biological progeny, or that of members of their group.

Anzumana, a young *karamogo*, or Qur'anic scholar, was married to Salimata, a girl of about sixteen. The morning after the wedding night, there is always a celebration if the bride proves to be a virgin. A gun is fired in front of the hut where they have spent their first night together, and a gift of white kola is presented to the bride's mother. Should the bride fail the test, her mother will be presented instead with a mixture of red and white kola. At the wedding celebrations I attended, the failure was approximately 50 percent, although I was assured that this would never have occurred in the "good old days." Nowadays, brides who fail the test are beaten by their male relatives; in some cases, their mothers may also share the blame, and even the beating, on the grounds that they are well informed about their daughter's sexual behavior. However, such failure never constitutes grounds for divorce or for annulling the marriage.

In any case, a gun was fired outside the hut at Anzumana's wedding, and the bride formally declared a virgin. The celebration turned out to be short-lived and unwarranted. To Anzumana's great dismay, it turned out that Salimata was already pregnant on her wedding day. When I first found this out from Anzumana, he was livid. A good husband should abstain from sexual relations during his wife's pregnancy, and afterwards until she has finished weaning her child. This meant, in the first place, that the bridegroom might have to wait as long as three years before resuming sexual relations with his wife. Under the circumstances, an ordinary man of Anzumana's age would be expected to indulge in extra-marital affairs. But Anzumana was, as a Qur'anic scholar, expected to behave in an upright fashion; in his case, such affairs were out of the question. In any case, it is considered entirely inappropriate for pregnant women to undergo the marriage ceremony. Even in the case of "shotgun weddings" where the woman marries the father of her child, the ceremony is performed after its birth. I was told that the bride's family (and especially her mother) ought to have known that the girl was pregnant and, under the circumstances, to have canceled or postponed the ceremony. Anzumana was within his rights to send back his bride.

Whatever Anzumana's rights, it did not follow that it was in his interest to repudiate the marriage. The considerable expenses of Anzumana's (or any other) wedding were not refundable, and represented considerable contributions from a wide range of kin. Were he to send back his bride, he would have to wait a long while before these contributors would be willing to underwrite another marriage. Anzumana and his immediate family were of modest means, and in no position to finance a marriage on their own. Effectively, Anzumana was confronted by the choice of accepting his pregnant bride or remaining single for several more years, until another marriage could be arranged. To a certain extent, his career was at stake. Marriage is an essential stage of social adulthood. No one takes a bachelor seriously, and a young Qur'anic scholar needs to be taken seriously. Last but not least, Anzumana is a gentle, mild-mannered man. I suspect that, once his anger had cooled, he began to feel pity for his bride. He chose not to send her back.

But what was to become of the unborn child? It was, of course, a *nyamogoden*, belonging, properly speaking, to the bride's family. Again, Anzumana would have been within his rights to repudiate the child, and to send it packing once it was old enough to survive without its mother. However, such an action would have boded ill for the future of the marriage, publicly shaming both the bride and her kin. Faced with such an affront, the bride's kin could be expected to urge her to abandon her husband and return home, if under the circumstances she needed enticing. Moreover, it would have made a public fool of Anzumana, bad publicity for a young Qur'anic scholar. It was clearly in everyone's interest to treat the whole affair as if it had never happened. This is precisely what Anzumana, perhaps in keeping with his own personal inclinations, chose to do.

For similar reasons, children of adulterous unions – and adulterous liaisons, in small communities, are always "common knowledge" – are very rarely publicly branded as *nyamogoden*, though they will certainly be so labeled in private gossip. In the first place, to all intents and purposes, a husband who repudiates such a child also repudiates his marriage. In fact, adultery is rarely grounds for divorce among the Dyula, provided that a wife found guilty puts a stop to the liaison. Of course, the situation is quite different when the wife runs off with another man. The dynamics of such cases are exactly like the elopements of unmarried women. Until a divorce is pronounced, children are *nyamogoden*, and they belong to the husband. After the divorce, a *furu* can rapidly be performed for the couple; the *furu* for a widow or divorcee is a rather perfunctory affair. Under the circumstances, most husbands are willing enough to be rid of their wives. Occasionally, out of stubbornness or vindictiveness, a husband will refuse to divorce a runaway wife; again, I know of one such case. Such a husband's claims over his wife's children, however justifiable, are unenforceable. They will grow up as members of the wife's lover's kin group, where their status as *nyamogoden*, though common knowledge, will be passed over in silence.

The conspiracy of silence

We have seen how individuals are incorporated as full members into *kabila* by means of the deliberate occultation of information about the circumstances of their birth; information which would otherwise stigmatize them and bar them from the rights and privileges of full membership. But why are groups concerned with imposing this conspiracy of silence? A somewhat puzzling statement by a friend of mine provides a clue. He asserted, as a bit of conventional wisdom, that bastards will seek out their biological fathers to go live with them. When I asked why, he answered that it was because they do not feel wanted, that they are stigmatized and disfavored, driven out to seek the natural affection of their natural fathers. I was surprised, in the first place, because it is clear that the biological father has no right to his child. Such rights belong either to the mother's father or her husband. It is by no means obvious that either the mother's father or her husband would be able to enforce – assuming they were even interested in enforcing – such "rights." Even so, why would a *nyamogoden* receive better treatment among his father's kin, in a group to which he has no claim to belong?

What struck me as most curious about my friend's assertion is that I know of no case where it is borne out. I certainly cannot claim that "bastards" never seek out their biological fathers, but it cannot be a common phenomenon, whatever the tenets of conventional wisdom. However, conventional wisdom, even if it is false, must at least be plausible. The dynamics of kinship among the Dyula involved the acknowledgment of a degree of flexibility on the part of junior kinsmen, their ability –

whatever the "rules" – to affiliate themselves with one senior kinsman rather than another; and countervailing strategies on the part of senior individuals to limit this field of maneuver. The idea that a "bastard" might choose to live with his biological father rather than with his "rightful" family is conceptually akin to a situation where a young man might choose to work for – and live with – his mother's brother rather than his elder brother. The scenario of "bastards" moving away in search of their natural fathers depicts what would *plausibly* take place in the absence of active attempts to keep them in place, specifically by refusing to stigmatize them in public.

To the extent that the political influence of any *kabila* was partly a function of its size, it was clearly in the interests of the group as a whole to attract and retain as many members as possible, "bastards" or otherwise. In addition, as we have seen, young men were valuable for the labor they performed on behalf of elders, and young women (whose labor was not negligible either) as brides to reward dutiful young men. On the other hand, individual members had unequal stakes in the interests of the "group" as a whole. By the same token, its cohesiveness could hardly be taken for granted.

As far as "bastards" are concerned, we might consider what categories of individuals had an interest in occulting the circumstances of their birth, and consequently of retaining their allegiance; and which individuals might have an interest in revealing the "truth," relegating them to a position of social inferiority. First of all, the political leaders of the group, those who effectively tended to dictate its policy in factional maneuvers, had an interest in mobilizing as many dependents as possible, whether slaves, clients or junior kinsmen. As long as "bastards" were willing to back them, it was in their interests to uphold their effective "legitimacy," perhaps quietly reserving the threat of revealing their origins in public as a way of keeping them in line. It was certainly in a husband's interests to maintain rights over his wife's children, legitimate or no, given that he controlled the labor of his sons and the marriages of his daughters. After his death, heirs to his position of authority in the family had exactly the same interests. Again, threats to expose the origins of "illegitimate" dependents might have kept them in line; otherwise, senior kinsmen had a vested interest in maintaining silence as the price of allegiance and labor.

Who, on the other hand, might have wished to "expose" *nyamogoden*? Such exposure would disqualify them from office, notably that of head of the clan ward. Headship is ascribed according to strict criteria of seniority, devolving automatically on the eldest free male in the senior generation. The very rigidity of the process minimizes the real power of the office, ultimately rendering it an unattractive "prize" for factional infighting (Launay 1988b). People do not fight for the office, and would have no reason to disqualify a successor on grounds of illegitimacy unless, in a specific context, some other hidden agenda were at stake. The individuals with the clearest interest in denouncing a *nyamogoden* are younger siblings, those who would normally fall under his authority, especially after the death of the father, and consequently have the greatest reason to get him out of the way. However, full siblings cannot denounce a *nyamogoden* without in the process denouncing their own mother, a shameful act which would expose them to the terrible power of a mother's curse, and which would call the circumstances of their own legitimacy into question. To do such a thing to the child of one's own mother – legitimate or not – would be such a flagrant breach of norms of decency that it would far outweigh any conceivable benefits. Of course, junior half-siblings, children of a different mother, would have no such scruples. On the other hand, the authority of an elder half-sibling is far more tenuous than that of a full sibling. There are socially far more acceptable means of escaping a half-sibling's authority after one's father's death, notably by attaching oneself to some other senior kinsman.

I have phrased the issue rather crudely in terms of calculated self-interest, in order to demonstrate that it was very definitely in the interests of some individuals to conceal or ignore the origins of "bastards" in the group, whereas no one had a real interest in revealing such information, or, more properly, making it a public issue. However, the threat of making such information public could indeed be very useful. In this way, two parallel systems of discourse coexist neatly within the confines of the group, one public ("Bastards? We have no bastards here!") and one private ("By the way, did you know that *x* was born before his parents were married, that *y* was born five months after his mother's wedding, that *z*'s mother was guilty of an adulterous liaison with so-and-so, etc.?"). However, the conspiracy of silence which governs the public (but only the public) realm of discourse is not simply a question of calculated self-interest. It is a moral imperative, one of the many unspoken rules about what it means to be a decent human being, that one ignores any embarrassing anomalies surrounding the birth of fellow members of one's own group, and that what goes on in other groups is none of one's business. To violate such norms flagrantly, except in the name of some even higher principle, is to behave ignominiously. People who behave that way are to be neither trusted nor respected; their word carries no weight, and will not be taken into account. The moral reasoning is circular: anyone who would publicly denounce a kinsperson as a *nyamogoden* does not deserve to be listened to! It takes a powerful private motive and a convincing public pretext to dare to violate such norms.

The new regime: An epidemic of illegitimacy

So far, the cases we have discussed involve the children of women who either are married or have eloped. The scenarios are typical of what might be called, for lack of a better word, "traditional" marriage patterns among the Dyula, where girls were betrothed at an early age and married quite young, at the age of sixteen or so. Such marriages have by no means disappeared, especially in village communities. Typically, such girls have, at most, very rudimentary schooling. Such early marriages minimize the likelihood of premarital pregnancy (or, as in the case of Anzumana's marriage, disguise its occurrence). Elopement is the only means these young women have of exercising choice of a husband; even then, the family of the young man must actively connive. The situation of young women, mostly in town, who have received a formal education is quite different. In the first place, it is considered inappropriate that they marry husbands with less education. This presents obstacles for "traditional" arranged marriages within the *kabila*. The more educated the young woman, the less likely it is that any appropriate candidate would be available. The principle that educated girls should choose their husbands has gained currency in town, and their less educated siblings and cousins are beginning to insist on similar privileges. As long as girls remain in school, they remain unmarried. But age at marriage is bound to rise for all women, educated or not, whose marriages have not been arranged beforehand.

One striking consequence of the increasing freedom of young women in towns to choose their husbands and to remain unmarried has been an "epidemic" of premarital pregnancies, and consequently of *nyamogoden*. Older Dyula deplore the decline in standards of sexual morality among the younger generation, though "sexual morality" is not necessarily the culprit. It is possible to deny, or cover up, the illegitimacy of children of married women, provided that their husbands are willing, for whatever reason, to acknowledge them as their own. This is not possible for the children of unwed mothers, at least as long as the women remain unmarried. In 1984, I would estimate that in the neighborhood of Koko in Korhogo, as many as one in four (perhaps even more) young women between the ages of sixteen and twenty were unmarried mothers – a proportion all the more remarkable when one bears in mind that many of the others, still subject to the "traditional" regime, were already married. Moreover, these women are finding it increasingly hard to find a suitable spouse. One unwed mother complained bitterly that she continually had to ward off propositions for sexual favors, but was never offered marriage. The problem is much less acute if the genitor of the child can be persuaded, or coerced, to marry its mother, but this is hardly always the case.

The question remains: what happens to these *nyamogoden* once their mothers marry? For a variety of reasons, some explored by Caroline Bledsoe in Chapter 6, husbands are less likely to accept these biologically unrelated children as their own. Formerly, when marriages were arranged, husbands were usually related to their wives, and could be pressured very effectively by the mutual kin of both spouses. Nowadays, the kin of an unwed mother are happy enough to find her a suitable husband at all, and are in no position to convince or coerce him into acknowledging the children.

The case of Nasaran illustrates what may happen to such children. Nasaran dropped out of secondary school when she became pregnant, refusing at all costs to name the father. Shortly after her son Bakary was born, a well-to-do bureaucrat proposed that she marry his nephew, who was living in another part of the country. Nasaran's father pressured her into accepting. Her parents accepted the responsibility for raising her young son, fearing that his presence would jeopardize the future of the marriage.

Bakary was raised by Nasaran's parents as if he were their own child, and not an illegitimate grandchild. His presence in the household could easily be taken for granted; some of Nasaran's siblings and half-siblings were scarcely older. He was treated by his grandfather and grandmother as affectionately as any of their own children. As a toddler, he suffered no stigma whatsoever. He was an exuberant two-year-old until Nasaran returned and this apparent stranger claimed to be his "mother." Bakary had always addressed his grandparents as "father" and "mother." The example of Bakary suggests that illegitimate children may not only be fostered but sometimes virtually adopted by their maternal grandparents.

Rights or responsibilities?

Changing marriage patterns are partly responsible for the production of, not necessarily more, but rather more highly "visible," *nyamogodens*. However, the issue is not simply marriage alone. At stake is the importance of group membership to individuals, and of individual members to groups. I have stated the case in terms of group membership and group norms. However, the stakes have steadily changed. The *kabila* has become an increasingly irrelevant unit in the factional politics of the region, and of the nation as a whole; only at the micro-political level, the village or a single urban neighborhood, where the stakes are increasingly marginal, does it make any difference. Formerly, the kin group supplied senior members with a pool of dependents, allowing elders to control the labor of young men and the marriages of young women. Particularly since the end of World War II, weaving and the cloth trade have become progressively marginal. Dyula men weave as a fallback option, if they are incapable of finding any other work. It makes no sense for sons to work for their fathers, much less for other senior kinsmen. Instead, young men work in the wage sector, if they can find work. The labor of young men has slipped forever out of the hands of their elders. Over the years, I have seen the marriages of young women escape increasingly from their control. Under these circumstances, the rights of individuals to claim membership in such groups and, even more acutely, the rights of groups to claim individuals as members, have become less and less relevant.

As rights fade into the background, responsibilities assume greater importance. Who is willing to, or can be expected to, raise and support the child? A priori, a woman's husband has no vested interest in her children by other men. He has little control over either their labor or their marriages, and probably cannot count on their support when he is old. Similarly, there is no reason why the husband's kin group should wish to lay claim to such children. Assuming he is unrelated to his wife, it also follows that *his* relatives will not pressure him into recognizing such children. The child's biological father, unless he marries the mother, is highly unlikely to provide support either. If, indeed, he is interested in keeping the child, the mother's natal kin, who "rightfully" claim it, will use this as leverage to induce him to marry the mother; if not, they will probably not cede the child. On the other hand, it is next to impossible to coerce the father into supporting a child who is not in his custody. If only by default, most such children are raised and supported by the mother and/or her close kin – usually parents and elder siblings.

To the extent that it makes sense to say that these children are "claimed," then they are claimed by individuals and families, rather than by whole kin groups. Still, the kin groups continue to exist, and such "bastards" are considered members of their mothers' groups provided they and their mothers wish it so. Recalling the example of Bakary, they do not even suffer considerable stigma. Such children are conceivably at a disadvantage, but not noticeably more so than "legitimate" orphans or children of indigent parents. In all such cases, the welfare of the children depends on the willingness and ability of other members of their kin network to assume responsibility for their upbringing and their upkeep. Despite the fact that all Dyula are Muslims – and many of them devout – religious beliefs do not seem to interfere in such decisions. *Nyamogoden* will be welcomed or rejected by their mother's family on other grounds than on the circumstances of their birth.

Conclusions

The issue of "illegitimacy" among the Dyula is of particular interest because of the light it sheds on the relationship between rules, categories and behavior. An illegitimate child is one who is "not born 'according to the rules'" (E. Goody 1982:12). The rules in question are both *logical* – a question of how individuals are assigned to specific categories – and *sociological* – questions about social behavior. The critical social behavior at issue is "marriage." It follows logically that if marriage is an easily identifiable event, then "illegitimacy" should be a relatively unambiguous category; on the other hand, if marriage is rather a long drawn-out process, rules of deciding who is or is not illegitimate should be far less straightforward. By and large, anthropologists have been sensitive to the implications of ambivalence. In cultures where the legitimacy of individuals is not always – perhaps never – a foregone conclusion, it is likely to be a central issue of debate in matters of inheritance or accession to office; the attribution of illegitimacy becomes a political issue, in a broad sense, where the outcome depends less on the "rules" themselves than on the ability of either party to impose its construction of the situation. The Dyula example is virtually the diametrical opposite of this more "typical" scenario. The rules concerning the attribution of illegitimacy are as clear-cut as possible. In spite of these rules, there is a "conspiracy of silence" which prevents them from being applied, specifically in cases of inheritance and accession to office.

The emphasis on ambivalence fits very neatly with the current anthropological preoccupation with agency.[10] Ambivalence clearly provides individuals with space to maneuver within given "systems" or "structures." However, the notion of ambivalence, important as it is, is sometimes too convenient. Whatever the paradoxes of illegitimacy among the Dyula, they have little to do with ambivalence – either with questions about what the rules "really are" or about how they are to be applied to specific situations – but rather with the circumstances in which rules are deliberately ignored.

The very real changes which have taken place among the Dyula – the very noticeable "epidemic" of apparent illegitimacy in recent years – have not been accompanied by any changes in the "rules" at all. More importantly, they are not necessarily the result of changes in sexual behavior per se. Rather obviously, if many young women, particularly in towns, are marrying later and later, the likelihood that sexual encounters will lead to premarital pregnancy is dramatically increased. Marriage, not sex, is at issue. This is a point that has been repeatedly stressed by anthropological discussions of illegitimacy, most forcefully by O'Neill (1987). It is not that proponents of the neo-normative approach have ignored marriage, but rather that they have put the cart before the horse. Marriage is not a "force" or "factor" affecting illegitimacy; illegitimacy is a *feature* of systems of marriage. Marriage, however, is not the only issue. New patterns of illegitimacy are also a result of the growing unwillingness of husbands to claim as their own any "illegitimate" children of their wives.

All of these changes, in turn, have to do with the implications of kin group membership. Let me make it quite clear that the *kabila* has not ceased to be a salient, indeed a central, feature of Dyula social organization. But no *kabila* is, or has ever been, an island unto itself. The very identity of the Dyula as an ethnic and religious minority specializing in local and long-distance trade has involved their society at every level in a regional and supra-regional political economy. However, the ways in which *kabila* have been embedded within this wider political economy have changed radically. In the political domain, the *kabila* was a significant unit in local, factional politics. It is important to point out that, well before the colonial period, politics was not a strictly local affair. Korhogo and its region fell within the spheres of influence of neighboring states and empires. Even so, such states were rarely interested in imposing a high degree of central control. French colonial control was not only more centralized, but much more removed from any local "influence." In real terms, however, the difference was not immediately apparent. The incursion of central authority on local autonomy has been a gradual, but not easily reversible, process.

Even more radical than this loss of political control has been the loss of economic control. Dyula social organization was geared to the establishment and maintenance of monopolies or quasi-monopolies. Control over sectors of the economy, specific techniques of production, access to strategic markets, restricted commercial networks, and the labor of producers and porters were all critical. Such control kept strategic resources out of the hands of outsiders while allowing the maximum latitude for initiative among insiders. Arguably, high rates of in-marriage constituted an ideal means of keeping everyone "in the family." This control depended on the articulation of local, regional and inter-regional economies. Control over the labor of a few weavers was enough to establish one in the cloth trade; profits from the cloth trade might, in turn, be invested in long-distance ventures. Initially, colonial rule disturbed rather than destroyed this control. The death blow was dealt after World War II, with the advent of a modern infrastructure of transportation which definitively marginalized micro-scale enterprises: weavers had to compete with mass-produced textiles; goods were counted by the truck load rather than the head load.

It is misleading to say that the *kabila* "lost" control over its members (though not, by and large, their loyalty). Rather, control over its members is less and less of a strategic resource, either politically or economically. The outcome has been a sense of freedom on the part of younger members. Young men are "free" to work in the wage sector, outside the control of their elders (provided they can find a job); young women are "free" to marry whom they please (provided they can find a husband). Illegitimacy is both a symptom and a consequence of the new-found independence of young people from their senior kin. The price of this freedom is the narrowing of responsibility for raising and supporting children. Fewer and fewer people have a vested interest in "claiming" children; on the contrary, they arguably have an interest in evading potential responsibility. The problem is not that "bastards" will increasingly find themselves excluded, but rather that there is nowhere to include them in the first place.

Notes

This article is based on fieldwork among the Dyula of northern Côte d'Ivoire in 1972–73 and 1984–85. I wish to thank the National Science Foundation and the National Endowment for the Humanities for funding this research. I am also very grateful to my colleagues Caroline Bledsoe, Susan Greenhalgh, and Allan Hill for their extremely helpful comments on a previous draft.

1 The anthropological literature on the West Indian family is far too vast to be cited here extensively. Notable contributions, by way of example, include R. T. Smith 1956; 1988; Edith Clarke 1957; M. G. Smith 1962.

2 Cf. Khera 1981.

3 On the Ivoirian Civil Code of 1965, see Launay 1982:139–145.

4 The difference between "African" and "Eurasian" family systems has been discussed extensively by Jack Goody (1976).

5 For a detailed account of the Dyula of northern Côte d'Ivoire, see Launay 1982, 1992.

6 On Dyula wedding ceremonial in general, and the *furu* in particular, see Launay 1975.

7 The implications of these pushes and pulls on Dyula social organization are discussed in more detail in Launay 1988b.

8 See Launay 1982:150–156 for a fuller discussion of rates of in-marriage.

9 On the notion of *nambaga* among the Dyula, see also Launay 1988a:56.

10 See, for example, Karp 1986.

6 Marginal members: Children of previous unions in Mende households in Sierra Leone

Caroline Bledsoe

The social roots of resource distribution

Just as resources are not distributed equally throughout national populations or communities, neither do they necessarily trickle down equitably within households. Stratification and differentiation can produce selective allocations of food, medical treatment, and educational support among children in the same household.

My previous work has attempted to instill interpretations of reproduction outcomes with a dynamic view, highlighting people's social efforts to *manage* or *achieve* demographic outcomes by restructuring household compositions and influencing obligations, rather than by acting strictly within the biological bounds or cultural norms that seem to be imposed on them (e.g., Bledsoe 1990b). Instead of being tethered to demographic facts, people try to tinker with them, to create or undo them, or to construe "official" (Bourdieu 1977) versions of them. By fostering in children, for example, adults try both to meet their current labor needs and to stake future claims in a broad array of children besides their own. Here I examine people's active efforts to shed those conjugal ties whose advantages have waned and build loyalty in new directions by tracing resource allocations to children.

Anthropological works have long accustomed us to the idea of *accreting* family members through reproduction or marriage; practices such as marriage, adoption, and fosterage are examples. Yet arguments that groups are shaped socially must acknowledge equally the opposite potential: eliminating some ties and rendering others marginal. Divorce and infanticide are examples. However, radical efforts to sever ties are measures of last resort. Dissatisfaction between spouses, for example, is usually expressed more subtly, by neglecting sexual or domestic duties. It may also be expressed by marginalizing individuals. (Robert Launay's chapter in this volume suggests one way in which this might be done.)

A key symbolic medium through which social relationships can be managed is through resource distribution to individuals central to these relationships. As Audrey Richards (1932) pointed out long ago: "the gift of sharing of food is a legal symbol of union" (p. 190). Because children are symbols of links between adults, resource allocations to children, like the performance of sexual or domestic duties, become barometers of adult relations. How a foster child, for example, is treated reflects less the guardian's sentiments toward the child than the ties between parents and guardians. If the caretaker occupies higher status than the parent, the child may receive less to eat than other children in the household and be treated as a servant. Similarly, how a man treats his new wife's child by a previous union, whether with magnanimity or resentment, may reflect more his sentiments toward her or her former spouse than those toward the child. And a woman seeking to prove her loyalty to her new spouse may even slight her own children by a previous union. These observations suggest that in the realities of everyday life, fertility, child mortality, and child migration are not simply demographic outcomes. They may be signs of broader adult relations as well.

In Africa, as elsewhere, one of the key factors affecting children's access to resources is their mothers' conjugal status. Yet in the context of a massive rise in short-term or informal relationships across much of the continent (van de Walle 1993), we know virtually nothing about what happens to the children of these unions as their mothers enter subsequent ones. This paper shows that because both women and men feel pressure to allocate resources disproportionately to children by unions they most value currently, the children of extant unions often fare better than do those of broken ones: an observation that bears relevance elsewhere.

The paper draws on ethnographic and demographic data from the Mende of Sierra Leone. During 1981–82 and 1985 I worked in a rural chiefdom in the Eastern Province, and carried out a follow-up study in December of 1985 in a large town in the Southern Province. While I present some results from my 1982 survey of 179 households and a 1985 survey of 860 women, the most compelling data consist of open-ended interviews, observations, and case studies. The quotes used in this paper are particularly powerful statements of moving conjugal dilemmas surrounding children.

Economic and political inequalities and the household

It would be wrong to attribute intrahousehold inequities to "bad" African caretakers or to the evils of polygyny or divorce. Microlevel politics are shaped and intensified by larger economic and political inequalities (see Greenhalgh 1990 for an overview).

In previous eras, the benefits of rearing children in rural Sierra Leone considerably outweighed the costs. Even today, most children, particularly girls, work hard in the household until they leave home for marriage or work, after which many send remittances and backstop parental emergencies. But nowadays, to educate children up to a level that would qualify them for white-collar employment exerts enormous drains on scarce rural incomes. Students incur costs ranging from perhaps $25 per year for government primary schools to thousands of dollars for prestigious secondary schools. Paying school expenses also poses an increasing gamble. Because of the shrinking market for wage employment, the chances have diminished that any one child will become highly successful. Even for those few children who do, their own urban commitments make it difficult to remit benefits to elders who invested in them. Analogous pressures apply to medical expenses incurred from serious illnesses requiring periods of hospitalization and expensive remedies. The costs of producing a healthy, successful child may detract substantially from the chances of the other siblings succeeding.

Changes in economic expenditures for, and returns from, children operate against a broader political context of patron–clientelism. In Sierra Leone, jobs, scholarships, money, and land are dispensed through personal ties to powerful brokers who can intervene with national institutions. Legal cases can be trumped up against those with weak patronage support, stripping them of land, property, and dependents. With precipitous declines in the national economy, people have even greater need for patrons well connected to the urban and government bureaucracies to bypass cumbersome bureaucratic channels during shortages, and to provide crucial ties to the international world for travel, jobs, and access to hard foreign currency.

How, then, do children figure in this political arena? Needless to say, juxtaposing children with patronage politics is not standard practice. We usually try to extract children from the messy business of politics, relegating them to Meyer Fortes' (1969) safe moral haven of "kinship." Yet the Mende place fertility and successful childraising at the heart of adult power struggles. A son who acquires a good job and elite political connections is expected to distribute his earnings and use his connections on behalf of his extended kin, all of whom claim to have supported him during his formative years, and try to undermine those who failed to support him. In such a context, a boy with educational promise becomes at once the object of feverish investment by some family members and the target of discrimination by those who seek to "block his progress," lest he gain power over them.

Particularly for women, bearing and raising children lie at the heart of political power and economic wellbeing. As in much of West Africa, women control many of their own financial enterprises and take responsibility for most of their children's costs of rearing. Yet male support fills crucial gaps when funds are short. It also pays for expenses beyond ordinary childraising costs: expenses such as large hospital bills or tuition bills.

Largely because of the polygynous – or potentially polygynous – character of married life, women need children to justify making demands on their husbands' wealth and estate. Infertility or subfertility, an anguishing problem in general for African women, is particularly severe in the context of polygyny. A subfertile wife must watch whatever productive effort she exerts for the household going to benefit her co-wives' children. No matter how well they get along, co-wives jealously observe how many children the other wives bear and how many survive. Fearing to shortchange any of his wives, a polygynous man is a reluctant advocate of birth control.

In his illuminating discussion of resource distribution, Sen (1981) argues that most starvation deaths stem not from external factors such as food shortages, drought, or economic depression, but from legal and social forces that produce inequitable food "entitlements" *within* countries. Such insights have been applied to widely differing contexts. Tilly (1983), for instance, argues that wage earners in eighteenth- and nineteenth-century Europe were deprived of food entitlements as capitalist development advanced; and Hill (1990) shows that during recent Sahelian droughts, poor herders suffered disproportionate losses of resource entitlements while many urbanites scarcely felt any effects.

Inequalities and struggles over scarce resources at the broader societal level take graphic shape within households, where children are born and raised. Like assumptions of harmonious integration at the national level, assumptions of households as homogeneous units face critical scrutiny. Folbre (1986) points out that in economics, both neoclassical theory and its unlikely bedfellow Marxian theory "have diametrically opposed theories of the firm, but remarkably similar theories of the household" (p. 245): both conceive of the household as an undifferentiated, sharing unit. While neoclassical theory, including the "New Household Economics" (Becker 1976), treats households like individuals or firms, as the primary actors in the economy, Marxian political economists see macrolevel inequality, within the nation or among nations, as the cause of underdevelopment. Although Marxian theory grew out of concerns with conflict and the exploitation of labor, Folbre charges that it is largely unconcerned with relationships of production within domestic units (1986:246–247). In contrast, she casts doubt on assumptions of joint utility within households (see also Guyer 1981) and of families as undifferentiated, sharing units:

> it is somewhat inconsistent to suggest that individuals who are entirely selfish in the market . . . are entirely "selfless" within the family, where they pursue the interests of the collectivity. The vision of pure altruism within the family resembles nothing so much as the Marxian vision of utopian socialism. There is something paradoxical about the juxtaposition of naked self-interest that presumably motivates efficient allocation of market resources and a perfect altruism that presumably motivates equitable allocation of family resources. (Folbre 1986:246–247)

Polygamy as a basis for differentiation among children

Although poverty clearly affects children's access to health care and food (Scrimshaw 1978; Scheper-Hughes 1985; and Cassidy 1980), stratification and differentiation can result in selective neglect of children within the same household. Sierra Leoneans point to predictable distinctions among children such as age, sex, sibling order, and "cleverness" as bases for intrahousehold differentiation. Yet they also point to children's relationships to adults that draw potential lines of discrimination within households. Unlike a child from a high-status family, for example, a fostered child from a low-status family may be treated as a servant and given food and medical treatment of poorer quality.

A key distinction among children stems from plural conjugal unions. Not every man is a polygynist. Yet even a man who is technically monogamous may produce children by different women over his lifetime as he remarries after divorce or a spouse's death, or if he contracts informal "outside" unions. Because of the cultural salience of polygyny, some of the most important distinctions among children stem from their mothers' characteristics (Bledsoe 1993). Anthropologists have long noted that a polygynous man, despite ideals of equal treatment, usually shows favoritism among his wives according to their seniority in the house, educational level, social and political connections, business success, or special designations such as the "favorite" wife or the "official" wife who appears in "civilized" public contexts.

Whereas polygyny and its inevitable jealousies have been well described, less noted is the fact that how a man values his various women has a considerable influence on how he supports their children. Despite his claims to treat all his offspring equally, a man readily produces money to send a sick child of his favored wife to the clinic and he strains the household budget to educate the children of a wife from a high-status family whose good will he is cultivating. Multiple unions – whether extant or defunct – lay the groundwork for bitter rivalries. Small favoritisms, whether real or perceived, among the children of different co-wives portend advantages for some children at the expense of others.

That men differentiate not only among these women but also their children by them follows the logic of polygyny. More surprising is the fact that the plural unions surrounding women present a parallel case. Women cannot have more than one legal spouse at a time. Yet because of high rates of divorce, widowhood, and remarriage, and because of extramarital unions, women, like men, may well produce children by different conjugal partners over their life course. Equally logical, then, is the possibility that women themselves, like men, favor certain of their children over others: usually those by partners from whom the women currently receive most support.

If resource distribution to children is linked to conjugal viability, then recent transformations in marriage have considerable import for children's welfare. Only thirty years ago, Evans-Pritchard (1965) argued that in "simple" African societies, there was no such thing as an unmarried adult woman, and preferences for polygyny predominated. Although considerable deviation from these patterns arose in different times and places, recent history has witnessed truly dramatic changes. Under pressure from missionaries as well as policy makers some African countries have decreed polygyny illegal, at least on paper (Ngondo a Pitshandenge 1994), and in most urban areas, the outward form of marriage has shifted to monogamy, especially among educated people. Even among such populations, however, the logic of polygyny thrives in new forms: "serial monogamy" (Comaroff and Roberts 1977), "outside wives" (Baker and Bird 1959; Mann 1985; Karanja 1987), "informal unions," "polyandrous motherhood" (Guyer 1994), and, in francophone countries, *"la femme de coeur"* or *"le deuxième bureau"* (Lacombe 1983; Clignet 1987).

In the context of economic decline, these shifts toward legal monogamy have eroded the security that some women derive from marriage. Elite spouses can define their unions as legitimate monogamy, while marginalizing lower-status wives and children as stemming from "country" or "outside" marriages (Gage and Bledsoe 1994). While these trends make conjugal relations more tenuous, they also induce women to strike up "outside" or short-term relationships to support themselves and their children. As a Mende woman asserted: "People are anxious to have this material wealth, and they can't get this money unless they go to their boyfriends." While we should not underplay the affective realities of conjugal relations, the economic bases of unions are the ones to which women themselves draw attention: problems that threaten to intensify as national conditions worsen.

Writing on Nigeria, Guyer (1994) broadens such observations, pointing out that whereas *lineal* fertility theories stress the long-term benefits to be gained from children in their maturity, increasing economic instability is pressuring women to establish immediate *lateral* links to different men and their resource networks. Lateral strategies can produce dividends in a shorter time frame, with greater breadth and flexibility. (For a parallel, see Browner and Lewin's (1982) description of Colombian women in San Francisco.) At the heart of these lateral strategies are children. A woman can press her demands on a man, whether or not they call their relationship a marriage, with far greater leverage if she has a child by him: a strategy Guyer calls "polyandrous motherhood." Marriage, in fact, becomes almost incidental to a woman's reproductive career: "the child [is] the key to stabilizing an otherwise fleeting relationship; without the child there is no basis to claim any longer-term assets" (Guyer 1994; see also Bledsoe 1990a).

In the wake of rising rates of union rupture and reconfiguration, fertility, like marriage, becomes an ambiguous process that partners can use to test their relationship. A young woman may try to bear a child to bolster a new relationship or one she wishes to continue. She can also try to press her claims on a former partner who continues to show interest in the child she bore him. Although such strategies may appear to have all payoffs and no costs, the risks are high. If a relationship deteriorates, this child can become an economic burden as well as a social hindrance for a woman trying to initiate a new union.

The result is that a child from a previous union holds a tenuous status. If the mother's relations to the father and his people are genial and provide support, then the mother and her kin view the child with favor. If, however, the father and his kin maintain a bitter distance, then the child is seen as a hindrance now and a likely burden later in life when more resource-intensive training becomes necessary.

Kinds of children from previous unions

Rivals for paternal resources can include women and children from present unions as well as previous and even future ones. Among children from previous unions, there are three principal types.

An *orphan*, first, is technically a child whose mother and father have died. The Mende term for "orphan," however, usually refers specifically to the child of a dead mother because her conscientious, day-to-day care is hard to replace. Orphans appear to suffer considerably from neglect; other women in the household have their hands full with their own children's needs and sicknesses, and orphans necessarily make demands on household wealth. Chinua Achebe's Novel *Arrow of God* (1969:2–3) describes a new moon as being "as thin as an orphan fed grudgingly by a cruel foster-mother." And the following Mende proverbs underscore cultural perceptions that orphans are perpetually hungry:

An orphan stands, watching for food.
An orphan eats too much [i.e., more than caretakers want to provide].

For these reasons, many fathers prefer to send the child of a dead woman to be raised by relatives. But because relatively few children suffer the loss of a mother at an early age, and because of the growing importance of multi-partner conjugal strategies, the rest of this paper will concern the children of conjugal dissolution or of non-marital unions.

Second, *children of a divorce* necessarily accompany only one parent into a new union. If this is the mother, such a child is called a "met-in-the-hand" child. Although people insist that children legally belong to the husband's lineage, most young children (and many older ones) live with their mothers or their mothers' kin after divorce.

Finally, an *illegitimate child*, following local English translations, is a child resulting from a pre- or extramarital union (see Harrell-Bond 1975:124–156, for Freetown). Because illegitimacy is increasingly singled out in local debate, we need to look more closely at this category.

People express considerable ambiguity about exactly what illegitimacy is. Some ambiguities surround the kind of union the parents claim to have, whether conducted through the church, civil authorities, or customary procedures (see, for instance, Comaroff and Roberts 1977; Burnham 1987; Gage and Bledsoe 1994; Nelson 1988; van de Walle and Meekers 1994; Locoh 1994). Others surround the marriage event itself. African marriage is less a definitive event than a process consisting of visiting, token exchange, initiation of sexual relations, coresidence, childbirth, nuptial ceremonies, and bridewealth payments – often occurring in markedly different sequences from couple to couple. All this makes it unclear when a couple was actually married. In many cases, the union is defined after the fact: if the relationship is intact, it is a marriage; if it broke down, it was not. Whether the child was born well before most of the significant events defining the union occurred seems to be less important than whether the union has lasted.

A final source of ambiguity concerning legitimacy is whether a woman's current man claims paternity for her child. Some scholars argue that in sub-Saharan Africa, all children belong in theory to either their mother's or father's lineage, meaning that there is no such thing as an illegitimate child. But in everyday life, distinctions are increasingly drawn between children who came in the "right" versus the "wrong" way (see, for example, Launay, this volume). The category of illegitimate child – a child with no acknowledged father – is highly charged, and calling someone illegitimate, a horrendous insult, is grounds for lawsuit. The following terms reflect a stigma that requires little explanation:

night-time child
window (or back-door) child
disgraceful-business child
thieving-here, thieving-there child (refers to the lover's theft of the husband's sexual rights)
go-and-wait-for-me-there child
come-and-close-the-door-quickly child
hurry-up-I'm-going child (refers to the woman worrying about discovery)
corner-corner child (refers to secret, illicit acts)
tricky child ("tricky" referring to the mother's behavior)

Many men are willing to recognize their children, regardless of the union's legality. But what "recognition" entails in terms of actual support over the life cycle of the child or of recognition by the man's family is another matter, especially since this implies relationships to a wider kinship network reaching far beyond the man himself. Indeed, Folbre's generalization seems to hold for Africa: "the more costly children become, the more likely women are to be assigned primary responsibility for rearing them" (1990:40). In more elite urban circles, family pressures to maintain the appearance of formal monogamy induce many men to draw hard lines between their "inside" and "outside" children. But whereas people refer readily to a woman's child as "illegitimate," they do so less for a man since a pregnancy by an "outside" woman can be construed as a step toward a legitimate polygynous union.

A man who allows his wife's illegitimate child to remain in his house often draws clear symbolic and economic distinctions between this child and his own, but less because he resents the child than to punish and embarrass the mother. A man explained:

> I'll say [to the child], "Look, keep far . . . The way your mother brought you here was not satisfactory, so you have to be quiet. Otherwise, I'll send you to your grandmother in no time." So really, it's not the child I am vexed at: it is the woman. This is why I say all this in her presence: so she can hear.

Besides the kind of illegitimacy resulting from an extramarital affair is that of a child born to an unmarried woman. Prominent among these nowadays are the ill-timed births of teenaged schoolgirls (Bledsoe 1990c; National Research Council 1993). Most schoolgirls who bear children do not return to school, fearing taunts and harassment. But some leave their babies with their mothers and try to resume schooling elsewhere or strike up new unions, unfettered by damning evidence of the past.

Despite the apparently clear distinctions among these two principal kinds of children of previous unions – children of divorce and illegitimate children – the two tend to conflate in practice. In neither case is the mother still with the father, earning necessary paternal blessings through good behavior toward him, that people consider essential to children's welfare. The implications of this problem are immense. While, as we saw above, lateral fertility strategies give women access to multiple male networks, people resent attempts by a new woman and her children of a prior union to exert claims on their own family's meager resources. Similarly, a responsible father who provides support to his children by a previous union runs the risk that their mother and her kin will "poison their minds" against him, provoking his children to use all his investments to benefit the woman he rejected or even to seize his properties, in the name of patrilineality, to share with their mother's kin. Such suspicions almost inevitably result in resentment toward the children of former unions and also toward adults with whom the children are associated.

The treatment of children of previous unions

The foregoing descriptions have suggested that children can come, well after the biological event of birth, to have different values to their mother – values deriving from the ebb and flow of her conjugal relations and strategies of polyandrous motherhood. It should not be surprising, then, that children from former unions may have quite different health and welfare prospects than those from intact unions. The following survey results bear out this conclusion. We begin early in the fertility sequence, using some traditional "proximate determinates of fertility" indicators, then move toward the welfare of older children. (The numbers of such children are not trivial: the 1982 survey indicated that about one-third of all unmarried living children from 0 to 18 were from either broken unions or had at least one dead parent.)

Pregnancy outcome

One indicator of how children of prior unions are likely to fare is whether defunct unions are less likely than intact ones to produce live births. Taking the first three pregnancies as the units of analysis, the 1,335 instances in which women were married to the biological father when the pregnancy ended resulted in a higher proportion of live births than the 103 cases in which they were not married to the father (92 percent vs. 86 percent, respectively). These instances also resulted in fewer "spoiled pregnancies" (4 percent vs. 11 percent), a category including both miscarriages and abortions (see Caldwell and Caldwell 1994, for parallel observations), differences that are likely to be understated because women are reluctant to report abortions and illegitimate pregnancies (see Bleek 1987). While these differences might reflect more fragile pregnancies for young women, young Fula and Mandingo women in the sample, who typically marry very early, experienced fewer "spoiled" pregnancies than young unmarried Mende women.

Higher "spoiled" pregnancy rates can result from taking active measures such as abortion or, possibly, infanticide. Higher rates among non-marital pregnancies may occur also through medical steps *not* taken: antenatal clinic visits and medications not paid for, blood transfusions not given. A local physician related a dramatic case in point. A woman in acute labor distress was brought into the hospital at 1:30 in the morning. After a rapid examination, the doctor told her husband an emergency Caesarian was

Table 6.1 *Whether the woman was married to the biological father of the pregnancy when it ended, by average years to next pregnancy – 1985 survey (first 3 intervals only; N = total number of intervals)*

married	Years to next pregnancy			N
	1st interval	2nd and 3rd intervals	all 3 intervals	
yes	1.7	1.6	1.6	1093
no	2.8	1.2	2.2	55

necessary. He urged the husband to sign a statement permitting the operation, and to pay 60 leones ($51 US in 1982) to cover the expenses. The husband, though, was oddly reluctant to sign. He wavered, then refused, then wavered some more. Finally, he was dispatched to borrow some money from relatives in town. He came back some time later with only 10 leones, and still refused to sign for the operation. Finally, at 6 a.m. he signed, just as the doctor was suctioning out the now-dead baby. When the man heard the outcome, he commented that the baby was not his anyway.

Breastfeeding duration

The 1985 data for the first three births show that once a child survives past the neonatal phase, whether a union is recognized as a marriage has a pronounced effect on the number of months the child is breastfed. Children of women who were married to their fathers when they were born were breastfed almost a year on average (0.95 year; N = 1,116). In contrast, children of women who were not married to their biological father were breastfed for only 9 months (N = 81).

Time to next pregnancy

Whether a woman is married to the child's father when she gives birth also appears to affect the length of time to her next birth, an interval that can decisively influence the health of the previous child. The top row of Table 6.1, which considers the first four births, shows that women married to the progenitors of their pregnancies reported virtually no difference in any of their first three pregnancy intervals. However, there are acute differences between married and unmarried women. The mean interval from birth till the next pregnancy is 1.6 years for women who were married to the progenitors, and 2.2 years for women who were not. This long first interval for unmarried women may reflect the irregular unions of young women such as schoolgirls who, after a first pregnancy, may take extra precautions to avoid a second one. When we look at the combined second and third intervals, it becomes clear that women who are not married to the fathers of their last children have much shorter intervals than do women whose relationships are recognized as marriage (1.2 vs. 1.6 years).

Paternal support

Whereas it is not entirely clear how paternal support affects a child's welfare, the 1985 data on the first three surviving children show that whether the mother and father recognize their union as a marriage is crucial to whether the father will support the child financially. Of those children whose parents were currently married to each other, 74 percent, mothers reported, were receiving paternal support (N = 939), compared to only 51 percent of those whose parents were not married (N = 71). (The two variables, however, are not wholly independent: one sign that the man recognizes a union as a marriage is whether he supports the children resulting from it.)

Fosterage

One of the most important findings of the study is that children of prior unions are far more likely to be fostered, defined here as being away from mothers, than those whose parents' marriages are intact.[1] The principal reasons are fears that the child will suffer from overwork and indifferent care in the hands of step-parents, or aversion by a new husband to a graphic reminder of the wife's former husband. Whatever the immediate cause (or the polite excuse given) for sending children away, whether the parents' union is intact strongly affects fosterage: among all children from 2 to 16 years, 71 percent of those whose parents were married to each other were with their mothers (N = 235), compared to 23 percent of children with unmarried parents (N = 66). Age strongly affects these results: small children more often remain with mothers after a divorce, regardless of the mother's marital status, while older children of divorced women usually live elsewhere.

The sex of the child has a very marked effect on whether a child will be fostered out if the parents divorce. Among the children of divorced parents, sons are much more likely than daughters to be away from mothers (61 percent vs. 39 percent, respectively; N = 41), perhaps because it is considered appropriate for them to be with fathers or because they pose threats to step-fathers. Among the children of married parents, however, more girls were fostered out than boys (56 percent vs. 44 percent; N = 52).

Because many young women want to continue their schooling or look for new men unburdened by children from prior unions, grandmothers often end up with children (in the 1982 survey, 30 out of 112 fostered children were with "grannies"). Most people argue that because "grannies" love and pamper their small charges, they are the best caretakers for young children (Bledsoe and Isiugo-Abanihe 1989). Though many grannies live upcountry with untreated water, diminishing supplies of food, and few clinics or immunization programs, they generally treat grandchildren as well as their means allow. Because grannies tend to have fewer means or skills to educate children, grannies tend to be given young children. In my survey, almost half (48 percent) of in-fostered children less than 6 years old were living with real or classificatory grandmothers, compared to fewer than a quarter (21 percent) of in-fosters from 6 to 17. To leave a child with the maternal grandmother past the age of 6 or 7 hints at illegitimacy, for it reflects paternal disinterest in the child's advancement. In only two instances out of 19 had any children over 5 of still-married parents remained with grannies. These children, however, were still relatively young (7 and 8), both had come from small villages to the larger survey town, and both were slated to leave their grandmothers soon to enter school.

Besides fosters with grandmothers, many fosters are treated well, particularly those sent to a barren or subfecund woman who wants a child of a close relative to raise as her own. On the whole, however, out-fostered children of defunct unions are less likely than those from extant unions to go to prestigious urban households, and more likely to remain in rural areas with bleak chances for advancement. As fosters, they may receive arduous work assignments, and suspicious caretakers may dismiss their complaints of illness as tricks to avoid work. Many receive little animal protein and are given food of poor quality, such as the crusty, burnt rice at the bottom of the cooking pot. They are required to "earn" their food through good behavior, and are punished frequently by "starvation": food deprivation. People articulate a strong cultural perception that a small fostered child may become a "watch-pot child," who goes around to other compounds, begging silently as food is cooked and dished out. At older ages, however, fosters become adept at foraging for wild animal and vegetable foods, hawking, stealing, embezzling from market customers, and appealing to sympathetic outsiders for food or money (Bledsoe 1989).

As for illegitimate fosters, abundant evidence about their welfare comes from Sierra Leoneans. An official at the Ministry of Social Welfare charged that particularly in the heavily-Christian south, such children suffer intense stigma, and their mothers seldom visit. To be sure, many fosters may fare better than they would with their own mothers, particularly if the mother is young and single or in an unstable union (Bledsoe et al. 1988). Still, the above factors, compounded by negligible paternal support, suggest that illegitimate fosters may suffer high health and mortality risks.

Nutritional status

Two other possible indicators of children's welfare as a correlate of their parents' marital situations include nutritional status and survival chances. My own quantitative data on these questions are thin. However, studies from southern and eastern Africa report that one of the most salient correlates of a child's nutritional status is a lack of paternal economic support, through desertion, divorce, or illegitimacy. (See also Williams 1933; Sachs 1953; Pretorius et al. 1956; Scragg and Rubidge 1960; and Moodie 1961 for South Africa; Thomas 1981 for Ciskei; Burgess et al. 1972 for Malawi; LeVine and LeVine 1981 for Kenya.)

Child's survival chances

If pregnancy, like marriage, is an ambiguous process that continually reflects and tests the relationship between the partners and their families, then shifting relations among these parties can alter the social status of a child. A young woman may try, for example, to get pregnant to bolster a wavering relationship to a man. If he loses interest, or makes moves toward another woman, the perceived failure of this union can have unfortunate consequences for the child. Analyzing World Fertility Survey materials for nine African countries, Adegbola (1987) found that in five – southern Nigeria, Ivory Coast, Cameroon, Benin, and Ghana – illegitimate children suffer higher mortality rates in general: a pattern that increases, rather than decreases with age.[2]

A young urban woman in Sierra Leone exemplified such a case. She had borne one child by a man who claimed social and financial responsibility for it. But a second child arrived less than a year later, resulting from an affair with a man who denied paternity. The girl's family was angry because the short birth interval implied that she had failed to observe a decent period of postpartum sexual abstinence. They were also annoyed that the needs of this second child would endanger the life of the first, whose paternity was secure. Under such pressure, the mother badly neglected the second child. She frequently failed to feed him and left him alone for long periods in dirty diapers. Not surprisingly, his health deteriorated, and he suffered from bouts of untreated illness. Finally, the mother decided to "throw him away." She put him in a plastic bag and left him in a dump, but was caught in the act. The baby was saved, and she was arrested and later released. But the baby began to get sick again and finally died.

Factors influencing the care of children of previous unions

To explore in more depth the social factors that influence access to household resources for children from previous unions, I outline a case study of Vani (all personal names in this paper are fictitious), a boy of whom I have kept track for several years. Like many other older boys, Vani stayed with his father after his parents divorced. In other ways as well, the case highlights problems common to children of prior unions.

A case study

Vani, generally a bright, gregarious 13-year-old when I first met him, had enormous ambition to advance in school. His mother and father had divorced, however, and his main obstacle was his father's new wife, who made it clear that she resented spending household reserves on this child instead of her own young son, Ansu: Vani's half brother. She saw Vani's secondary-school expenses as a thankless sacrifice by the household. Vani, however, saw them as resources properly due him, as his father's son, and as investments in Ansu's future. He envisioned himself helping Ansu to continue school once he himself graduated from college and acquired a job. In a number of incidents, the son and the new wife squared off in bitter conflict.

In one telling event, Vani complained that he could not grind the household's cassava leaf in preparation for a meal because he had hurt his wrist at school. His step-mother accused him of bluffing, and threatened him with no food until he completed his work. This stalemate lasted four days, during which Vani managed to eat a bit of food secretly at a friend's house. Finally his father called a crisis "house palaver." During the session, no one mentioned Vani's hand. Instead, the debate focused on the tension between the boy and his step-mother. Vani charged, "If it had been your own child, you wouldn't have done this." She retorted, "All I have been doing for you, you have not appreciated it. So I know that in the future you will not [recognize] me." Vani's irate father accused his son of ingratitude, a devastating charge in the Mende moral vocabulary, and of being a cocky braggart whose educational achievements had made him too proud to perform demeaning household chores for a woman with no education.

A deep source of the step-mother's resentment was indeed Vani's school successes. Although her own son Ansu did well in school, Vani did better. And because he was older than Ansu, she feared that he would likely advance more quickly, a situation older siblings sometimes exploit to seize the family properties and money. Vani's school honors, therefore, only intensified the step-mother's jealousy and determination to halt his academic progress.

At one point Vani expressed a desire to visit his mother, whom he had not seen for five years. His step-mother seized this statement as proof that regardless of how many sacrifices she made on his behalf, he would eventually turn his primary loyalties to his own mother. In retribution, she "starved" him for a day and grew ever more resentful of him. On other occasions as well, he got nothing to eat and fell asleep in school from hunger.

Vani's step-mother put increasing pressure on his father to avoid paying his mounting secondary-school expenses, and threatened to leave if he capitulated. On one occasion, when the father's payments for Vani's schooling left little for immediate household expenses, she fumed, "You have gone and spent all your money on your son [Vani]. And now we are still staying here and suffering, suffering!"

One year she pressured Vani's father to refuse to pay his school fees, using the excuse that the family was going to move to another town before the school year was over. This, however, meant that Vani would not pass to the next class. From a diary he kept, I excerpt the following:

> School was over. I came home with my hunger and illness [a boil]. I was unfortunate that there was no food prepared for me, so I went to the town to [walk] around. When I came I eat [a meager meal] and I took bathe and pack my books and went for evening studying. When I went, was unable to study because my boil and stomach was aching. Deliberately I just have to keep myself on the floor for satisfaction [lying on the stomach to suppress hunger pangs]. I was unable to study [or sleep].
>
> [The next morning]: When I went to school I was unable to study for my stomach was empty. I try to force myself to study but I was reading while nothing remains in my head. So I decided to go home and have food. I came home and have food, but it was not enough, therefore I drank a lot of water to get my stomach fill . . . At that night I study for I was worry whether I will be allowed to sit to the examination for my father hasn't pay my fees; for that worry I immediately decided not to study . . . So I went to sleep for that night.

The next day, the national promotional exam results were announced in school, but the name of the student who had placed first in the class (whom everyone knew was Vani) was not announced, because he had not paid his fees. Vani's diary entry for this day reveals great depression.

Forced to turn elsewhere for support, Vani moved in with his mother's brother, who fed him and took on some of his school expenses. But this uncle had started his own young family, and his wife watched apprehensively as money was diverted to Vani. She began to scrimp on Vani's food, and demanded that he turn off his studying lantern early at night to save on kerosene, the lifeblood of rural students. Sensing his wife's growing hostility, his uncle had to cut down Vani's support, forcing him to fend increasingly for himself.

Eventually, Vani managed to complete his requirements to enter college, but was unable to muster the necessary fees. He had no one to lobby on his behalf with his father: usually the crucial role of a mother in a polygynous household. He wrote despairingly to me:

> I am from a polygamous family wherein my mother had separated long since from my father and I have no body to advocate for me to my father to put serious attention in my education . . . . [Even] if I go to university who will help to finance my education? Of course my father will say [he will do it], but will not do it because of my step-mothers influence . . . . My [own] mother who I was thinking could help me when I attain university level is seriously sick that only God knows whether she will survive, so my plan at home has ruin.

To a large extent, Vani's step-mother appeared to be using both Vani and her own son Ansu to test her husband's loyalty to her. She expected her husband to shower attention and resources on Ansu and ignore Vani. Despite Vani's stated affection for his brother, his frustration foreshadowed future strains between them:

> There is one thing bringing the situation to a worse position. My father has grown *too* much love for the lad [Ansu] again. *Too* much love. *More* love . . . . Because the lady is there, working, taking care of him [the father] . . ., he has to pay more attention to the son of the lady. [His emphasis.]

Socioeconomic factors determining the treatment of children of previous unions

Vani's case highlights several factors that determine how children are situated on a continuum ranging from warm acceptance to hostile maltreatment by step-parents.

Whether they stay with their father or their mother can spell large differences for children of previous unions. Children staying with fathers will likely suffer more deprivation and work harder because a step-mother oversees them and feeds them. Since men try to keep the messy business of childcare at arm's length, the father may be unaware of discriminations. More likely, he is aware, but remains silent to avoid antagonizing his wife. Although Vani faced such hardships, they are particularly important for small children, who rely on their female caretakers for time-consuming nurturance. Most people argue that despite the patrilineal ideology, a young child is better off with the mother and her new man.

Vani's case also highlights economics as a fundamental determinant of how children of previous unions are treated. A woman's ambivalence toward her step-child can turn into ill will if the husband fails to cover the child's expenses, forcing his current wife to absorb these costs as well as those of her own children. She also resents, as Vani's step-mother did, expenditures for the child of a woman no longer contributing to the household and who, moreover, is benefiting from the household's scanty wealth. Even step-parents who currently enjoy amicable relations with their step-children fear that their investments in such children will be wasted.

The impact of economic strains also affects grandparents who believe, probably correctly, that the more they do to feed and clothe an illegitimate grandchild, the less the father, if his identity is known, will help. Hoping the father will come to pay for any needed medical treatment, they may delay treatment until the child's condition is critical. Yet I also heard a surprising number of cases of explicit neglect: grandparents giving indifferent care to children with no paternal support because they view such a child less as their own grandchild than as the father's unmet responsibility. One person explained that if

> the boyfriend will be tipping [his mother] small-small, she will take care [of the child]. But if she doesn't get something from the young man, she wouldn't want to know what the child is doing. Since the father is not interested, the granny also will not be interested. Even the woman's mother will not be interested. If the granny is not fully supported, how do you expect her to bring up that child?

Because of the growing frequency of union ruptures, many children are caught in multiple economic binds: both parents as well as grandmothers may have new spouses who pose new financial conflicts. The Ministry of Social Welfare official I talked to cited a case in which a grandmother with two small children of her own had to take in two of her daughter's illegitimate children. Her own husband, however, who was not her daughter's father, resented the burden these children posed, and pressured her to give them back.

Another determinant of how children of former unions are treated, as Vani's case shows, is whether step-parents have their own children in the household. A childless woman may seek to bolster her tenuous position in the home by treating her husband's children as her own. But even genial relationships can dissolve into competition once she begins to bear children. A man related:

> My wife did take . . . the boy by my other [divorced] wife, but at that time, she didn't have a child. Everything was alright then, but when she began to have her own children, she began to show some favoritism.

A father who pays the school fees for his children by a departed wife while making his present wives pay for their own children, not only angers his wives; he also drives a deep wedge between the sets of siblings. These gulfs typically widen over time, as the former union's children grow older, posing ever-larger economic and political threats. A man explained:

> This is a bad mistake. You cannot tell which of these children is going to be somebody tomorrow. And when that happens, then the child who becomes somebody will be ready to victimize these from the other woman who is not there.

The treatment of children as a symbol of adult relationships

The three factors outlined above – who children stay with, financial strain, and the presence of step-parents' own children – clearly influence how step-parents treat their spouses' children by previous unions. But such explanations tend to restrict attention to the relationship between the child and the caretaker. Relationships among adults are almost always overlooked when asking about caretaking quality (see also Bateson 1972). A Mende proverb expresses the tendency to extend one's sentiments for certain individuals to their dependents: "If you like the monkey, you must like its tail."

Using children as symbols of adult relationships is especially common to female step-parents who, because of their subordination, find it safest to express conjugal resentments indirectly. But husbands like Vani's father who do not wish to escalate quarrels into conjugal rupture also tend to divert their hostility toward children. Such principles apply to any children that spouses bring into the household; not simply those from previous conjugal unions. A man named Joseph explained that when he was a foster child in his uncle's household, he knew exactly how his guardians were getting along with each other by how the woman treated him. When the spouses were on good terms, the woman would invite Joseph to the parlor, an unusual privilege for a fostered child, where she served him some coffee and a bounteous meal with his uncle. When he returned from an errand, she would casually pocket the change he returned without counting it. He would have few chores that day, and if he were tired the woman would suggest that he wait till morning to bring water. But when the uncle and his wife were at odds, Joseph's treatment was quite different. The woman would acidly explain his minute rice allocation as "what your uncle provided [today]," implying that the allocation had been miserly. She would painstakingly count the change from his errands, reporting any embezzlement immediately to her husband, and demand that he work late into the night, if necessary, to finish his chores.

What, then, are some of the pivotal adult–adult relationships that affect how children of previous unions are treated? To simplify some of the permutations, I divide the discussion into how step-parents and natural parents treat children, as a function of the adults' wider relations with other adults.

Step-parents' treatment of children

The most relevant social component that affects a child's treatment is relations between the new couple itself. Tensions between natural and step-parents make step-parents more likely to maltreat step-children. Some of these tensions stem from a man's suspicion that the woman he recently married is using the child she brought with her to maintain a secret connection to the child's father. But there are many cases as well in which a step-parent's affection and generosity toward the spouse extend to the spouse's children. An older boy described his own relationship with his step-father in these terms:

> Presently my mother's husband loves my mother so much. So the love extends to us. He is willing to accept us, he is glad over us. Because of the love. Last year he got sports [shoes] for me. I was so glad, because I hadn't shoes at that time. That was my complaint. He bought that for me. I was so happy. So happy!

The relationship between the spouses – more than the step-parent's relationship with the children themselves – determines even how a man will treat his wife's illegitimate child. Testimonies such as this one from a remarkably frank man bear witness:

> If the father loves his wife very dearly . . ., he will *never* expose [the illegitimacy]. If the woman is arrogant, he will say, "I am going to expose you," and he will do it. He will say, . . . "There is a reason why you are being proud. Because you are loving [having an affair] . . ." But if it is a quiet woman, you will keep things very cool and dark. You won't expose it at all . . . There are some women who love, who have more than 20 boyfriends. But as long as your wife is obedient, she does not disturb you at home, you wouldn't mind this. If, with this "up and down" [love affairs] if she happens to [bear] any child, you just have to claim that child to be your son or daughter. You don't have to expose it at all.

Relations between step-parents and absent parents also figure strongly in children's treatment. For children staying with their father, whether their step-mother and absent mother were on good terms is critical. If not, as is often the case – indeed, disputes between the women may have led to their mother's departure – then such children are considered at high risk of poisoning or witchcraft, especially if the current wife perceives any signs of paternal favoritism toward them. In Vani's case, he and his half-brother Ansu had become symbols through which the father and the new step-mother tested their loyalty to each other. Though a man may assure his present wife that his past marital ties are broken, she faces the daily reminder of a woman who may have been her bitter enemy. The more her resentment grows, the more she interprets any paternal attention toward his child as a sign of her fall from favor and even of his renewed interest in the departed woman. Sensing this, the father feels even more pressure to remain silent about how she treats his child.

Parents' treatment of their own children
Although the role of adult relationships in determining child treatment is understandable in the case of step-parents, more dramatic are instances of relationships normally considered inviolate: the grandparent–child bond.

In one striking case, a father drove his secondary-school daughter out of the house after she bore an illegitimate child, and threatened to disown her – unless the child died. I quote the grandfather himself:

> my daughter . . . had been attending school and was "pregged" . . . So she told me she had [given birth to] a baby boy. I said, "Look, Mary, let me tell you one thing. I am not going to touch that child until he dies. Otherwise, you and I are not going to be one." I drew away . . . She was gone about 6 months, and the child died. When she came back, I accepted her because I was not seeing the [boyfriend] again . . . . I never wanted to *know* how he died, since I said I was not going to touch that baby . . . She came to meet me and apologize. I later forgave her . . . But later, she came with her own choice [a real husband]. I said, "Well, now I am happy. But I wouldn't want you to be going up and down without a legal husband. My name is too big. They would say, 'Look at [X's] daughter. She is a street girl.' This would be a big shame to me." This is why I drove her away.

Final evidence for the assertion that women and men allocate resources disproportionately to children by unions they most value currently is found in the fact that parents may express discontent with their spouses (present or past) through their own children whom they bore with those spouses.

Because children are associated with their mothers in the polygynous context, it makes logical sense that a father might discriminate against his own children if he and their mother are at odds. (One man, enraged at the woman he was divorcing, drove her three sons – his only surviving children – out of the house after her, and deliberately focused his affections and money instead on his new wife's daughters by her former husband.) Yet compelling evidence that adult relationships in new unions influence the care of children consists of discrimination by mothers – in theory, a child's ultimate refuge – against their own children. If women are facing growing pressures to use their children as links to men's resources and, as a result, find themselves juggling multiple men through various children, jealousies are inevitable. Women with new partners face strong economic and social pressures to shore up these new unions by displaying disinterest in their old ones. Such demonstrations may include withholding resources from their own children. Recognizing these pressures, a man vowed that should he ever divorce, he would send his children to his sister because she would take better care of them than would their own mother:

> The mother would love a new child with her new husband more than those from a previous husband . . . So this is why sometimes when a man and woman divorce, the man has to take the children away. When the woman gets the child with her new husband, she would want to satisfy the husband by taking good care of his child. He would in fact be vexed to see her taking care of the previous husband's children so well, and there will then be

misunderstanding between the new couple, and the woman wouldn't want that. So it is not that the woman loves her older children less, but that she knows she must take better care of the new ones to make sure that no palaver arises between her and the new husband.

Analogous pressures apply even to mothers who are still with their children's fathers. Women are particularly likely to express through their own children their anger at men who threaten to undermine the economic viability of the union through taking on outside women. Under such conditions, they may give more privileges and food to their fostered children than their own. A man related that when he gave his wife no money for the day or "slept out" with a girlfriend, she would beat "his" children and deprive them of food for small infractions. By contrast, she would treat royally her sister's son, whom she was fostering. One time, after the man "slept out," he returned to find his wife and her nephew eating, her own children looking on in hungry silence. Referring indirectly to the money he spent on his lover, she said spitefully, "Let [your children] eat the food you have provided."

Most cases of women neglecting their own children involve only brief periods of symbolic neglect – with the exception, perhaps, of illegitimate children whose presence exposes their mothers to continual shame. Furthermore, a child's death is most likely a by-product than a goal of indirect adult communications about conjugal loyalties. Still, exceptions occur. Hospital workers report that mothers who have new boyfriends or who are experiencing marital discord often take indifferent care of their children in the hospital. They may be gone for long periods, leaving the children with no one to feed and tend them. And startlingly frank comments from mothers also surface. One young woman in my 1982 survey voiced defiant relief to my surveyor at the death of her child by a husband who had given her little money to run the household or buy food: "Lest my child suffer, let him die, because the father wasn't taking care of him."

Conclusions

A considerable body of literature draws attention to two key factors that appear to precipitate child abuse or neglect: cultural views of children as non-persons (e.g., deMause 1974; Shorter 1975) and demographic/economic constraints in high-mortality/high-fertility regimes, wherein parents may invest selectively in children by sex, sibling order, temperament, or physical imperfections (e.g., Stannard 1977; Stone 1977; Scrimshaw 1978; Scheper-Hughes 1987; for a brief review, see Bledsoe and Hirschman 1989). In contemporary Sierra Leone, selective allocations to children stem also from competition that the wider system of patronage and political instability imposes, even at the household level, among shifting arrays of conjugal partners. In sum, the same pressures that make adults' lateral fertility strategies more viable also increase the health and mortality risks for young children of former unions.

Provocative parallels occur elsewhere in the world. In the US, the highest rates of child abuse and neglect appear to be in father-only homes or homes with one step-parent and one natural parent. Some studies that seek to explain these patterns argue that step-parents are abusive because they have little to gain from children with whom they share no genes (e.g., Wilson et al. 1980; Lightcap et al. 1982). Although such explanations could be debated in detail, I simply point out that they focus almost exclusively on the child/step-parent relationship, without recognizing the likely hostilities stemming from the reminders of the old union or tensions arising in the new one.

By focusing on the socially constructed character of families, rather than on biological fertility, the analysis has revealed that a woman's various children can come to have different values to her – values depending on her relations with the children's respective fathers. Analyses stopping at the level of household or even of individual women may overlook striking imbalances in resource distribution among the children present: a woman's children by her current husband versus those by previous men. Such analyses may also overlook imbalances among the children *not* seen: the products of former unions who are absent because their presence undermines the stability of the current union.

The more complicated message from viewing families as socially constructed is that demographic phenomena such as fertility, marriage, divorce, and child mortality cannot be considered in isolation from each other or in simple causal relations in a proximate-determinates framework. Children and their wellbeing become cultural symbols which adults use to shape their own relations with each other.

Notes

For generous institutional support of the project I am grateful to the National Science Foundation, the Population Council, the Ford and Rockefeller Foundations, the Population Studies Center at the University of Pennsylvania, and the Department of Anthropology at Northwestern University. For help during the fieldwork or analysis of the chapter, I thank Anne Ferguson, C. Magbaily Fyle, Jane Guyer, Allan Hill, John Janzen, Robert Launay, David Lucas, and William Murphy. I am also grateful to the Population Research Center at the University of Chicago for comments during a presentation of the paper on which the chapter is based.
1 Similarly, Page (1989) showed, using WFS data, that whether a woman had

divorced was a better predictor of fostering out children than any other tested. See also Fraenkel (1964:215–216) and Findley and Diallo (1988) for discussions of the impact of union rupture on fosterage.

2 Apparently contrary evidence on the circumstances surrounding first births only is found in the work of Meekers (1994), who concludes, using Côte d'Ivoire WFS data, that the presence of a man is more important to children's survival than legitimate paternity.

Gender, class, and clan: The social inequality of reproduction

7   Women's empowerment and fertility decline in western Kenya

Candice Bradley

Two recent news stories about Kenya have turned international attention to the changing African family. The most far-reaching of these news items was the September 1989 announcement that fertility transition had begun in Kenya (*N.Y. Times International* 1989). This much-anticipated announcement was based on data from the 1989 Kenya Demographic and Health Survey (KDHS) which indicated that, for the second time in ten years, Kenyan fertility had declined and contraceptive use had increased (NCPD 1989; van de Walle and Foster 1990). The KDHS presented reliable evidence of "the first significant decline in fertility in Africa ever," corroborating other data showing that Kenya, Botswana, and Zimbabwe are the first three African nations to move toward lower fertility. Authors comparing DHS data from eleven African countries focused on women's education and relative economic stability as factors that might explain the trend:

> It is noteworthy that these countries have been relatively less affected by the economic crisis of the recent decades, and have a more educated female population, than the other countries that had a DHS survey. (van de Walle and Foster 1990:13)

The other major news story from Kenya, ultimately less important but perhaps more revealing of the internal dynamics of Kenyan society, gained international attention in August, 1991. A group of boarding-school boys in Meru, Kenya, had gone on a "rampage" which resulted in the deaths of nineteen of their female classmates and the rape of seventy-one others (*N.Y. Times* 1991; The *Weekly Review* 1991). The headline in the *N.Y. Times* – larger than the one announcing Kenya's turn toward lower fertility – read "The Evil Men Do To Women In Kenya." The article quoted Kenyan leaders arguing that this event "was not an isolated case," though shocking in its unprecedented scale. They felt that an atmosphere condoning

157

violence toward women is responsible for sanctioning the kinds of behaviors which led to this horrifying incident:

> At St. Kizito, the principal and some of the teachers told Kenyan reporters that they regarded the raping of girls by boy students as a normal occurrence . . . In this country, where girls join boys in an educational system that provides more children with a better education than do those in most other African nations, the rampage is a cruel reminder that the place of women has not shifted with progress . . . The Professional Women's Organization and Maendeleo ya Wanawake, or Women in Development, the official women's group of the Kenyan African National Union, described events at St. Kizito as "a mirror of the kind of abuse and violence that women and girls are going through in Kenya, at home, at the work place and in public places . . . St. Kizito boys found legitimacy from the way the Kenyan society subordinates women and girls." (*N.Y. Times*, 4 August 1991, Section 4, p.4)

Historical evidence of violence toward women in East Africa is documented by both Kenyan and non-Kenyan researchers. Violence toward women was present precolonially among the Abaluyia (Wagner 1949), Iteso (Karp 1978), Gusii (LeVine 1959), Samia (Kilbride and Kilbride 1990), and Kikuyu (Wamalwa 1989). Members of the Kenya Parliament based their opposition to the Marriage Bill of 1969 on their understanding that "wife beating was a normal customary practice" among Kenyan ethnic groups, evidence that such violence has been perceived by many Kenyans as usual practice (Wamalwa 1989:71).

There is substantial evidence that the physical safety of Kenyan women and girls has deteriorated over time (Kilbride and Kilbride 1990; LeVine and LeVine 1981). The general consensus among both Kenyan and non-Kenyan observers is that these events are growing in frequency as the traditional family structure breaks down and stresses of Westernization and modernization increase (LeVine and LeVine 1981). Wamalwa states:

> Although it is difficult to generalize for all ethnic groups in Kenya, wife beating has become much more severe and frequent with the breakdown of the African socio-cultural system. The social limits on men are often non-existent as the extended family system continues to break down and women become marginalized. (1989:72)

The juxtaposition of these two seemingly unrelated events – fertility decline and violence toward women – underscores a conflict between the growing empowerment of Kenyan women and a corresponding atmosphere of domestic uncertainty. While educational and career opportunities have become more equitable for many Kenyan women, economic and advanced educational opportunities are limited for both men and women, and domestic violence may have increased.

Relationships in the demographic literature which link women's empowerment to declining fertility, primarily as an outcome of universal primary education, fail to pay attention to three factors which call this linkage into question. First, the mechanism through which education leads to declining fertility is often attributed to Westernization (e.g. Caldwell 1982), though there is evidence that education alone may not lead to lower fertility (Handwerker 1986b, 1989, 1991, 1993a). The Westernization hypothesis assumes that there are changes which improve women's status relative to men's, yet women's status may change multidirectionally as traditional norms and behaviors which protected women and girls break down. Second, the empowerment of women through routes such as education ultimately depends on the availability of economic opportunities for both men and women. An atmosphere of scarcity, whether real or perceived, may create tension between men and women who must compete for resources, educational opportunities, and employment. Third, the linkage between women's empowerment and fertility decline is usually made at the macrolevel, ignoring important status differences between individual women. Women's decisions to contracept may differ according to their education and economic opportunities brought about by age and other social statuses.

The focus of this chapter is the relationship between women's empowerment, domestic violence, and fertility. Using data from a Maragoli sublocation in a highland farming region of western Kenya, I demonstrate that, while fertility has declined and contraceptive use has increased, there are some important areas in which Maragoli women have lost ground. Domestic violence may be one of these areas. I also question the link between contraceptive use and education, demonstrating that women of different ages have access to different forms of empowerment and contracept at different rates, perhaps even for different reasons.

Women's empowerment, violence, and fertility

The empowerment of women is defined as decreases in inequalities between men and women, including increases in the range of real opportunities or choices, and the power to control or influence social, political and economic decision-making both within and beyond the household (Cain et al. 1979; Handwerker 1993a; Safilios-Rothschild 1980; Sanday 1981).

Power differs from status, often defined as the overall position of women in a society (Safilios-Rothschild 1982; Mason 1984), and from autonomy, "the extent to which women are free of *men's* control" (Mason 1984:6; see also Cain 1984; for the theoretical roots of these and other gender-related terms see Chapter 1). Autonomy compares women's power with men's, usually in a single setting, while women's status may be compared across settings. Although status may be discussed diachronically, it is used more as a static category, like class or caste, whereas empowerment implies agency, or causal power where action is constitutive (Karp 1986:137). By using the term empowerment, I am concerned with the degree to which women are social actors, able to affect their own positions (Collier and Yanagisako 1989; Lamphere 1989; see also Fuchs and Moch, this volume). Both empowerment and agency imply that women are able to resist, in favor of their own interests, the actions of institutions and more powerful individuals who might limit their abilities to act.

The link between fertility and the position of women, be it status or empowerment, is built into most contemporary theories of fertility decline (e.g. Cain 1984; Caldwell 1980, 1982; Hammerslough 1990, 1991; Handwerker 1986a, 1989, 1991, 1993a; Mason 1984; van de Walle and Foster 1990). For example, improved status or empowerment of women is hypothesized to result from increased educational (Caldwell 1982) or economic opportunities (Handwerker 1991; Hammerslough 1991), leading to increased contraceptive use and declining fertility.

Though Caldwell implies that changes in women's status are central to the processes of fertility decline, he rarely focuses directly on women (1982:323). For example, in one paper, Caldwell discusses the "patriarchal family head" (1982:301). The patriarch in pre-transitional societies is the decision-maker both in the household and the larger community, manipulating relationships in a system that rewards both age and maleness (pp. 311, 317). Both men and women in pre-transitional societies benefit from high fertility. Low fertility, on the other hand, is related to a more egalitarian family structure (pp. 314, 322) in which women demand greater cooperation in financial matters (pp. 320, 322) and, by looking out for their own interests as well as the educational and economic interests of their children, are implicated in the breakdown of a traditional family value system which supports high fertility (pp. 317–324).

Caldwell's perspective may be contrasted with Handwerker's (1986a, 1986b, 1989, 1991, 1993a). Handwerker argues that women begin to reduce fertility when they have opportunities besides having children for the attainment of adult status, prestige, and wealth. In Handwerker's view, fertility decline results from "changes in opportunity structure that increasingly reward educationally acquired skills and perspectives" (1986b:402). These opportunities may be more available to educated women.

However, Handwerker argues that education is only one route that women may use to free themselves from traditional power structures in which children are "gatekeepers" for certain kinds of wealth. In his research on Barbados and Antigua, Handwerker found that education by itself had no effect on fertility, but that education combined with opportunities for employment had major impacts on fertility (1986b, 1989, 1991, 1993a).

Hammerslough (1990, 1991) connects women's status and empowerment with lower fertility in his study of women's cooperatives throughout Kenya. Hammerslough finds that contraceptive use increases with women's participation in women's groups, especially if women are participating in groups that are more economically oriented. Nevertheless, Hammerslough attributes this increase not to the presence of economic opportunities, but to increased knowledge of family planning that comes with women's group participation as well as increased bargaining power within the household.

These theories, and others like them (Bulatao and Lee 1983; Cain 1984; Easterlin and Crimmins 1985) share the notion that improvements in women's status or empowerment of women leads to fertility decline. While it is generally recognized that women's status does not necessarily change uniformly along a single dimension (Mason 1984; Whyte 1978), theoretical models of the relationship between women's status or empowerment and fertility generally posit a strong negative relationship between the two.

Handwerker (1993a, 1993b) has also linked women's empowerment, violence toward women, and fertility. In his research on Barbados and Antigua, Handwerker found that women who are empowered are less likely to be beaten by their husbands or sexually abused. He found that family violence declined in a single generation as women, freed from childbearing and empowered by increased job opportunities and better education, gained better relationships with their spouses. "Power inequalities may elicit violence; power equalities may elicit good behavior" (Handwerker, 1993c:11).

The focal community

"Maragoli" is the traditional place-name for one of seventeen Abaluyia subnations occupying the hills of western Kenya for the past 500 years. Maragoli, in Kenya's Western Province, is a highland farming area located between Mount Elgon in the north and Lake Victoria in the south. Western Province is divided into four districts, which are further divided into divisions, locations, and sublocations. The Maragoli region is in Vihiga District in the southern portion of Western Province. The research reported here took place between 1988 and 1991 in Igunga Sublocation, W. Maragoli Location, Sabatia Division, in what is now Vihiga District.

Maragoli residents are called Logoli.[1] They are patrilineal, patrilocal horticulturalists who intercrop a variety of grains, trees, roots and vegetables, and who keep some cattle for milk, meat and bridewealth. Though plowing is sometimes done using oxen or tractors, most farms are cultivated with hoes because plots are too small to turn a plow around on. Women do most of the farm work in Maragoli, though men may help out in any phase of the agricultural cycle (Bradley 1995; Munroe and Munroe 1990; Ssennyonga 1978; Wagner 1949; Were 1967).

High fertility has probably been a feature of the Logoli for at least a hundred years. Early visitors remarked on the very high population density of Logoli communities, and there are estimates as early as the 1930s of densities as high as 1,000 persons per square kilometer (Farson 1949; Wagner 1949). Population densities in areas of Maragoli now exceed 2,000 persons per square kilometer. Researchers in western Kenya have described Maragoli as a "neighborhood" or "bedroom community" because the houses are so close to each other (Karp 1978; MPND 1989; Moock 1976; Nichols 1978; Ssennyonga 1978; Wagner 1949).

Igunga is a Logoli sublocation located about a kilometer off the paved international truck route running through the center of Western Province. Igunga is on the northern end of Vihiga District, several kilometers from the bustling Maragoli towns of Vihiga and Majengo but closer to the home areas of other Abaluyia subnations such as Kisa and Idaxho. Igunga is on a hill surrounded by rivers that watered lush communal grazing lands as recently as the 1950s. A busy murram road runs through the center of the sublocation. This road is lined with churches, schools, a dozen small shops, and scores of market women who arrive daily to sell grains, vegetables, dried fish, and sundries.

The classic ethnographic account of Maragoli comes from Gunter Wagner's 1937 research (Wagner 1949), although other social scientists have contributed important studies (e.g., Moock 1976; Munroe and Munroe 1990; Ssennyonga 1978). The findings reported in this chapter build upon previous research. My work is a restudy of a sublocation studied from 1974 to 1976 by an African anthropologist, Joseph Ssennyonga. Using data from two points in time, I was able to determine that fertility was declining in Igunga, and to test a series of sociocultural hypotheses related to declining fertility (Bradley 1994).

The data reported in this chapter come from three sources. These are: (1) a 1989 census of Igunga Sublocation (a total of 3,487 persons in 652 households); (2) a 1989–90 survey of 303 women between the ages of 15 and 49, collected in collaboration with a University of Nairobi graduate student, James Onyango Ndege; and (3) ethnographic and interview data from a smaller sample of 25 Igunga households, selected for closer study. Time allocation, interview, health, and household budget data were collected in the focused sample between December 1988 and November 1989. The 25 households in the smaller sample included eleven from Ssennyonga's 1974–76 research.

The larger survey of 303 women covered such topics as fertility, socioeconomic status, health, and women's empowerment, as well as husband–wife communication about contraception. The survey data presented in this chapter include nine variables to measure women's empowerment or agency. These are activities that an Igunga woman may engage in that enable her to accumulate wealth in the form of cattle or land, to hire her own laborers, or to earn, borrow, or save her own money through such activities as selling beer, selling crafts, trading, banking, obtaining credit, or participating in a cooperative. These economic and political activities are ways in which Igunga women gain more control over their lives. Some of these activities, such as cooperative participation, bring women together where they are able to act jointly in obtaining loans, saving, or speaking out as a group. Women in cooperatives may call upon local leaders to complain about actions that displease them, and have met jointly with officials as high up as the Kenya Parliament. Maragoli women who trade or sell beer are notoriously independent. Hiring laborers, or owning cattle and land, are activities previously restricted to men. Women who do these things are relatively powerful, and more in control of their futures and the fortunes of their children.

These activities variables are coded dichotomously (0 if she does not do the activity, 1 if she does). We also collected information on age, number of births, size of homestead, number of years married, and number of years educated. An additional variable, women's statements of how frequently they are beaten by their husbands, is discussed in detail later in the chapter.

Evidence of declining fertility

Total fertility rates (TFRs) for Kenya have been among the highest in the world. However, Kenya's TFRs for women aged 15–49 have declined over the past decade (NCPD 1989) (see Table 7.1). Recent data confirm a fifteen-year trend of declining fertility that is also supported by evidence of increased contraceptive use. Twenty-seven percent of married women aged 15–49 were planning their families in 1989, compared to 7 percent in 1977–78.[2] These trends provide convincing evidence that fertility decline has begun in Kenya (Bradley 1994; Hammerslough 1990, 1991; NCPD 1989; van de Walle and Foster 1990).

TFRs for Western Province and Kakamega District, where Maragoli is located, have been consistently higher than national-level statistics. Family planning use in Western Province and Kakamega District, both about 14 percent in 1989, is below the national average (CBS 1984; NCPD 1989). During 1989 Western Province women were less likely to use any kind of contraceptive than married women elsewhere in Kenya.

There is substantial evidence of declining fertility and increased contraceptive use in Igunga. TFRs for Igunga women aged 15–49 were 8.6 births in 1976 (Ssennyonga 1978) (see Table 7.1). Less than one percent of the women Ssennyonga sampled planned their families, though family planning clinics were nearby and easily accessible. TFRs for Igunga fell to 7.1 by 1989–90, and 31 percent of Igunga women were planning their

Table 7.1 *Total fertility rates, Kenya and subnational localities*

	1977–79	1984[a]	1989–90	1993
Kenya	7.9	7.7	6.7	5.4[b]
Western Province	8.6	7.9	8.1	n.d.
Kakamega District[c]	8.7	9.2	7.0	n.d.
Igunga Sublocation	8.6[d]	n.d.	7.1	n.d.
	(N = 398)		(N = 303)	

Notes:
[a] Since no Igunga Survey was conducted in 1984 or 1993, no sample sizes are presented for these columns. The other data are from national-level statistics.
[b] Data from NCPD 1993.
[c] Kakamega District was recently divided into two districts, one with Kakamega town as its headquarters and the second with Mbale as its headquarters. These changes took place after my 1988–89 fieldwork, although they were ongoing during Ndege's fieldwork (discussed in text).
[d] 1976 data for the eastern portion of what was then Vihiga District (from Ssennyonga 1978).
Source: Bradley (1994), CBS (1984), NCPD (1989), Ndege (1991), Omurundo (1989), Ssennyonga (1978).

families (Bradley 1994; Ndege 1991). The dependency ratio for Igunga (the ratio of young- and old-age dependents to adults of working age) has declined significantly from 134 in 1976 (Ssennyonga 1978) to 118.3 in 1989, and the proportion of children under age 15 has also declined, though not significantly (Bradley 1994). These and other data support the notion that fertility is declining in Igunga.

Changes for Maragoli women

In another paper (Bradley 1994), I argue that there is ethnographic evidence of changes in intergenerational wealth flows which increase advantages to younger people and women in Igunga while decreasing the flow of wealth and power to the older generation (Caldwell 1982). But these have not been the only kinds of changes in Igunga. While women have more education as well as economic opportunities and decision-making power, there are more incidents of violence against girls and women of all ages, as well as increased ideological and sexual conservatism in the community.

Women and girls in Igunga have made considerable gains. Girls are now educated equitably with boys and have more career choices. As they grow up, they select among several marital and parenting options outside the male-negotiated bridewealth system, choosing not to be married, or opting to leave children born in their natal homes with mothers and grandmothers while they pursue jobs in Kenya's major cities. Women exercise a greater voice within the community via such institutions as church organizations, women's cooperative societies, and participation in the previously male-dominated political system. At home, girls and younger women are more likely to defy their parents or husbands than in the past, for example, by using contraception, by keeping the money their husbands send home rather than giving it to their mothers-in-law, or by refusing to cook for their mothers-in-law. Let us examine each of these changes more closely.

More equitable education

The Republic of Kenya has been committed to universal free education since independence in 1963 (Eshiwani 1990). Although education is considered free in Kenya and teachers are paid by the national government, even the most reasonable fees and donations can be prohibitive for poorer households.[3] In Maragoli, as well as elsewhere in Kenya, the cost of schooling includes the cost of shoes, uniforms, books, and materials as well as fees and "harambee" (local community fundraising) donations.

Primary-school attendance sex ratios for Kenya in 1987 were encouraging, with 107 boys for every 100 girls. That dropped to 144 boys for every 100 girls in secondary schools (Republic of Kenya 1989). Although education at secondary school was less equitable, the proportions of girls educated at both levels was among the highest in Africa (World Bank 1984). In some Kenyan provinces, overall attendance was below national averages, while in others, boys attended more than girls. This was the case for the coastal region where the majority of the Muslim population lives, as well as in the arid herding areas (Eshiwani 1990). Western Province, an agricultural zone with nearly a century of Christian church-sponsored schooling, has one of the highest school-attendance rates in Kenya. Fifty percent or more of primary-school children in Kakamega District were girls (MPND 1989).

Ssennyonga (1978) argued that education was less than equitable during the 1970s, and that girls missed school more often than boys when school fees were lacking. By 1989, all primary and secondary school-aged children in a focused sample of 25 Igunga households, with the exception of the poorest household, attended school. In addition, there were no gender differences in school-fee debts for nursery, primary, and secondary-school children in the 25 households in 1989. Boys were absent slightly *more* often than girls at the primary school level because boys played hooky more often. Similarly, *both* boys and girls were found at home when there were school-fee debts.

The high level of female education, and the fact of its increase, is evident from differences between means in the survey data, shown in Table 7.2. Women under 30 have significantly more education than older women (7.5 versus 5.2 years). Current family planning users also have significantly more education than non-users.

Table 7.2 *Means for family planning, age and domestic violence, Igunga sublocation (N = 303)*

Variable name	Family Planning[a]		Woman's Age		Domestic Violence[b]	
	Users	Non-users	Under 30	30 & over	Never/ rarely beaten	Beaten some/ often
Age of woman	32.00*	30.00	–	–	30.50**	32.80
Years educated	7.10*	6.10	7.50**	5.20	6.60	6.20
Years married	13.00	11.20	6.10**	18.70	11.10*	13.20
Plot size (acres)	1.40*	1.10	1.20	1.30	1.30*	0.99
No. births	5.06	4.60	2.90**	7.00	4.45**	5.39
Plans family (%)	–	–	28.00	37.00	32.00	33.00
Banks (%)	14.00**	1.00	7.00	3.00	n.d.	n.d
Sells beer (%)	1.00	3.00	1.00	4.00	2.00	3.00
Has cows (%)	9.00*	5.00	3.00*	10.00	6.00	8.00
Sells crafts (%)	10.00	5.00	6.00	7.00	6.00	7.00
Uses credit (%)	3.00**	0.00	2.00	1.00	n.d.	n.d.
Rents land (%)	13.00	4.00	4.00*	10.00	7.00	7.00
Hires labor (%)	28.00**	15.00	21.00	17.00	21.00	16.00
Trades (%)	36.00	28.00	23.00*	41.00	32.00	30.00
Frequency beaten[c]	2.96	2.99	3.11**	2.82	–	–

* t-test for difference between means $p < 0.05$
** t-text for difference between means $p < 0.01$
Notes:
[a] Family planning includes all modern and traditional methods, including the pill, IUD, injection, sterilization, and periodic abstinence.
[b] This is the self-reported domestic violence variable. It is scored 1 if woman reports she is beaten often, 2 if she is beaten sometimes, 3 if she is rarely beaten, and 4 if she is never beaten. For this table, the variable is dichotomized: Never/Rarely Beaten for values 3 and 4, Beaten Some/Often for values 1 and 2.
[c] See note b.

Both men and women in Igunga place higher priority on education than on traditional subsistence activities of farmwork, herding, and meal preparation. This is consistent with Ssennyonga's (1978) finding that during 1975–76 educational expenses often constituted more of a household's budget than food. In 1989, Igunga women ranked education as the most important of seventeen common Maragoli activities, whereas Igunga men placed education behind such activities as attending church, getting water, and resting while sick.

The emphasis on education in Igunga is no surprise. In general, the Abaluyia have taken advantage of education throughout this century (Wagner 1949). However, small plot size, averaging less than a hectare, means that agricultural yields are too small to sustain most Igunga households (Bradley 1994). Both Ssennyonga (1978) and Moock (1976) argue that "gardening" is viewed by Maragoli residents merely as a supplement to outside employment, although school fees often come from sibling networks, other relatives, etc. The high value placed on education in Igunga reflects a dependence on outside sources of income for survival. Women are more aware than men of the wider realm of opportunities – and potential remittances – that education can bring.

The reality of more equitable education for Igunga girls may be considered a positive change. However, the value of that education in the Kenya job market must be considered separately.

Career options

The most common occupation listed by married Igunga women is "farmer," although many women combine farming with other activities. These include selling vegetables, grains, or dried fish on the road, running a shop, making pots to sell in a regional market, working part-time as a community health worker, working as a day laborer (commonly, weeding or picking tea), teaching primary school, or assisting a husband in a small business. Few women consider themselves as housewives.

The street running through the middle of Igunga is lined with marketwomen selling food, grains, vegetables, a variety of dried fish, and small household products. During one week in 1989, we counted thirty-three businesswomen and one businessman on the road. They ranged in age from 24 to 71. The average marketwoman is 37 years old, in a country where women born in 1960 had a life expectancy of 48 years (World Bank 1984). A small business gives a woman a way to earn money if she is not married, and supplements other income if she is married or receives regular remittances. Yet it is generally a business for older women, and one that does not interest many younger women. Table 7.2 shows that 41 percent of women age 30 and over trade, while 23 percent of women under age 30 trade. Some of the older women have been selling on the road since the 1950s. In 1989, a 22-year-old Igunga woman offered the following explanation:

> Most women who are unemployed are now self employed, i.e., selling vegetables, maize, tomatoes, onions, sweet potatoes, clothes; and others own shops. The only problem we are facing in development is youth of 1980s are very much ignorant about what is taking place. The reason why they are ignorant is 'coz they think they can't do such business. So they stick at home, waiting for better jobs which are nowhere to be found . . .

Igunga girls aspire to a somewhat wider range of careers than their mothers. Teacher is the most desired job, and at any one time several Igunga girls are enrolled in teachers' colleges throughout Kenya. Many girls apply for teachers' college but few are accepted. Due to the sheer number of applicants, it is difficult for both boys and girls to gain admission to Kenya's colleges and universities (*Standard* 1992). This is a terrible disappointment to the young people who are left behind, but the demand for these slots far exceeds the supply. Other jobs, such as agricultural extension worker, are viewed as undesirable by girls despite a teaching component and the fact that admission to agricultural colleges is less competitive.[4] Young women from Igunga also work as office workers, domestics, health-care workers, and numerous other occupations in larger towns and cities all over Kenya.

Girls who leave Igunga may be thought of as prostitutes despite their stated motives for leaving. This is not to say that some girls don't become prostitutes (see White 1990). Others may go to Nairobi to visit a boyfriend, returning with gifts and money. They sometimes return to give birth in their natal homes, and their children may remain behind with grandmothers while the women return to the city. At least 13 percent of Igunga households included grandchildren or great-grandchildren. Since jobs are scarce in Kakamega District, girls who want to expand their career options almost certainly must leave home (MPND 1989; Oucho 1988). The girls' mothers and grandmothers facilitate these long-distance careers by acting as foster parents.

White (1990) has shown that there was an historical tradition in Kenya through which women migrants, even as prostitutes or marketwomen, acted as entrepreneurs. As such, they were able to look out for their own interests as well as the interests of their families. In contemporary Igunga, women – especially educated women – have a broader range of career choices. Nevertheless, opportunities for advanced education are slim, especially in teachers' colleges where the demand is so high. Jobs are scarce for both men and women in Western Province. To be employed almost certainly means a move elsewhere, and to do so often means leaving small children behind. While having career options seems empowering on the surface, the job market limits how much women may act. In 1989, an Igunga woman in her early twenties wrote the following:

> Life after school is no longer sweet, unless you pass with high credit and have someone who has a long hand to help you so that you may get employment. Even if you pass highly compared to the person who flopped, the ones who failed may find a job . . .
>
> Kenya, my Motherland, is full of job-seekers. Myself, I find tears dropping down my cheeks when I see that [my education has] ended up being useless.

Political voice

Research in Western Province nearly always emphasizes the political roles of men (Wagner 1949). De Wolf (1978–79), for example, discusses the structure of local leadership in Bungoma District, Western Province, with very little mention of women's roles. This is probably because women do not participate in the formal leadership structures in these other communities.

However, women in Abaluyia communities typically participate in organizations and cooperative societies through which they have access to savings accounts, small business loans, self-help projects, women's communal work groups, family planning and nutrition information, as well as social activities such as singing and dancing (Davison 1985; Hammerslough 1991). Women make up the majority of the congregation in five of the seven church denominations in Igunga.[5] Many hold important women's offices in the church, but are always subordinate to male leadership. The Igunga branch of Maendeleo wa Wanawake (literally "Development of Women," the official women's branch of KANU, a political party in Kenya) claims fifty-three active members. It collects money for savings, gives out loans, organizes cooperative work groups, and has been involved in government-sponsored self-help projects. As stated previously, cooperative participation has also given Igunga women access to leaders at every level with whom they can air grievances. Slightly more older women belong to cooperatives than do younger women (30 versus 21 percent) though this difference is not significant.

Igunga women in cooperatives are significantly more likely to use family planning than women who do not belong to cooperatives. This may be due to information accessible at cooperative meetings, including family planning information. However, cooperative participation is an activity in which older women are more likely to engage (though not significantly). Participation in cooperatives in contemporary Kenyan society is an outgrowth of traditional work groups in which women helped each other weed or harvest (Wagner 1956:27–28).

Although Logoli women did not own land and cattle precolonially, renting of land and ownership of cattle by contemporary Logoli may be activities which, like trading, women are more likely to do they grow older (see Table 7.2). Thus, the difference between old and young women for these activities represents a reproduction of older, gerontocratic forms of power which now include older women as well as men.

In addition, Igunga has a formal women's leadership structure, probably a recent development, that parallels men's.[6] The men's structure in Western Kenya, described in detail by both de Wolf (1978–79) and Karp (1978), includes a chief who is appointed for each location and who is the lowest-ranking paid government employee. Each chief presides over a regularly scheduled local men's *baraza* (community meeting) and has several assistant chiefs (one for each sublocation). Sublocations consist of several villages, each with village headmen (*luguru*). Igunga sublocation has eight villages. In addition to having male *luguru*, the villages were led in 1989 by two female *luguru* and four female deputies. The chief female *luguru*, Josie, was a great-grandmother of at least 69 years. Josie led a weekly women's *baraza* and, with the assistance of the other women, collected money for funerals, supervised women's activities, and maintained water sources. Women may be fined at the *baraza* for violations such as neglecting children or allowing animals to run amok in neighbors' gardens. The female *luguru*, always older women, have numerous other jobs in the community. For example, Josie is an herbalist, a midwife, a go-between for traditional marriages, and a women's leader in her church.

Some Igunga women have non-traditional leadership roles. The 33-year-old mother of four who headed the Igunga cooperative in 1989 was also the community health worker. At least two women had been formally trained by the government as herbalists and midwives, and one, a grandmother, had taken responsibility for rescuing and placing children of "incestuous" relationships (unions between men and women from the same clan). Older women have clearly gained in their leadership roles in Igunga, although some activities that may empower women – cooperative participation, trade, cattle ownership, and renting of land – are either a continuation of precolonial ways in which women gained power as they grew older, or represent the reproduction of a gerontocratic power structure of Logoli men in the community of women.

Women at home

Fifty-six percent of the households in the focused sample of 25 are headed by women because husbands are either deceased or involved in long-term labor migration. This is slightly more than the 47 percent Ssennyonga (1978) found. Nevertheless, focused household budgets indicate that Igunga households with male heads are generally better off than households with female heads.

As is the case throughout much of Kenya, there are more marriage choices in Igunga. In addition to a traditional marriage in which bridewealth is exchanged, marriages may take place in church, in a civil ceremony, or not at all. Bridewealth is declining in Igunga, as it is elsewhere in Kenya; however, civil and church marriages, which may or may not involve bridewealth, are increasingly common (Bradley 1993, 1994; Hammerslough 1990).

In more traditional Maragoli households, wealth flows upward from daughters-in-law to mothers-in-law. This means that older women benefit not only from any remittances the younger woman receives, but also from her labor. A symbol of this subordination is the fact that the young family eats with the in-laws. This obligation may mean that the young bride is under the control of the mother-in-law until a ceremony takes place in which cooking stones are set up in her own house. This ceremony may not take place for several years, and when it does the young couple may already have several children.

In contemporary Igunga, young wives sometimes reject traditions that keep them at the mercy of their mothers-in-law. Older women complain, for example, that their daughters-in-law are hoarding money and food. Nowadays, the younger woman may refuse to wait for the ceremony to begin cooking for her own family in her own kitchen. It is true that older women have always complained about the stinginess of their daughters-in-law. Nevertheless, the perception of the community and local leaders is that, oftentimes, daughters-in-law no longer care for the older generation the way they should. The belief is that something has changed. In some senses, the empowerment of the younger women has been at the expense of the older women.

These transformations probably reflect the kinds of education-induced value changes Caldwell (1980) discusses. Younger women usually read and speak at least three languages (Lulogooli, Kiswahili and English), and are known to consume large quantities of English-language (British, North American) women's magazines, romance novels, and newspapers. They often express interest in marrying men with good jobs, owning nice clothes, and having a small number of children. Not all young Igunga women are able to achieve these goals.

Ideological and sexual conservatism

Maragoli was the site of Christian missionization early in the century, initially through the Friends African Mission. The first schools were started by missionaries, and were firmly entrenched in western Kenya by the 1930s (Wagner 1949). The Friends African Mission, with its simplicity, is associated throughout the century with the abolition of many of the traditions of precolonial Abaluyia. In Igunga, these included prohibitions on beating of drums and some of the other traditions that surround death. Until recently, the Friends African Mission was the dominant mission in Igunga.

It is typical for Igunga residents to identify people as belonging to one of three categories: Christians, *chang'aa* (bootleg) drinkers, and backsliders. Christians are not supposed to drink, smoke, or practice polygyny. They are also not supposed to be "superstitious." In precolonial Igunga, misfortune and death were attributed to multiple causes, including ancestors, curses, and sorcery. The Christians I know regard attributions of causality to these factors as superstition. When these beliefs were associated with a particular death, they were roundly criticized by community leaders at the funeral. One such statement about the "true" (worldly) cause of an Igunga death even appeared in a national newspaper.

Christian beliefs also carry with them notions that in the United States are associated with radical Christian fundamentalism, e.g., that AIDS is the result of sexual misconduct, sin, and promiscuity. Conservatism about sexual conduct is widespread. Even girls who travel to nearby towns may be accused of prostitution. Girls' houses, where girls and small boys lived with real or classificatory grandmothers, are now nonexistent in Igunga. Few people even remember them, though Wagner (1949) documents their presence. One young woman told me that girls would never be allowed to sleep in a separate house because it would be too dangerous and their morals would be questioned. They now sleep in kitchens, which may now be inside or connected to the main house. Girls and women are also not supposed to go out at night. Unless there is a night-time funeral celebration, the only people out at night are thieves and *chang'aa* drinkers.

Many Abaluyia groups have derogatory names for girls who give birth premaritally. This is indicative of long-standing concerns about morality. Though not as rigid as Europe before this century, rules about premarital chastity existed, and remnants of them continue today. The fact that so many Igunga women have premarital pregnancies does not contradict the reality that premarital liaisons and pregnancies were, and still are, disapproved of.

The demise of girls' houses is one way in which the safety of girls has deteriorated over time. Girls learned about marriage and sexuality from older women, who protected them, participated in selecting their spouses, and supervised their activities. Paradoxically, conservative values about sexuality and behavior, present precolonially and reinterpreted by Christian missionization and education, were accompanied by a decline in supervision of girls and a resultant loss of control over their sexual behavior.

Violence toward women in Igunga

One cannot live in Igunga for very long without becoming aware of the grave difficulties many Igunga women face in their daily lives. These difficulties represent a microcosm of the kinds of problems women often face in Kenya, and include hunger, poverty, neglect, inability to access medical services, divorce, and physical and sexual abuse.

Perhaps the most striking events in Igunga were those involving violence, abuse, and neglect of women. After living in Igunga for only a few weeks I learned that an old woman had died as a consequence of sexual abuse. She had been raped repeatedly by her grandson, who was sent to live with her as a helper and companion. She is believed to have died of syphilis. The Logoli think of grandparents and grandchildren as being closely related, and it is not uncommon to find people of alternate generations living together. So shocking was this event that, although everyone knew what had happened, great efforts were made to keep the story away from the anthropologist.

Shortly thereafter, I learned that a girl had died from puncture wounds to her genitals. Only her brother had been home at the time and had reported a convoluted sequence of events in which the girl had fallen on an iron bed rod while trying to reach a schoolbook. The boy had not been suspected of sexual abuse.

Around the same time an old woman was found dying in her thatched house, neglected by her three daughters-in-law who had not bothered to check on her. These women were neighbors living on the same compound. Sublocation and village leaders were so shocked at the neglect of this woman that several of them scolded the mourners at her funeral.

The situation which disturbed me the most was the events surrounding the divorce of my neighbor, Rhoda, a woman whose household was part of my focused sample as well as Ssennyonga's. This 35-year-old woman had been married for fifteen years and had five children. Rhoda lived in a mud house with an iron-sheet roof on her in-laws' compound, where her husband, Jack, was born. The little land they had was not fertile and the maize was quickly gone. The smallest child had been battling malaria and was not doing well, and when Jack's father broke his arm that year, he could not even afford transport to a clinic. Jack had a small but successful business halfway across the country, and had taken a second wife there. He rarely sent money and never came to Maragoli.

One day, Rhoda decided to travel to see Jack and ask for money. Jack was infuriated by the intrusion, returning to Maragoli to divorce her. He arrived wearing pleated slacks, dress shoes, and a bright orange shirt in a dollar-bill print. His clean clothes and round belly contrasted sharply with the ragged thinness of his parents, wife, and children. That night Jack beat Rhoda, and threw her and her children out of the house. Forced to sleep outside during the cold part of the year, the children wailed the entire night. The in-laws opened their doors to the family at 4.00 in the morning, but Rhoda and the children were sitting on the road again the next day. She went to sublocation leaders for assistance, but Jack beat her again, telling her if she reported it this time he would take the iron sheet roof from the house and never return.

The sublocation leaders met that weekend to mediate the divorce. Though they were angry with Jack and sympathized with Rhoda, they nevertheless approved a traditional divorce and, as is customary, sent Rhoda back to her parents' home without her children. Jack returned to his second wife, and the children were left in the hands of their elderly grandparents. The door to Rhoda's house was locked.

These events as well as others occurred during the eleven months I spent in Igunga. They were not considered commonplace by the community, but rather were thought of as both disturbing and uncharacteristic.

How pervasive was spouse abuse in Igunga during the time I lived there? My research assistants and I asked the 303 women sampled in the Igunga survey what happens when they and their husbands disagree, as well as how often they are beaten by their husbands. The first question was open-ended, and women gave a variety of answers. Most commonly, they told whether or not they discussed problems, either immediately or after a cooling-down period, or whether there was no discussion or resolution to the argument. A few women (only 5 percent) commented on the impact on their children and their households (such as the husband withholding food or support from the household), or whether they chose to accept the husband's decision rather than engage in an ongoing battle on the topic.

As to whether or not they were beaten, women were asked to answer "never," "rarely," "sometimes," or "often." Sixty-five percent of these women had been beaten by their husbands. Only 2 percent of these reported that they were beaten often. Half of those reporting being beaten often were women in the oldest age group (ages 39–48). Women in the youngest age group (ages 15–28) were beaten the least often. Indeed, only the age-related variables, including the length of the woman's marriage, the total number of births she has had, and her age, are significantly different between women who state they are rarely or never beaten, versus women who state they are beaten sometimes or often (Table 7.2).[7] Variables hypothesized to be related to women's empowerment, including years of education, and her participation in cooperatives, trade, manufacture of goods for sale, land ownership, etc. are not significantly different between the two groups. Current use of family planning is not significantly different between the two groups.

Unlike Handwerker's Barbados and Antigua samples, there is no evidence that the empowerment of women reduces domestic violence in this sample. What is evident is a life-cycle difference. Either there is less abuse in younger marriages, which increases as the marital partners grow older, or something has changed for younger women and men. Perhaps younger people experience less violence in their marriages. Nevertheless, the variables I am using to measure empowerment do not explain the difference between the two groups.

Scarcity, competition, and family planning

The evidence I have presented for Igunga Sublocation in Maragoli calls into question hypothesized relationships between fertility decline, women's empowerment, and domestic violence.

Though fertility is declining and contraceptive use is increasing in Igunga, these cannot be connected unproblematically to a single factor. For example, it is clear from the data that current family planning users have more education than nonusers (Table 7.2). On the surface this appears to confirm arguments, such as those made by Caldwell (1982), that Westernization, through the route of education, can bring about fertility decline. Indeed, many Igunga women read widely from a variety of sources, speak several languages, and aspire to a broad range of careers through which they hope to improve their circumstances. But aspirations are not achievement, and in the absence of other opportunities, many women have no way to make their educations work for them. The mechanism through which education is related to contraceptive use and lower fertility in Igunga is still unclear. The relationship may also be spurious.

The data also appear, on the surface, to support the notion that factors empowering women are associated with family planning; to wit, women who use contraception are significantly more likely to bank, to participate in cooperatives, to rent land and hire laborers, and to have larger plots of land. However, family planners are also significantly older and have had more births. The age data present a similar picture. Older women are more likely to use family planning and to gain economic power through cattle ownership, hiring of land, trade and, to a degree, cooperative participation. Older women also hold leadership positions in the community, and may therefore be in positions that enable them to teach others about family planning.

I would argue from these survey data that Igunga women usually begin to plan their families after they have given birth to several children. It is then that they also begin to have more control over their lives. Perhaps it is because younger women are restricted by small children that they do not trade or join cooperatives as much as older women. It is also possible that older women choose to end childbearing around the same time that they begin to participate in cooperatives, to farm more land, and to trade. These are ways that Igunga women access wealth and power separately from men, but they are not necessarily causally related to the decision to end childbearing. The global generalization that education and/or the empowerment of women result in lower fertility fails to pay attention to ways in which women of different ages may differ. Younger women in Igunga have more education because the achievement of universal primary education for Igunga women is relatively recent. At least, most of the inequities between boys' and girls' educational opportunities have disappeared since Ssennyonga's research in the 1970s. We have seen that older women access wealth and power differently than younger women. This cohort of young women might not choose to move into trading at the rate that the older cohort has. In other words, women of different ages may be coming to family planning for different reasons and through different routes.

Domestic violence is appallingly common in Igunga, and local discourse, like discourse at the national level, supports the notion that it has increased. The fascination of women throughout Kenya with the Anita Hill/Clarence Thomas coverage, as well as the Mike Tyson hearings,[8] reflects a newfound concern over Kenyan women's own physical safety, which is perceived as deteriorating. In Igunga, the frequency with which women are beaten is unrelated to education or contraceptive use. Domestic violence in Igunga is related almost exclusively to life-stage factors. Older women are beaten more frequently than younger women. Though most of the empowerment variables are in the same direction as Handwerker's Antigua and Barbados findings, education and empowerment do not prevent domestic violence in Igunga.

An alternative explanation is that both violence and declining fertility are related to competition for scarce resources. Women gain access to education, land, animals, and credit in an atmosphere of unemployment, job insecurity, inflation, and a shortage of slots in the higher education system. I hypothesize that there are three outcomes of this environment of scarcity. First, lower fertility may come about as children become more of a burden. The prospect of having several unemployed children may loom as a long-term cost rather than a potential benefit. Unemployed or underemployed parents may also feel reluctant to have large families. Second, women are put into competition with men. This may result in an increased incidence of violence toward women. Finally, conservative values may be used to keep women in line when they become too much of a threat.

The discourse among Kenyans surrounding the St. Kizito incident reflects both an historical tradition in which men were accustomed to abusing women as well as the breakdown of a system that protected women from violence.[9] A core component of the dialogue was the fact that women were being educated equitably with men, and the realization that the increased status of women had somehow led to their abuse (*New York Times* 1991). In fact, the precipitating event at St. Kizito was the girls' refusal to join the boys in a strike. At St. Kizito before the riots, the boys had perceived themselves to be in competition with the girls for scarce resources. The boys felt the girls had better living conditions; furthermore the boys demanded additional tutoring for themselves (*Weekly Review* 1991). The violence against the girls was a result of the boys rejecting their empowerment, not a reenactment of old traditional values. The girls were beaten, raped, and killed after asserting their independence (*Weekly Review* 1991). Leaders were later quoted questioning the wisdom of educating girls alongside boys (*New York Times* 1991).

The St. Kizito incident draws our attention to what may seem like a paradox, namely that women may be empowered on the one hand but may lose ground on the other. This is the case in Igunga, where women have gained in such areas as education, career choices, and political voice. These gains have enabled women to act positively on their own behalf in many arenas. On the other hand, some women are not able to protect themselves from violence at their husband's hand. Like the St. Kizito tragedy, Igunga women may be experiencing increased violence as they become more of a political and economic threat to men. More equitable education and broader career choices do not occur in a vacuum. In an atmosphere of growing scarcity, both men and women feel the pinch. It may be scarcity, rather than empowerment, which is fueling a turn toward lower fertility.

Notes

This research was funded by the National Science Foundation (BNS 870977) (BNS 9011986), a Fulbright Hays grant, the Wenner-Gren Foundation (Gr. 5076) and the Ford Foundation through the Population Studies and Research Institute of the University of Nairobi, where I have been a member of staff since 1988. The following people contributed to the success of the field project: Prf. H. W. O. Okoth-Ogendo, Prof. John Oucho, Prof. A. B. C. Ocholla-Ayayo, Dr. Joseph Ssennyonga, Mrs. Mwango of Kenya's Office of the President, Mike Seidenstricker of the US Embassy Nairobi, PSRI graduate students John Kwendo Omurundo and James Onyango Ndege, UCI undergraduate Brian Fulfrost, and Maragoli field assistants Phyllis Keith, Edith Manono, Cubic Mugera Mudiri, Lilian Mwasiagi, Josephine Mwasiagi, Anne Nyangasi and Rose Nyangasi.

1 Some people erroneously refer to the Logoli as "Maragoli." Logoli is used most often by North American anthropologists, but Avologoli is the more correct term, and means Logoli people.
2 Family planning use in these statistics includes abstinence and other methods categorized as natural family planning.
3 Recent efforts on the part of the Kenyan government to make education more available to the general public include ceilings on school fees.
4 The perception that attendance at the agriculture schools was undesirable comes from my own experience with several young women secondary-school graduates, as well as conversations with local leaders.
5 Igunga church leaders claim the following memberships: Friends African Mission (400), African Divine Church (1,000), Pentecostal Churches (PAG 400, PEFA 120), Holy Spirit (300), Salvation Army (260), Catholic (127). Women outnumber men in all but the ADC. Most members of the Catholic church are children. Friends, PAG, and Salvation Army have three branches in Igunga.
6 Josie, the chief female village headman, claims to have held this job since 1962. Although the names and roles of women's leaders at the village level were confirmed by various informants, how long the institution has existed is difficult to know. Ssennyonga (1978) makes no mention of female headmen and was surprised when I asked him about it. My explanation is that there have been women's leaders in the community doing these tasks for a long time, but that the roles have recently been formalized.
7 The results do not change when the variable is dichotomized differently.
8 Both the Anita Hill/Clarence Thomas hearings and news reports of the Mike Tyson trial were carried on CNN in Kenya as well as in Kenyan newspapers. Both incidents involved African Americans and occurred in the US during the early 1990s. The former involved accusations of sexual harassment by Hill, a

previously little-known but now prominent US law professor, against Thomas, a Republican nominee for the Supreme Court. The latter situation involved accusations of rape by a well-known African American beauty queen against boxer Tyson.

9 This event is in no way considered "normal" by anyone in Kenya. The *Weekly Review* (1991) notes: "Many who visited the scene could only gape and shake their heads in saddened incredulity. 'How could this happen?' some of them asked repeatedly, addressing the question to no one in particular. President Moi described it as the 'most ugly' incident he had ever encountered in his entire life" (p. 6). The article describes the entire nation as being in a state of "shock and disbelief" at the "unprecedented" event.

8 High fertility and poverty in Sicily: Beyond the culture vs. rationality debate

Peter Schneider and Jane Schneider

Until the turn of the twentieth century, the rural town of the Sicilian interior that we call Villamaura conformed to what may be a characteristic premodern population dynamic. Surrounded by large, wheat-producing and pastoral estates, the town was differentiated into strata of unequal power and wealth. Members of an affluent gentry class enjoyed large families, but for the great majority in other groups – artisans, landed peasants (called *burgisi*), landless and landpoor peasants – high fertility was offset by high rates of infant and child mortality. Family size more or less corresponded to family wealth and income and served as one of the visible indices of local social standing.

Villamaura's incorporation into the structures of capitalism during the late nineteenth century led to an overall decline in mortality, rising fertility, and a total reversal of this relationship between family size and standard of living. Around 1900, members of the town's landed gentry began to limit their fertility, mainly through the use of coitus interruptus. Between the world wars, artisans adopted and then perpetuated the same strategy for family limitation. The town's small number of landed *burgisi* clung to a different mechanism for articulating fertility with resources: the delay of the marriages of both daughters and sons until an adequate dowry or inheritance could be accumulated. Given the strict code of virginity then in place in Sicily, with its associated arrangements for monitoring the behavior of young women, this mechanism could – and from the 1930s did – postpone childbearing by several years. In contrast to these birth-reducing measures, the most numerous class, consisting of sharecroppers and agricultural day laborers, experienced an *increase* in family size. We shall refer to this group collectively as the *braccianti* (plural; singular, *bracciante*), to mean workers who possess virtually no land, and no tools other than their own arms (*braccia*).

Finally, during the late 1950s and 1960s, a land reform and the mechanization of agriculture, together with universal compulsory education,

created conditions in which most of Villamaura's peasants, landed and
landless, also adopted coitus interruptus for the purposes of birth control.
Until this happened, however, the town exemplified what Italian political
leaders as well as sociological and historical demographers had in mind
when they compared Sicily and the Italian South to the "underdeveloped"
third world, i.e., to areas in which population pressure coincided with
economic dependency to create a synergistic interaction between falling
mortality, high fertility and increasing immiseration (e.g. Rocheforte 1961).

It is that "second stage" of demographic transition that this paper
addresses. It sketches two models, one "culturalist" and the other
"rationalist," that have more or less dominated the interpretation of such
"demographic traps." Then, with Villamaura as a focus, it charts how the
"trap" developed in Sicily, in order to suggest a third, historical, approach
in which a population's fertility behavior is neither attributed to the
expression of an undifferentiated worldview, nor reduced to an aggregate
of discrete individual choices, but is examined in relation to the interactive
unfolding of political-economic and cultural processes over several decades.
In light of this approach we replace the question "Why did Villamaura's
braccianti continue to adhere to a high-fertility regime of multiple births
and no birth control even as their resource base declined?" with an
alternative statement of the problem: "In the historical formation of this
class, what undermined its ability to formulate a new set of values
concerning family respectability until the land reform decades that followed
World War II?"

High fertility in low-mortality populations: Two interpretations

Interpretations of high fertility in low-mortality populations that are also
impoverished tend to cluster around one of two poles. For one group,
exemplified by historical demographers of the Princeton-based European
Fertility Project, "traditional cultural norms," especially norms associated
with religion, blind people to the possibility of "rational" fertility control.
(For more on this Project and its culture concept see Kertzer, this volume.)
In a 1977 publication, Massimo Livi-Bacci, the Project's specialist on Italy,
showed statistically that the Italian south (including Sicily) "lagged"
behind the north in the demographic transition to small families. Arguing
that there was a greater degree of homogeneity in southern than in northern
fertility patterns, he attributed both phenomena – the homogeneity and the
lag – to a seamless worldview:

> What seems to be at work is the force of residual factors, which we cannot
> measure statistically. Attachment to traditions; a more extended and tightly
> knit family system; the stronger weight of social control; the lack of women's

emancipation; the weight of the often very conservative teaching of the Church – these are some of the manifold factors of Southern culture [that] affect, in a degree not appreciably different, all sectors of the population without regard to income, profession, or residence. (1977:244)

This culturalist approach to the problem of "overpopulation" has taken several forms. In its mainstream form, as represented by the Princeton Project, overpopulation is deemed likely when, notwithstanding falling mortality, people are led by their culture (usually in the form of religion) to reject or fail to embrace the idea that fertility can be brought "within the calculus of conscious choice" (Coale 1973). A more exaggerated version of this cultural determinist outlook emphasizes "fatalism," whether derivative of a religious outlook – reproduction is up to God – or of poverty itself. Since the late eighteenth-century writings of Thomas Malthus, the discourse on poverty in Western societies has promoted the concept of a "culture of poverty" that induces people to abandon control of their bodies and hyper-reproduce. Assessing situations of demographic entrapment, "culture of poverty" theorists characteristically presume lower-class promiscuity (see Leacock 1971 for interesting discussions of this issue).

A second, competing approach to "overpopulation" views fertility behavior as generically rational – that is, governed by the actor's considered and calculating self-interest. Anthropologists and demographers pursuing a "demand for children's labor" theory of population growth exemplify this approach. Marshalling evidence from rural ethnography (e.g., Cain 1977; Nardi 1981; Ross 1986; B. White 1973, 1982), and from comparative analyses based mainly on survey data (e.g., Fawcett 1983; Lee and Bulatao 1983; Lindert 1983), proponents stress how, from the age of seven or eight, children are able to weed, hoe, and help with harvests; work alongside their parents in mines, quarries, or cottage industries; earn wages and, eventually, care for their parents in old age. Where household labor is subject to exploitation by rapacious overlords, as described by Benjamin White for colonial Java and Eric Ross for pre-famine Ireland, these benefits of children are the more significant. Either way, birth rates must be attributed not to cultural inertia in the face of declining mortality, or to a fatalistic culture of poverty, but to parents' conscious preference for multiple offspring. Although severe population pressure may be the outcome at the societal level, its causes must be sought in processes external to culture: in the property system that constrains opportunities, and in the aggregation of individual calculations that are rational for each family, even if "irrational" for society as a whole.

Outside of anthropology, the rationalist approach to fertility behavior focuses on the extent to which behavior can be accounted for through an analysis of the costs and benefits of children to their parents. Economic demographer Peter Lindert, for example, argues that couples are always capable of economic consciousness and "roughly aware of the economic consequences of children" (1983: 495). Fertility therefore remains high until the cost of having and rearing offspring outweighs their benefit and there is a "transition in demand." But Fawcett, in a review article on "perceptions of the value of children," unearths little empirical support for the proposition that the financial *costs* of children have a consistent impact on parents' fertility behavior. The studies he reviews show that expectations about the positive *benefits* of children are more likely to be associated with fertility decisions than are expectations about cost (1983). And to Mead Cain, a "curious myopia" underlies the assumption that parents calculate the cumulative benefits and costs of a possible *nth* child, relative to the cumulative costs and benefits of some alternative commodities that could be purchased instead of that child, over what is left of their "lifetime planning horizon in years" (1983: 688–689; for comprehensive reviews of this literature see Lee and Bulatao 1983; Leibenstein 1974; Simmons 1988).

Cain's early research in Bangladesh produced fine-grained analyses linking fertility behavior to the exigencies of family-household economies and the productivity of children. From the perspective of parents, he argued, "high fertility and large numbers of surviving children are economically 'rational' propositions" even for impoverished landless peasants (Cain 1977: 224). Among such peasants in the socially stratified village of Char Gopalpur, female children produced no outside wage income. But, according to Cain, the average male child became a net producer by age 12, "paid back" the *cumulative* costs of his own subsistence by age 15, and paid for the cumulative costs of his own subsistence as well as that of his nearest sister by age 22 (provided that she married and left the family by her age 15, which usually happened).

Cain's argument was conservative, in that, if anything, he underestimated the importance of non-wage contributions made by daughters to the peasant household economy. From his own report, however, it appears that the "average son" was likely to have married and left the family by his twenty-second year. This means that just as that son began to produce a net profit over the cumulative subsistence costs of himself and a sister, the family of origin was deprived of his labor. In other words, although Cain's analysis demonstrated that in a high fertility regime the children of large families may well "pay for themselves" with their own labor, it did not show that having children materially *improves* the parents' standard of living, or that of the family as a whole. Under such conditions the cost of a large family would certainly not be a disincentive to high fertility; but, on the other hand, one cannot on the basis of these data argue that the net return on children's labor would be a significant positive incentive to reproduction.

In subsequent work, Cain himself broached this issue, arguing that demographers' "preoccupation with the more immediate costs and benefits of children leads to the neglect of yet another major class of potential economic benefit – the value of children as insurance against the risk of income insufficiency in parents' old age and in a variety of other circumstances" (1983: 688–689). The corrective he proposed was to think of fertility as "an adjustment to risk" in which parents, contemplating a possible *nth* child, consider the likelihood that the birth of that child will increase their probability of avoiding a precarious old age. In South Asia, at the time of his research, the following conditions promoted this calculus: First, that the early cost of children was sustained by the children's own labor, or by support that comes from outside the family/household. Second, that alternative sources of subsistence in old age, such as financial and insurance markets and extrafamilial welfare institutions, were non-existent or inadequate. And third, that at least some children would, as adults, be able to contribute to their parents' subsistence. Cain noted that there could be no guarantee of such support, but argued that intelligent people everywhere make decisions on the basis of increasing probabilities of return in the presence of risk.

Whether an economic model of fertility behavior treats children as rewarding to their parents in the short or in the long run, its fulcrum is the parents' rational approach to reproduction. It is time to ask whether this outlook is an advance over cultural determinist explanations for high fertility among impoverished social groups. We would not be the first to raise serious questions about microeconomic models of fertility behavior (e.g., Carter, this volume; see Simmons 1988:123–124 for a summary of the relevant literature), but we would like to underline certain problems that in particular have to do with questions of agency, and the relationship between culture and rationality in fertility behavior.

The first and most glaring problem stems from the tendency for rationalist models to conflate "the couple" with a single, decision-making "firm," as if it were an individual. In the absence of evidence to the contrary, it is better to view even joint fertility behavior as the outcome of exchange, bargaining, or constraint between a woman and a man. Just as firms are internally differentiated entities in which decisions are negotiated among individuals with unequal power, the husband and wife dyad do not automatically generate a single "family utility function" or unified set of "merged wants" (Ben-Porath 1978:58; for ethnographic examples, see the chapters of Bradley and Bledsoe, this volume).[1]

But even if a married couple could, for purposes of analysis, be construed as a single decision-making unit, there is a further problem concerning the conditions under which – rather than the *presumption* that – such an individual, or a dyad acting as one, would make rational fertility decisions.

Rationality has to do with reason, calculation, deliberation in human action. So the term invokes the concept of planning prior to action – literally, forethought or foresight. (If reason is brought to bear after the fact, we may refer to *rationalization*.) Following Weber, rational action depends upon the application of mental processes that follow accepted canons of logic and lead towards an appropriate alignment of means and ends (Parsons 1947:87–90). The ends might be determined through some individual or personal calculus (Weber's *zweckrational* – "rational orientation to a system of discrete individual ends"), but they may just as well derive from cultural or institutional convention (Weber's *wertrational*; Parsons 1947:115).

Herbert Simon, in an essay on "The Psychology of Administrative Decisions," presents what is in social psychological terms a most startling challenge to the economic rationality model: "It is impossible," he says, "for the behavior of a single, isolated individual to reach any high degree of rationality" (1976:79). This because rational decision-making requires a panoramic search for alternative means to a desired end, considering the consequences that would follow on the choice of each, and choosing the most satisfactory path from among the alternatives considered. An isolated individual's knowledge of possible pathways and the likely consequences associated with each is bound to be fragmentary and incomplete. Even regarding those alternatives that the individual does know or could know, in reality only a few ever "come to mind." And finally, as the actual consequences lie somewhere in the future, the values attached to them can only be imperfectly anticipated. So we might best think of rational behavior as a social/collective, rather than individual, enterprise. In this sense, "culture driven" behavior is no less rational – indeed, in Simon's terms more likely to approach rationality – than behavior based on so-called "individual choice."

This formulation shifts our attention to social groups – small communities, social classes, and other reference groups – whose members both generate, and act in relation to, systems of value. In the domain of fertility, these systems may specify what features characterize a respectable, or worthy, family. Fertility behavior may, of course, reflect individual idiosyncratic considerations of sexual preference, health or economics (although even these considerations are inevitably *conditioned* by wider cultural practices). More generally though, the number of children responds to a cultural "imperative" – such as, "respectable couples have at least one, but no more than three children." Are we thereby falling back on a culturalist approach to fertility? Not at all, for in contrast to treating tradition as determinative, we emphasize the mutability of beliefs and values, through the "cultural work" of thinking and acting human groups. Action in relation to values is not, as the cultural determinists would have it, unthinking and therefore "irrational". Rather, such action satisfies Weber's second sense of rationality: the selection of appropriate means in relation to valued ends.[2]

In the account to follow, we first lay out the history of declining mortality and rising fertility among Villamaura's *bracciante* class, showing those developments to have been relatively unproblematic until the end of World War I. Then Sicily, and with it Villamaura, experienced the twin crises of blocked migration to the United States, and a severe economic depression. Based on retrospective interviews and a survey of material culture, we portray the *braccianti* during the inter-war years as at least temporarily trapped in a fertility regime which added to the misery of both men and women, although for different reasons. Our interpretation of this process questions the proposition that large birth parities during this difficult time resulted from rational choice. But rather than attribute the large parities to a fatalist or traditional mindset, we specify the life-circumstances that obstructed a collective *bracciante* response to unwanted high fertility, at least until well after World War II.

Declining mortality, rising fertility: Villamaura, 1860–1919

Villamaura, with its 8,982 inhabitants in 1861, 9,884 at the turn of the century, and over 11,000 in the 1920s, contributed modestly to the overall growth of the Sicilian population. Until the years after World War I when railroad construction brought an influx of laborers, no significant in-migration added to the town's numbers; on the contrary, the 11 percent increase of the second half of the nineteenth century occurred in the face of significant out-migration, beginning in the 1880s (see Gabaccia 1988:50–51). A falling death rate was, of course, relevant. It was 36.4 per 1,000 in the 1860s, but had dropped to 25.7 per 1,000 by the turn of the century.

Significant for the falling mortality rate, food supplies were becoming more abundant and predictable as local crop rotations improved. Yet the impact of better resources on nutrition depended on social circumstance. Villamaura's municipal archive contains records of the military draft which, for the decades in question, show gentry sons to have measured on the average nearly a head taller than the sons of the *braccianti*. Many of the latter, in fact, were ineligible for military service because of their short stature, inadequate chest development, or general poor health.

In the 1870s, national legislation was passed requiring local communities to construct piping systems for the supply of water from the countryside, as well as to create cemeteries to replace burial of the dead in church vaults and catacombs, a practice which was declared to be unhealthy. Other laws mandated that localities provide for sanitation officers, doctors, midwives,

Table 8.1 *Births and deaths in the first five years per couple (Villamaura)*[a]

Class	Marriage cohort								
	1860–1861			1870–1871			1880–1881		
	Born	Die[b]	N[c]	Born	Die	N	Born	Die	N
Braccianti	5.1	2.5(49)	96	5.3	2.6(50)	80	4.8	2.2(45)	85
Burgisi	6.2	2.2(35)	10	5.2	2.0(39)	22	4.2	1.6(39)	19
Artisans	6.0	1.4(24)	7	4.5	1.3(29)	14	5.3	1.9(36)	9
Civili	3.8	0.3 (9)	6	6.6	1.4(22)	7	5.7	1.3(23)	7
Total	5.2	2.3(44)	147	5.3	2.3(44)	150	4.8	2.0(42)	149

[a] Excluding childless couples.
[b] The number of children who die in the first five years is given by the mean per couple and percent (in parentheses).
[c] N is the number of childbearing couples in each category.

and veterinarians. But an analysis of local council proceedings makes it clear that these provisions were not actually enacted until two or more decades later.

Although we are unable to calculate overall rates of death by social class for late nineteenth-century Villamaura, a family reconstitution study comparing marriage cohorts at ten-year intervals does permit a class comparison of infant and child mortality. For the cohorts 1860–61 to 1880–81, gentry couples lost between 9 and 23 percent of their offspring in the first five years of life; artisans between 24 and 36 percent; *burgisi* between 35 and 39 percent; and poor peasants or *braccianti*, the most numerous group, lost between 45 and 50 percent of their newborns (see Table 8.1).

The period from the 1890s to the 1920s was introduced by capitalism's first "Great Depression," in which drastically falling cereal prices and mounting tariff battles with other countries destabilized not only agrarian Sicily, but Italy as a whole. In interior, latifundist towns like Villamaura, members of the landed class managed to stave off their own decline by shifting the burden of contraction onto their peasant sharecroppers and day laborers. For example, they used local political power to retain a regressive tax structure even in the face of mounting opposition and the inability of peasants to pay. As bosses of the local towns, moreover, they called on mafiosi and other "strong men" to enforce agricultural contracts and break peasant resistance (see M. Clark 1984:19). Records of the town council of Villamaura in the early 1890s indicate that many citizens could not pay their taxes, that the annual religious festival was deeply in debt, and that the town was lending money to peasants for their daughters' dowries. Bread riots were a threat while, as the notarial archives for the same years show, peasants were regularly forced to borrow seed or money from the gentry at usurious rates of interest (Schneider and Schneider 1976:123).

As the confrontational events unfolded, however, southern Italians and Sicilians joined what became, by the turn of the century, a massive out-migration to the Americas, "voting with their feet." Because no authority kept accurate records of migration and return migration, it is difficult to know the full magnitude of the migratory streams, but historians estimate that between 1900 and 1914 at least a million people departed Sicily, of whom perhaps a third returned (see Caroli 1973). Quite apart from the immediate demographic consequences of such an out-pouring, the earnings that the Italian "birds of passage" eventually remitted or carried home as savings helped change the context in which poor peasants married and reproduced.

All told, this context improved considerably from around 1900 until a new conjuncture developed after World War I. Emigration remittances sent from abroad, and the savings of returned migrants, enabled peasants to buy or rent small plots of land and to improve their housing. As emigration and new landholdings absorbed landless laborers, sharecropping contracts and wages paid to day laborers also improved. Most important, more *braccianti* and sharecroppers were able to acquire a mule or, more commonly, a donkey. With such an animal, the cultivator gained both manure and the means to carry it (or the means to carry chemical fertilizers, if he could afford them) to the fields. This in turn allowed for the integration of legumes, especially nitrogen-rich fava beans, into the rotation cycle, and these miraculous legumes enriched the soil while providing cheap food for both the donkey and the hungry children at home. No wonder, as Lorenzoni put it, that the peasant "loves his donkey as he loves his wife" (1910:128–145; see also Scrofani 1962:253–256; De Stefano and Oddo 1963:164).

In addition to the proceeds of emigration, Sicilian peasants benefitted from a general economic recovery that supported higher prices for wheat and other agricultural products, and from political and economic reforms that promoted a network of agrarian banks. These banks (the *Casse Rurali*) offered relatively low-cost loans to finance peasant cooperatives that rented latifundia under long-term contracts and helped individual cultivators purchase seed, animals, and fertilizers. For most peasants, meat was still a luxury, consumed only once or twice a year, on festival days. But other sources of protein – cheese, sardines, fava beans – became more plentiful than in the preceding period. Fava beans, especially, gave substance to soups made of wild vegetables that could be collected in the mountains surrounding the towns.

In the early twentieth century, towns like Villamaura at last came into de facto compliance with the sanitary law of 1888 that assigned a doctor and

Table 8.2 *Mortality and fertility rates for Sicily, 1862–1971*

Intercensus years	Mortality (deaths per 1,000 per year)	Fertility (births per 1,000 per year)
1862–1871	32.0	38.8
1872–1881	29.2	40.2
1882–1891	28.4	41.9
1892–1901	25.2	36.6
1902–1911	23.8	33.1
1912–1921	20.6	27.4
1922–1931	16.7	28.7
1932–1941	15.1	26.4
1942–1951	13.1	24.2
1952–1961	9.3	22.8
1962–1971	9.4	21.1

Source: Somogyi 1974: 36, 41.

midwife to every community of its type in Italy. Many Sicilian towns, Villamaura included, could now boast a municipal sewer and a public cemetery to replace churchyard burials. The national government and the Red Cross combined to distribute quinine in zones that were infested with malaria, and although the measures were not universally effective, the incidence of malaria did decrease, as did deaths due to the combined effect of malaria and malnutrition (Lorenzoni 1910).

The developmental process did not significantly alter the class structure, but it did contribute to a dramatic fall in mortality rates among the poorest groups. As a result, population growth in the early 1900s more than compensated for the massive out-migration (see Table 8.2). Especially significant were the improved life chances of infants and children in the most numerous class of landless laborers and sharecroppers. Aggregate statistics for the region do not reveal this breakthrough but we do know it for the sampled marriage cohorts in Villamaura: losing between 45 and 50 percent of their children by age five in the latter half of the nineteenth century, *braccianti* couples lost 23 percent if they married in 1899 (N = 18), 24 percent if they married in 1910 (N = 26), and 21 percent if they married in 1920 (N = 50). Whereas in the 1870s through 1890s, falling infant and child mortality had enhanced the formation of large gentry and artisan families, after 1900 this trend became a reservoir for population increase among the rest.

At the same time that mortality was declining, there was little to discourage peasants from marrying. According to Caroli (1973:46), young men, going to America, returned with sufficient frequency to keep the marriage pool alive. Moreover, in the context of emigration, both widowers and widows remarried quickly. According to some contemporaries, the existence of Catholic charities that provided dowries for impoverished girls played a role as well. As for age at marriage, Lorenzoni reported men marrying between twenty and thirty, with twenty-five as a likely age if they served in the army. Eighteen was a likely age for women, whose overall average was 15 to 25. According to Foerster, the proportion of men and women married in Sicily was higher in 1911 than in 1872, 1882, and 1901 (1969 [1924]:470). Consistent with this claim was an overall rise in the rate of marriage from 7.24 in the 1890s to 7.86 in the decade of 1902–11 (that rate fell to 6.79 during the decade of World War I).

Disaggregating marriage age in relation to social class, it is possible to argue that for Villamaura of the early twentieth century there was a higher rate of marriage among *braccianti* than among other groups, with a consequent rise in marital fertility (Schneider and Schneider 1984). Surely, the main observable demographic trend was in family size. Under late nineteenth-century conditions, infant and child mortality in the *bracciante* class undermined the fertility maximizing consequences of youthful marriage and close birth spacing (the latter not discussed here). After 1900, however, this ceased to be the case. Moreover, although the agrarian crisis and development of out-migration led the members of Villamaura's gentry class to redefine their image of the ideal family from one that was grandly prolific to one that was modestly small, we have no evidence that poor peasants suffered their increasing "demographic success" as a burden. On the contrary, we might imagine that, in contrast with the previous epoch, and because of the extent of migration, the new large families were welcome. Even so, the eventual reversal of the premodern correspondence between high social standing and large families had begun.

The first Great War and the second Great Depression

Villamaura was hardly a bystander to World War I. Its peasant population, having grown somewhat healthier over the preceding decade, harbored more youths who were draft eligible. There were other, related disruptions: the recruitment of settlers for would-be Italian colonies in Africa, then their return when the colonies failed; and the war-spawned 'flu epidemic of 1919. The wartime decade also saw an influx of migrants from neighboring towns to work on the construction of a nearby railroad spur (see Gabaccia 1988:155). Although World War I interrupted out-migration to America, it did not mark the end of the exodus, and return-migration, conditioned by the threat and fact of hostilities, became stronger still (Gabaccia 1988:156–157).

Villamaura was not isolated from the surge of labor and peasant unrest that swept through Italy at the end of the war. Along with a severe price inflation during this time, the land claims of returning war veterans stoked this militance. In 1919, the national government promulgated decrees providing for the orderly occupation of uncultivated holdings by certified leagues and cooperatives of former soldiers. At the same time, leagues with a socialist or Catholic-populist orientation mobilized to claim land too (see Ganci 1980:94–97). In Villamaura, artisans led the local socialist movement, which in 1913, aided by an expansion of the suffrage, gained a voice on the town council. According to Gabaccia, who has chronicled these events, in 1916, 150 Villamaura socialists had "organized one of the earliest Sicilian protests against the war" (1988:161). In 1919, larger strikes, especially nearby Ribera's "four days of Bolshevism," prompted three peasant leagues in Villamaura – one socialist, one Catholic, and one of veterans – to occupy the latifundia (Ganci 1980:154–158). Finally, in 1921, the town's "maximal" socialists founded a section of the Communist Party (Ganci 1980:102–109; Gabaccia 1988:161; Schneider and Schneider 1976:128).

Suppression of these "revolutionary" initiatives took different forms in Italy's varied regions. In the case of Sicily, only the economically most developed Province of Ragusa in the southeastern quadrant of the island generated indigenous fascists. Nevertheless, titled elements of the landed class, resident in Catania and Palermo, countered the "poisonous" specter of peasant power by creating an "anti-Bolshevik" agrarian bloc. When, after Mussolini's March on Rome in 1922, the national government set about consolidating a fascist presence in the South, its leaders sought out an alliance with this group, eventually gaining the allegiance of interior landowners as well. Local gentry magnates in towns like Villamaura thereby lessened their dependence on mafiosi as guardians of their property.

Whereas in the early twentieth century, the national government had nourished free trade and open borders, fascism took Italy in an opposite, bellicose direction. The changed global context of the postwar years encouraged this step. The United States Immigration Acts of the early 1920s heavily restricted, indeed virtually dammed up, the migration stream from Italy. With the transatlantic connection severed, Italy faced new and serious balance of payments problems, which were in part the motivation for a turn-around in tariff and agricultural policy. In 1925, Mussolini launched a "Battle for Grain," designed to put pastures back into wheat, reclaim unused land, and thereby break reliance on imported cereals. But, as historian Salvatore Lupo has documented, these policies, and the protectionist bent that underpinned them, encouraged a return to latifundism in Sicily (1981:49–70).

As we have seen, in the early twentieth century, peasant latifundism had begun to fragment the large estates of the Sicilian interior; some latifundi had been divided, others rented out to peasant cooperatives, but Mussolini's Battle for Grain established a context in which the gentry could regain their hold over the largest properties. The renewed consolidation satisfied the goal of class vengeance as landowners sought to recoup "complete control over productive activity and the social fabric" (Lupo 1981:70; also see Mack Smith 1968:516). Agrarian reform projects designed by Rome were poorly articulated with local patterns of culture and agriculture, and tended to be misused or abandoned, only adding to the pent-up demand for reform that exploded among peasants after World War II. Meanwhile, the 1926 revaluation of the lira undermined the market for the specialty crops produced by peasant proprietors and, as the world depression set in after 1929, many smallholders were brought to their knees (Lupo 1981:76). Most vulnerable to indebtedness and bankruptcy were those whose land was recently acquired and marginal, who lacked the necessary capital for improving it, or who suffered from price declines in the food crops they produced. In Lupo's words, the inter-war years saw a "veritable inversion" of the tendencies of 1900–14 (1981:77).

Between smallholders' vulnerability to bankruptcy, and the loss of transatlantic migration as leverage for peasants in Sicilian labor markets, peasant latifundism declined. The agricultural economy lost its capacity for reabsorbing labor, whether that of demobilized soldiers returning from the front after World War I, or the increasing number of *Americani* who repatriated. Absorption became yet more difficult as the world depression instigated processes of ruralization everywhere. Although some Sicilians went clandestinely to America, and although colonization efforts in Libya and Ethiopia held out opportunities for a few, the inter-war years for Sicily – and Villamaura – were plagued by underemployment in agriculture and a trapped labor reserve.

Villamaura's *braccianti*: Fertility control delayed?

During the inter-war years, Sicily's population continued to grow, although probably not because of the populationist measures undertaken by the Fascist government in support of its autarchic and bellicose posture in the world community of nations. There is virtually no evidence that people in Villamaura took these measures seriously and it is more likely that a continued decline of mortality and return migration accounted for most of the growth. Especially important to people's recollections of the inter-war years was an increasingly visible and acknowledged association between large families and poverty – a reverse of the past when large families bespoke wealth. Contributing to this perception, at the time, was the initiative of local artisans to commit themselves to a strategy of family limitation. Among artisans who married in Villamaura in 1920, none had more than three children but over half of the landless peasant couples who wed in that year (excluding those who were childless) ended up with five to thirteen offspring. Given what we know about the structural conditions of the *braccianti*, and the testimony of their own historical memories, we cannot attribute these large families to the parents' self-conscious decision to maximize a return on child labor or reduce the risk of insecurity in old age. Nor is there evidence that religious adherence to traditional values produced "fatalistic" attitudes that would induce people to forswear the practice of family limitation. Instead, we conclude that the persistence of high fertility and the production of large families was linked to a broader problem: interclass relations in the local community that created insurmountable obstacles to upward mobility for the *braccianti*, and made it difficult for them to construct and realize a new family ideal.

Let us begin with evidence regarding a "demand for children's labor" explanation for *bracciante* high fertility. Villamaura's landless and landpoor peasant men found precarious employment through a combination of annual sharecropping and day-labor contracts on the large estates. Except for supplementary work – for example in preparing and hauling construction materials, or gathering palm leaves for women to weave into brooms – they were typically idle for about one hundred days of each year (see Blok 1966; Rochefort 1961). Adult women combined the care of their own hearths and families with gleaning, broom-making and, to their shame, work as domestic servants. Occasionally they worked for the *burgisi*, washing floors, preparing feed for the animals, perhaps baking bread. *Padroni*, the gentry lords of three-storey houses as well as of the land, liked to have four or five live-in servants and several others on call. They engaged peasant men as day-laborers or sharecroppers and, as a condition of employment, claimed the domestic labor of the men's wives and daughters. Because they were already in debt to the landlord for seed and other advances, the peasants were usually constrained to comply.

The typical *bracciante* household also dispersed its children into an array of occupational niches, some of which gave almost no return. Young girls, by the age of 9, learned to bake bread and make pasta on their own, but their main activity in their mother's absence was swaddling, feeding, and otherwise caring for younger siblings. As teenagers, girls found employment in domestic service, their work being remunerated with combinations of room and board, gifts of food, and a monetary wage. Surplus earnings were earmarked for the preparation of a trousseau of bed linens, necessary for their marriage. When the family was desperate, however, a daughter's earnings went directly to the mother's kitty for food, clothing, festivals, and illness. Such constraints often led the mothers to ignore an assault on their daughter's honor by an employer or his son, even hiding the fact from the girl's father to ensure that he would not do anything rash that would jeopardize the daughter's continued employment.

Boys worked outside the home – at 7 or 8 years old alongside their father or grandfather, and then from age 9 or 10 minding sheep for landowners. Memories of child labor are harsh and, as with the girls, desperate parents tried to disregard the abuses, sometimes even urging an employer to discipline a homesick son. In the case of landed peasant families, sons' earnings from casual labor were managed by the father for the eventual purchase of land and houses, but in poor families, boys either gave their earnings to their mothers to purchase food or, at their father's invitation, put something aside to pay for their own simple wedding and the few pieces of furniture they would need to create a new household. A boy's earnings might also help purchase the bed linens for a sister's minimal dowry – but child labor rarely improved the family's standard of living as a whole. Relations of employment are instead remembered for the parasitic way they drained energy and resources from the peasants' own family life.

This characterization is dramatized by a comparison with landed peasants in Villamaura of the 1920s and 1930s, whose families were also large. Having some land and livestock, a *burgise* father mobilized his children to maintain and enhance the family patrimony, putting his sons to work for him, or claiming their earnings if they worked for others. As such he could establish a fund for his daughters' dowries and the sons' marriage settlements, and insist that the sons remain single and work with him until their sisters were wed. A single household fund underwrote the preparation of trousseau for these girls and in hard times both they and their brothers delayed their marriages for years. Hence the tendency, evident in the marriage records of the 1920s and 1930s, for the mean ages at first marriage for both men and women in the *burgise* class to fluctuate, rising as high as 28.8 for women and 32.8 for men. In *bracciante* families, by contrast, each child worked for his or her own account and the sooner one married the better. For *bracciante* women, the mean age at marriage in the inter-war years was 23, for men 26.

It is possible that some *burgise* parents decided to have an *nth* child with considerations of the family patrimony or their eventual old age in mind, and we have no evidence that would rule that out. Indeed, the conditions of the *burgisi* were most similar to those postulated by Cain as likely to promote a link between fertility decisions and concern for security in old age. Given the centrifugal and precarious employment structure of *bracciante* families, however, it would in their case be misleading to elevate parents' "demand" for children's labor or "old age insurance" into an explanation for high fertility. Although the cost of feeding children did not become burdensome until after World War II, and even though *bracciante* children earned some income, most often they could contribute little more to their family household economies than the cost of their own subsistence and marriage. As for children's contributions to household labor, this took mainly the form of older daughters caring for younger siblings. Nor were children a reliable source of support in later years, owing to their persistent poverty. Among emigrant children, some were a source of remittance money, but others dropped off the map and, in any event, prospects for emigration had dwindled greatly during the inter-war years. In reconstructing this period, several of our interviewees resorted to a proverb: "One father can support ten children, but a hundred children would not be enough to care for one father."[3]

Perhaps the most convincing challenge to the notion that the high fertility of Villamaura's *braccianti* reflected a calculated response to demand, lies in women's experiences of pregnancy. In the cohort of women who married in 1920, peasants showed an average birth interval of 28 months, against 31 months for artisans and 30 months for the gentry – a difference that suggests a disruption of lactation among the poorest groups. The busier a mother, the more likely she was to wean her babies early, with the result that she would lose the protection of lactational amenorrhea against a new conception. Interviewees reported introducing supplementary foods and mobilizing sibling caretakers as early as three months, then discovering with surprise that their breast milk was losing its substance, "turning to *colostra*" or becoming "'spoiled" (*guasto*), because they were pregnant again. In such cases, the first signs of pregnancy were not the familiar nausea and "cravings," but evidence that the suckling baby had stomach disorders caused by "damaged milk." A postpartum taboo on sexual intercourse was not practiced in Sicily, as it is in many places, to protect women from this situation, perhaps because past lactation patterns had been sufficiently exclusive and intense to render such a rule unnecessary. In its absence, and in a context of decreasing infant and child mortality, many women felt confused by their own biology. "In those days," they told us, "we had babies with *occhi chiusi*, with our eyes closed." This was the will of God (*la vogghiu di Dio*), who would provide. As a local proverb had it, "*ogni bimbo, providenza di Dio*," "every child, the providence of God."

In summary, the *bracciante* children survived, earned their keep, even earned enough to marry, and did not cost their parents much. But neither did they add much to the family economy, and the labor of some was even lost entirely through migration. As for children's contributions to household labor, this mainly took the form of older daughters caring for younger siblings. Of course today's *braccianti* have lived through the 1950s and 1960s when their class undertook the transition to low fertility. As a result they too participate in the labeling and shaming of the very few remaining non-conformists – poor families with more than five children. One cannot discount the likelihood that today's outlook colors their memory of the past. Yet we were struck by how rarely an image of the large family as interdependent and pulling together emerged in our conversations with them, compared with the other classes. More characteristic were recollections of worn-out mothers, colds and diarrhea, and proverbs such as, "If nothing is enough for one, it will do for ten."

If the high fertility of inter-war *braccianti* families cannot be attributed to a rational calculus of the benefits over the costs of additional children, could an explanation reside in peasants' world view? Were poor peasants hostage to a stubbornly persistent cultural fatalism or traditionalism, even in the face of such destabilizing changes as a falling rate of infant and child mortality and an increase in immiseration? The women's claim that in the past, "we had babies with our eyes closed" compels us to take a look at this hypothesis. Of the cultural traits inimical to family planning noted by Livi-Bacci, one resonates strongly with this claim: "the lack of women's emancipation" (1977:244). We begin our discussion there.

In Sicily, as elsewhere, the idea of patriarchy has been important to many, but its workings vary considerably by social class (Saunders 1981; Schneider and Schneider 1976, 1992). For men to have full authority over their families they needed to have a reliable source of income without long absences from home. Whereas landed peasants, the *burgisi*, worked holdings in the vicinity of the rural town and always slept at home, landless day-laborers commuted to distant fields under daily contract and were constrained to sleep there during peak planting and harvesting seasons. Unlike the *burgisi*, who mobilized family work groups, day-laborers joined groups of peers, their wives and sons and daughters dispersing as well. Most significant, where wives and daughters served as domestics in gentry households, they were vulnerable to the sexual predations of their employers.

For the *bracciante* men of Villamaura, life consisted of alternate rhythms: days of intense physical exertion from sun-up to sun-down, and days with virtually no employment at all. Often men spent their idle hours at one of the local taverns, called *bettole*, playing cards and enjoying the repartee of the male peer group. In interviews, aging *braccianti* described how in this context, the announcement of a wife's new pregnancy was celebrated as evidence of her husband's sexual efficacy.

Women, meanwhile, met each other in the daily rounds of drawing water at the neighborhood fountain, doing laundry (their own, or a landlord's) at a stream on the edge of town, collecting wild vegetables and making brooms in small family groups. For the Villamaura women, as for the Parisian women described by Fuchs and Moch in Chapter 4, opportunities to talk and gossip were frequent and were probably the occasion on which women could share information and support with those who might be seeking an abortion. We were told that local experts, resident in the town's peasant neighborhoods, administered both herbal remedies and curettage; that after World War II, "outsiders" offered other invasive procedures using metal instruments as well. Under both conditions, most of the "clients" were older married women who had already given birth to several children and who, usually without their husband's knowledge, sought relief from once more having to bear a child (see Borruso 1966; Triolo 1989).

Yet women were in no position to elaborate a public or collective discourse to this effect. On the contrary, abortion was very nearly a tabooed subject for wider discussion. Proscribed by Church doctrine, abortion was also illegal in Italy until 1976. Of the ten narratives we collected from *bracciante* women on this subject, all drew attention to medical danger as another drawback, in three instances citing the proverb "better children than illness." According to the narratives, complications from hemorrhaging or infection required the clandestine and costly intervention of an officially licensed midwife or doctor and even then, one could die. Virtually every woman interviewed said she remembered a neighbor or a relative who had died after an abortion.

Without question, in Villamaura of the 1920s through 1950s, women were subordinate to men and to a legal, religious, and medical context that limited their sphere of autonomy *vis-à-vis* abortion. Yet there are other aspects of the *bracciante* situation that contradict the main obstacle to family limitation cited by Livi-Bacci: the "weight of social control (and) the often very conservative teaching of the Church" (1977:244). Although the local clergy strongly opposed abortion, elderly priests claimed to have been non-interventionist regarding another route to smaller family size: coitus interruptus. Artisans were embracing this practice in just these years and, as we describe elsewhere (Schneider and Schneider 1984;n.d.), artisan men talked about it, joked about it, and celebrated it in their various manufactories and shops. Doing so they furthered an understanding of this technique as "rational" and "progressive" – a civilizing practice that enabled enlightened parents to have the number of children they could afford.

Peasants, including the *braccianti*, were not cut off from artisans on whom they depended for many goods and services. There were even occasional instances of intermarriage between these groups. Most important, artisans were among the leaders of the peasant leagues that occupied large estates after World War I, and prominent in the founding of local sections of the Socialist and Communist Parties. Both artisans and peasants shared the experience of the fascist repression of these parties, including a few cases of political imprisonment or exile. Not surprisingly, a minority of *bracciante* parents emulated artisans' redefinition of the respectable family as "two or three children soon after marriage, and then 'stop.'" To suggest a generic fatalism produced by blind religiosity as the reason why most, or all, did not also follow suit is, we think, to underestimate the complexity of local social and political experience, and the peasants' capacity for rational analysis. One artisan told us in detail how a *bracciante* man, upon quizzing him about coitus interruptus, concluded that, given his life circumstances, embarking upon such a regime would be ridiculous. The point is to know more about these circumstances.

Australian demographer, Gigi Santow, is one of only a few scholars who have looked carefully at the world distribution and characteristics of coitus interruptus. Her survey emphasizes how completely the efficacy of this technique is dependent upon men's motivation, aided by mutuality between the practicing partners (Santow 1993; Schneider and Schneider n.d.). We have already noted the bifurcation of gender relations in Villamaura's *bracciante* class and can imagine that married couples communicated rather little about their respective orientations toward sexuality and reproduction (see Triolo 1989). Mutuality would seem an unlikely or distant ideal. Below we examine the relationships of domination and humiliation that undermined the development of motivation among *bracciante* men. Lacking economic resources relevant to family formation – in particular, property with which to reward children who delayed getting married – the men were no more likely than women to generate a discourse of family planning, let alone convince their peer group that large birth cohorts were worthy of opprobrium, rather than prestige.

The social relations of domination and humiliation: Demographic implications

In Villamaura, the more affluent landed peasants, artisans, and gentry had, by the twentieth century, entered the fashion system of Western capitalism, their consumption habits leaving poorer peasants in the dust. The *braccianti*, we were told, wore patched clothes, handed down to them by the rich or sent in packets from relatives in America. Nor could they apprentice their daughters to the local seamstresses or have sewing machines at home.

Burgise and artisan women prepared their own trousseaux of elaborately embroidered or lace-enhanced sheets and bed covers, and gentry women often commissioned this work at the local monastery. But women of the *bracciante* class, marrying earlier, and with far fewer resources, had neither the time nor the money to assemble more than three beds' worth of simple, appliquéd cotton – the minimum required for marriage, it was said (see J. Schneider 1980). Those in the most numerous group, the *braccianti*, also lived in the humblest dwellings. Some had a one- or two-room second storey over a combined stall and kitchen on the street level, but as late as the 1961 census the majority still occupied houses with two or more of the following deficits (as defined by the census): three or fewer rooms, prior existence as a stall or magazine for the gentry, rental rather than ownership status, the absence of such amenities of the postwar years as water, a latrine, electricity, and gas. In addition, most *braccianti* married with debts and began married life in rented housing, failing thereby to achieve an important symbol of respectability, because neither they nor their parents could provide the new family with housing of its own (see Gabaccia 1984:46–54). In the eyes of others, large families in substandard housing could not possibly conform to the rules of sexual modesty that constituted the basic foundation for respect – especially the rules that humans should live separately from beasts and boy and girl children sleep separately, in alcoves, if not in separate rooms. "Boys with boys and girls with girls, or God cries and the Devil laughs," was the proverbial expression of this concern.[4]

The *braccianti* were malnourished. Able to eat meat no more than once or twice a year, they subsisted on thin soups enriched by wild vegetables, and on *pitirru*, a porridge of grains threshed by hand to avoid the tax on milling. Whereas *burgise* women kept rabbits or hens, *bracciante* women prepared eggplant to simulate meat. Infant nutrition was a special problem. *Bracciante* women spent hours away from home collecting wild capers or asparagus for barter or sale; they collected other vegetables for the evening soup, and worked as laundresses or servants in gentry homes. Perhaps in the very early morning, they also made brooms for a local merchant. Whatever the activity, it often meant leaving infants in the care of older siblings, who fed them a pap containing grain, sugar and goats' milk. In poor families, children had an up-hill struggle against respiratory and stomach ailments. As in the past, they grew up shorter in stature than the children of other classes, even if with a much reduced chance of dying.

Poverty created other humiliations. Landlords in Villamaura gave out coins and sometimes soup on Sundays. Aging *braccianti*, their children too poor to care for them, sometimes begged. Landlords built elaborate mausoleums in the new cemetery, with stone carvings copied from pattern books, and transported their dead in a glass-enclosed, gold-painted (and eventually motorized) hearse. The *braccianti* bore their dead to the cemetery in a rustic, mule-drawn wagon, and buried them in underground graves marked only by a cross. Having little or no education in the local elementary school that was first established in the late 1860s, peasants in general spoke only the Sicilian dialect whereas many of their class superiors were able to speak in Italian. The latter were not only the necessary intermediaries of any bureaucratic transaction, but had to be called on to read letters from America.

These humiliations must be understood in the context of the contributions that *bracciante* men and women made to the health, wealth, and viability of gentry households. Among *bracciante* women, breast milk circulated from haves to have-nots in a relatively non-commoditized system of favors and generosity. A woman with plenty of milk might offer her breasts to the fretting infant of a neighbor whose milk was "spoiled." *Padroni*, in contrast, paid women, some of whom were *braccianti*, to nurse their babies, but expected the relationship to include servile qualities of loyalty and affection. It was preferred, for example, that the wetnurse live-in and favor the employer's child over her own. The "ideal wetnurse" had milk to spare because her own baby had just died, and was a "brunette" – according to the belief that "the sweat of blond women repels the suckling child."

Interclass sexual relations were similarly constructed. It is not possible to know how many landlords or their sons actually committed sexual assaults on peasant women who served in their households, but local gossip assumed that this was the norm. Indeed, to raise the topic of servitude with older *braccianti* in Villamaura, as we did during fieldwork in the 1980s, almost always evoked stories about fallen honor. In several interviews we heard of *bracciante* women who had kept the knowledge of a *padrone*'s abuse of their daughter from their husbands, fearing the helpless rage of what Sicilians call a *"cornutu bastonatu"* – a cuckold who structurally has no recourse other than to accept his horns. Especially indicative, because it brings out the element of parasitism in gentry–*bracciante* relations, is the often repeated story of a married servant who, trying to escape the advances of her employer, fell down a staircase, suffering injuries so disabling that she could no longer care for her own home, husband, and children.

Among the elderly *braccianti* in our sample, several recalled being told or made to feel that only the rich were governed by "brains, culture, civilization," whereas the poor, like animals (*le bestie*), were governed by instincts. "Sexual amplitude is the festival of the poor," and "the poorer they were, the more children they had," are among the proverbs that our interviewees recall. Some *braccianti* claimed that the rich had promoted this opposition in their own self-interest, purposely hiding knowledge of birth-control techniques from "class inferiors." One woman of *bracciante* background also remembered that the administrator of the landlord for whom her husband sharecropped had pointed to her belly during one of her pregnancies, saying, "that one is for the baron."

Like many other Sicilian towns, Villamaura had a system for allowing someone to anonymously abandon an unwanted infant, who would then be provided nutrition and care by a woman "receiver" employed by the town for that purpose (see Kertzer 1993). Some unknown number of foundlings were the legitimate children of parents too poor to raise them and, if they did not die, were later reclaimed. Many of the others, however, were born of brief unions between a gentry father and peasant mother. Town officials, all of gentry status, registered the foundling babies with tell-tale disparaging names of their own invention such as "Fortunate Pilgrim," "Clear Telegraph," and "Giulietta Romeo." The appearance of these names in the birth registers of a face-to-face community like Villamaura suggests that landed patriarchs exploited poor women in lieu of their own, their truncated birth parities and "quality" children being won at the price of a population of *"creati"* – illegitimate children who would also become servants and agricultural laborers (if they survived infancy).

In effect, servile relations drained energy from one group of families to add it to another. Like wolves, said an old peasant man, the rich "sucked the blood of the poor." *Bracciante* men recall with resentment the gentry's expectation that "we give up our lives as well as our labor" to be "*sempre spostata*" – always at their disposition. This meant forsaking one's own family to care for that of another, being available on Sundays and late at night to take bread dough to the bakery, fix broken furniture, and help prepare for festivals. It also meant lending manpower to the seasonal migration of entire gentry households from town dwellings to country villas and back again. As if to symbolize the unequal incorporation of the *braccianti* into their families, landowners addressed them with the intimate "tu" form of the pronoun "you", but exacted formal terms of address like Signore, and "baccio la mano" ("I kiss your hand"), in return. In local memory the patronizing gifts of landlords to servants of hand-me-down clothes and left-over food hardly compensated for the flow of family services that had to go the other way.

The result was the interdependent reproduction of the two classes: *bracciante* milk nurtured gentry infants, *bracciante* mothers cared for them and, as gentry couples reduced their fertility, the *braccianti* increased theirs. It is against this background that we return to the problem of *bracciante* men's potential to redefine the respectable family, motivating themselves and each other to contracept. To the extent that their wives and children were not fully their own, but in a dependency relation with a *padrone*, their *machismo*, if indeed they expressed this, masked a profound resignation with regard to family formation. A pregnant wife, and a newborn child, affirmed their masculinity but in a superficial sense. Parallel to women's confusion about the loss of contraceptive protection against new pregnancies, and claims to have conceived multiple offspring with their "eyes closed," was men's sense of situational powerlessness in general. It was this, we think, rather than a generic or religiously inspired fatalism (or, as we have seen, the economic utility of children), that made members of their class slower than the others to respond to the imbalances that emerged between people and resources once mortality rates began to decline. "If nothing is enough for one, it will do for ten," they said.

Notes

1 Ironically, in a way, culturalist approaches to "overpopulation" are more sensitive in this regard. As in the case of Livi-Bacci, they often target women's subordination to patriarchal values as a reason for the "lagging" adoption of birth control.

2 Nor are the means to an end neutral in terms of cultural values. As Simon suggests (1976: 64), alternative means embody or imply particular ends while,

over time, intermediate ends become the means to more remote goals. Through a process of cultural construction, what begin as instrumentalities can become valued ends-in-themselves. In the domain of fertility behavior, for example, sets of parents might "decide" to maintain the integrity of their property into the next generation (end) by limiting family size (means). If, over time, members of the local propertied class became ideologically committed to the notion that only small families are respectable, then what was once the means would have turned into an end.

3 To the contrary, they remarked that only since the establishment of old-age pensions in the late 1970s had children shown much interest in caring for their parents (clearly with an eye on the old folks' monthly pension checks).

4 The degree and incidence of *bracciante* overcrowding may be exaggerated in the popular memory (and in our narrative) because the pressure on rental space may have been mitigated by emigration (at least in the years prior to 1924), and by the fact that some children slept where they were employed, boys as shepherds in the countryside, and girls as servants in gentry homes.

9   History, marriage politics, and demographic events in the central Himalaya

Tom Fricke

Anthropology's contribution to the study of population processes has crossed many watersheds in the years since John Caldwell's pioneering development of micro-demography. No longer is it unusual to find village studies on the graduate reading lists of our population training centers. The issues of familial context, intergenerational relations, and, to a slightly lesser extent, relationships between household and family groups give entry to discussions in which anthropologists and more sociologically trained demographers share common ground. At the same time, the mutually reinforcing strengths of community studies and larger representative efforts are well recognized. Examples of the best of this work by non-anthropologists are found in Caldwell's research in Africa and South India where attention to local sociocultural contexts provide greater explanatory texture (Caldwell 1982; Caldwell et al. 1988). Related work by other non-anthropologists also hints at the explanatory possibilities of relatively localized studies (Cain 1982).

In spite of these developments, however, direct borrowing from anthropology has centered mostly on the methodological innovations in micro-demographic data collection (Caldwell et al. 1988; Axinn et al. 1991) or a small range of theoretical contributions from British social anthropology most amenable to stressing intergenerational relationships. Powerful as these innovations have been, this chapter shows how more recent attention to political economy may bring additional value to the merger of anthropology and the understanding of demographic events in pre-transition settings. I view this enlargement of theoretical common ground between disciplines as a furthering of the prospects initiated by many from within the demographic tradition (Caldwell et al. 1987; McNicoll 1980).

The theoretical motivation for this analysis emerges from two strains of political-economic inquiry in anthropology, one recently surveyed by Greenhalgh (1990) and the other not yet applied to demographic data, but embodying a somewhat different approach to social transformation

202

(Ortner 1984; 1989). This analysis forms part of a larger investigation into social and family transformation and their implications among a Himalayan people known as Tamang. Here I am concerned with the village of Timling, a setting in which fertility was not consciously controlled through the 1987–88 field period.

Most current anthropological treatments of the political economy of fertility deal with societies that are undergoing or have recently undergone a demographic transition, and approach the transition in terms of class-differentiated processes (Kertzer and Hogan 1988) or in terms of state–local relationships with respect to population policy (Greenhalgh 1994). Greenhalgh's 1990 review itself most explicitly focuses on fertility decline. Here I argue that many of the same political issues that color connections among local, regional, and national levels and which are linked to fertility transition in these other settings are properly implicated in the variation that exists within non-contracepting populations, too. This is especially true if the meaning of political is taken to include "all relations in which the relative power, authority, agency, legitimacy . . . of actors is negotiated and defined . . . [S]uch issues are at stake not just in formal institutions defined as 'political' or 'public,' but in most forms of relationship, and in most contexts of interaction" (Ortner 1989:194). Taken this way, political-economic approaches to population processes open the possibility of merging the intrafamilial and intergenerational foci of Caldwell's work, the more explicitly class-conscious work surveyed by Greenhalgh (1990:86–87), and the ethnographic history of more recent anthropological theory (Ortner 1989).

Political economy and fertility

Greenhalgh's 1990 review and her discussion of a "cultural and political economy of fertility" in Chapter 1 of this volume are useful starting places since they so clearly outline one proposal for a political-economic approach. She begins by asserting that such an agenda is a variant of other institutional approaches, differing in its tendency to begin with regional, national, and international historical forces impinging on local contexts and individual fertility behavior (1990:87). Methodologically, an anthropological political economy relies on the long-term residence and techniques that have come to define more general ethnographic work. It combines these with an interest in quantifying dependent variables of interest to demographers: the timing and nature of life-course transitions such as marriage, birth, and death. At the same time, it suggests the possibility of quantifying independent variables novel to most demographic inquiry (Dahal et al. 1993; Fricke and Teachman 1993). Underlying the kinds of explanatory data collected, however, is the assumption that local processes are penetrated by larger events, notably those related to the process of state formation and global systems of relationship. Thus, as with political-economic anthropology more generally, a political economy of fertility must turn toward history to avoid past assumptions that local systems developed in isolation from a larger world (Wolf 1982; Roseberry and O'Brien 1991). The political economy of fertility is "concerned with the social, cultural, *and* political and economic forces underlying demographic change" (Greenhalgh 1990:95). It follows, finally, that demographic political economy be equally concerned with both the structural forces implicated in population processes and the concrete behaviors that emerge from human agency.

Stated this way, the political-economic framework makes use of narrative forms of explanation associated with historical analysis in addition to the proximate explanations centered on mechanisms. Narrative explanation allows us to ask which groups in a particular setting may be differentiated demographically by actions based in their relations of inequality. It directs attention to the historical processes giving rise to group differences while suggesting the historical depth of relationships of inequality. In the contexts typically studied by anthropologists, the bounds of these groups can only be known through an unusual degree of immersion in highly localized settings. Narrative reconstruction of historical process tells us which groups may be relevant for exploring behavioral differences related to inequality. Social theory and the understanding of these contexts in their own terms guides the attention to specific details in that narrative (Lloyd 1986; Macfarlane 1986).

At the same time cultural analysis informs us about both the worldview motivating and framing behaviors and the structure of local relationships channeling strategies (Hammel 1990b; see also Kertzer, this volume). It is here that proximate mechanisms for the expression of demographic processes are explained. From the point of view of culture theory, the extent to which the motivation for actions extends to a conscious manipulation of numbers of children born is an empirical issue (for elaboration see Carter, this volume). Irrespective of the real effects that behaviors may have on fertility, numbers of children ever born may be an unintended consequence of decisions made for other culturally relevant ends (Lesthaeghe 1980) and it is here that the anthropological political-economy framework permits an extension to those societies characterized as "seamless":

> In relatively unchanging societies no one sees these separate bonuses conferred by fertility. The society is made of a seamless cloth. . . . Indeed, the respondents' ability to see clearly the separate aspects of children's value show that the old system is already crumbling and that children's roles are not as certain as before. (Caldwell 1982:139)

In such societies, often organized by kinship, local relationships between families and larger groups are inherently political. While sophisticated analysis of these relationships and their implications for particular forms of marriage dates from the work of Leach (1961), their incorporation into the political-economic framework argued for by Greenhalgh has lagged. I argue here that such a connection enlarges the scope of a political economy of fertility by drawing attention to the reproduction of relations in pre-transition settings.

Procedurally, then, a political-economic perspective within anthropology is concerned with the multiple dimensions that structure relations both within societies and outside. It draws together a wider set of considerations than those found in more typical demographic study. As with demography, the primary variables to be explained are numerical and have to do with individual behavior (Greenhalgh 1990). Unlike much demographic research, however, investigation begins with internally relevant categories of social difference, the relationship of these local status hierarchies with encompassing regional and state systems, and the strategic behaviors that constitute social reproduction. Recent ethnographic work demonstrates that these strategies are also embedded within the local systems of meaning that link family relationships with wider politics.

Objectives

This chapter examines the demographic consequences of culturally motivated political strategies implied by relationships created and maintained by marriage within a natural fertility society. It explores the creation and maintenance of stratified groups as an outcome of historical patterns of migration buttressed by the needs of authority during the consolidation of the Nepali state. Once these groups are defined, it demonstrates that their members manipulate culturally given possibilities of marriage with a view to orchestrating advantages in the flow of obligations and labor.

While the goals motivating individual marriage behavior are not consciously related to fertility in the population examined here, the relationship between marriage timing and fertility is well-established (P. Smith 1983; see also Kertzer, this volume). To the extent that differential strategies relate to women's age at first marriage, they may be expected to affect exposure to the risk of childbearing and will be investigated in that light. A second exploration will focus on the relevance of marriage-linked political dimensions to the timing of childbearing. Since age at first birth is directly related to the total fertility of women in a non-contracepting population, this variable is worthy of independent investigation.

Following this logic, then, I first provide a narrative history of status-group formation in Timling. Subsequent sections explore the implications of these hierarchies for marriage strategies, age at marriage, and age at first birth.

Timling and the Tamang

In 1988 Timling was a nucleated village of 142 households and 669 people in north central Nepal. Located near the Tibetan border on a narrow shelf of land at about 7,500 feet, its residents are Tibeto-Burmese language speakers whose social structure and agro-pastoral economy bear broad similarities to other Tibeto-Burmese language groups forming large segments of the Nepali population. Like these other groups, Timling people are notable for their exchange ethic, their organization into exogamous patrilineal clans, their expressed preference for various forms of cross-cousin marriage, and their incorporation into the Hindu-dominated monarchy of Nepal in the closing years of the eighteenth century. Today's population includes two groups, the Tamang and Ghale, who see themselves as distinct in spite of their speaking the identical Tamang language and over two centuries of intermarriage.

Timling's location within encircling ridges formed by the Ganesh Himal range kept it from the main routes of travel between Nepal and Tibet and sufficiently marginal to be ruled through intermediaries. During the 1987–88 field period, Timling continued to be a remote site relative to the capital, lying some five to six days' walk from the nearest roadhead.

The Tamang are one of many peoples of the Nepal Himalaya claiming ancestral origins in Tibet (Holmberg 1989; Fricke 1994; Höfer 1969). In their general relations with the Nepali state, the Tamang have had the misfortune of residing in the mountainous country surrounding the Kathmandu Valley. Urban elites living there have always considered them a ready source of corvée labor; proximity to the valley has long been associated with heavy labor extraction by dominant Hindu peoples. Early nineteenth-century British reports already recognized the Tamang as laborers without "any share in the government" (Buchanan 1971[1819]). Not long after the unification of the contemporary Nepali state in 1768, a number of Tamang villages to the north of Kathmandu participated in an unsuccessful rebellion. Since that time, however, they have not taken up arms as a group and were used heavily for state labor throughout the nineteenth century (Regmi 1971, 1978).

Marriage and politics within a culture of exchange

In societies organized by kinship, marriage often structures interfamilial relations of hierarchy and equality (cf. Kelly 1993). While an earlier tradition within anthropology characterized whole societies as practicing a certain marriage form, more recent approaches have looked at the nature of concrete marriages in terms of their reproduction of social relationships (Gutiérrez 1991; Collier 1988; Bourdieu 1976). The stress is on political behavior and the manipulation of marriage as strategy and implies variation in the forms of marriage contracted in a single society. Thus, the cross-societal implications of various cross-cousin marriage forms may be said to hold within settings for the relationships between particular families united by marriage.

Societies in which patrilateral cross-cousin marriages are preferred, for example, often allow other forms of marriage including those with matrilateral cross-cousins and non-relatives. The choice of one over another has implications for the relationship between families since these societies typically rank wife-giving families higher than wife-receivers. While patrilateral, or exchange, forms of marriage imply a good deal of equality between families, matrilateral forms indicate some kind of enduring hierarchy since they involve a continued one-way movement of women between lineages for multiple generations (Barnard and Good 1984; Fricke 1990). Marriages contracted between previously unrelated families are intermediate in terms of this hierarchy. Far from being merely symbolic, these hierarchies have practical outcomes in settings where labor and ritual obligations toward wife-giving families are an expectation of marriage.

Among the Tamang, marriage ideally unites two families in an alliance affirming multiple kinds of exchange – labor, goods, services. Wife-receiving groups owe labor and obligations to a wife's natal kin. These are affirmed at important life-cycle rituals centering on marriage, a son's first haircutting, and mortuary rituals. Other service is offered in tasks from wood-cutting to help in agriculture and pastoralism. Although the practice of bilateral cross-cousin marriage imposes a reciprocity on these obligations in time, Tamang often manipulate their alliances by marrying other than cross-cousins or by engaging in matrilateral forms as a means of maintaining unequal status between patrilines across generations (Fricke 1990).

Tamang kinship terminology is categorical so that actual first cousins are called by the same terms as other orders of cousin. Categorically, they are the same and the implications of marriage to either is felt to be quite similar in its statement of relations between groups. Nevertheless, the political charge of marriage to first cousins is made distinct by drawing actual families into direct exchange undiffused by wider lineage networks. While categorical links may also be called upon to legitimate status distinctions, real social power can be diluted by the distance of apical ancestors linking people within the same category (cf. Bourdieu 1977). Power derives from the real lived experience of contact between social actors. Not only is the exchange more direct when first cousins are involved, but it ratifies concrete relations between families and turns on culturally significant relations between actual brothers and sisters. The significance of these first cousin versus categorical cousin marriages will become more clear in the empirical discussion of marriage strategies in Timling where a mother's brother is spoken of as having a "right" to her daughter for his son.

The marriage process itself can take multiple forms with the ritually most elaborate, called *milsing bhyaa*, usually arranged by seniors and involving a series of prestations including drink, food, small amounts of money, and cloth from the groom's to the wife's family. These prestations include a widening circle of kin. First visits center on the woman's immediate household and later visits expand to other neighborhood households patrilineally connected to them. At every stage, the acceptance of drink and food implies a simultaneous acceptance of the marriage and the social relationships implied by it. These formal marriages are notable public events marked by feasting and ritual prestations of cloth to a wife, her father, and her mother.

Other, less formal, marriages are distinguished by greater autonomy of spouse choice and decreased ritual elaboration. These marriages are more likely to revolve around the wishes of the couple themselves and lack the firm, public acknowledgment of the full set of social relationships implied by the ideal Tamang marriage process. Even when retroactively formalized at the birth of a child, they seldom draw as wide a circle of kin into acknowledgment of rights and obligation.

All marriages are considered to draw affines into relations of inequality and differential obligation, but the quality of any particular marriage must be affirmed through the actions of its principal actors. Women are crucial players here, both as signifiers of alliance and as active agents in the construction of affinal ties buttressed through their continuing links to natal kin (March 1984; Fricke et al. 1993). These links endure as an outcome of cultural ideologies of descent and transmission of bodily substance common among Tibeto-Burmese groups (Levine 1981). Thus, clan membership is inalienable and transferred across generations through the patrilineal inheritance of bone (*nakhrut*). Since women receive this bone from their fathers they stand in marital homes as constant reminders of links between families. In the ideal, these close links will culminate in the request of a woman's daughter for her brother's son as a part of the exchange cycle between patrilines.

The formation of local status hierarchies in Timling

Although Timling people explicitly stress their egalitarianism in ways consistent with a widespread Tamang ethos of reciprocity and exchange, the Tamang clans and the Ghale are accorded ranked statuses associated with royalty, ministers, priests, and commoners in imitation of a general Tibetan state pattern (Fricke 1990). The Ghale claim highest and royal status relative to the Tamang clans.

Contrary to the longstanding tradition seeing Himalayan villages as internally homogeneous and made distinct by their different ecologies and elevations, Timling's contemporary organization is intimately connected to the history of incorporation into the state over the past two centuries (cf. Zurick 1989). The earliest migrations to the area were a part of a continuing movement of populations from Tibet into the upper Himalayan valleys of Nepal about 300 years ago. Oral traditions suggest that ancestors of the Tamang clans arrived first, followed by Ghale conquerors from the northwest shortly before conquest by the nascent Nepal state before 1800.

Ghale dominance of local politics was, paradoxically, buttressed by their incorporation into the state. As with other northern border communities, government sensitivity to threats from Tibet caused it to grant some measure of local autonomy to Timling and to choose already established local elites to aid in administering the area. Although serving at the behest of the state, these intermediaries had a good deal of local power in gathering taxes, apportioning corvée tasks among households, and adjudicating local disputes (cf. Regmi 1971, 1978). The heavy use of Tibeto-Burmese populations surrounding the Kathmandu Valley for corvée labor comprised the most direct state intervention in local affairs (Regmi 1986, 1989). Because of Timling's remoteness, however, representatives of the Nepali state never resided in the community, preferring instead to collect taxes by bolstering Ghale authority.

Although the state elsewhere treated Ghale as just one clan among others within a common ethnic group (Höfer 1979: 144; Macfarlane 1976), within areas of ancestral Tamang habitation they were categorized as of separate and higher rank, thus helping to preserve their privilege relative to others.[1] Even though the Ghale validate their claims to higher status with reference to mythic charters and culture-specific theories of inheritance, their concrete status in Timling was necessarily reaffirmed by state authority looking out for its own interests. The history of other settings in which Ghale do not hold the role of "kings" (Messerschmidt 1976) indicates that traditions of kingship in the absence of state support were not sufficient to support claims to higher status.

Local Ghale were themselves segmented into antagonistic patrilines as a result of a land dispute in the 1870s. This dispute turned on the issue of expansion into lands set aside for the establishment of a Buddhist temple in 1804. Originally donated by Ghale brothers, the huge tract of land was closed to farming, hunting, and logging until population pressures motivated one segment of the Ghale clan less involved in the temple to encroach on it. This caused a split into distinct and named patrilines, the Gangle and the Chetgle. Government officials took advantage of this dispute to consistently appoint members of the Gangle as intermediaries in tax collection, thus dissipating the potential for a competitive power base to form around a unified Ghale clan.

From the time of this land dispute until the 1950s Timling's social order was more or less stable with the Gangle clan at the top of the hierarchy. Timling's people continue to relate the stories of elite village personages from the higher-ranking patriline. One Gangle ancestor, son of the headman who originally encroached on temple lands, is remembered as establishing alliances with southern villages through the strategic marriages of his sons. He parlayed his power into monopolizing the village salt trade with Tibet and commanded enough labor to build rest houses along the trail over the high passes to Tibet.

Two events transformed this stability in the 1950s. In the early years of the decade, a revolution overthrew the old social order in Kathmandu. After experiments with various democratic forms, a new political system was installed in 1960, destabilizing the relations which bolstered Ghale power in Timling. At about that same time, the escape of the Dalai Lama from Tibet and the subsequent closing of the border between Tibet and Timling cut the salt trade which the Ghale had monopolized. The reorientation of Timling's external economic links to the south led to a substantial transformation of individual activities and allowed members of all clans to compete equally for the wage-labor jobs becoming available in Kathmandu, further destabilizing Ghale dominance in the area.

This sketch of Timling's history and marriage culture suggests some of the dimensions along which demographic differences may be found. These include elements of marriage strategy revolving on marriage formality and the nature of relationships between families, the changing nature of individual experience and its implications for relations between daughters and parents, and the nature of local hierarchies. Local status groups defined by clan and patriline membership include two Ghale patrilines – Gangle and Chetgle – and the Tamang clans. The political and economic contexts of social action, moreover, are divisible into periods centering on 1960.

In what follows I explore the relationships between politically charged marriage strategies, clan membership, and demographic events among all ever-married women in Timling aged 22 and over.[2] Beginning with the strategic manipulation of marriage, subsequent analyses follow the implications of social hierarchy for ages at first marriage and first birth.

Hierarchy and marriage strategy

In order to look at the extent to which marriage strategies reproduce social inequalities, Table 9.1 displays relevant dimensions of women's experience and marriage characteristics for three ranked clan and patriline groups. The first four panels under section A explore women's premarital experience outside of Timling, the extent to which marriage involves the interests of seniors, and the extent of formality among these groups. The premarital

Table 9.1 *Selected characteristics of Timling women by natal group*

(N)	TAMANG 84	CHETGLE 36	GANGLE 32	TOTAL 152
		Ghale clan		
	A. Percentages of women in categories at left			
	%	%	%	%
Outside experience before marriage				
None	76.2	77.8	68.8	75.0
Lived or worked out	23.8	22.2	31.3	25.0
Spouse choice				
Senior	39.3	33.3	59.0	42.1
Joint	31.0	33.3	25.0	20.3
Respondent	29.8	33.3	16.0	27.6
Cloth exchange				
None	54.8	58.3	38.0	52.0
Exchanged	45.2	41.7	62.5	48.0
Spouse choice and cloth exchange				
No cloth exchanged	54.8	58.3	38.0	52.0
Respondent & cloth	15.5	25.0	6.3	15.8
Joint & cloth	8.3	2.8	18.8	9.2
Senior & cloth	21.4	13.9	37.5	23.0
Degree of relation				
No relation	32.1	30.6	21.9	29.6
FZD/categorical	38.1	13.9	18.8	28.3
FZD/1st cousin	16.7	16.7	18.8	17.1
MBD/categorical	9.5	30.6	18.8	16.5
MBD/1st cousin	3.6	8.3	21.9	8.6
Relative land in spouses' families				
Equal/husband >	70.2	55.6	56.3	63.8
Wife family >	29.8	44.4	43.8	36.2
	B. Average ages at first events			
Age at 1st marriage	19.4	18.6	18.4	19.0
Age at 1st birth	22.5	21.5	21.4	22.0

Notes: FZD = Father's sister's daughter (patrilateral cross-cousin marriage).
     MBD = Mother's brother's daughter (matrilateral cross-cousin marriage).

experience of living and working outside of the village is an indicator of social transformation and increasing independence for these women. Here we see that Gangle patriline women are slightly more likely to have had these experiences than women of the Chetgle patriline and Tamang clans.

Spouse choice, as an indicator of strategic interest in the connections formed by marriage, can be seen to vary for these ranked groups. Women from the high-ranking Gangle are most likely to have seniors involved in their marital decisions. Only 16 percent of the marriage decisions for this group were left entirely up to daughters while 59 percent were entirely made by seniors. Senior choice of spouse is, on the other hand, much reduced for the Chetgle patriline and Tamang clans.

Prestations of cloth to a woman's family at marriage indicate the relative importance of formal and public marriages for these groups. We see here that the highest-ranking Ghale families are most likely to receive cloth in the marriage process. Since senior participation together with cloth exchange are crucial elements of *milsing bhyaa*, I have joined these two dimensions into a single variable in the table. Gangle women are again shown to be the most likely to have *milsing bhyaa* for their first marriages. Moreover, when joint- and senior-decision marriages involving cloth exchange are considered together, over half (56 percent) of Gangle women are married in this way compared to 30 percent of Tamang and 17 percent of Chetgle women.

Cloth exchange and spouse choice indicate the extent to which individual marriages involve the interests of seniors and are marked by public ceremony but do not in themselves reveal the political implications of marriages. The final two panels in section A provide an entry into the content of relationships created by marriage alliance by relating the status implications of marriage form and relative family wealth to status groups. Here we find that Gangle women are most likely to be involved in matrilateral cross-cousin marriages with first cousins, marriages which least ambiguously assert a status claim. Moreover, the percentages of women involved in these marriages increase regularly with rank in the local hierarchy of natal groups, from 4 percent for Tamang women to 22 percent for Gangle women. Expanding the net of matrilateral marriages to categorical cross-cousins suggests that even Chetgle families are able to manipulate marriage alliances of this type at fairly high levels.

Finally, as an indicator of economic difference between families joined by marriage, the last panel in section A makes it clear that Ghale women are more likely to come from families of greater wealth than those of their husbands. Where 44 percent of Ghale women from both patrilines enter into marriages with families having less land, only 30 percent of Tamang women do so.

Section A in this table reveals some of the implications of locally constructed hierarchy and suggests that marriage itself is a mechanism by which status is reproduced. While Gangle ascendancy was reaffirmed by their designation as intermediaries between the village and the state in the past, their maintenance of privilege has been through manipulation of marriages in ways that legitimate rank in culturally relevant terms. Thus, their orchestration of matrilateral marriages at higher levels than other clans validates their status in acceptable ways within the village.

Section B of Table 9.1 extends the exploration of hierarchy-based difference to average ages at first marriage and first birth. Here we see that although differences are small they nevertheless distinguish Tamang and Ghale women. Patriline differences within the Ghale clan are trivial, yet Ghale women as a group both marry and bear their first children at younger average ages.

Interestingly, many differences among the groups are consistent with their relative rank, yet there is also a fairly clear break into two groups when the most obvious indicators of status, together with the timing of events, are looked at. Thus Gangle and Chetgle differentiate from Tamang in relative family land at marriage and the same line holds if all matrilateral marriages, categorical and first-cousin are considered together. For this reason and the relatively small numbers of women in the two Ghale patrilines, subsequent multivariate analyses join the Chetgle and Gangle into their single clan identity.

While Table 9.1 suggests that marriage practice and strategic outcomes for alliance differ by the hierarchical positions of Timling's patrilines and clans, the relationships between these differences and the timing of demographic events remain to be examined. In thinking about these implications we need to be aware that unlike other South Asian societies a woman's age does not by itself have any significance for the value of a marriage alliance. As such, their age does not generally figure in the conscious manipulation of transfers cementing marital connections between groups. This lack of explicit attention raises the issue of how the differential strategies might be reflected in marriage timing. The answer lies in the overall context of Timling marriages and the different interests of the whole set of actors involved in any marriage. In the next section I develop expectations about the relation of age at marriage and first birth to the politics of marriage and test these against empirical patterns in Timling.

Marriage politics and demographic events in Timling

As recounted above, all marriages in Timling join families into politically and economically meaningful unions, but some forms of union are more charged than others. The Ghale and Tamang of this region have long recognized multiple pathways for establishing these connections. Formal marriages, *milsing bhyaa*, draw in the widest range of family and intergenerational interests. The agreement of actors to the implied relations of marriage are ratified by cloth exchange. Less formal marriages entered into at the discretion of the couples themselves do not explicitly require the assent of this range of kin but are recognized as no less legitimate. These less formal unions may occur when seniors lack the necessary cultural and material capital to arrange a desirable alliance – in a sense, parents can choose not to choose and accept the lower level of cooperative alliance implied in an own-choice union. Such marriages may also occur because a daughter has preempted parental strategies by marrying on her own. In such cases, her parents are presented with a *fait accompli* in which they are expected to make do with the level of services expected from any son-in-law and forego the political advantages that come when wider kin are involved in the marriage process.

Since Timling parents are aware of this possibility – that their daughters may act independently to form alternative marriages – seniors who wish to manipulate marriages toward strategic ends need to act fast. It follows that the more politically charged marriages will occur at younger ages for daughters. Thus, younger ages at marriage are an unintended consequence of the prior decision to engage in the strategic politics of marriage.

We have seen above that Ghale families are more likely to engage in these forms of marriage manipulation, that *milsing bhyaa* are most likely to involve such considerations, and that first cousin matrilateral marriages are the most highly charged of all marriages for statements about inequality. By this logic, all of these characteristics should be reflected in younger ages of first marriage.

Other marriage characteristics with strategic implications include the relative land of families united by marriage and the distance between affines. Where a wife's family has more land than a husband's, the people of Timling often give usufruct rights over excess fields to their daughters' marital families. These rights are not necessarily tied to *milsing bhyaa*, allowing even poor families unable to afford full marriage ceremonies to take advantage of such opportunities. The desirability of usufruct makes it more likely that these women will be sought as wives, with the implication that such material inequality will be associated with lower ages at marriage irrespective of marriage formality. Similarly, affinal connections outside of the village area may be sought for access to resources such as summer or winter pasture. We might therefore expect that these marriages would involve younger ages for women.

Finally, earlier discussion argues for the relevance of different eras marked by the 1960 watershed when trade links with Tibet were cut just as national political developments altered the kin context of internal village politics. In the post-1960 environment, the salience of kin for reproducing stable interclan relations was reduced and the motivation for controlling the activities of women also declined.

We might expect this transformation in the activities of women to be associated with later ages at marriage. Seniors, for their part, are less inclined to orchestrate the marriages of independent daughters because they perceive these marriages to be at higher risk of divorce.[3] Since divorce cancels the advantages of marital alliance while creating its own problems for interfamilial relations, the safer course is to let daughters decide for themselves. Since these daughters are preoccupied with other activities such as wage labor and travel outside of Timling, they are likely to marry at later ages than women who remain in the village, working only in agriculture.

Following statements of the link between marriage age and fertility in the technical demographic literature, earlier analysis (Fricke 1994) has shown that the largest part of the explanation for Timling's overall fertility is explained by exposure to the risk of childbirth. Were Timling's women to be married throughout their fecund years, women would bear an average of 7 children rather than the 5.4 reported in that earlier analysis (Fricke 1994:101–105). Age at marriage is thus straightforwardly related to fertility experience since childbirth is sanctioned only within marital unions and Timling's is effectively a natural fertility population.

Because age at first birth bears a close relationship to total fertility in these populations, the exploration of the impact of marriage strategies on fertility focuses on this transition rather than on number of children ever born. Doing so allows the analysis to include all 144 women 22 years old and above who have ever borne a child, rather than being limited to the small numbers of women who have completed their childbearing. The expectations explored in the analyses below are that the timing of first births is largely an unintended consequence of age at marriage. Thus, those characteristics of marriage associated with younger ages should also be associated with earlier ages at first birth.

Expectations for ages at first marriage and first birth are examined in Tables 9.2 and 9.3 using multiple classification analysis (Andrews et al. 1973). Multiple classification analysis is an appropriate method for exploring such relationships because of its easy to understand presentation and because it allows a look at average ages at first marriage for the whole set of dimensions discussed here. In the tables below, I provide, but do not discuss, information for several levels of statistical significance. These levels, strictly speaking, relate to probabilities that statistical results from a random sample reflect true population parameters (Blalock 1972:159–166). Because these analyses include the entire population of Timling women 22 years old and above in 1987, Tables 9.2 and 9.3 present real population means rather than estimates. My argument therefore focuses on magnitudes of difference among categories. This point notwithstanding, readers who prefer may evaluate results by using the indicated significance levels.

Age at marriage

Table 9.2 presents three columns showing the average age at first marriage for women by each of the variables discussed above. The "unadjusted" column presents the simple averages for each category as we would observe them. The "adjusted" columns present the expected average ages at first

Table 9.2 *Women's mean age at first marriage by family characteristics and marriage process variables*

Variable	Mean age at 1st marriage			Number of women
	Unadjusted[a]	Adjusted[b]	Adjusted[b]	
Marriage cohort				
<1960	18.3	18.7	18.8	60
≥1960	19.4	19.2	19.1	92
	**	**		
Natal clan				
Tamang	19.4	19.4	19.3	84
Ghale	18.5	18.5	18.6	68
	*	*		
Pre-marital non-family experience				
None	18.2	18.2	18.2	114
Lived or worked out	21.5	21.4	21.3	38
	****	****	****	
Relationship with spouse				
Not related	18.6	–	18.5	45
Categorical FZD	20.3	–	19.7	43
1st cousin FZD	18.4	–	18.7	26
Categorical MBD	19.6	–	20.1	25
1st cousin MBD	16.2	–	16.8	13
	****		**	
Marriage decision & formality				
No cloth exchanged	19.6	–	19.5	79
R's choice/cloth	19.9	–	19.5	24
Joint choice/cloth	18.4	–	19.2	14
Senior choice/cloth	17.3	–	17.6	35
	***		**	
Relative family land				
Husband ≥ Wife	19.3	–	19.3	97
Husband < Wife	18.5	–	18.4	55
			*	
Affines' location				
Same village	19.4	–	19.4	100
Different village	18.3	–	18.2	52
	*		**	
Grand mean	19.0			
Total cases	152			
R^2		0.145	0.261	

Notes:
FZD = Father's sister's daughter (patrilateral cross-cousin marriage).
MBD = Mother's brother's daughter (matrilateral cross-cousin marriage).
[a] Observed mean.
[b] Controlling for other variables in column.
   Significant at: * 0.15 level ** 0.10 level *** 0.05 level **** 0.01 level

marriage controlling for the effects of all other variables in the column. That is, the average ages in these columns represent the effect of the variable of interest taking into account the effect of other variables. The interpretation of changing averages for a variable across columns is made clear by an example. Looking at marriage cohort, we see that women who married before 1960 marry 1.1 years younger than those whose first marriage occurred in the later period. In the first adjusted column we see that this difference is reduced to 0.5 years, suggesting that some of the change is the result of changes in the other two variables in the column. In this case, we might interpret the changing age at marriage to be the result of an increase in the percentage of women who have worked at wage labor or lived out of the village before marriage. In the second adjusted column, the age difference for marriage cohort is further reduced to 0.3 years, suggesting that changes in the additional variables in that column explain these additional changes in age at first marriage through time.

This example indicates that historical changes in age at marriage are related to transformations in both the individual activities of women and the practice of marriage itself and supports the historical arguments made above. Turning to the other variables, we see in the unadjusted column that nearly all the characteristics of marriage associated with political strategy have implications for marriage age argued for above. Ghale women marry about a year younger on the average. Women in the most politically charged unions – with matrilateral first cousins – marry from two to four years earlier than those in other marriage relationships. Women in *milsing bhyaa* in which the choice of spouse is entirely up to seniors marry at least a year and often more than two years younger than women whose unions are arranged in other ways. Women who marry outside their natal village marry younger than those who marry endogamously, and women whose families own more land than their husbands marry younger than those whose husbands have more or equivalent amounts of land.

Most of the differentials, apart from that of marriage cohort already discussed in the example above, continue even after controlling for the effects of other variables in the adjusted columns. The magnitude of differences in average marriage age is most pronounced for differences in premarital experience of women, kin relationship with spouse before marriage, and the formality of marriage process. These results suggest that differences in age at first marriage among Timling women are most strongly related to the individual life-course experience of women. At the same time, controlling for the effects of all other variables, the two most direct measures of social inequality, relative land and marriage form, have the expected relation with age at marriage. In both cases, women whose natal families rank higher through material advantage and post-marital relations marry at younger ages. For land, a material indicator of relative status, the difference is only about a year. Matrilateral first-cousin marriages, on the other hand, are associated with a two to three year difference from other forms when considered simultaneously with other variables.

Age at first birth

Table 9.3 uses multiple classification analysis to look at the differentials in average ages at first birth for each of the dimensions of marriage politics, village history, and individual experience examined in Table 9.2. The unadjusted averages again show the observed differences for these variables. The first adjusted column presents average ages at first birth net of all other effects in the column while the second adjusted column includes the effects of age at marriage itself and a variable for first marriage ending in divorce (not shown in the table).

I control for the impact of divorce in this last column since a broken first marriage would be expected to effect exposure to the risk of childbearing by increasing time out of the married state. By including age at marriage in this column, on the other hand, we are able to determine whether the marriage strategy variables have any effect on age at first birth over and above their association with marriage age. The persistence of effects for any variable in this column would indicate that some feature of the relationship between spouses in a given category affects a woman's exposure to the risk of pregnancy even after the marriage has been made (Fricke and Teachman 1993). Conversely, a reduction in the effect of a variable in this column would indicate that its impact on childbearing is largely a result of its implications for marriage age alone. As an example, note that the unadjusted average age at first birth for women who have lived outside of the village or worked at wage labor before marriage is 23.7, some 2.4 years later than those women who did not have these experiences. While there is little change in this difference in the first adjusted column, when the effects of age at marriage and divorce are added in the next column, the difference is reduced from 2.4 to 0.8 years. This suggests that nearly all of the impact of this variable on age at first birth is through its effect on marriage age rather than through its implications for spousal relations.

Looking at the other variables in the unadjusted column, we can see that many of the effects of these variables on age at marriage are still present, although moderated, when we look at childbirth. Measures of social hierarchy show a relationship with age at first birth. Ghale women bear their first children an average of 1.4 years younger than Tamang women. Women in matrilateral marriages with first cousins experience their first births at the youngest ages, two years earlier than the average age of 21.9 for all women and nearly three years younger than women married to categorical patrilateral cousins. The formality of the marriage process, on

Table 9.3 *Women's mean age at first birth by family characteristics and marriage process variables*

	Mean age at 1st birth			Number of women
Variable	Unadjusted[a]	Adjusted[b]	Adjusted[c]	
Marriage cohort				
< 1960	21.5	21.9	22.2	59
≥ 1960	22.2	21.9	21.7	85
Natal clan				
Tamang	22.5	22.5	22.4	82
Ghale	21.1	21.0	21.3	62
	***	***	***	
Pre-marital non-family experience				
None	21.3	21.2	21.7	106
Lived or worked out	23.7	23.8	22.5	38
	****	****		
Relationship with spouse				
Not related	22.0	22.1	22.5	41
Categorical FZD	22.7	22.0	21.5	42
1st cousin FZD	21.2	21.4	21.6	25
Categorical MBD	22.2	22.6	21.9	23
1st cousin MBD	19.8	20.6	21.9	13
	*			
Marriage decision & formality				
No cloth exchanged	22.2	22.1	21.9	78
R's choice/cloth	21.6	21.4	20.9	22
Joint choice/cloth	20.9	21.1	21.4	13
Senior choice/cloth	21.8	22.1	23.0	31
			***	
Relative family land				
Husband ≥ Wife	21.9	21.9	21.8	91
Husband < Wife	22.0	21.9	23.2	53
Affines' location				
Same village	22.1	22.2	21.8	94
Different village	21.5	21.3	21.8	50
Grand mean	21.9			
Total cases	144			
R^2		0.170	0.540	

Notes:
FZD = Father's sister's daughter (patrilateral cross-cousin marriage).
MBD = Mother's brother's daughter (matrilateral cross-cousin marriage).
[a] Observed mean.
[b] Controlling for other variables in column.
[c] Controlling for other variables in column plus age at 1st marriage and whether first marriage ended in divorce.
Significant at: * 0.15 level ** 0.10 level *** 0.05 level **** 0.01 level

the other hand, shows almost no observed relationship with age at birth, while the effects of other variables such as relative landed status and affinal distance are almost nonexistent or quite small.

The picture changes little when all of these variables are considered together in the first adjusted column. Natal clan is still related to age at first birth while the small difference for women in the two marriage cohorts disappears entirely. Matrilateral first-cousin marriages are still associated with the youngest ages at marriage although the magnitude of difference is reduced. Furthermore, the two youngest ages at first birth are for women married to first cousins, suggesting that when all elements of marriage strategy are considered together the differential here has more to do with kin distance than with the hierarchical implications of marriage itself.

Turning to the second adjusted column, we see that nearly all of the observed differences in age at first birth work through age at marriage and divorce. The impact of affinal distance disappears while the effects of kin relationship with spouse are further reduced. Interestingly, the impact of Ghale versus Tamang affiliation lingers on at an only slightly reduced level while the effect of marriage formality becomes more pronounced when age at marriage and divorce are considered. Ghale women in this column bear their first children an average of 1.1 years younger than Tamang women, while women whose marriages are arranged by seniors and which include cloth exchange bear their children at least a year later than others. Since age at marriage is controlled for in this column, the implications are that these two variables have an impact on exposure to risks of pregnancy apart from their impact on entry into marriage itself. Since natal clan status is a recognized indicator of status in Timling, we have evidence that some aspects of hierarchy have an impact on the quality of conjugal relations themselves, while other measures of inequality have their impact on first-birth timing as an outcome of their association with marriage age. The effect of marriage decision-making and formality, on the other hand, is likely to be a result of the Timling practice of delaying cohabitation and increasing the number of natal home visits in marriages involving formal cloth exchanges (Fricke et al. 1993).

Discussion

Tables 9.2 and 9.3 together reveal the extent to which the demographic events of first marriage and first-birth timing are structured by locally relevant hierarchies and their reproduction through marriage politics in Timling. If, as I have argued, age does not by itself constitute an exchange value within the narrow ranges of difference in these tables, then the variation must be seen as an unintended outcome of strategy and circumstance motivated by other ends. The discussion of Timling's history and culture of marriage suggests that these motivations have to do with a political economy of relationships involving state intervention in village affairs and the differential interests of social actors.

Thus, clans in Timling are hierarchically ordered with their ranking buttressed at critical periods by the needs of an expanding Nepali state. While the use of Ghale headmen as intermediaries responsible for local tax collection, delegation of corvée responsibilities, and local order created an advantage for this group, their translation of this political capital into advantage needed to be conducted in locally meaningful cultural terms revolving around concrete marriage strategies. These strategies result in younger ages at both marriage and first childbearing for Ghale women.

While Table 9.2 suggests that natal clan membership is less important to an explanation of differential marriage age than the marriage strategies themselves, the results in Table 9.1 indicate that the high-ranking Gangle patriline families are more likely to pursue these demographically significant strategies. Gangle women are more likely to have their marriages arranged in accordance with senior interests and in formal and public ceremony. Pursuit of these interests requires younger ages at marriage to circumvent a daughter's potential alternative desires. Similarly, Gangle are more likely to arrange marriages that link affines as direct matrilateral kin and these forms of marriage are associated with younger ages for their daughters. Here the value of an anthropological political economy is illustrated in its ability to uncover the composition of active strategists. The result is a more complete understanding of internal context and motivation.

External political events also have an indirect impact on the timing of marriage. The different contexts of pre- and post-1960 relations with the outside world transformed the kin-based rationality of internal village politics. Trade links with Tibet under the direct control of Ghale patrilines were broken by the border closing at precisely the time when a new electoral politics was instituted in Nepal. The result was a reduced incentive for controlling the activities of young people, giving way to greater mobility and outside wage-labor participation for daughters and consequent later ages at marriage.

The implications of these statuses and processes for age at first birth are confirmed in Table 9.3. Ghale women bear their first children at younger ages than Tamang women, while marriage forms connoting the highest level of inequality between affines are associated with the youngest average ages at first birth. The analyses in this table also explore the mechanisms by which these ages are younger and confirms that much of the difference results from their association with age at marriage as we would expect in a natural fertility population. Nevertheless, the influence of hierarchy, even after age at marriage is accounted for, is indicated by the continuing difference in average age at first birth for Ghale and Tamang women. The analysis does not reveal the proximate cause of these differences but they are likely to be due to behaviors related to exposure to the risk of pregnancy differing between the two groups.

Conclusion: A political economy of demographic events

Recent developments in anthropological theory have converged around theories of practice that explicitly integrate concepts of power, inequality, and social reproduction into ethnographic data collection and analysis. Although the practitioners of this new agenda have arrived from various traditions within anthropology, differing on the degree of emphasis on cultural versus social analysis (Ortner 1984, 1989; Roseberry 1989), there exists a remarkable agreement on the salience of the political and historical dimensions of social action. One emerging framework in this new social theory requires that explanation consider political-economic relations at multiple levels of inclusion – within families and localized settings and between these levels and larger political entities. Nearly all practitioners agree that these relationships are mediated by cultural models which guide perceptions, motivate strategies, and define the universe of opportunities for individual actors. This framework suggests, moreover, more complexly argued models of explanation asserting no a priori primacy for either economic or cultural sources of causation. The framework also suggests a merger of once distinct interpretive and explanatory accounts of social action. Such arguments have been paralleled in recent treatments of demographic transition (Kertzer and Hogan 1989).

Although practice and political-economic models constitute a framework for understanding all forms of social action, their application to demographic events has been halting and partial. Greenhalgh summarizes the impediments to such application in her 1990 review and her discussion of the intellectual and institutional history of demography in Chapter 1 of this volume: non-anthropological demographers, even as they acknowledge the value of anthropological approaches, lack the necessary grounding in cultural theory, tend to confine their borrowing to field methods, and are less interested in local context for its own sake; anthropologists most associated with these new theoretical developments, on the other hand, are among the least quantitatively inclined in the discipline.

Nevertheless, empirical work by anthropologists and theoretically informed historians has begun to draw demographic analysis into current social theory. Much of this work focuses on the political economy and culture of class relations within state societies (Kertzer and Hogan 1989; Schneider and Schneider 1984; Gutiérrez 1991; Greenhalgh 1994). The analyses in this chapter complement these efforts by showing that social inequality and political economy structure demographic events in societies where kinship organizes social relations. Timling provides an example in which nascent state-building bolstered local hierarchies even as their reproduction was made dependent on Nepal's bureaucratic system of resource extraction. It suggests that even "seamless" natural fertility settings have long histories of relationship with external political entities (Wolf 1982; Roseberry 1989) and that, in these societies lacking conscious strategies of fertility manipulation, the timing of births may be an outcome of the interaction between encompassing state systems and internal, politically motivated strategies.

Finally, this chapter suggests the components of a political economy of demographic events for such settings. The framework assumes that all societies include social inequalities which structure the differential interests of their members. It redefines the political to include all relationships which involve unequal distributions of power and advantage and seeks to link the multiple levels at which these are realized: between generations, between families and patrilines, and between local and state levels.

While the events to be explained are the individual numerical events of demographic research, the levels of contextualization called for go well beyond standard analyses. Because the different status groups are locally defined, our understanding of their genesis and reproduction requires attention to highly localized historical processes that emerge from ethnographic investigations. Explanation in this approach joins narrative and quantitative analyses in novel ways, by giving attention to both the historical processes and the cultural logics which define the strategies of social actors seeking to reproduce their positions. Here, we find the mechanisms by which the actions directed to other ends may have consequences for demographic variation.

Notes

Support for data collection and analysis was provided by the National Institute for Child Health and Human Development (Grant HD22543) and the National Science Foundation (Grant SES-8607288). Thanks to Tschering Lama, Meena Tamang, Sirman Ghale, Nyemsar Ghale, and Ramleka Tamang for help in data collection. Thanks also to Laura Ahearn, Susan Greenhalgh, Nancy Levine, Sherry Ortner, Catherine Panter-Brick, Arland Thornton, and two anonymous reviewers for comments on an early draft of the chapter.
1 The codification of Nepal's Hindu caste hierarchy in the first pan-Nepal legal code in 1854 was itself part of the felt need of its rulers to legitimate Nepal's existence in response to the threat of the British Raj. By establishing a national code, the *Muluki Ain*, they saw themselves as affirming their nationhood in terms recognizable by the British (Höfer 1979; Burghardt 1984; English 1985). While the *Muluki Ain* classifies the Ghale as one clan among an ethnic group known as

Gurung, an 1874 government document found in Timling's Buddhist temple distinguishes between Ghale and Tamang.

2 This age limits potential truncation biases inherent in analyses confined to ever-married women (see the discussion in Appendix B of Thornton and Lin 1994). The mean age at marriage for all Timling women is 19, while about 80 percent of all women have married and 50 percent have experienced their first birth by age 22. The pattern found for women aged 22 and above is similar to that for later age cut-offs but retains a larger number of cases for multivariate analyses.

3 A perception communicated to me by several informants with good reason. Risks of divorce have increased markedly over the years. Within the first five years of marriage only 3 percent of marriages entered into before 1960 ended in divorce. For marriages made between 1960 and 1974, 15 percent ended in divorce in five years; for those between 1975 and 1987, 34 percent ended in divorce in the first five years.

10 Economics 1, culture 0: Fertility change and differences in the northwest Balkans, 1700–1900

E. A. Hammel

This paper brings data from ethnography, history, and family reconstitution to bear on the understanding of fertility differences and an early fertility decline under quasi-medieval institutions, in an area of Europe poorly known to demographers.[1] Its theoretical intent is to sharpen the debate set by the general results of the Princeton European Fertility Project and critics of economic theories of fertility, from which sources one may draw the broad conclusion that economic factors are of lesser utility in explaining fertility differences and change, while cultural factors are more convincing.[2]

Two points dominate the theoretical enterprise. The first shows the difficulty of using simple cultural or linguistic labeling as an explanatory device, but demonstrates the utility of economic explanation. The second shows that characteristics of political organization, working through control of economic resources, also had an effect on demographic behavior. Finally I propose that where ethnic labels are effective proxies, they are useful largely because elites have employed ethnic criteria to allocate sub-populations to positions in political and economic structures. Where the linkage between ethnic group definition and structural allocation is precise, ethnicity will proxy the underlying structural factors well and will serve as an explanatory device. Where distinctly different ethnic groups are allocated to similar structural positions, or where the same ethnic group is allocated to different structural positions, ethnicity will not proxy the structural factors well, with consequent loss of its explanatory power in the elucidation of demographic behavior. Ethnicity, to paraphrase the words of an earlier materialist, is the opiate of social analysis.

Overview

The northwest Balkans is an ideal place to test the importance of cultural differences. It is one of extraordinary cultural diversity. Ethnicity is for resident social actors the primary organizing principle for explanation of

225

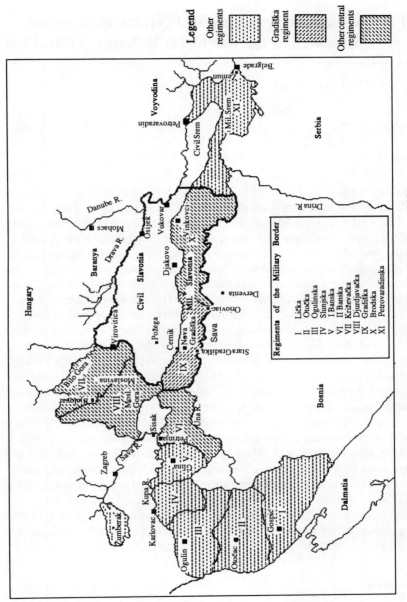

Figure 10.1 Slavonia and environs c. 1800

behavioral differences and the ordering of social life. This proposition is shown clearly on the front and editorial pages of the newspapers of 1991–93, for the narrower study region (Slavonia) was the center of the early phases of the Yugoslav Civil War.[3]

The languages of Slavonia and its environs include one that is not Indo-European (Hungarian), German, and several of Slavic stock, primarily distinctive dialects of Serbo-Croatian. Turkish was spoken in the region between 1526 and 1691. The religions include Roman Catholicism, Orthodox Christianity, two Protestant sects (Lutheran, Calvinist), and some Uniate churches. Islam was represented widely in the area from 1526 to 1691, and is still a dominant force in nearby Bosnia. Three distinct orthographies were used to write the languages of the northwest Balkans and served as important ethnic markers. These cultural differences of religion, language, and writing systems define interacting communities of shared communication, cultural values and tradition, and demographic characteristics, especially fertility, should conform to those cultural variations.

That is not what the data show. The data show that fertility control and long term decline are shared by Calvinist and Catholic Hungarians and by Catholic Croatians but not by some other Hungarians or by Orthodox Serbians (who, with the Croatians, speak mutually intelligible dialects), or by some other Catholic Croatians speaking the most closely related dialect. Further, different fertility behaviors characterize politically and economically different subsets of a group of Catholic Croatians otherwise having a unique subculture, speaking a single dialect in a contiguous set of seven parishes. While on theoretical grounds culture in its most general sense must inform behavior, if it is taken in its simplest sense of ethnic labeling, the score in this analysis is Economics 1, Culture 0.[4]

General historical background

The research area is part of Slavonia, in Croatia. Figure 10.1 shows the study region, plus all of Croatia and adjacent parts of Dalmatia, Bosnia, Serbia, and Hungary. Slavonia is a triangle of land bounded on the north by the Drava, on the south by the Sava, on the east by the Srem region which terminates in the Danube–Sava confluence at Belgrade, and on the west by the Ilova river and the Moslavina region, which was once considered part of Slavonia. Slavonia is roughly 300 km east to west and 100 km north to south along its western base. Across the Drava is Hungarian Baranya, part of the same ecological zone and subject to the same political authority from 1102 to 1918, already known for the early appearance of conscious fertility control in the late eighteenth century.[5]

The Balkans from the eastern Tyrol to the Black Sea were occupied by Slavic tribes in about the seventh century. Beginning around the ninth century, a German wedge split the Balkan Slavs from their northern brethren, assisted by Magyar penetration westward over the Carpathians. In the late fourteenth century the Ottomans began to move northwest, and they were at the gates of Vienna by 1683.

As the Ottomans moved, they pushed before them a no-man's land or border. A corresponding zone developed on the Christian side of the frontier. Both frontier zones were populated largely by nomadic shepherds known in that period generically as Vlachs, usually members of the Serbian Orthodox faith but sometimes Roman Catholic, speaking dialects of South Slavic, or what is now Serbo-Croatian. Many Christians, both Orthodox and Roman Catholic, fled the Turks across the Sava into non-Ottoman Slavonia before its invasion in 1526 and again after the Turkish retreat in 1683–91.

Ethnicity

Ethnic or cultural differences, as locally perceived, were and are partly conditioned on language or dialect and partly on religion.

All of the Balkan Slavs speak local dialects that are mutually intelligible over close distances, even though their modern standard languages often emphasize difference for political reasons. Croatian and Serbian are transparently close, and the urban dialect of Zagreb and that of its hinterland are close to Slovenian. Many of the populations of the area are customarily also bilingual in second languages that are quite different from the Slavic, such as Italian, Hungarian, and German. Thus while differences across major linguistic boundaries make communication between mono-linguals impossible, there is enough bilingualism to override apparent barriers to communication.

Description of dialect differences in the study area requires some recounting of the classification of Serbo-Croatian dialects. These are usually classified in three ways. The first way is according to the word for the interrogative pronoun, "what," which takes the forms *kaj*, *ča*, and *što*. Thus dialects of Serbo-Croatian are called *kaj*kavian, *ča*kavian, or *što*kavian. The second differentiation is based on the divergent modern pronunciations of a Late Common Slavic vowel as *i*, *e* or *je*. The dialects of the region are thus classified as *i*kavian, *e*kavian, and *je*kavian. A third factor is a shift in the stress accent toward the front of the word. The shifted form is more recent and is called "neoštokavian." These three analytic dimensions intersect to produce a number of local vernaculars.

Writing systems are also important ethnic markers. The original alphabet for the Slavic translation of the Scripture was Glagolithic, based on the Greek minuscule. Later translations were based on a simpler alphabet from the Greek uncial, now known as Cyrillic and used today in those Slavic languages whose speakers are traditionally Orthodox. By contrast, those traditionally Roman Catholic use the Latinic alphabet. The use of these alphabets has become a bond of communion, and they have achieved extraordinary symbolic value in ethnic definition.

Religion is the third factor. The formal schism of the Roman and Orthodox Churches occurred in 1054. The Roman Church was centralist, under the authority of the bishop of Rome. The eastern Churches were not organized in that way, each ethnic group having its own patriarch. Some of the eastern Churches ultimately recognized the primacy of the Roman Pope but retained their own liturgy as Uniates. Each of the Orthodox Slavic congregations developed into an ethno-linguistic-religious entity, worshipping with a written liturgy common to all, in an orthography based in the original Cyrillic. Glagolithic was used for the Latin liturgy and for Protestant scriptural and secular writing in the Reformation, contrasting local community even within a more universal Church. Ultimately it was replaced by the Latin alphabet. Orthographic usage thus defined three broad communities reasonably congruent with religious differences.

Ethnic identification in this area, based on these details of dialect, religion, and writing is deeply felt by the inhabitants of the region. Narrow definitions of ethnic allegiance condition every social act, and the ability to engage in social action is determined by subtle indicators of membership. These are the boundaries of love and of hate and thus of the sexuality that concerns demographers.

The core area

Ethnicity in the core

Within this kaleidoscopic field the population of the narrow study area (central Slavonia) is ethnically ancient, distinctive, and relatively homogeneous. It is Catholic, ikavian, arguably once čakavian, and employs the old accentual pattern. It is separated from its ikavian and čakavian relatives on the Dalmatian coast by a wedge of neoštokavian jekavian driven northwestward along the Dinaric Alps as populations fled the Turks in the fifteenth century. The population is sufficiently distinctive to be recognized as a special ethnic group, the *Šokci*. The inhabitants were arguably part of the pre-Ottoman population that persisted through the Turkish period into the present. They are also the population involved in an early and extreme decline in fertility that became a matter of political note and dispute in the nineteenth and twentieth centuries.

History in the core

After the Turkish conquest Slavonia was heavily occupied by Islamicized Slavs and their Orthodox Vlach allies. The population was about a quarter million before the Turkish defeat at Vienna in 1683 (Mažuran 1988). Over the next half-dozen years more than three-quarters of the population fled the advancing Catholic armies. The first known post-Ottoman census of the region counts only about 50,000 persons in 1698. After that, the population increased through in-migration of refugees from Bosnia and Serbia, both Catholic and Orthodox, as well as settlers from Hungary and Croatia. Land was abundant. Annual population growth rates were initially above 10 percent, declining to 5 percent in the 1740s and 1750s, to 2 percent by 1770, and around 1 percent or less thereafter, with growth concentrated largely in the market towns. The lands liberated from the Ottomans were held in part by the Hapsburg Crown as a royal fief and in part distributed to magnates under a system often called the Second or New Feudalism. Peasants lived as serfs on both categories of these lands. These events re-established the ancient division of the Balkans between East and West, left a mélange of distinct ethnic groups scattered across the borderland, re-instituted feudal tenure, and provided large amounts of unoccupied agricultural land because of the massive exodus of the Turks and their allies. In fact, they set up a natural comparative experiment for the frontier fertility hypothesis (Easterlin 1976).

That part of the region administered directly by the Emperor became part of the famous Military Border of Austria. Into it the Hapsburgs invited refugees to settle as military colonists, giving land free of most feudal obligations on the condition of perpetual military service. In the study area of this analysis, centered on the civil parish of Cernik (pron. *tsernik*) and the Gradiška Regiment in central Slavonia, the Border was not separated from the civil administration until 1749. Some villages were entirely civil, others entirely military, and a few were mixed.

The flow of refugees and the settlement policies of the Hapsburgs led to broad ethnic differentiation of the settlement pattern in Croatia. West of Slavonia the population of the Border was heavily Orthodox. Moslavina and central Slavonia were mostly Catholic. To the east in Srem and the Vojvodina, the Orthodox proportion increased again, and some Protestant enclaves appeared. Table 10.1 shows the Orthodox proportion in 1857 for eleven regiments; the residuum is almost entirely Roman Catholic, except in the Petrovaradin Regiment in Srem, where 10 percent of the population was Protestant. There were few if any Jews and almost no Uniates. The regiments are arranged west to east in the table, and it can be seen how the Orthodox proportion declines along that transect, only to rise again at the

Table 10.1 *Regimental areas by religion, 1857*

Regiment	Proportion orthodox
Lička	0.66
Otočka	0.44
Ogulinska	0.46
Slunjska	0.47
Križevačka	0.27
Djurdjevačka	0.21
1. Banska	0.67
2. Banska	0.59
Gradiška	0.24
Brodska	0.08
Petrovaradinska	0.72

Table 10.2 *County areas by proportions in each religion, 1880*

County Civil Croatia	Catholic	Orthodox	Uniate	Protestant	Jewish
Rijeka	0.9714	0.0273	0.0000	0.0006	0.0007
Zagreb	0.9800	0.0089	0.0010	0.0015	0.0084
Varaždin	0.9926	0.0014	0.0000	0.0002	0.0056
Požega	0.6193	0.3455	0.0000	0.0247	0.0104
Virovitica	0.7565	0.2009	0.0001	0.0218	0.0206
Srem	0.8378	0.1402	0.0027	0.0097	0.0093
Former Military Croatia					
Lika-Otočac	0.4549	0.5451	0.0000	0.0000	0.0000
Ogulin-Slunj	0.4986	0.4535	0.0476	0.0001	0.0003
Križevačka	0.9073	0.0828	0.0002	0.0006	0.0040
Djurdjevačka	0.7850	0.2102	0.0002	0.0006	0.0040
Banska	0.3729	0.6252	0.0000	0.0002	0.0016
Gradiška	0.7228	0.2737	0.0000	0.0007	0.0028
Brod	0.8875	0.0809	0.0003	0.0203	0.0107
Petrovaradin	0.2680	0.6306	0.0025	0.0895	0.0090

Notes:
The census of 1880 classifies Križevci and Bjelovar in Civil Croatia and not in the Former Border. I have placed the areas of the corresponding Križevačka and Djurdjevačka regiments into the Former Border in Table 10.2 to make comparison with Table 10.1 simpler.

eastern terminus. The religious nature of this transect will be important to us in later exploration.

Table 10.2 shows a more detailed count by religion, for broader areas of the Border and for additional areas of Civil Croatia in 1880. Here it can be seen that Civil Croatia was overwhelmingly Catholic, while the military area was heavily Orthodox, except in the more Catholic regiments of Križevačka, Djurdjevačka, Gradiška, and Brod. These four are the Border areas in which fertility decline occurred most strongly. The proportion of

Protestants is minuscule except in the extreme east in Petrovaradin, an area in which fertility decline happened last and least. To find the sharpest declines in Catholic areas and the lowest in Protestant ones calls some of our stereotypes into question.

The social organization and status of serfs

Both the civil and the military regions were well known for their complex household structure in the Slavic populations – a patrilocal joint or extended family around an agnatic core of father and married sons, or of brothers, sometimes of patrilateral cousins. These are the classic *zadruge* of Slavic tradition, characterized by a continual cycle of expansion and fission.[6] They are important to demographic analysis because they permit early marriage without the necessity of establishing an independent economic unit, making nuptiality less sensitive to economic pressures. Thus we might expect that controls on population exerted by resource availability would depend less on institutional controls of nuptiality (the "marriage valve") and more on control of fertility, per se.

Military households received an amount of land deemed necessary to provide men for active military duty and at the same time maintain the homestead. Household division and recombination were strictly controlled to maintain the military labor supply. Military serfs were in principle free of the usual feudal obligations, except military service and state and community corvée, but these corvée obligations, as in the construction of fortifications, could be very heavy. Military service involved rotation on local border duty and mobilization for foreign wars. Although Austrian policy exploited the military population for its labor, it also buffered it from economic shocks by controlling land allotments, provisioning in times of need, and preventing the emergence of a land market. These policies could be expected to lead to differentiation of demographic responses between the military and civil population. A significant factor in the life of military households must have been spousal separation and the morbidity and mortality attributable to military service. Major campaigns were not infrequent, and the mortality toll in them was about one in six. These factors could be expected to have both direct and indirect effects on fertility.

But in general and apart from the losses of war, civil serfs were less fortunate than military serfs, liable for money taxes and corvée labor on the landlord's estate according to the amount of urbarial land they held. They could also work for wages on the estate. There were distinct economic groups among civil serfs, whose status might be expected to lead to demographic differences: *coloni*, *inquilini*, and *subinquilini*. *Coloni* had at least an eighth of a session of urbarial land, *inquilini* less than that and sometimes only a house plot, while *subinquilini* had nothing.[7] Civil serfs were in competition with the estate for access to common land, which the landlord could arrogate to increase commercial production, and which the serfs could arrogate to increase subsistence. Such common land arrogated by serfs was called "industrial land," and serfs worked it as sharecroppers, paying a portion of their production on it to the landlord. When land redistributions occurred, industrial land might be allocated as urbarial land to the serfs holding it. This conflict over the commons was not characteristic of the Border, where military serfs had free access.

Peasant plots were smaller in the civil zone than in the Border and smaller in Civil Slavonia than elsewhere in Civil Croatia. Foreign observers unanimously deplored the level of agricultural technology and management, in both the civil and military zones, but especially in the latter, where there was no commercial grain production. Grain was commercially produced on the civil estates and shipped up the Sava, then by primitive road to Adriatic ports.

Civil serfdom was ended in 1848. Civil serfs received (in 1853) the land they had held in feudal tenure, were relieved of all feudal dues, but had to compensate the former owners over a twenty-year amortization, and pay land taxes, so that their burden was in some sense increased by emancipation. Nevertheless, their perception of economic opportunity and the increased possibility of working for wages, not to mention the final achievement of freedom, may have given a flush of optimism. The common lands were divided, the former lords' shares becoming their personal property, while the serfs' shares were communally held in land associations.[8] Increasingly, joint families began to divide, either legally or clandestinely, not only because the new political climate encouraged the economic independence of households, but also because the pressure from landlords to maintain large *zadrugas* intact to preserve the reliability of corvée labor had collapsed. Indeed, since the economies of scale present in large mixed-farming households were diminished, the labor shortfall could only be made up with increased fertility and nuclear family size. Thus, any internal pressures for control of fertility in the household would have lessened.

At the same time there was some relaxation of corvée for the military serfs and an effort to open a market in land, taking effect around 1853. Military obligations were lifted by 1873 and the military serfs acquired their land without having to recompense a former owner. They continued to have access to most of the common land they had exploited for pasturage, which had been an important source of income, especially in the pasturing of swine. The Border was finally incorporated into Civil Croatia under Hungarian jurisdiction in 1881. Thus at the same time the burdens of the military serfs were diminished and their resources stabilized. We might expect from these differences that there would be less downward pressure on fertility among the military than among the civil serfs.

The maintenance of reasonable peasant household land endowments to avoid impoverishment was a continuing concern of the state, and Croatian laws of 1853, 1889 and 1902 established minimal farm sizes for all constituent units of a household, if it were to be permitted to divide, just as the old military regulations and earlier civil law and feudal practice had done. However, households often divided secretly, and there was a clandestine market in land. Control over division, and reallocation of land seem to have been more rigorously pursued in the military zone. Again, we would expect to see stronger evidence of economic pressure in the civil zone than in the military, both before and after emancipation.

Micro-local background

Kinds of records and geography

This analysis is based partly on published records of vital events and population 1830–47, 1857, 1870–83, 1890, and 1901–10 in the entire Border, for 1857, 1870–83, 1890, and 1901–10 in several civil counties of Moslavina and central Slavonia, and on the parish records of seven central Slavonian parishes that raggedly span 1714–1900. The aggregate data cover populations of various ethnicities. Depending on the date of the records and the level of aggregation, information is sometimes classified by religious adherence, sometimes by mother tongue, and by categories of sex, age, and so on. The definitions are seldom perfectly consistent from one source to another. The parish data, on the other hand, are only for the Catholic population. They permit classification by military versus civil status of the village of residence, and sometimes by wealth, where tax and corvée records could be linked to demographic records. The area, centered on the old market town of Cernik, was only thinly populated after the liberation of Slavonia but filled rapidly. In the earliest census there is little evidence of complex family organization, while such evidence is strong in the last half of the eighteenth century, suggesting that the initial immigrants may have come as nuclear families, settled on assigned plots, and then filled them with complex family organizations.

The records of the parish of Cernik begin in 1714; over time it divided into several others, and new ones came into existence in 1789, yielding seven. Figure 10.2 shows the villages and relevant boundaries in the study region around 1800. The civil villages were all part of the estate of Cernik, founded in 1707, with its main house in the town, where there were a Franciscan monastery and some artisanal and trade activity that became increasingly important into the nineteenth century.[9] One civil village (Mala) was a suburb of Cernik with a population of mostly *subinquilini* who were probably wage laborers, and there were two other villages within

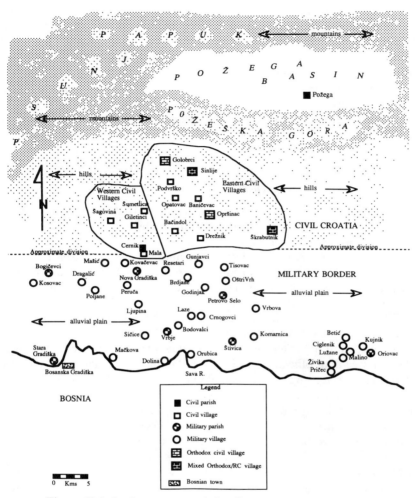

Figure 10.2 Study area around Cernik

about a thirty-minute walk. As much as a day's walk to the east was a group of ten other civil villages, including some that were partly Orthodox or wholly Orthodox. To the south and southeast toward the Sava lay about forty military villages that were never part of the estate or that were separated from it in 1749; their center was the regimental headquarters town of Nova Gradiška, once a minor command post three kilometers south of Cernik.

There was a major ford and ferry across the Sava 15 km south of Nova Gradiška at Stara Gradiška. Traffic was strictly controlled. There was substantial river traffic along the Sava. The major overland routes were from Stara Gradiška to Cernik to Požega, which was the hub of the regional system, and a military road running east–west at the foot of the central Slavonian massif along the Sava plain; these were augmented and supplanted by railroad construction only in the last quarter of the nineteenth century. Thus, although the study region was literally on the edge of Europe until the Austrian occupation of Bosnia in 1878, it was at a crossroads between East and West. With some whimsy, one may observe that from 1809 to 1813 the border of France was only 100 km away at Karlovac, occupied by the troops of General Marmont.

Historical events and influences

Some important historical events might be expected to have affected economic wellbeing and thus perhaps fertility. One of these was the massive in-migration that characterized settlement of the area after 1691, followed by the slowing of that migration by the middle of the eighteenth century and its virtual cessation within eighty years. We would expect high fertility in the presence of abundant resources, then a slackening of fertility as resources became scarce.

There was a thorough reorganization of the Border and tightening of regulations under Joseph II from 1786 to 1799. This reform effort, the so-called "canton" system, established a dual hierarchy in the Border, with Austrian civilian officials parallel to the military command and charged with the care, feeding, and maximal exploitation of the military serfs for non-combat purposes. The canton system was abandoned because of the extreme hardship it worked on the military serfs.

There was a war with Turkey between 1788 and 1791, in which the Bordermen were heavily involved, and a spate of new immigration as Serbian and Croatian refugees followed the retreating Austrians.[10] A war with the French Republic began in 1792, with a respite in the late 1790s, followed by the Napoleonic War itself. This conflict, the most substantial to which the Bordermen were exposed after Austria's war with Prussia, began in 1804 and led to loss of the western Border as far as Karlovac in 1809, until its restoration in 1813. The Napoleonic War led to substantial impoverishment in the Border and general deterioration of economic conditions in the civil zone, especially by strangulation of trade through Adriatic ports. The next major crisis was in 1848 when Croatian troops put down the Hungarian revolt, but this episode was brief. The Bordermen probably mobilized for the Crimean War, 1853–56, but Austria did not enter it, and our usable demographic data scarcely reach that point.

The initial distribution of land to the civil serfs of Cernik must have begun with the establishment of the estate in 1707, but the earliest useful listing was in 1757, consequent on a recent urbarial distribution, and there are two other listings in 1821 and 1854.[11] In 1821 there was a second distribution of urbarial land. Farm sizes were small. In the western villages 69 percent of farms were a quarter-session or less in 1757, 72 percent in 1821, and 86 percent in 1854. In the eastern villages, farms were larger, only 23 percent being less than a quarter-session in 1757, 43 percent in 1821, and 46 percent in 1854. The 1821 distribution seems to have been directed principally toward the enlargement of the smallest farms and the provision of land to the landless; thus it had its greatest impact in Cernik and immediate environs. The main trend is a general increase in allotments in 1821 over 1757 and a general decrease in 1854 over 1821 as parcelization took hold once again. These fluctuations can be expected to have effects on fertility levels. We would anticipate higher fertility just after a land distribution, decreasing as population overtook available resources. There is no detailed economic information on the local Border zone, but differences there can be expected to be less because of continual state adjustment of resources and household size.

General ethnographic background

Early evidence

There can be no doubt of early concern about and knowledge of techniques of fertility control in this region. Coitus interruptus is reported from Baranya in the late eighteenth century, and recent work indicates it was practiced not only by Hungarian Calvinists but also by Hungarian Catholics and perhaps by Croatian Catholics as well.[12] In Croatia, Bačić in 1732 describes magical methods to prevent pregnancy. Došen in 1767 and 1768 (1969) relates folk poetry suggesting prostitution, illegitimacy, infanticide, and prevention of birth. The epic poetry of a Slavonian captain in the Austrian Border, Matija Antun Reljković, written in 1762 (1973), refers to concern about pregnancy and the preservation of female beauty, and alludes to birth control methods. Engel in 1786 (1971), is already lamenting the depopulation of Slavonia, a phenomenon that later came to be called the "white plague." Buturac (1930, 1941a–e), writing on the history of the Požega basin, finds evidence of birth limitation in some villages as early as 1780, widespread by 1880. Describing the population of Moslavina, he notes a decline in fertility from 1800 to 1880 on account of contraception and abortion. He identifies the adjacent regions along the Drava, the Sava, Moslavina and Pokuplje as those with the lowest fertility and describes them as "nests of lust, adultery, and abortion."

By 1850, Slavonia was beginning to earn its infamous reputation for limitation of births and low fertility, and numerous articles appeared in lay, medical, and ecclesiastical journals. Some of these related low fertility and problems of household organization.[13] Some denounced contraception and abortion as sinful.[14] Medical journals and ethnographic accounts describe abortion, contraception, and infanticide.[15] The earliest ethnographic monograph on the region, written in 1897, is explicit on abortion in passages from girls' folk songs.[16] The periodical literature and the pronouncements of churchmen and nationalist politicians through much of the nineteenth century and into the twentieth were full of denunciations of Slavonian women for their low birth rate. They were accused of caring more about their appearance and their trinkets than about the wellbeing of the nation.[17]

Modern and retrospective evidence

In 1940 a socialist feminist, Nada Sremec, published results of extensive interviews with Slavonian peasant women, in order to defend them against such charges. She was explicit about abortion, and the reported dialogues also indicate the use of coitus interruptus. They demonstrate concern over the parcelization and impoverishment that resulted from having too many children. Mothers-in-law in the senior generation of joint households exerted pressure on the more fecund daughters-in-law to diminish their fertility for the general benefit of all the grandchildren. Since property was divided per capita, a more fecund ramage of the household would diminish the shares of the children in a less fecund one; thus there were household-level negative externalities to childbearing. Less fecund coresident sisters-in-law also exerted pressure on the more fecund ones to limit fertility.[18] Such pressure was sometimes extreme enough to involve threats of physical harm or even of death. Children were seen as increasingly expensive, with the investment in education unlikely to yield returns to the family.

Sremec was not an unbiased, objective ethnographer. The condition of women was for her a cudgel to beat the capitalists. She does not flinch at detail but is unlikely to have invented it. We get it all – coitus interruptus, the goose quill from the barnyard, the sharpened dogwood or lilac branch, mallow root straight from the earth, hellebore, willow-bark tea, gunpowder, oleander, quinine, massage, no knowledge of the germ theory of disease, no money for the doctor – pain, guilt, tetanus, peritonitis, and death. It is a powerful account.

From the same period comes a less evocative but penetrating report by a medical statistician, Bojan Pirc (1931). He distinguished marriages according to whether both members of the pair were old settlers in the region, mixed, or both new settlers. The lowest fertility was found in regionally endogamous marriages (2.1 children), the next higher in regionally exogamous marriages (2.8 children), and the highest in those in which both spouses came from outside the region (3.7 children).[19] Pirc notes, as did Sremec, the concern about parcelization, the conflicts in the joint family when one of the wives had "too many" children and threatened the level of shares for the others, and the desire of women to hand over their dowry intact to a single daughter. The most probable inference is that spouses in locally endogamous marriages had been under land pressure for the longest time, while entrants from outside who had bought into the land market were not so pressed, or simply brought with them attitudes that had not yet come into conformity with the prevailing economic constraints of the region. Pirc notes that husbands and wives seemed to be in almost perfect accord about the need for limitation of births.[20] He calls attention to the very high levels of infant and child mortality and suggests that these phenomena indicate intentional neglect as a mechanism of limiting family size – when the small church bell tolls the death of a child, his informants relate, "Again some mother rejoices." He disposes of theories of biological degeneration, the effects of venereal disease on fertility, and puts the onus (for such is his point of view) squarely on culture, on a "new sexual morality" characterized by individualism. But he acknowledges that it is not really new, finding the roots of that morality in the eighteenth and nineteenth centuries with references to Reljković. And although his embrace of culture would have been welcomed by the critics of economic theories of fertility, much of the culture to which he points has to do with reactions to economic circumstances. Certainly the culture of which he speaks has nothing to do with ethnic labeling.

General evidence for fertility control and decline

Evidence of deliberate fertility control from studies of short-term variation

Analyses of short-term fluctuations in fertility and grain prices or harvest yields for the entire Border 1830–47 and in a set of military and civil parishes from Moslavina and Slavonia 1760–1860 show significant decreases in fertility coupled with short harvests. The fertility response in a given year is to the price or harvest changes occurring within the last year or two, suggesting control through contraception or abortion in the context of recent economic experience or its anticipation.[21] The responses are weaker in military parishes than in civil ones. Overall, about 30–60 percent of the variance in births can be accounted for by such analysis. In general, the causal chain seems to rest on conditions that affect harvest yield and adult morbidity. First marriage rates show virtually no significant response to price fluctuations or to non-infant deaths, so that the supply of reproductive individuals entering the population is not affected. Thus new household formation seems an almost autonomous process, unaffected by the economy, while the responses to economic change are in fertility itself.

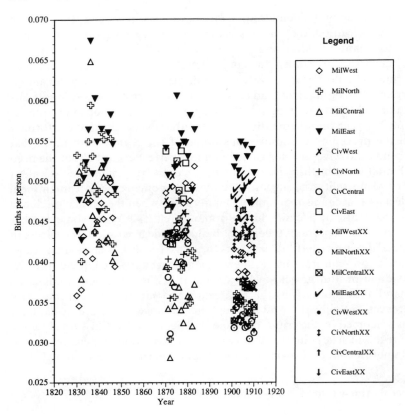

Figure 10.3 Crude birth rates, Croatian regions 1830–1910

Fertility control seems to have been institutionalized as a response to unfavorable economic conditions at least in the short term.

Aggregate evidence of fertility decline

Crude birth rates (CBR) can be compared for regimental (county) areas of the Croatian Military Border 1830–47, 1870–83, and 1901–10, using Austrian military and later Croatian civil statistical sources.[22] The CBR can also be computed for the civil counties for the second two time periods. Figure 10.3 shows the distribution for individual years, while Table 10.3 shows mean CBRs for the major regions in three time periods.

Table 10.3 *Mean crude birth rates, Croatian regions, 1830–1910*

Region	1830–47	1870–80	1880–83	1901–10
Military West	0.0432	0.0458	0.0497	0.0407
Military North	0.0506	0.0404	0.0390	0.0344
Military Central	0.0471	0.0353	0.0350	0.0358
Military East	0.0529	0.0528	0.0545	0.0519
Civil West	–	0.0472	–	0.0336
Civil North	–	0.0429	–	0.0434
Civil Central	–	0.0406	–	0.0442
Civil East	–	0.0484	–	0.0449

Notes:
Military West includes the six regiments from Lika to the Second Banska, Military North the Križevačka and Djurdjevačka, Military Central Gradiška and Brodska, and Military East the Petrovaradinska. Civil West is Rijeka alone, Civil North is Zagreb, Varaždin and Virovitica, Civil Central is Požega, and Civil East is Srem. In 1870–80 and 1901–10 the counties of Križevci and Bjelovar are included twice, once as Military North and once within Civil North, since the census materials classified them as civil even though they were former border regions.

These data show little drop in the western or eastern military counties, and a substantial drop in the northern and in the central ones, within which the Cernik-Gradiška area falls. Most of the decrease had occurred in the central military counties by 1870–83, which had been close to the level of the other counties in 1830–47. Although there are no aggregate data for the civil counties 1830–47, the central ones already had a lower CBR than the western or eastern ones by 1870–80. The decline in Rijeka (Civil West) is then rapid to 1901–10, reaching the level of the northern and central military counties, while fertility in the civil north and center rises slightly to meet the falling fertility in the civil east.

Fertility in Dalmatia in general is problematic. The earliest firm reports available, from the 1820s, show rather low fertility, with crude birth rates in the low thirties (Gelo 1987), and then an increase to the low forties by 1900 and a drop only in the 1920s. Some of this nineteenth-century increase in fertility may have been a strategy to increase remittances from emigrating sons (Olujić 1991). Temporary labor migration, increasing in this period, may also have led to undercounts in the denominator of the crude birth rate. In any case, Dalmatian fertility does not show the same pattern as Slavonian fertility, despite the close relation between the dialects, a common religion, and the contiguity of the two populations before the fifteenth century. In this we have an example of different fertility within a linguistically and religiously defined (Croatian Catholic) unit.

Krivošić (1983) has calculated crude birth rates for three counties of Civil Croatia just outside the Military Border in northwest Croatia, in some instances from the early 1700s. There is an indisputable decline to 1855, and the picture is similar to that for civil serfs in the study area examined here.

Table 10.4 *Crude birth rates, microregions, 1830–1910*

County	1838	1875	1905
Virovitica		0.047	0.044
Požega		0.043	0.045
Srem		0.048	0.045
Bjelovar	0.050	0.041	0.034
Križevci	0.051	0.039	0.031
Gradiška	0.049	0.038	0.041
Brod	0.045	0.033	0.033
Petrovaradin	0.053	0.048	0.052

There are major fluctuations to the end of the Napoleonic War, then a stabilization and a final decline after about 1835. These populations showing an early fertility decline are Catholic like those of the study area, but speak a distinctive dialect, different from that in the Sava–Drava drainage, and substantial portions of that population speak varieties of *kajkavian*. In this we have the same fertility behavior within a religiously defined unit but across a rather sharp linguistic boundary.

Buturac's analyses of Moslavina show a CBR of 46 in 1820–30, falling to 24 in the next decade and then fluctuating between 24 and 34 to 1930. Although his data are not strictly comparable to the aggregate census materials, since they are restricted to the Catholic populations, they also suggest an early decline in the regions of Moslavina and central Slavonia. Table 10.4 gives the average crude birth rates for microregions (counties) surrounding the Cernik–Gradiška study area. Rates fell between 1838 and 1905 from 45–51 to 31–34 in Bjelovar, Križevci and Brod and to 41 in Gradiška (thus in the former northern and central military zones), staying high in the eastern military zone (Petrovaradin) and falling less in the northern and central civil counties of Virovitica and Požega. The picture that emerges is one of an arc of similar fertility behavior, surrounding and facing out into the Hungarian plain, crossing linguistic boundaries even to the extent of including Hungarian populations.

It is also possible to examine data from the civil parish of Cernik and the regiment of Nova Gradiška (Fig. 10.4). The CBR in Cernik parish was around 60 about 1760. There is very substantial annual variation, and except for a few high points around 1805, a downward trend to around 50 during the Napoleonic War. Fertility then recovers to its earlier levels and then declines in the parish data to between 40 and 45 around 1850. Overlapping data from Austrian military censuses 1830–47 for the Gradiška Regiment show fertility in the low forties for that period. Austrian civil censuses in the 1870s, 1880s and 1900–10 show the CBR to be about 30 from the 1870s to around 1900–10. Despite remarkable medium-term

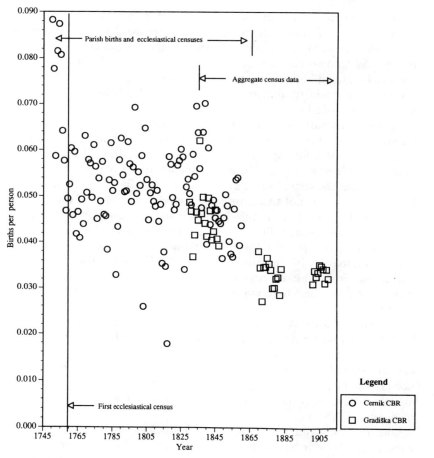

Figure 10.4 Crude birth rates for Cernik parish and Gradiška regimental areas

fluctuations, there is an overall decline of about a third between 1760 and 1850 and of about 50 percent between 1760 and 1900.

All of these aggregate sources seem to tell us the same story. There is a fertility decline, it is early, it seems to cross linguistic boundaries, but it seems to be geographically concentrated.

Explaining the aggregate fertility decline – will culture help?

The differences between the central Border (that is the regiments encircling the Slavonian mountains and plains) and the eastern and western regions coincide generally with major differences in the ratio of Catholic to Orthodox populations earlier indicated. The areas that had high proportions of Orthodox had higher fertility. Further, in the eastern area and out into the Vojvodina where there were Catholics of Slavic and German ethnicity, the areas that had high proportions of Germans had higher fertility. Thus, it seems that to be Croatian and Catholic resulted in relatively low fertility and in fertility decline.

These associations suggest a strong cultural determination of fertility decline. We can think of culture either in the sense of inherited tradition or in the sense of contemporary shared communication. Thus both the precepts of Catholicism and the habits of community may have exerted an influence. But the second sense may be more meaningful, since intentional birth control seems not to accord with the usual precepts of Catholicism. The intimate and often ritualized subjects of marriage, birth, death, and sexual behavior are more likely to be discussed in the local dialect, even the household dialect. But the Catholics in this region spoke more than one dialect of Croatian and had different origins. Thus, while those apparently sharing the fertility decline shared some linguistic and cultural characteristics, they differed in others that had substantial symbolic importance for ethnic identity.

Hungarian Calvinists and Roman Catholics, as well as Croatian Catholics in Hungary, also seem to manifest fertility decline and control. While all of the southern Slav dialects in the area are mutually intelligible, these Slavic dialects are not mutually intelligible with Hungarian, Czech, or German, nor are the last three with one another. It is thus not a simple matter to attribute the fertility differences to "cultural" differences by simple ethnic or linguistic labeling.

One might imagine that some of the fertility variation across the study zone could be attributed to ecological factors. The western (Serbian, Orthodox) regions were much poorer and predominantly pastoral, and the intensity of agriculture steadily increased with descent from the Dinaric Alps into the lower hills of central Slavonia and eventually into the riverine and Pannonian plains. Perhaps child labor was more important in the herding areas. Malaria was a major force in the Pannonian lowlands, and wells were shallow. High infant mortality from malaria and gastrointestinal disease from polluted drinking water may have led to higher, replacement-induced fertility. However, it is exactly in the rich alluvial zone of the Danube–Sava–Drava confluences that one finds the contrasts between Hungarian Catholics and Calvinists and Croatian Catholics of low fertility on the one hand, and Serbian Orthodox, and German and Czech Protestants and Catholics of high fertility on the other. All of them shared the same ecological conditions. Simple ecological differentiation will not explain the differences any more than simple linguistic or cultural identity.

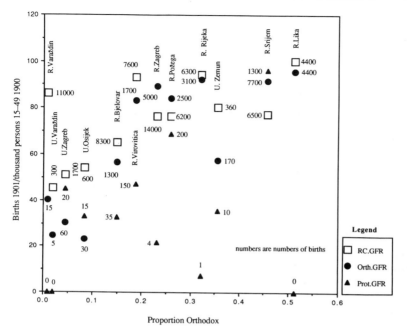

Figure 10.5 Births per 1,000 persons 15–49, Croatia, 1901, by county by religion

Perhaps the most convincing "anticultural" evidence that can be gleaned from the census materials comes from the 1901 census. Fig. 10.5 shows data for the principal regions, with the General Fertility Rate (GFR) plotted against the proportion of the region that was Orthodox. The higher the proportion that is Orthodox, the higher is the GFR. But in nine of the twelve regions, Roman Catholic fertility is actually higher than Orthodox fertility. Protestant fertility is generally lowest, but the data are unreliable because sample sizes are minuscule, except in rural Srem. In Srem, Protestant fertility is the highest in the region and almost the highest in all of Croatia. This violates most of our preconceptions. Thus religion, long held to be the major cultural determinant in the region, does not tell us much about fertility levels. We do no better by focusing on language as a proxy for cultural identification.

We can contrast "cultural" with other explanatory variables at an earlier date. The census of 1857 has the earliest consistently recorded data across the entire zone of Civil Croatia, Dalmatia, and the Border. It permits calculation of a crude index of fertility, the child–woman ratio (children under age 6 to women aged 14 to 39) and of important economic and ethnic

Table 10.5 *Regression analysis of the census of 1857*

Variable	Coefficient	Std. Err.	Std. Coeff.	t	p
Intercept	−1.166				
Marrat	0.815	0.629	0.138	1.297	0.198
Urban	0.063	0.024	0.203	2.606	0.011
Flfp	−0.068	0.029	−0.166	−2.387	0.019
Primocc	0.065	0.035	0.161	1.864	0.066
Bigstock/pop	0.004	0.023	0.015	0.151	0.880
Sheepgoat/pop	0.024	0.006	0.412	4.292	0.000
Pig/pop	−0.053	0.025	−0.212	−2.117	0.037
Catholic	0.903	0.638	2.498	1.417	0.160
Orthodox	1.004	0.643	2.722	1.560	0.122
Lutheran	1.450	1.035	0.164	1.401	0.165
Calvinist	2.679	0.894	0.303	2.995	0.004
Croatia	0.062	0.029	0.289	2.123	0.037
Military bord	0.093	0.051	0.349	1.828	0.071
Zagreb	−0.071	0.033	−0.052	−0.515	0.608
Moslavina	−0.091	0.057	−0.139	−1.595	0.114
Osijek	0.033	0.048	0.076	0.687	0.494
Požega	0.037	0.045	0.089	0.821	0.414
Varazdin	0.000	0.031	0.001	0.005	0.996
Istra	omitted	omitted	omitted	omitted	omitted
Westborder	0.102	0.053	0.217	1.900	0.061
Midborder	−0.041	0.051	−0.116	−0.809	0.421
Eastborder	omitted	omitted	omitted	omitted	omitted
Centdalmatia	omitted	omitted	omitted	omitted	omitted
Southdalmatia	omitted	omitted	omitted	omitted	omitted

Notes:
N = 109
R^2 = .705
Adjusted R^2 = .638
p = .0001

characteristics for 109 county-sized areas. These characteristics are: the balance of married males and married females, urban versus rural location, female labor-force participation, the proportion of the population in agriculture, forestry and maritime occupations, indicators of concentration on grain agriculture, shepherding, or swine herding, religion, military versus civil peasant status, and locality itself as a residual ethnic identifier.

A regression of the CWR on these factors shows that the balance of the sexes and thus of gender-specific emigration was not a significant factor, that urban fertility was higher than rural fertility (perhaps confounded by illegitimacy rates), that high female labor-force participation depressed fertility, that high concentration in the primary sector was associated with high fertility, that concentration in large animals and thus in grain agriculture was associated with lower fertility than concentration in sheep and goat herding, as was concentration in swine herding. Religion shows no consistent association with fertility, except for Calvinists, among whom fertility was high. Military fertility was higher than civil fertility. Any residual ethnic factors embedded in location showed significance only for the Western Military Border, but the meaning of that result is not clear, since religious and at least some ecological factors were already removed in the regression. Thus we see that in 1857 economic, ecological, and political-organizational factors had a substantial influence on fertility, while religion was of almost no importance, and any residual ethnic factors contained in sheer locality were less important than the economic, ecological, and political.

We may conclude from these explorations of census materials that cultural differences, as we are able to specify them according to language and religion, or residually as location, are of little assistance in explaining fertility differences at the small-area ("county") level. By contrast, variables apparently more closely related to the activities of extracting a living from the land and the exchange system, such as female labor-force participation, the strength of the primary sector, and the kind of agriculture, seem strongly predictive of fertility differences. We now pursue the enterprise at a still lower level of aggregation, namely parish-level records within the seven-parish area surrounding Cernik. The attempt here will be to uncover non-cultural sources of fertility differences within a population that is culturally relatively homogeneous. All of the persons included are Catholic, since the records are parochial, and most are Šokci, speaking the archaic ikavian.

The reconstitution data

This analysis focuses on about 13,000 first marriages with at least one child. I limit examination to period fertility because the impact of exogenous events is in principle clearer. The period analysis starts in 1770 when the number of women at risk is high enough to lend some statistical stability to the data, and ceases in 1857 when marriage recording stops. The measure of fertility used is the duration-specific total marital fertility rate, namely the number of children a married woman would expect to have on average, if her marriage lasted as long as the longest marriage among her peers.

Analysis

This analysis uses the level of grain prices and fluctuations from that price. No one imagines that military or civil serfs were buying or selling grain; rather, the price of grain is a proxy for grain supply. The period fertility rates for 3,736 military serf families and 2,892 civil serf families are given in Figure 10.6. The plot shows 11-year moving averages of the duration-specific

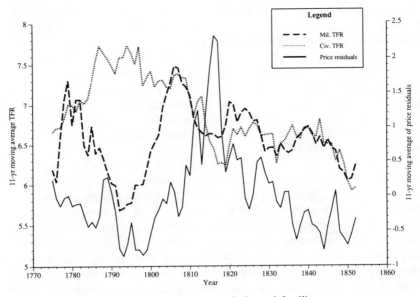

Figure 10.6 Military and civil period total fertility rates

total marital fertility rate and a similar average of price fluctuations. Because of this averaging the plots run from 1775–1852.

Military fertility first increases from about 6 to over 7 between 1775 and 1790. The trend may reflect the gradual diminution of Border conflicts that accompanied stabilization of the frontier and generally improved living conditions and abundant food supplies, as shown in the early part of the price series. Military fertility then shows a sharp decline to under 6 between 1780 and 1792, then a recovery to over 7 about 1805, a decline with a small recovery around 1820, and then a ragged decline with a small recovery about 1840 to about 6 in the 1850s. The early sharp decline is coterminous with a drastic reorganization of the Border under Joseph II that made military existence more stringent, the war with Turkey, and the early North Italian campaigns against the French Republic. Some of the decline is probably due to harsher living conditions under the reform, some to spousal separation. But the price series, showing falling grain prices almost to 1800, suggests that these difficulties were not primarily economic but organizational and military. With the suspension of hostilities, fertility rebounded sharply until the early years of the Napoleonic War, and then declined again, with a recovery after 1814. One cannot separate economic from military effects during the Napoleonic War. Price inflation, reflecting not only poor harvest conditions and a strangulation of trade that lowered supply but also increased buying to provision the armies, was extreme. But so also was spousal separation. The recovery around 1840 may be plausibly attributed to unusually high grain production in the late 1830s. But fertility declined after 1840, a phenomenon that may be plausibly attributed to increasing land shortage prior to the first appearance of liberalizing tendencies in the mid-1850s, and perhaps to the mobilization and military involvement in 1848.

Civil fertility behaves quite differently than military before the onset of the Napoleonic War, with an apparent rise from under 7 to under 8 by 1790, then a ragged fall to about 6 around 1820, a quick recovery to just under 7, a ragged plateau, then a final fall to about 6 by the 1850s. The early increase, like that for the military, may reflect amelioration of living conditions and abundant grain supply. It may also reflect the attraction of high-fertility migrants to the new lands made available in a land distribution of 1757. The increase is in almost perfect opposition to the behavior of grain prices; when prices begin their phenomenal rise around 1795, fertility begins to fall. Since the civil population was not mobilized during the war, the effects are probably only economic, including grain shortage and possibly the quartering of troops. The recovery around 1820 reflects a fall in prices and increased food supply, but also the special land distribution of 1820–21. The subsequent fall probably reflects increasing land shortage. In sum, civil and military fertility behave similarly after the early 1800s, when military and economic causation are difficult to distinguish, but they behave very differently before 1800, when military fertility seems to respond to mobilization and war activity, while civil fertility seems to respond to economic conditions, i.e. food supply.

Civil fertility was heterogeneous, and we can attempt to tease out some differences. For lack of space I only summarize the evidence. Some serfs lived in the market town of Cernik, others in the countryside. Both groups evince the early increase, but the fertility of the town serfs was higher. After about 1790 the fertility of town serfs declines sharply but raggedly until the late 1830s, while that of the rural serfs stays on a ragged plateau until about 1810. Rural fertility then declines sharply during the Napoleonic conflict, recovers in the 1820s, and then declines after 1840. Rural fertility seems driven by economic conditions as reflected in the price series, out to 1820, then by the land distribution of 1821, and the decline after 1840 surely reflects emerging land shortage.

There are some geographical differences as well. Civil rural serfs in the western part of the estate near the feudal demesne and the town manifest fertility rather like that of town serfs, while rural serfs in the eastern part show a different pattern. All of the town serfs were of course in the western part of the estate.

A cautionary note must be inserted on these interpretations of fertility. The period rates are calculated only to 1857, and the running average is shown only to 1852. The effects of emancipation in 1848 or the collapse of the military feudal system beginning in the early 1850s scarcely had time to be reflected in period fertility data, since they would have been strongest in the expectations of the youngest marital cohorts, beginning around 1848–53. Thus the apparent decline in period fertility out to the 1850s does not give us the temporal reach that cohort fertility would, in which we would examine the full marital histories of women marrying as late as 1857 and bearing children perhaps out to the 1870s or even 1880s. What such a display would show (if we had the space for a cohort exposition here), would be a sustained increase in cohort fertility, both for former civil and former military serfs. This cohort increase begins about 1835 for military serfs (and its effects can just be seen in the period fertility average around 1850), and somewhere between 1835 and 1845 for civil serfs (the effects of which may also be visible at the very end of the period fertility averages). These cohort fertility increases can be interpreted as the results of anticipation of better times and a freer life, with the ultimate economic correction coming again, as it did after previous booms, in the form of land shortage, immiseration, the full fiscal burden of emancipation, and consequent fertility restraint that is clearly visible in the census data out to 1910.

To summarize: The long-term decline is stronger for civil than for military serfs, stronger for urban than for rural, stronger for western (at the core) than for eastern (on the periphery). Military activity of reorganization, mobilization, or war depresses military fertility but not civil fertility. In the beginning, grain prices have a negative effect on civil fertility but not on military fertility; later on, when the two populations become more similar in political status, the effect of price changes is the same for both groups.

The graphical analysis can be extended with a simple statistical exercise by regressing the 11-year moving averages on a vector of predictors. These predictors are three major time phases (early, middle, and late), civil versus military status, intensity of military activity, the general level of grain prices, the deviation of grain prices from the long-term average, the presence of military activity for military serfs only, the intensity of grain-price fluctuations for civil serfs only (this last factor for the early time period only), and the intensity of grain-price fluctuations for all serfs in the late period only. The general level of grain prices exerts a strong influence, depressing fertility when high. Wartime has the hypothesized depressant effect on military fertility as do high grain prices on civil fertility. There is an additional such effect of high grain prices on civil fertility in the early period, and a similar effect on all fertility in the late period. War years, net of the measured effects on the military and of the associated price effects on civilians, increase fertility. Given the earlier specifications, this effect must be manifested among civil serfs in wartime. High prices, net of the

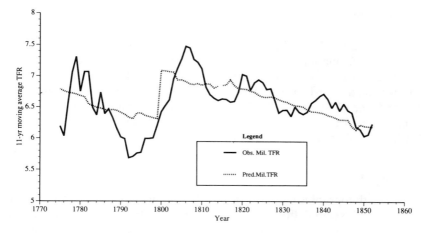

Figure 10.7 Observed and predicted military period total fertility rates

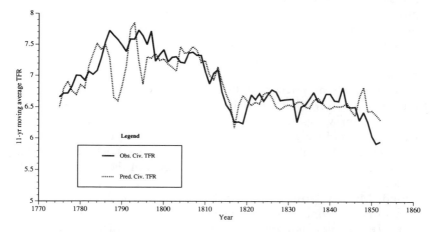

Figure 10.8 Observed and predicted civil period total fertility rates

measured effects in the late period and of those on the civil serfs in general and on the civil serfs in the early period in particular, increase fertility. Given the earlier specifications, this effect must be manifest largely among military serfs in the early period. Finally, in the context of all of these, fertility in the late period is higher than would be expected, while military period fertility is lower than would be expected, although neither of these effects is significantly different from zero. Figures 10.7 and 10.8 show the observed values of fertility and those estimated from this regression model. The fit between model and data is reasonably good for the military serfs, although the model fails to pick up some medium-term fluctuations after 1810, and it underestimates the decline between 1780 and 1800 and the recovery from it. The failures of the model in the early period are doubtless related to our inability to know the intensity of military conflicts; we are restricted to knowledge only of their presence or absence. The model of civil fertility fits the data extremely well, with the only important discrepancies lying between 1790 and 1800. Generally speaking, the fits are good and thus demonstrate the utility of political and economic variables in accounting for long- and medium-term fertility fluctuations.

Conclusion

General ethnographic and historical information leave no doubt about the concern in this population for the limitation of birth, as early as the earliest reliable records we have in the first third of the eighteenth century. Knowledge of contraception, abortion and infanticide is attested. Indirect evidence on the importance of economic conditions to the level of fertility is provided by analysis of short-term fluctuations in demographic rates and prices and harvest data; this area shows high negative elasticities of fertility with respect to the economic indicators, while the response of nuptiality is virtually nil. The importance of economic conditions is confirmed by historical and ethnographic acccounts.

Data from family reconstitution provide information from a period preceding but overlapping with the earliest censuses. They give a picture of medium-term swings in fertility in a generally descending cascade, fertility responding positively to amelioration of material conditions (or their perception, as in 1848–57), and negatively to material deterioration. They suggest that there was a major difference between the demographic and socioeconomic regimes of the military and of the civil serfs early in the period. Military fertility responded most clearly to military conditions rather than to economic ones, declining with military involvement even as general economic conditions were improving, while civil fertility responded to the economic conditions. After the onset of the Napoleonic War, grain prices were more driven by war conditions, and the two effects cannot be separated. Military and civil fertility then behaved similarly, with a general decline from about 1805 to the 1850s. Since war had abated, the decline could have been driven by continually rising prices indicating general grain shortages, or by shortages of land available for the grain supply of individual households, or by some tidal wave of cultural influence. But relative prices were falling, and there is no evidence of a cultural tidal wave that would have affected Croatian civil serfs, Croatian military serfs, and by comparison with other data, Serbian military serfs in the same way. It is more likely that even though grain was globally abundant, individual households were being squeezed between increases in their population and a supply of common land increasingly constrained either by military regulation or by competition from civil landlords engaged in the modernization and commercialization of agriculture.

The general decline in fertility seems steeper and less interrupted among urban dwellers than among rural serfs, suggesting a fairly steady set of anti-natalist conditions. Price fluctuations seem to affect the rural serfs more sharply, as does the special land redistribution of 1821. Fertility changes in the western part of the estate reflect the concentration of town dwellers there, with fertility higher in the west than in the east before 1800, and with a decline between 1800 and the beginning of the Napoleonic War. Fertility in the east does not respond much to the land redistribution of 1821, since there were few poor civil serfs in the east. The fertility of wealthier serfs seems more sensitive to price fluctuations than that of the poor before 1800, and the poor respond more dramatically to the land redistribution of 1821.

This analysis shows a commonality of demographic trends across major cultural and linguistic differences, but demographic differences *within* much more closely defined cultural commonality. These commonalities across the boundaries and the differences within them seem associated with economic and political factors, notably those of the Second Feudalism in civil areas liberated from the Ottomans, or of military feudalism in the Border. Within a small region characterized largely by a single dialect and within the confines of a few adjacent parishes, analysis shows the importance of socioeconomic differentiation and of simple hypotheses having to do with land, labor, the value of children, the threat they bring to the continued welfare of the corporate family group, and intensification of these forces in a modernizing environment. The basic hypotheses about parcelization and the value of children come not only from general theory but from the mouths of the social actors and their descendants living under similar circumstances. As one looks at these disaggregated graphs of fertility decline in the eighteenth and nineteenth centuries, the voices of Sremec's informants ring in the ear, and Pirc's separation of migrant newcomers and stable peasants long under land pressure comes forward in the mind's eye. In this most turbulent area, there is a striking consistency of behavior over time, if we examine it finely enough, and most of that behavior seems economically driven.

But the economic forces that impinge on populations do not do so at random. They bear on populations that have been selected by history. That selection has often been political, and indeed ethnic, especially in the Balkans where the tides of empire have swept local groups about like froth for millennia. The political forces have brought economic weight to bear on those populations, contingent on their social position, on their self-definition,

254   E. A. HAMMEL

and on their definition by other groups. Although the economic forces are here taken as the proximate causes of fertility behavior and change, they work their action on groups defined by political relations of ethnicity and existing in particular historical contexts. Thus, while it may seem to us that ethnicity is an important predictor variable, ethnicity may only proxy the political relations that define those economic relations within which demographic behavior is embedded. From these data we see that while understanding the historical position of populations is properly grounded in appreciation of ethnicity and the political events that have placed them in those positions, understanding the behavior of their actors must take into account the more proximate effects of political status and finally the hard facts of economic reality. At the historical macrolevel, ethnicity is a proxy for political assignment. At the individual microlevel, ethnicity is a proxy for the economic consequences of such assignment, with no obvious direct relevance for the explanation of behavior. At that microlevel, in these data, Economics 1, Culture 0.

Notes

Limitations of space prevent inclusion of much relevant information on the history and culture of the study region (especially on the complex history of the Military Border), on technical details of the analysis, as well as full citation of the sources (especially those in Croatian). Interested readers should consult Hammel 1993c, which may be obtained from the Department of Demography, University of California, Berkeley, CA 94720.

 1 This research was supported by initial grants from the Joint Committee on Eastern Europe of the Social Science Research Council and the American Council of Learned Societies in 1983–84, the Wenner-Gren Foundation for Anthropological Research in 1985, the Center for Slavic and East European Studies at the University of California, Berkeley, in 1985–86. Major funding was provided by Grant No. BNS 84-18760 of the National Science Foundation in 1985–89, continuing as DBS 91-20159 and NICHD RO1 HD29512. Facilities in the US were provided by the Department of Demography and the Quantitative Anthropology Laboratory at the University of California, Berkeley. The research was made possible by the hospitality and collegiality of the Institute for the Study of Folklore, Zagreb (now the Institute for Ethnology and Folkloristics), especially Dr. Dunja Rihtman, Olga Supek, and Jasna Čapo, by the Archive of Croatia, especially Mr. Josip Kolanović, by Professors Vladimir Stipetić, Alica Wertheimer-Baletić, and Jakov Gelo of the Faculty of Economics of the University of Zagreb, Professors Igor Karaman and Mirko Valentić of the Faculty of History, Dr. Stjepan Krivošić, the Franciscan Monastery of Cernik, local civil registry offices and police stations in the Cernik region, and by the kindness of Professor and Mrs. Vlado Ivir of Zagreb. I am indebted to Ruth Deuel and Carl Mason for programming assistance, to Jasna Čapo, Dubravka Mindjek, Andrew Ruppenstein, Marija Olujić, and Rada Božić for research

assistance and to Ronald Lee, Kenneth Wachter, and Patrick Galloway for analytic advice and commentary. I am especially obliged to Dr. Jasna Čapo for her continuing cooperation in the analysis. None of the institutions or persons named are responsible for any errors of fact or interpretation. Preliminary reports of the research are to be found in Hammel 1990a, 1992, 1993c.

2 The failure to find generally valid economic explanations for fertility behavior has led to a recognition of the importance of cultural factors, in more extreme arguments to calls for substitution of the cultural for the economic. Cf. Coale and Watkins 1986; Knodel and van de Walle 1979; Lesthaeghe 1983; Levine 1986; van de Walle and Knodel 1980; Tilly 1986; Watkins 1987, *inter alia* on the results of the European Fertility Project, Cleland and Wilson 1987 for a critique of microeconomic explanations, and Hammel 1990b on the use of cultural explanation.

3 For a view of this war, see Hammel 1993a, 1993b. For an introduction to the history, ethnography, and economy of the area, useful initial sources are Tomasevich 1955; Moačanin and Valentić 1981. Čapo's dissertation (1990, 1991) contains an excellent review of Slavonian feudal institutions. On the Military Border see especially Rothenberg 1960, 1966.

4 Having been myself schooled in the importance of ethnic differences during extended ethnographic research in the Balkans, I expected, on beginning the present study, to find ethnic explanations paramount. The contrary outcome, except for the anticipated importance of the political status of military colonists was a surprise.

5 See Andorka 1971, 1972, 1976, 1979a, 1979b, 1984, 1986; Andorka and Balazs-Kovacs 1986; Andorka and Farago 1983; Demeny 1968; Hölbling 1845; Lengyel-Cook and Repetto 1982; Vassary 1989.

6 Hammel 1968, 1972, 1976, 1980a, 1980b.

7 The size of a session of land depended on the time period, the place, and the quality of the land. See Čapo (1990, 1991) for a discussion of these measures and their uncertain definitions.

8 For details see Tomasevich 1955: 84–88. Landless peasants received no land in this distribution, and landed serfs received only the allotments that had been held in formal tenure (see below), not land they had held under nonfeudal sharecropping or other arrangements. Amelioration of their contractual relations was not achieved until 1876. For details see Karaman 1981.

9 The Military Border was almost entirely lacking in activities other than subsistence farming, military construction, military activity, religion, and administration. However, the Gradiška Regiment that borders the estate of Cernik was the most "industrialized" of all the regiments; in 1857 it had 57 priests (about average for a regiment), 475 artisans (the highest number in any regiment), and 49 merchants (the next to highest after the 53 in Brod, the next regiment to the east), comprising 9 percent of the population. The commercial activity centered in Nova Gradiška was right next to Cernik town, and both were on the trade route from Požega to Bosnia and from Zagreb and Sisak to Zemun and Belgrade.

10 Unfortunately, it is virtually impossible to determine from the published

sources the involvement of specific regiments, especially the Slavonian ones, in military conflicts.

11 See Čapo (1990) for a detailed account. Land in the civil region was of four types: allodial land (the landlord's feudal holding), urbarial land (the land allocated to serfs in feudal tenure), industrial land (land taken from the commons by serfs and placed in agricultural production), and the common lands, which were available to all for wood gathering, pasturage, etc. In the military zone serfs held land as though it were allodial, as direct feudal tenants of the Crown, even though its allotment and distribution were closely controlled by the military authorities.

12 Rudolph Andorka, personal communication.

13 Družtva gospodarskoga hervatsko-slavonskoga 1850. Several of the accounts refer to the pressures generated within joint households when a less populous segment had to work hard to support a more populous segment. The resistance of adults to support their brothers' children was an important force in household division, as were the usual conflicts between the diligent and the lazy, the selfish and the altruistic.

14 Biskupija Djakovačko-srijemska 1873a,b, 1874; Pavlinović 1875; Kornfeind 1907.

15 Guči 1880; Kršnjavi 1882; V. Bogišić 1874; Valjevec 1901; Mirković 1903; Lulek 1914; Lukić 1921, 1926; Buturac 1941a–e.

16 Lovretić and Jurić 1897:376. See also Ilić Oriovčanin 1846, Jančula 1980, Jović 1962, Matić 1970, Stojanović 1852.

17 Viz. Reljkovic's references to female beauty two centuries earlier. Women's "trinkets," usually necklaces of gold ducats, were the form in which family liquid wealth was kept, and were usually transmitted as dowry directly from mothers to daughters. Only males inherited real property and livestock. It is of some interest that a major cultural contribution of early modernization in this area was to transfer control of women's bodies from their husbands' lineages to the state, with pious churchmen continuing to cluck in the background.

18 The history of inheritance in this region is unclear. The classic system of zadruga inheritance is agnatic and *per stirpes*, or division by successive generations of male heirs (*po kolenima*, "by knees," "by generations"). Under *per stirpes* inheritance the negative externalities generated across ramages do not occur, since the division of property is executed conceptually, step by step, in each generation. *Per stirpes* division is still the traditional form among Orthodox Serbs, and this factor may account for their more persistent high fertility in the Border (see later comments in the text). The alternative form of inheritance is *per capita* (*po glavi, po muškoj glavi* – "by the head, by the male head,") among surviving heirs. *Per capita* inheritance to survivors at the time of division does generate externalities. There were efforts to legislate *per stirpes* inheritance in the late nineteenth century, perhaps to strengthen the traditional zadrugal system by diminishing internal pressures for fission that resulted from differential fertility of the constituent nuclear families. That suggests that an original *per stirpes* inheritance may have been replaced by a *per capita* system, and that there were then attempts to restore the more ancient tradition, but one can only speculate. The debate is confused by issues having to do with the preservation of

ancient Slavic tradition and pressures to liberalize the economic system (see Hammel 1980a).

19 Pirc carried out his most detailed survey for the village of Otok near Vinkovci, in Eastern Slavonia. His technique is really quite remarkable for its time, in computing duration-standardized completed fertility rates for marriages that differed in duration across the different exogamic–endogamic categories. There are a few arithmetic errors in his results, which I have recomputed from the original data given. My report here omits the marriages in which both partners came from the old Military Border, since there are only 44 of those out of 1,440 total marriages. Such marriages had fertility rates between those of the locally exogamous and the externally endogamous marriages, namely 3.4 children.

20 Some of the earlier ethnographic sources claim that men had no ken of matters concerning birth and that abortion and contraception were practiced without their knowledge, being the province particularly of old women, especially midwives. It is certainly possible that male knowledge of and participation in fertility control increased over time. Sremec's account indicates that at least by the early years of this century a good husband was expected to practice *coitus interruptus* and that adult males applied moral, verbal, and physical pressure *inter se* to control fertility in joint households. I cite my favorite South Slavic proverb, "*Da je brat dobar, i Bog be ga imao*" ("*If brothers were so good, then God would have had one*").

21 See Hammel 1985 for analysis of short-term fluctuations in the Military Border 1830–48 and Čapo 1986 for the parish of Cernik 1760–1860. Other data are for six parishes of central Slavonia 1760–1860, gathered by Čapo for Hammel, and reanalyzed in cooperation with Patrick Galloway (viz. Galloway 1987, 1988). Although this population was composed almost entirely of subsistence agriculturalists, price data on basic food commodities still serve as a reasonable indicator of food supply. It is as yet difficult to make precise comparisons between military and civil Croatia and between these areas and others in Europe. However, the elasticity of births in Croatia, with respect to economic indicators and net of endogenous demographic effects, seems among the highest in Europe. At the same time, nuptiality responses are correspondingly weak. The control mechanism thus seems not to have been a marriage valve but a birth valve. A full analysis of the comparative data will be published separately. See Komlos 1985, 1986 for a more general picture of immiseration as reflected in nutrition in the Hapsburg Monarchy.

22 Although the border was administratively merged with the rest of Croatia in 1881, the regimental districts of the former border region were clearly distinguished in the immediately subsequent censuses and can be tracked to 1910. I am indebted to Andrew Ruppenstein for organizing and recording these data. The western area comprises five regiments from the Lika Regiment, headquartered at Gospić, around the shoulder of Bosnia to, and including, the first Banska Regiment, headquartered at Glina. The central regiments are the second Banska, headquartered at Petrinja, and then the four stretching from the Djurdjevačka through the Križevačka and Gradiška to the Brodska. The eastern zone consists of one regiment, the Petrovaradinksa, which is in Srem.

The five central and the eastern regiments lie on a great arc that runs from the Drava, south around the curve of the Sava, and to the confluence of these waters at the meeting of the Sava and Danube at Belgrade. Technically, Slavonia extends from the western border of Srem only to the Ilova river. But formerly the region of the Djurdjevačka and Križevačka regiments was considered as part of Slavonia. This great arc, of course, surrounds and faces the central Slavonian massif and the Pannonian plain, including Baranya, within which fertility control seems to have appeared at an early date.

Afterword: (Re)capturing reproduction for anthropology

Susan Greenhalgh

In Chapter 1 I outlined the analytic moves by which this book has sought to remake demographic analysis to incorporate the roles of culture and history, gender and power in reproductive life. In this brief afterword I turn to anthropology, suggesting how the discipline might be stretched, and thereby enriched, through closer attention to demographic and reproductive matters. I do so in two ways: by looking backward to review what has been accomplished here, and by looking forward to sketch out domains for future research.

Old themes and new

During most of this century anthropological interest in reproductive issues has been muted, depressed perhaps by the demographic construction of them as matters of modernization and mathematics. Nevertheless, anthropologists have not neglected these issues entirely. A close look at the history of our field indicates that reproduction was not a consistent theme in *anthropology*, but it attracted the attention of a good number of individual *anthropologists*, including leading practitioners of our craft. For reasons that cannot be pursued here, the interest in fertility was stronger among British than American anthropologists, at least in the early and middle decades of this century. Bronislaw Malinowski's *The Sexual Life of Savages* (1987 [1929]), Raymond Firth's *We, The Tikopia* (1936), and Meyer Fortes's *The Web of Kinship Among the Tallensi* (1949) come readily to mind. On the other side of the Atlantic, Margaret Mead may have been demography's greatest champion within anthropology, arguing vigorously for the liberating potential of birth control for women and calling for inquiry into cultural practices that shape its use.

Surprisingly, at least at first blush, some of the central motifs of this earlier work are precisely the themes that have emerged from contemporary theory to inform and organize this volume. Perhaps in disciplinary resistance to the biologization of fertility in other fields, throughout the twentieth century anthropologists have been fundamentally concerned with the cultural regulation of fertility. Collectively we have devoted thousands of pages to detailing the myriad cultural practices people have deployed to shape their families. Following contemporary theory, the contributors to this book have framed the issue as the "social construction of demographic reality," simultaneously historicizing, politicizing, and macro-contextualizing it, but the fundamental theme – that fertility is humanly constructed – has endured.

A second, broadly political-economic theme has pervaded our work, surviving continuous transformation of the political and economic structures of reproductive life. From early twentieth-century accounts of colonialist destruction of indigenous fertility regimes (e.g., Firth 1936:408–417) to mid-century critiques of the "population bomb" mentality in the US and associated efforts to defuse that bomb by inundating the "underdeveloped world" with contraceptives (e.g., Mamdani 1972), anthropologists have underscored the centrality of power in reproductive life, the global reach of some reproductive actors, and the culture-altering consequences for the powerless. Re-reading this history of anthropology's engagement with fertility, one is struck by the fact that the anthropology of reproduction, or at least part of it, has always been a critical field. While today's political-economic demographers within anthropology are more self-reflective about the histories they construct and more attentive to the resistances as well as the dominations, both the specific issues they address and the critical thrust of their work are strikingly similar to the work of anthropologists past.

Although developing relatively recently, with the emergence of feminist concerns within anthropology, a third, feminist theme has run through our work at least since the early 1970s. The last twenty-five years have witnessed a veritable explosion of research on the social construction and cultural elaboration of women's reproductive experiences. While the feminist study of reproduction today, including that presented in this book, differs from studies of the 1970s in its concerns with women's agency, with politics, and with gender more broadly, earlier and later work are tied together by the central insight that gender and reproduction are mutually constituted and fundamental to society and culture as a whole.

That these three motifs – the cultural construction of biology, the encounter between Europe and those Eric Wolf (1982) has called "the people without history," and gender as a structuring element of social life – have perdured is perhaps not surprising, since they, or at least the first two, are fundamental, almost boundary-defining preoccupations of the discipline. Equally unsurprising, and for the same reason, is the utter lack of anthropological interest in what the other social sciences find so fascinating, namely, the convergence of reproductive behavior around the world on the Western norm of two children per family.

While this triad of meta-concerns is likely to move with us into the twenty-first century, changes in the world we live in will thrust a host of new, more concrete issues onto our intellectual agenda. As technological and biomedical research creates previously inconceivable reproductive possibilities, understanding the social and cultural construction of reproduction will require attention to such issues as the prenatal manipulation of gender, the genetic engineering of families, and the implications of such options for both cultural and social constructions of family and kinship. As the globe becomes more compressed, understanding the political economy of reproduction will require attention to such matters as the flows of children from East to West, and the populationist ethics and activities of environmental movements worldwide. As feminism becomes more political and more fractionated by ethnic, class, and national "difference," understanding the mutual construction of gender and reproduction will require increased sensitivity to the reproductive politics of women's groups, and the voices and values of women for whom woman is a secondary identity.

As this very brief review of past and present research indicates, anthropologists have rarely been interested in the issue of fertility per se, viewing it as a means to larger analytic ends, whether cultural and political, as stressed here, or ecological and evolutionary. Yet as this book hopefully has made clear, the subject of human fertility deserves attention in its own right. Since it is through birth that most societies recruit most of their members, the social management of fertility is a major element in the making of human society. When we neglect this subject, we overlook a fundamental part of life that occupies large amounts of our informants' time and, as A. F. Robertson (1991) has recently shown, has profound implications for the structures of society and economy. While demographers, sociologists, and economists have done a good job of quantifying the trends in fertility and identifying their social and economic concomitants, far too little is known about the culture and politics of reproduction. And the socioeconomics of reproduction needs to be further illumined at the local and global levels, which are lightly treated in these other fields. We need, in short, to capture this subject for anthropological analysis. This volume has shown some of the ways that might be done.

Analytic accomplishments and tasks

Understanding the complex issues surrounding reproduction requires analytic approaches capable of embracing the multidimensional, multi-leveled, and historically variable character of reproductive process. Recognizing the diversity of reproductive regimes across time and space, in this volume we have not essayed a unified analytic framework or, even more, a general theory of fertility dynamics. Rather, we have sought to capture the complexity of reproductive process, more specifically, to show its character as a human construction forged within historically specific political economies. We have endeavored to avoid breaking demographic behavior up into discrete chunks – marriage, fertility, mortality – and separating its underlying processes into discrete domains – culture, society, politics, economics. Our aim, instead, has been to show the interconnections between these, over time and space.

In pursuing this analytic agenda the contributors to this volume can claim to have made conceptual progress in five areas. First, using primarily narrative forms of explanation, they have devised ways to combine the culture, politics, and socioeconomics of reproduction into a single analytic framework. Although the emphases vary, with some authors paying more attention to socioeconomics and politics, and others giving greater weight to culture and politics, every chapter combines these elements into "whole demographies" that both respect and reflect the interrelations of the cultural and political, social and economic in everyday life.

In demography and much of anthropology, the study of fertility has historically been a resolutely microlevel endeavor. A second accomplishment of these chapters has been to show the importance of actors and processes operating on other levels of social organization and the interrelations of different levels in the construction of reproductive outcomes. While more remains to be done, in particular, in tying the global to the national level, these essays leave no doubt about the centrality of global (Schneider and Schneider), national (Kertzer, Fuchs and Moch, Fricke, Bradley, Hammel), and regional (Bledsoe, Launay) political-economic developments in the construction of local reproductive regimes.

A third contribution has been to restore the wholeness to reproductive life. By emphasizing the social management of fertility rather than simply the number of children born, the chapters have shown that marriage, fertility, and child mortality are not separate domains of behavior, as they appear in demographic research, but parts of a single micro-historical process of the shaping and reshaping of the family.

A fourth achievement has been to historicize demographic analysis. By placing reproductive practices within the macro-history of the global and national political economies (Fuchs and Moch, Schneider and Schneider, Bradley, Fricke, Hammel) and the micro-history of community and individual lives (Launay, Bledsoe, Carter), the authors have made history an ingredient in the making of reproduction and actors an ingredient in the making of history.

Fifth and finally, the chapters have pointed the way to a more gendered type of reproductive analysis. Although more work needs to be done to bring out the centrality of gender in reproductive life, the chapters of Fuchs and Moch, Bradley, and Carter, in particular, have made important advances in shifting conceptual ground from women's roles and status to gender – with its notions of agency and power, among other things – as an organizing concept in the analysis of reproductive life.

Considerable progress has thus been made in mapping out the conceptual terrain for an anthropology of fertility. Yet much more remains to be done. Three tasks in particular demand attention. First, we have made time central to reproductive analysis, but space remains underconceptualized. An important task for future research is to theorize the spatial dimension of reproductive processes and chart its empirical contours.

A second task is to turn a critical eye on our own demographic praxis. In recent years anthropologists have grown increasingly aware of the politics of their own research and the ethnographies they produce. In demographic anthropology too we need to problematize the relation between observer and observed, and to study the political implications of our methods, our modes of presentation of research results, and our funding arrangements to see whether we too are not complicit in perpetuating relations of unequal power.

Finally, we need to foster intra-disciplinary dialogue about reproductive research. In this volume we have sought ways to integrate three perspectives on fertility that are currently popular within the cultural branch of the field. But these are not the only perspectives on reproduction competing for anthropological attention today. Within cultural anthropology, a variety of ecological and evolutionary perspectives have flourished, while still other approaches are being elaborated within the biological and archeological branches of the field. A crucial task for anthropology is to initiate a dialogue between these largely non-communicating discourses. If we are to make reproduction more central to the anthropological project, we need to begin by sorting out the various approaches, agreeing on their strengths and weaknesses, and cataloging their separate and collective contributions to the understanding of central anthropological problems.

References

Abernethy, Virginia D. 1993. *Population Politics: The Choices that Shape our Future*. New York: Plenum.

Achebe, Chinua. 1969. *Arrow of God: A Novel of an Old Nigeria and a New Colonialism*. Garden City, New York: Anchor Books.

Adegbola, O. 1987. "A comparative analysis of children of informal and formal unions." Paper presented at the IUSSP seminar on Mortality and Society in Sub-Saharan Africa. Yaoundé, Cameroon.

Akhter, Halida H. and Rowland V. Rider. 1983. "Menstrual regulation versus contraception in Bangladesh," *Studies in Family Planning* 14, no. 12: 318–323.

Alonso, William and Paul Starr (eds.). 1987. *The Politics of Numbers*. New York: Russell Sage.

Alter, George. 1988. *Family and the Female Life Course: The Women of Verviers, Belgium, 1849–1880*. Madison, WI: University of Wisconsin Press.

Amin, Samir. 1988. *Eurocentrism*. New York: Monthly Review Press.

Anderson, Barbara. 1986. "Regional and cultural factors in the decline of marital fertility in Western Europe," in Ansley J. Coale and Susan C. Watkins (eds.), *The Decline of Fertility in Europe*. Princeton: Princeton University Press, pp. 293–313.

Anderson, Michael. 1971. *Family Structure in Nineteenth-Century Lancashire*. Cambridge: Cambridge University Press.

Andorka, Rudolph. 1971. "La prevention des naissances en Hongrie dans la region Ormánásag depuis la fin du XVIIIe siècle," *Population* 25: 63–73.

1972. "Une example de faible fecondité dans une region de la Hongrie, l'Ormánásag à la fin du XVIIIe siècle et au début du XIXe: Controle de naissances ou faux-semblant?" *Annales de Demographie Historique* 23–43.

1976. "The peasant family structure in the eighteenth and nineteenth centuries: Data from Alsönyék and Kölked in international comparison," *Acta Ethnographica Academiae Scientarium Hugaricae* 25: 321–348.

1979a. "Family reconstitution and types of household structure," in J. Sundin, and E. Soderlund (eds.), *Time, Space, and Man*. Stockholm: Almquist and Wicksell, pp. 11–33.

1979b. "Birth control in the 18th and 19th centuries in some Hungarian villages,"

Local Population Studies 22: 38–42.

1984. "Early birth control in marriage in some Hungarian villages." Population Association of America. 5 May. Minneapolis: Minnesota.

1986. "Review. Review symposium: The decline of fertility in Europe, Ansley J. Coale, and Susan Cotts Watkins (eds.)," *Population and Development Review* 12, no. 2: 329–334.

Andorka, Rudolph and Sandor Balazs-Kovacs. 1986. "The social demography of Hungarian villages in the eighteenth and nineteenth centuries (with special attention to Sárpilis, 1792–1804)," *Journal of Family History* 11: 169–192.

Andorka, Rudolph and T. Farago. 1983. "Pre-industrial household structure in Hungary," in R. Wall, R. Robin, and P. Laslett (eds.), *Family Forms in Historic Europe*. Cambridge: Cambridge University Press, pp. 281–307.

Andrews, Frank, James Morgan, John Sondquist, and Laura Klem. 1973. *Multiple Classification Analysis*, Second Edition. Ann Arbor: Institute for Social Research, University of Michigan.

Angeli, Aurora and Athos Bellettini. 1979. "Strutture familiari nella campagna bolognese a metà dell'ottocento," *Genus* 35: 155–172.

Anker, Richard, Mayra Buvinic, and Nadia H. Youssef (eds.). 1982. *Women's Roles and Population Trends in the Third World*. London: Croom Helm.

Axinn, William G., Tom Fricke, and Arland Thornton. 1991. "The microdemographic community study approach: Improving data quality by integrating the ethnographic method," *Sociological Methods and Research* 20, no. 2: 187–217.

Bačić, A. 1732. *Istina katoličanska* (The Catholic truth). Buda.

Baker T. and M. Bird. 1959. "Urbanisation and the position of women," *The Sociological Review* 7: 99–122.

Barnard, Alan and Anthony Good. 1984. *Research Practices in the Study of Kinship*. Orlando: Academic Press.

Bateson, Gregory. 1972. *Steps to an Ecology of Mind*. New York: Ballantine.

Becker, Gary S. 1960. "An economic analysis of fertility," in *Demographic and Economic Change in Developed Countries*. National Bureau of Economic Research. Princeton: Princeton University Press, pp. 209–231.

1976. *The Economic Approach to Human Behavior*. Chicago: University of Chicago Press.

Bellettini, Athos. 1978. "La popolazione di Bologna nel corso dell'ottocento," *Storia Urbana* 5: 3–23.

Ben-Porath, Yoram. 1978. *The F-Connection: Families, Friends and Firms and the Origin of Exchange*. Santa Monica, CA: The Rand Paper Series.

Berger, Peter L. and Thomas Luckmann. 1967. *The Social Construction of Reality: A Treatise in the Sociology of Knowledge*. New York: Doubleday.

Bertaux-Wiame, Isabelle. 1979. "The life history approach to the study of internal migration," *Oral History* 7: 28–29.

Bertillon, Jacques. 1911. *La dépopulation de la France: ses conséquences, ses causes, mesures à prendre pour la combattre*. Paris: Félix Alcan.

Betzig, Laura, Monique Borgerhoff Mulder, and Paul Turke (eds.). 1988. *Human Reproductive Behavior: A Darwinian Perspective*. Cambridge: Cambridge University Press.

Biskupija Djakovačko-srijemsko (Bishopric of Djakovo and Srem). 1873a. *Glasnik* (Herald), Podučavanje primalja (The education of midwives), Djakovo. 11: 82–84.

1873b. *Glasnik* (Herald). (A series of articles on the decline in population and annual numbers of births and deaths, compiled from parish registers starting about 1783, with various comments by local priests in 1873.) Vol. I, nos. 6, 9, 11, 13, 16, 17, 18, 19, 21, 24.

1874. *Glasnik*. Naš narod propada? (Is our nation falling apart? Article by F. F. Zašto.) Vol. II, nos. 13–18.

1930a. *Glasnik*. Slavonija umire. (Slavonia is dying. Article by Ivan Berti.) Vol. LVIII, no. 1: 6–8.

1930b. *Glasnik*. Statistics on births. Vol. LVIII, nos. 5, 19.

1930c. *Glasnik*. Problem nataliteta i mortaliteta, te depopulacije u Slavoniji. (The problem of natality, mortality, and thus depopulation in Slavonia. Article by Ivan Berti.) Vol. LVIII, no. 19: 159–161.

Blalock, Hubert M. 1972. *Social Statistics*. New York: McGraw Hill.

Blaut, J.M. 1993. *The Colonizer's Model of the World: Geographical Diffusionism and Eurocentric History*. New York: Guilford Press.

Bledsoe, Caroline. 1980. *Women and Marriage in Kpelle Society*. Stanford: Stanford University Press.

1990a. "The politics of AIDS, condoms, and heterosexual relations in Africa: Recent evidence from the local print media," in W. Penn Handwerker (ed.), *Births and Power: Social Change and the Politics of Reproduction*. Boulder: Westview Press, pp. 197–223.

1990b. "The politics of children: Fosterage and the social management of fertility among the Mende of Sierra Leone," in W. Penn Handwerker (ed.), *Births and Power: Social Change and the Politics of Reproduction*. Boulder: Westview Press, pp. 81–100.

1990c. "School girls and the marriage process for Mende girls in Sierra Leone," in Peggy Sanday and Ruth Goodenough (eds.), *Beyond the Second Sex: New Directions in the Anthropology of Gender*. Philadelphia: University of Pennsylvania Press, pp. 283–309.

1991. "The trickle-down model within households: Foster children and the phenomenon of scrounging," in John Cleland and Allan G. Hill (eds.), *The Health Transition: Methods and Measures, The Proceedings of an International Workshop, London, June 1989*. Canberra: Health Transition Centre, Australian National University, pp. 115–131.

1993. "The politics of polygyny in Mende education and child fosterage transactions," in Barbara Diane Miller (ed.), *Sex and Gender Hierarchies*. Cambridge: Cambridge University Press, pp. 170–192.

Bledsoe, Caroline, Douglas Ewbank, and Uche Isiugo-Abanihe. 1988. "The effect of child fostering on feeding practices and access to health services in rural Sierra Leone," *Social Science and Medicine* 27: 627–636.

Bledsoe, Caroline, Allan G. Hill, Umberto D'Allesandro, and Patricia Langerock. 1994. "Constructing natural fertility: The use of Western contraceptive technologies in rural Gambia," *Population and Development Review* 20, no. 1: 81–113.

Bledsoe, Caroline and Helen K. Hirschman. 1989. "Case studies of mortality: Anthropological contributions." Paper presented at the 21st General Conference of the International Union for the Scientific Study of Population, September, 1989. New Delhi, India.

Bledsoe, Caroline and Uche C. Isiugo-Abanihe. 1989. "Strategies of child fosterage among Mende 'grannies' in Sierra Leone," in Ron Lesthaeghe (ed.), *African Reproduction and Social Organization*. Berkeley: University of California Press, pp. 442–474.

Bleek, Wolf. 1987. "Lying informants: A fieldwork experience from Ghana," *Population and Development Review* 13, no. 2: 314–322.

Blok, Anton. 1966. "Land reform in a west Sicilian latifondo village: The persistence of a feudal structure," *Anthropological Quarterly* 39: 1–16.

Bogišić, V. 1874. *Gragja u odgovorima iz različnih krajeva slavenskog juga*. (Data in answers from various parts of the Slavic south.) Zagreb: Jugoslavenska Akademija Znanosti i Umjetnosti.

Bongaarts, John. 1978. "A framework for analyzing the proximate determinants of fertility," *Population and Development Review* 4, no. 1: 105–132.

   1980. "Does malnutrition affect fecundity? A summary of evidence," *Science* 208: 564–569.

Borruso, Vincenzo. 1966. *Pratiche abortive e controllo delle nascite in Sicilia*. Palermo: Libri Siciliani.

Boston Women's Health Collective. 1984. *The New Our Bodies, Ourselves*. New York: Simon and Schuster, Touchstone Books.

Bourdieu, Pierre. 1976. "Marriage strategies as strategies of social reproduction," in R. Forster and O. Ranum (eds.), *Family and Society: Selections from the Annales*. Baltimore: Johns Hopkins University Press, pp. 117–146.

   1977. *Outline of a Theory of Practice*. Cambridge: Cambridge University Press.

Bouvier, Jeanne. 1983. *Mes Mémoires: Une syndicaliste féministe, 1876–1935*. Paris: Maspéro.

Boxer, Marilyn. 1982. "Women in industrial homework: The flowermakers of Paris in the Belle Epoque," *French Historical Studies* 12: 401–423.

Bradley, Candice. 1993. "Altered promises and changed expectations: Fertility and the decline of bridewealth in Kenya." Paper presented at American Anthropological Association meetings, Washington, D.C.

   1994. "Declining fertility and wealth flows in Maragoli," in Thomas Weisner, Candice Bradley, and Philip Kilbride (eds.), *African Families and the Crisis of Social Change*. CT: Greenwood.

   1995. "The Abaluyia," in John Middleton and A. Rassam (eds.), *Encyclopedia of World Cultures*. Vol. 9, *Africa and the Middle East*. NY: G. K. Hall-Macmillan.

Browner, Carole. 1985. "Traditional techniques for diagnosis, treatment and control of pregnancy in Cali, Colombia," in Lucile F. Newman (ed.), *Women's Medicine: A Cross-Cultural Study of Indigenous Fertility Regulation*. New Brunswick, NJ: Rutgers University Press, pp. 99–123.

   1986. "The politics of reproduction in a Mexican village," *Signs* 11, no. 4: 711–724.

Browner, Carole and Ellen Lewin. 1982. "Female altruism reconsidered: The Virgin Mary as economic woman," *American Ethnologist* 9, no. 1: 61–75.

Browner, Carole and Sondra T. Perdue. 1988. "Women's secrets: Bases for reproductive and social autonomy in a Mexican community," *American Ethnologist* 15, no. 1: 84–97.

Buchanan, Francis H. 1971 [1819]. *An Account of the Kingdom of Nepal.* New Delhi: Mañjuśrī Publishing House.

Bulatao, Rodolfo A. et al. 1983. "A framework for the study of fertility determinants," in R. A. Bulatao and R. D. Lee (eds.), *Determinants of Fertility in Developing Countries*, Vol. I. New York: Academic Press, pp. 1–26.

Bulatao, Rodolfo A. and Ronald D. Lee (eds.). 1983. *Determinants of Fertility in Developing Countries.* 2 Vols. New York: Academic Press.

Burgess, H. J. L., S. Cole-King, and A. Burgess. 1972. "Nutritional status of children at Namitambo, Malawi," *Journal of Tropical Medicine and Hygiene* 73, 8: 143–148.

Burghardt, Richard. 1984. "The formation of the concept of Nation-State in Nepal," *Journal of Asian Studies* 54, no. 1: 101–125.

Burnham, Philip. 1987. "Changing themes in the analysis of African marriage," in D. Parkin and D. Nyamawaya (eds.), *Transformations of African Marriage.* Manchester: Manchester University Press, pp. 37–54.

Buturac, Josip. 1930. "Žiteljstvo u Moslavini. Problem nataliteta i mortaliteta u prošlosti i danas." (Population in the Moslavina. The problem of natality and mortality in the past and today.) Zagreb: *Hrvatska straža* II, no. 293: 10–11.

——— 1941a. "Bijela kuga u Požeškoj kotlini." (The white plague in the Požega basin.) *Katolički list* 92, no. 33: 390–391.

——— 1941b. "Natalitet djakovačke biskupije 1931–1939." (Natality of the bishopric of Djakovo 1931–39.) Zagreb: *Katolički list* 92, no. 23: 269–271.

——— 1941c. "Natalitet senjske i modruške biskupije 1931–1939." (Natality of the bishoprics of Senj and Modruška 1931–39.) Zagreb: *Katolički list* 92, no. 24: 279–281.

——— 1941d. "Natalitet u Bosni i Primorju 1931–1939. (Natality in Bosnia and the Littoral 1931–39.) Zagreb: *Katolički list* 92, no. 25: 291–293.

——— 1941e. "Žiteljstvo Zagrebačke nadbiskupije kroz 150 godina." (The population of the archdiocese of Zagreb over 150 years.) *Katolički list* 92, no. 26: 304–306, no. 28: 328–330, no. 29: 337–339, no. 30: 352–354.

Cain, Mead. 1977. "The economic activities of children in a village in Bangladesh," *Population and Development Review* 3, no. 3: 201–227.

——— 1981. "Risk and insurance: Perspectives on fertility and agrarian change in India and Bangladesh," *Population and Development Review* 7, no. 3: 435–474.

——— 1982. "Perspectives on family and fertility in developing countries," *Population Studies* 36, no. 2: 159–175.

——— 1983. "Fertility as an adjustment to risk," *Population and Development Review* 9, no. 4: 688–702.

——— 1984. "Women's status and fertility in developing countries: Son preference and economic security." Working Paper 110. NY: The Population Council Center for Policy Studies.

——— 1986. "The consequences of reproductive failure: Dependence, mobility, and mortality among the elderly of rural South Asia," *Population Studies* 40, no. 3: 375–388.

Cain, Mead, Syeda Rokeya Khanam, and Shamsun Nahar. 1979. "Class, patriarchy, and women's work in Bangladesh," *Population and Development Review* 5, no. 3: 405–438.

Caldwell, John C. 1976. "Toward a restatement of demographic transition theory," *Population and Development Review* 2, nos. 3/4: 321–366.

1978. "A theory of fertility: From high plateau to destabilization," *Population and Development Review* 4, no. 4: 553–577.

1980. "Mass education as a determinant of the timing of fertility decline," *Population and Development Review* 6, no. 2: 225–255.

1982. *Theory of Fertility Decline*. London: Academic Press.

Caldwell, John C. and Pat Caldwell. 1987. "The cultural context of high fertility in sub-Saharan Africa," *Population and Development Review* 13, no. 3: 409–437.

1994. "Marital status and abortion in sub-Saharan Africa," in Caroline Bledsoe and Gilles Pison (eds.), *Nuptiality in Sub-Saharan Africa: Contemporary Anthropological and Demographic Perspectives*. Oxford: Clarendon Press, pp. 274–295.

Caldwell, John C., Pat Caldwell, and Bruce Caldwell. 1987. "Anthropology and demography: The mutual reinforcement of speculation and research," *Current Anthropology* 28, no. 1: 25–43.

Caldwell, John C., Allan G. Hill, and Valerie J. Hull (eds.). 1988. *Micro-Approaches to Demographic Research*. London: Kegan Paul International.

Caldwell, John C., P. H. Reddy, and Pat Caldwell. 1982. "The causes of demographic change in rural South India: A micro approach," *Population and Development Review* 8, no. 4: 689–727.

1988. *The Causes of Demographic Change*. Madison: University of Wisconsin Press.

Čapo, Jasna. 1986. "Annual fluctuations in births, marriages and deaths in Cernik, Slavonia, from 1755 to 1855." Unpublished Master's thesis. Berkeley: Graduate Group in Demography, University of California.

1990. 'Economic and demographic history of peasant households on a Croatian estate, 1756-1848.' Unpublished doctoral dissertation. Berkeley: Graduate Group in Demography, University of California.

1991. *Vlastelinstvo Cernik: Gospodarstvene i demografske promjene na hrvatskome selu u kasnome feudalizmu* (The estate of Cernik: Economic and demographic change in the Croatian village in late feudalism). Zagreb: Institut za Etnologiju i Folkloristiku.

Caroli, Betty Boyd. 1973. *Italian Repatriation from the United States, 1900-1914*. New York: Center for Migration Studies.

Carter, Anthony T. 1984. "Sex of offspring and fertility in South Asia: Demographic variance and decision procedures in 'joint family' households," *Journal of Family History* 9: 273–290.

1985. "The seasonality of birth in the Punjab." Paper presented at the University of Wisconsin Conference on South Asian Studies, November 1985.

Casarrubea, Giuseppe. 1978. *I Fasci Contadini e le Origini delle Sezioni Socialiste della Provincia di Palermo*. Palermo: S. F. Flaccovio.

Cashdan, Elizabeth A. 1985. "Natural fertility, birth spacing, and the 'first demographic transition,'" *American Anthropologist* 87, no. 3: 650–653.

Cassell, Carol. 1984. *Swept Away: Why Women Fear Their Own Sexuality.* New York: Simon and Schuster.

Cassidy, C.M. 1980. "Benign neglect and toddler malnutrition," in Lawrence S. Greene and Francis E. Johnston (eds.), *Social and Biological Predictors of Nutritional Status, Physical Growth, and Neurological Development.* New York: Academic Press, pp. 109–139.

Central Bureau of Statistics (CBS). 1984. *Kenya Contraceptive Prevalence Survey.* First Report. Nairobi: Ministry of Planning and National Development.

Chabot, Paul. 1977. *Jean et Yvonne, domestiques en 1900: Souvenirs recueillis par Michel Chabot.* Paris: TEMA.

Chen, Lincoln C., Emdadul Huq, and Stan D'Souza. 1981. "Sex bias in the family allocation of food and health care in rural Bangladesh," *Population and Development Review* 7, no. 1: 55–70.

Chevalier, Louis. 1950. *La formation de la population parisienne au XIXe siècle.* Paris: Presses Universitaires Françaises.

Chisholm, James S. 1993. "Death, hope, and sex: Life-history theory and the development of reproductive strategies," *Current Anthropology* 34, no. 1: 1–24.

Clark, Gregory. 1988. "Economists in search of culture: The unspeakable in pursuit of the inedible?" *Historical Methods* 21: 161–164.

Clark, Martin. 1984. *Modern Italy, 1871–1982.* London and New York: Longman.

Clarke, Edith. 1957. *My Mother Who Fathered Me.* London: George Allen and Unwin.

Cleland, John. 1985. "Marital fertility decline in developing countries: Theories and the evidence," in John Cleland and John Hobcraft (eds.), *Reproductive Change in Developing Countries: Insights from the World Fertility Survey.* Oxford: Oxford University Press, pp. 223–252.

Cleland, John and Christopher Wilson. 1987. "Demand theories of the fertility transition: An iconoclastic view," *Population Studies* 41, no. 1: 5–30.

Clignet, Rémi. 1987. "On dit que la polygamie est morte: Vive la polygamie!" in D. Parkin and D. Nyamawaya (eds.), *Transformations of African Marriage.* Manchester: Manchester University Press, pp. 199–209.

Coale, Ansley J. 1973. "The demographic transition," in IUSSP (ed.), *International Population Conference, Liege, 1973*, Vol. 1. Liege: International Union for the Scientific Study of Population, pp. 53–72.

Coale, Ansley J. and Susan C. Watkins (eds.). 1986. *The Decline of Fertility in Europe.* Princeton: Princeton University Press.

Coffin, Judith. 1991. "Social science meets sweated labor," *Journal of Modern History* 63: 230–270.

Coleman, David and Roger Schofield (eds.). 1986. *The State of Population Theory: Forward From Malthus.* Oxford: Basil Blackwell.

Coleman, Samuel. 1983. *Family Planning in Japanese Society: Traditional Birth Control in a Modern Urban Culture.* Princeton: Princeton University Press.

Collier, Jane F. 1988. *Marriage and Inequality in Classless Societies.* Stanford: Stanford University Press.

Collier, Jane and S.J. Yanagisako. 1989. "Theory in anthropology since feminist practice," *Critique of Anthropology* 9, no. 2: 27–37.

Comaroff, John. 1980. "Bridewealth in a Tswana chiefdom," in John Comaroff (ed.), *The Meaning of Marriage Payments.* London: Academic Press, pp. 161–196.

Comaroff, John and Simon Roberts. 1977. "Marriage and extra-marital sexuality: The dialectics of legal change among the Kgatla," *Journal of African Law* 21, no. 1: 97–123.

1981. *Rules and Processes: The Cultural Logic of Dispute in an African Context.* Chicago: University of Chicago Press.

Comas d'Argemir, Dolors. 1988. "Household, family, and social stratification: Inheritance and labor strategies in a Catalan village," *Journal of Family History* 13: 143–163.

Connell, Robert W. 1985. "Theorizing gender," *Sociology* 19, no. 2: 260–272.

Coons, L. 1985. "Orphans of the sweated trades: Women homeworkers in the Parisian garment industry 1860–1915." Ph.D dissertation, New York University.

Corbin, Alain. 1975. *Archaïsme et modernité en Limousin au XIXe siècle.* 2 Vols. Paris: Marcel Rivière.

Cressy, David. 1986. "Kinship and kin interaction in early modern England," *Past and Present* 113: 38–69.

Czap, Peter. 1982. "The perennial multiple family household, Mishino, Russia," *Journal of Family History* 7: 5–26.

1983. "'A large family: The peasant's greatest wealth': Serf households in Mishino, Russia, 1814–1858," in R. Wall, J. Robin, and P. Laslett (eds.), *Family Forms in Historic Europe.* Cambridge: Cambridge University Press, pp. 105–151.

Dahal, Dilli R., Tom Fricke, and Arland Thornton. 1993. "The family contexts of marriage timing in Nepal," *Ethnology* 32, no. 4: 305–323.

Darrow, Margaret H. 1989. *Revolution in the House: Family, Class, and Inheritance in Southern France, 1775–1825.* Princeton: Princeton University Press.

Das Gupta, Monica. 1987. "Selective discrimination against female children in rural Punjab, India," *Population and Development Review* 13, no. 1: 77–100.

David, P. and T.A. Mroz. 1986. "A sequential econometric model of birth-spacing behavior among rural French villagers, 1749–1789." Stanford Project on the History of Fertility Control. Working Paper No. 19.

David, P., T.A. Mroz, and K. W. Wachter. 1985. "Rational strategies of birth-spacing and fertility regulation in rural France during the Ancien Régime." Stanford Project on the History of Fertility Control. Working Paper No. 14.

Davis, Kingsley. 1939. "The forms of illegitimacy," *Social Forces* 18: 77–89.

1945. "The world demographic transition," *The Annals of the American Academy of Political and Social Sciences* 237: 1–11.

Davison, Jean. 1985. "Achievements and constraints among rural Kenyan women," in Gideon Were (ed.), *Women and Development in Africa.* Nairobi: G.S. Were Press, pp. 268–279.

De Stefano, F. and F.L. Oddo. 1963. *Storia della Sicilia dal 1860 al 1910.* Bari: Laterza.

de Wolf, Jan. 1978–79. "Local leadership in northwestern Bungoma district, Kenya," *Rural Africana* 3: 61–78.

deMause, Lloyd. 1974. *The History of Childhood.* New York: Psychohistory.

Demeny, Paul. 1968. "Early fertility decline in Austria-Hungary: A lesson in demographic transition," *Daedalus* (Spring): 502–522.

Dérive, J., and M. J. Dérive. 1986. "Francophonie et pratique linquistique en Côte d'Ivoire," *Politique Africaine* 23: 42–56.

Devereux, George. 1955. *A Study of Abortion in Primitive Societies.* New York: International Universities Press (Revised edition publ. 1976).

di Leonardo, Micaela. 1991. "Introduction: Gender, culture, and political economy: Feminist anthropology in historical perspective," in *Gender at the Crossroads of Knowledge: Feminist Anthropology in the Postmodern Era.* Berkeley: University of California Press, pp. 1–48.

Dixon-Mueller, Ruth. 1993. *Population Policy and Women's Rights: Transforming Reproductive Choice.* Westport: Praeger.

Donzelot, Jacques. 1979. *The Policing of Families,* trans. Robert Hurley. New York: Pantheon.

Došen, Vid. 1969. "Aždaja sedmoglavna" (The seven-headed dragon), in Tomo Matić and Antun Djamić (eds.), *Djela Vida Došena* Stari pisci hrvatski XXXIV: Jugoslavenska Akademija Znanosti i Umjetnosti.

Društva gospodarskoga hervatsko-slavonskoga (Croatian-Slavonian Management Society). 1850. *List* (Newspaper), IX. Zagreb.

Dyke, Bennett. 1974. "Estimates of changing rates by simulation," in Bennett Dyke and Jean W. McCluer (eds.), *Computer Simulation in Human Population Studies.* New York: Academic Press, pp. 59–69.

Dyson, Tim and Mick Moore. 1983. "On kinship structure, female autonomy, and demographic behavior in India," *Population and Development Review* 9, no. 1: 35–60.

Easterlin, Richard A. 1976. "Population change and farm settlement in the northern United States," *Journal of Economic History* 36: 45–75.

1978. "The economics and sociology of fertility: A synthesis," in Charles Tilly (ed.), *Historical Studies of Changing Fertility.* Princeton: Princeton University Press, pp. 57–133.

Easterlin, Richard A. and Eileen M. Crimmins. 1985. *The Fertility Revolution: A Supply–Demand Analysis.* Chicago: University of Chicago Press.

Elliot, Vivian Brodsky. 1981. "Single women in the London marriage market: Age, status and mobility," in *Marriage and Society: Studies in the Social History of Marriage.* London: Europa Publications, Ltd, pp. 81–100.

Engel, Franc Štefan. 1971 [1786]. *Opis kraljevine Slavonije i vojvodstva Srema* (Description of the kingdom of Slavonia and the duchy of Srem). Zbornik matice srpske za književnost i jezik XIX (2): 289–356.

English, Richard. 1985. "Himalayan state formation and the impact of British rule in the nineteenth century," *Mountain Research and Development* 5, no. 1: 61–78.

Eshiwani, George. 1990. *Implementing Educational Policies in Kenya.* World Bank Discussion Papers: Africa Technical Department Series No. 85. Washington, DC: The World Bank.

Evans-Pritchard, E. E. 1965. *The Position of Women in Primitive Societies and Other Essays in Social Anthropology.* New York: The Free Press.

Farson, Negley. 1949. *Last Chance in Africa.* London: Victor Gollancz Ltd.

Fawcett, James T. 1983. "Perceptions of the value of children: Satisfactions and costs," in R.A. Bulatao and R. D. Lee (eds.), *Determinants of Fertility in Developing Countries,* Vol. I. New York: Academic Press, pp. 429–457.

Featherstone, Mike, Mike Hepworth, and Bryan S. Turner (eds). 1991. *The Body: Social Process and Cultural Theory.* London: Sage Publications.

Ferree, Myra Marx. 1990. "Beyond separate spheres: Feminism and family research," *Journal of Marriage and the Family* 52, no. 4: 866–884.

Findley, Sally and Assitan Diallo. 1988. "Foster children: Links between urban and rural families?" *Proceedings of the African Population Conference, Dakar, Session V2*, Vol. 2. Liège: International Union for the Scientific Study of Population, pp. 43–57.

Finkle, Jason L. and Barbara B. Crane. 1975. "The politics of Bucharest: Population, development, and the New International Economic Order," *Population and Development Review* 1, no. 1: 87–114.

1976. "The World Health Organization and the population issue: Organizational values in the United Nations," *Population and Development Review* 2, no. 3/4: 367–393.

1985. "Ideology and politics at Mexico City: The United States at the 1984 international conference on population," *Population and Development Review* 11, no. 1: 1–28.

Finkle, Jason L. and Alison McIntosh (eds.). 1994. *The Politics of Family Planning in the Third World*. Supplement to *Population and Development Review* 20.

Firth, Raymond. 1936. *We, The Tikopia: A Sociological Study of Kinship in Primitive Polynesia*. London: George Allen and Unwin.

Foerster, Robert F. 1969 [1924]. *The Italian Emigration of our Times*. New York: Arno Press.

Folbre, Nancy. 1986. "Hearts and spades: Paradigms of household economics," *World Development* 14, no. 2: 245–255.

1990. "Mothers on their own: Policy issues for developing countries. International Center for Research on Women." New York: The Population Council.

Fortes, Meyer. 1949. *The Web of Kinship Among the Tallensi*. London: Oxford University Press.

1954. "A demographic field study in Ashanti," in *Culture and Human Fertility*, by Frank Lorimer with contributors. Paris: UNESCO, pp. 255–339.

1958. "Introduction," in Jack Goody (ed.), *The Developmental Cycle in Domestic Groups*. Cambridge: Cambridge University Press, pp. 1–13.

1969. *Kinship and the Social Order*. Chicago: Aldine.

Foucault, Michel. 1978. *The History of Sexuality: An Introduction*, Vol. 1. New York: Vintage Books.

1979. *Discipline and Punish*, trans. Alan Sheridan. New York: Vintage Books.

Fraenkel, Merran. 1964. *Tribe and Class in Monrovia*. London: Oxford University Press.

Fricke, Tom. 1990. "Elementary structures in the Nepal Himalaya: Reciprocity and the politics of hierarchy in Ghale-Tamang marriage," *Ethnology* 29, no. 2: 135–158.

1994 [1986]. *Himalayan Households: Tamang Demography and Domestic Processes*. Expanded edition. New York: Columbia University Press.

Fricke, Tom, William Axinn, and Arland Thornton. 1993. "Marriage, social inequality, and women's contact with their natal families in alliance societies," *American Anthropologist* 95, no. 2: 395–419.

Fricke, Tom and Jay D. Teachman. 1993. "Writing the names: Marriage style, living arrangements, and family building in a Nepali society," *Demography* 30, no. 2: 175–188.

Fuchs, Rachel G. 1992. *Poor and Pregnant in Paris: Strategies for Survival in the Nineteenth Century.* New Brunswick, NJ: Rutgers University Press.

Fuchs, Rachel G. and Leslie Page Moch. 1990. "Pregnant, single, and far from home: Migrant women in nineteenth-century Paris," *The American Historical Review* 95, no. 4: 1007–1031.

Gabaccia, Donna. 1984. *From Sicily to Elizabeth Street: Housing and Social Change among Italian Immigrants, 1880–1930.* Albany: State University of New York Press.

1988. *Militants and Migrants: Rural Sicilians become American Workers.* New Brunswick: Rutgers University Press.

Gage, Anastasia and Caroline Bledsoe. 1994. "The effects of education and social stratification on marriage and the transition to parenthood in Greater Freetown, Sierra Leone," in Caroline Bledsoe and Gilles Pison (eds.), *Nuptiality in Sub-Saharan Africa: Contemporary Anthropological and Demographic Perspectives.* Oxford: Clarendon Press, pp. 148–164.

Gallagher, Catherine and Thomas Laqueur (eds.). 1983. *The Making of the Modern Body.* Berkeley: University of California Press.

Galloway, Patrick R. 1987. "Population, prices and weather in preindustrial Europe." Unpublished doctoral dissertation. Graduate Group in Demography, University of California, Berkeley.

1988. "Basic patterns in annual variations in fertility, nuptiality, mortality and prices in pre-industrial Europe," *Population Studies* 42: 275–302.

Ganci, Massimo. 1980. *La Sicilia Contemporanea: Storia di Napoli e della Sicilia.* Palermo, Napoli: Società Editrice.

Gaunt, David. 1983. "The property and kin relationships of retired farmers in Northern and Central Europe," in R. Wall, J. Robin, and P. Laslett (eds.), *Family Forms in Historic Europe.* Cambridge: Cambridge University Press, pp. 249–280.

Geertz, Clifford. 1973. *The Interpretation of Cultures.* New York: Basic Books.

1984. "Culture and social change: The Indonesian case," *Man* (n.s.) 19: 511–532.

Gelo, Jakov. 1987. *Demografske promjene u Hrvatskoj* (Demographic changes in Croatia). Zagreb: Globus.

Giddens, Anthony. 1979. *Central Problems in Social Theory: Action, Structure and Contradiction in Social Analysis.* Berkeley: University of California Press.

Gillis, John R., Louise A. Tilly, and David Levine (eds.). 1992. *The European Experience of Declining Fertility, 1850–1970: The Quiet Revolution.* Cambridge: Blackwell.

Ginsburg, Faye. 1989. *Contested Lives: The Abortion Debate in an American Community.* Berkeley: University of California Press.

Ginsburg, Faye and Rayna Rapp. 1991. "The politics of reproduction," *Annual Review of Anthropology* 20: 311–343.

(eds.). 1994. *Conceiving the New World Order: Local/Global Intersections in the Politics of Reproduction.* Berkeley: University of California Press.

Ginsburg, Faye and Anna Lowenhaupt Tsing (eds.). 1990. *Uncertain Terms: Negotiating Gender in American Culture.* Boston: Beacon.

Gold, Ann. 1988. *Fruitful Journeys*. Berkeley: University of California Press.

Goode, William J. 1964. *The Family*. Englewood Cliffs, NJ: Prentice Hall.

Goody, Esther. 1992. *Parenthood and Social Reproduction: Fostering and Occupational Roles in West Africa*. Cambridge: Cambridge University Press.

Goody, Jack. 1976. *Production and Reproduction: A Comparative Study of the Domestic Domain*. Cambridge: Cambridge University Press.

1990. *The Oriental, the Ancient, and the Primitive: Systems of Marriage and the Family in Pre-Industrial Societies of Eurasia*. New York: Cambridge University Press.

Gordon, Linda. 1977. *Women's Body, Women's Right: A Social History of Birth Control in America*. Baltimore: Penguin.

Granovetter, Mark S. 1973. "The strength of weak ties," *American Journal of Sociology* 78, no. 3: 1360–1380.

1974. *Getting a Job*. Cambridge, MA: Harvard University Press.

Greenhalgh, Susan. 1990. "Toward a political economy of fertility: Anthropological contributions," *Population and Development Review* 16, no. 1: 85–106.

1994. "Controlling births and bodies in village China," *American Ethnologist* 21, no. 1: 3–30.

Greenhalgh, Susan and Jiali Li. 1995. "Engendering reproductive policy and practice in peasant China: For a feminist demography of reproduction," *Signs: Journal of Women in Culture and Society* 20, no. 3.

Gribaudi, Maurizio. 1987. *Les itinéraires ouvriers: Espaces et groupes sociaux à Turin au début du XXe siècle*. Paris: Editions de l'Ecole des Hautes Etudes en Sciences Sociales, 113–122.

Guči, Ante. 1880. "Kako se može preranoj ženitbi u Posavini na put stati. (How to stop premature marriage in the Posavina), *Liječnički viestnik* IV (1): 1–9. Zagreb.

Guiral, Pierre, and Guy Thuillier. 1978. *La vie quotidienne des domestiques en France au XIXe siècle*. Paris: Hachette.

Gutiérrez, Ramón A. 1991. *When Jesus Came, the Corn Mothers Went Away: Marriage, Sexuality, and Power in New Mexico, 1500–1846*. Stanford: Stanford University Press.

Guyer, Jane I. 1981. "Household and community in African Studies," *African Studies Review* 24, no. 2/3: 87–137.

1994. "Polyandrous motherhood: Lineal identities and lateral networks in marital change in a rural Yoruba community," in Caroline Bledsoe and Gilles Pison (eds.), *Nuptiality in Sub-Saharan Africa: Contemporary Anthropological and Demographic Perspectives*. Oxford: Clarendon Press, pp. 231–252.

Hajnal, John. 1965. "European marriage patterns in perspective," in D.V. Glass and D.E.C. Eversley (eds.), *Population in History: Essays in Historical Demography*. London: Edwin Arnold, pp. 101–143.

1983. "Two kinds of pre-industrial household formation systems," in R. Wall, J. Robin, and P. Laslett (eds.), *Family Forms in Historic Europe*. Cambridge: Cambridge University Press, pp. 65–104.

Hammel, E. A. 1968. *Alternative Social Structures and Ritual Relations in the Balkans*. Englewood Cliffs: Prentice-Hall.

1972. "The zadruga as process," in Peter Laslett and R. Wall (eds.), *Household and Family in Past Time*. Cambridge: Cambridge University Press, pp. 335–373.

1976. "Some mediaeval evidence on the Serbian zadruga: A preliminary analysis of the chrysobulls of Decani," in R.F. Byrnes (ed.), *Communal Families in the Balkans*. University of Notre Dame Press, pp. 100–115.

1980a. "Household structure in 14th century Macedonia," *Journal of Family History* 5: 242–273.

1980b. "Sensitivity analysis of household structure in medieval Serbian censuses," *Historical Methods* 13: 105–118.

1984. "Opadanje fertiliteta u vojnoj krajini Hrvatske" (The decline of fertility in the military border of Croatia). Anthropological Society of Croatia and Ethnological Society of Croatia, Zagreb, 9 November.

1985. "Short term demographic fluctuations in the Croatian military border of Austria, 1830–47," *European Journal of Population* 1: 265–290.

1990a. "Early fertility decline in the Balkans." Annual Meetings of the Population Association of America, Toronto.

1990b. "A theory of culture for demography," *Population and Development Review* 16, no. 3: 455–485.

1992. "Cultural and economic factors in Croatian fertility decline." Annual Meetings of the Population Association of America, Denver.

1993a. "The Yugoslav labyrinth," in Harry Kreisler (ed.), *Crisis in the Balkans*. Berkeley: University of California, Institute of International Studies, pp. 1–33.

1993b. "Demography and the origins of the Yugoslav civil war," *Anthropology Today* 9: 4–9.

1993c. "Economics 1, Culture 0? Factors in early fertility decline in the northwest Balkans." Working Papers No. 34. Program in Population Research, University of California, Berkeley.

1993d. "Censored intervals in family reconstitution: A sensitivity test of alternative strategies with historical Croatian data," in D. Reher and R. Schofield (eds.), *Old and New Methods in Historical Demography*. International Studies in Demography. Oxford: Clarendon Press.

Hammel, E. A. and Beate Herrchen. 1993. "Statistical imputation in family reconstitution." *Proceedings of the IUSSP XXIInd International Population Conference*, Vol. 3. Montreal, pp. 245–258.

Hammel, E. A. and Nancy Howell. 1987. "Research in population and culture: An evolutionary framework," *Current Anthropology* 28, no. 2: 141–160.

Hammerslough, Charles. 1990. "Community determinants of demographic behavior in Kenya: First Report." Unpublished manuscript.

1991. "Women's groups and contraceptive use in rural Kenya." Unpublished manuscript.

Handwerker, W. Penn (ed.). 1986a. *Culture and Reproduction: An Anthropological Critique of Demographic Transition Theory*. Boulder: Westview.

1986b. "Culture and reproduction: Exploring micro/macro linkages," in W. P. Handwerker (ed.) *Culture and Reproduction: An Anthropological Critique of Demographic Transition Theory*. Boulder: Westview, pp. 1–28.

1986c. "The modern demographic transition: An analysis of subsistence choices and reproductive consequences," *American Anthropologist* 88, no. 2: 400–417.

1989. *Women's Power and Social Revolution: Fertility Transition in the West Indies*. Newbury Park: Sage.

(ed.). 1990. *Births and Power: Social Change and the Politics of Reproduction.* Boulder: Westview.

1991. "Women's power and fertility transition: The cases of Africa and the Caribbean," *Population and Environment* 13, no. 1: 55–78.

1993a. "Empowerment and fertility transition on Antigua, WI: Education, employment, and the moral economy of childbearing," *Human Organization* 52, no. 1: 41–52.

1993b. "Gender power differences between parents and high risk sexual behavior by their children: AIDS/STD risk factors extend to a prior generation," *Journal of Women's Health* 2: 301–316.

1993c. "Why violence?" Unpublished manuscript.

Harrell-Bond, Barbara. 1975. *Modern Marriages in Sierra Leone.* The Hague: Mouton.

Harris, Marvin. 1979. *Cultural Materialism.* New York: Random House.

Harris, Marvin and Eric B. Ross. 1987. *Death, Sex and Fertility: Population Regulation in Preindustrial and Developing Societies.* New York: Columbia University Press.

Hartley, Shirley Foster. 1975. *Illegitimacy.* Berkeley: University of California Press.

Hartmann, Betsy. 1987. *Reproductive Rights and Wrongs: The Global Politics of Population Control and Contraceptive Choice.* New York: Harper and Row.

Hassan, Fedki A. 1979. "Demography and archaeology," *Annual Review of Anthropology* 8: 137–160.

Henrey, Madeleine. 1951. *The Little Madeleine. The Autobiography of a Young Girl in Montmartre.* London: Dent and Sons.

Henry, Louis. 1961. "Some data on natural fertility," *Eugenics Quarterly* 8: 81–91.

Hietzinger, K. B.-F. and M. Stopfer. 1840. *Statistik der Militärgrenze.* Graz.

Hill, Allan G. 1990. "Demographic responses to food shortages in the Sahel," in Geoffrey McNicoll and Mead Cain (eds.), *Rural Development and Populations: Institutions and Policy. Population and Development Review,* Supplement to Vol. 15, 1989, pp. 168–192.

Höfer, András. 1969. "Preliminary report on a field research in a westernTamang group," *Bulletin of the International Committee on Urgent Anthropological and Ethnological Research* 11: 17–31.

1979. *The Caste Hierarchy and the State in Nepal: A Study of the Muluki Ain of 1854.* Innsbruck: Universitätsverlag Wagner.

Hogan, Dennis P. and David I. Kertzer. 1986. "The social bases of declining infant mortality: Lessons from a nineteenth-century Italian town," *European Journal of Population* 2: 361–386.

Hölbling, M. 1845. *Baranja Vármegyének Orvosi Helyirata* (Medical description of the county of Baranya). Pecs.

Holden, Constance. 1984. "Population studies age prematurely," *Science* 225, no. 4666 (7 September): 1003.

Holmberg, David H. 1989. *Order in Paradox: Myth, Ritual, and Exchange among Nepal's Tamang.* Ithaca: Cornell University Press.

Howell, Nancy. 1974. "The feasibility of demographic studies in 'anthropological' populations," in M. Crawford and R. Workman (eds.) *Methods and Theory in Anthropological Genetics.* Albuquerque: University of New Mexico Press, pp. 249–262.

1976. "Notes on collection and analysis of demographic field data," in John F. Marshall and Steven Polgar (eds.), *Culture, Natality, and Family Planning*. Chapel Hill, NC: Carolina Population Center, University of North Carolina, pp. 221–240.

1979. *Demography of the Dobe !Kung*. New York: Academic Press.

1986. "Demographic anthropology," *Annual Review of Anthropology* 15: 219–246.

Ilić Oriovčanin, Luka. 1846. *Narodni slavonski običaji* (Slavonian folk customs). Zagreb.

Ivić, Pavle. 1956. *Dijalektologija srpskohrvatskog jezika*. Novi Sad: Matica srpska.

1958. *Die serbokroatischen Dialekte, ihre Struktur und Entwicklung.* 's-Gravenhage: Mouton.

Jančula, Julije. 1980. *Povijest Cernička iz cernīka samostanska kronika* (The history of Cernik and the chronicle of the monastery of Cernik). Cernik: Julije Jančula.

Jeffrey, Patricia, Roger Jeffrey, and Andrew Lyon. 1984. "Female infanticide and amniocentesis," *Social Science and Medicine* 19: 1207–1212.

1988. *Labour Pains and Labour Power*. London: Zed Books.

Joffe, Carole. 1986. *The Regulation of Sexuality*. Philadelphia: Temple University Press.

Johnson, Mark. 1987. *The Body in the Mind: The Bodily Basis of Meaning, Imagination, and Reason*. Chicago: University of Chicago Press.

Jović, Spiridon. 1962. (1835) "Etnografska slika slavonske vojne granice" (Ethnographic picture of the Slavonian military border.) *Zbornik Matice srpske za književnosti i jezik* 9–10: 114–65.

Karaman, Igor. 1981. "Problemi ekonomskog razvitka hrvatskih zemlja u doba oblikovanja gradjansko-kapitalističkog drußtva do prvog svjetskog rata" (Problems of the economic development of the Croatian lands in the period of formation of civil-capitalistic society until the first World War), in Mirjana Gross (ed.), *Društveni razvoj u Hrvatskoj* (Social development in Croatia). Zagreb: Liber, pp. 307–342.

Karanja, Wambui Wa. 1987. "'Outside wives' and 'inside wives' in Nigeria: A study of changing perceptions in marriage," in D. Parkin and D. Nyamawaya (eds.), *Transformations of African Marriage*. Manchester: Manchester University Press, pp. 247–261.

Karp, Ivan. 1978. *Fields of Change Among the Iteso of Kenya*. London: Routledge and Kegan Paul.

1986. "Agency and social theory: A review of Anthony Giddens," *American Ethnologist* 13, no. 1: 131–137.

Kelly, Raymond C. 1993. *Constructing Inequality: The Fabrication of a Hierarchy of Virtue among the Etoro*. Ann Arbor: University of Michigan Press.

Kertzer, David I. 1984. *Family Life in Central Italy, 1880–1910*. New Brunswick, NJ: Rutgers University Press.

1985. "Future directions in historical household studies," *Journal of Family History* 10: 98–107.

1989. "The joint family household revisited: Demographic constraints and household complexity in the European past," *Journal of Family History* 14: 1–15.

1991a. "Household history and sociological theory," *Annual Review of Sociology* 17: 155–179.

1991b. "Gender and infant abandonment in nineteenth-century Italy," *Journal of Interdisciplinary History* 21: 1–25.

1993. *Sacrificed for Honor: Italian Infant Abandonment and the Politics of Reproductive Control.* Boston: Beacon Press.

Kertzer, David and Dennis P. Hogan. 1988. "Family structure, individual lives, and social change," in M.W. Riley (ed.), *Social Structures and Human Lives.* Newbury Park, CA: Sage, pp. 83–100.

1989. *Family, Political Economy, and Demographic Change: The Transformation of Life in Casalecchio, Italy, 1861–1921.* Madison: University of Wisconsin Press.

1991. "Reflections on the European marriage pattern: Sharecropping and proletarianization in Casalecchio, Italy, 1861–1921," *Journal of Family History* 16: 31–46.

Keyfitz, Nathan. 1984. "Introduction: Biology and demography," in Nathan Keyfitz (ed.), *Population and Biology.* Liège: Ordina Editions, pp. 1–7.

Khera, Sigrid. 1981. "Illegitimacy and mode of land inheritance among Austrian peasants," *Ethnology* 20, no. 4: 307–323.

Kilbride, Philip and Janet Kilbride. 1990. *Changing Family Life in East Africa.* University Park: The Pennsylvania State University Press.

Knodel, John. 1983. "Natural fertility: Age patterns, levels, and trends," in R. A. Bulatao and R. D. Lee (eds.), *Determinants of Fertility in Developing Countries*, Vol. I. New York: Academic Press, pp. 61–102.

1986. "Demographic transitions in German villages," in A. J. Coale and S. C. Watkins (eds.), *The Decline of Fertility in Europe.* Princeton: Princeton University Press, pp. 337–389.

1988. *Demographic Behavior in the Past.* New York: Cambridge University Press.

Knodel, John and Etienne van de Walle. 1979. "Lessons from the past: Policy implications of historical fertility studies," *Population and Development Review* 5, no. 2: 217–245. Reprinted in A. J. Coale and S. C. Watkins (eds.) *The Decline of Fertility in Europe.* Princeton: Princeton University Press, 1986, pp. 390–419.

Knorr-Cetina, K. 1983. "The ethnographic study of scientific work," in K. Knorr-Cetina and M. Mulkay (eds.), *Science Observed.* London: Sage Publications.

Kochanowicz, Jacek. 1983. "The peasant family as an economic unit in the Polish feudal economy of the eighteenth century," in R. Wall, J. Robin, and P. Laslett (eds.), *Family Forms in Historic Europe.* Cambridge: Cambridge University Press, pp. 153–166.

Komlos, John. 1985. "Stature and nutrition in the Habsburg Monarchy: The standard of living and economic development in the eighteenth century," *American Historical Review* 90: 1149–1161.

1986. "Patterns of children's growth in East-central Europe in the eighteenth century," *Annals of Human Biology* 13:33–48.

Kornfeind, Eugen. 1907. "Bračni griješi propast naroda" (Sins of marriage, the ruin of the nation), *Katolički list zagrebački* LVIII (2): 15–19, (3): 28–30, (4): 40–42, (5): 52–54, (6): 64–67.

Kreager, Philip. 1982. "Demography in situ," *Population and Development Review* 8, no. 2: 237–266.

1986. "Demographic regimes as cultural systems," in D. Coleman and R.

Schofield (eds.), *The State of Population Theory: Forward From Malthus.* Oxford: Basil Blackwell, pp. 131–155.

1993. "Anthropological demography and the limits of diffusionism," in *International Population Conference of the International Union for the Scientific Study of Population, Montreal 1993*, Vol. 4. Liège: International Union for the Scientific Study of Population, pp. 313–326.

Krivošić, Stjepan. 1983. "Stanovništvo i demografske prilike u sjevero-zapadnoj Hrvatskoj u XVIII i u prvoj polovini XIX stoljeća" (Population and demographic conditions in northwestern Croatia in the 18th and in the first half of the 19th century). Doctoral dissertation, Faculty of Economics, University of Zagreb.

Kršnjavi, Dr. Isidor. 1882. *Listovi iz Slavonije* (Newspapers from Slavonia). Zagreb.

Lacombe, Bernard. 1983. "Le deuxième bureau: Secteur informel de la nuptialité en milieu urbain congolais." Paris: Stateco. 35.

Lamphere, Louise. 1989. "Historical and regional variability in Navajo women's roles," *Journal of Anthropological Research* 45 (Winter): 431–456.

Laslett, Peter. 1972. "Introduction: The history of the family," in P. Laslett and R. Wall (eds.), *Household and Family in Past Time.* Cambridge: Cambridge University Press, pp. 1–90.

1980a. "Introduction: Comparing illegitimacy over time and between cultures," in Peter Laslett, Karla Oosterveen, and Richard M. Smith (eds.), *Bastardy and its Comparative History.* London: Edward Arnold, pp. 1–65.

1980b. "The bastardy prone sub-society," in Peter Laslett, Karla Oosterveen, and Richard M. Smith (eds.), *Bastardy and its Comparative History.* London: Edward Arnold, pp. 217–240.

1983. "Family and household as work group and kin group: Areas of traditional Europe compared," in R. Wall, J. Robin, and P. Laslett (eds.), *Family Forms in Historic Europe.* Cambridge: Cambridge University Press, pp. 513–563.

Laslett, Peter, Karla Oosterveen, and Richard M. Smith (eds.). 1980. *Bastardy and its Comparative History.* London: Edward Arnold.

Launay, Robert. 1975. "Tying the cola: Dyula marriage and social change." Unpublished Ph.D dissertation. University of Cambridge.

1982. *Traders Without Trade: Responses to Change in Two Dyula Communities.* Cambridge: Cambridge University Press.

1988a. "Sabati-ba's Coup d'Etat: Contexts of legitimacy in a West African chiefdom," in Ronald Cohen and Judith Toland (eds.), *State Formation and Political Legitimacy.* Vol. VI, *Political Anthropology.* New Brunswick: Transactions Books, pp. 45–67.

1988b. "Warriors and traders: The political organization of a West African chiefdom," *Cahiers d'Etudes Africaines*, 28, 3–4: 355–373.

1992. *Beyond the Stream: Islam and Society in a West African Town.* Berkeley: University of California Press.

Lave, Jean. 1988. *Arithmetic Practices and Cognitive Theory: An Ethnographic Inquiry.* Cambridge: Cambridge University Press.

Le Play, Frédéric. 1877–79. *Les ouvriers européens*, 6 vols. Tours: A. Mame et fils.

Leach, Edmund R. 1961. *Rethinking Anthropology.* London: The Athlone Press.

Leacock, Eleanor (ed.). 1971. *The Culture of Poverty: A Critique*. New York: Simon and Schuster.

Lee, Nancy Howell. 1969. *The Search for an Abortionist*. Chicago: University of Chicago Press.

Lee, Ronald D., and R. A. Bulatao. 1983. "The demand for children: A critical essay," in R. A. Bulatao and R. D. Lee (eds.) *Determinants of Fertility in Developing Countries*, Vol. I, New York: Academic Press, pp. 233–287.

Lehning, James. 1988. "The timing and prevalence of women's marriage in the French department of the Loire, 1851–1891," *Journal of Family History* 13: 307–327.

Leibenstein, Harvey. 1974. "An interpretation of the economic theory of children: Promising path or blind alley?" *Journal of Economic Literature* 12: 457–479.

1975. "The economic theory of fertility decline," *Quarterly Journal of Economics* 89: 1–31.

1981. "Economic decision theory and human fertility behavior: A speculative essay," *Population and Development Review* 7, no. 3: 381–401.

Lengyel-Cook, M. S. and R. Repetto. 1982. "The relevance of the developing countries to demographic transition theory: Further lessons from the Hungarian experience," *Population Studies* 36:105–108.

Lesthaeghe, Ron J. 1980. "On the social control of human reproduction," *Population and Development Review* 6, no. 4: 527–548.

1983. "A century of demographic and cultural change in Western Europe: An exploration of underlying dimensions," *Population and Development Review* 9, no. 3: 411–436.

1989. "Production and reproduction in sub-Saharan Africa: An overview of organizing principles," in R. Lesthaeghe (ed.), *Reproduction and Social Organization in Sub-Saharan Africa*. Berkeley: University of California Press.

Lesthaeghe, Ron and Johan Surkyn. 1988. "Cultural dynamics and economic theories of fertility change," *Population and Development Review* 14, no. 1: 1–45.

Lesthaeghe, Ron and Chris Wilson. 1986. "Modes of production, secularization, and the pace of the fertility decline in Western Europe, 1870–1930," in Ansley J. Coale and Susan C. Watkins (eds.), *The Decline of Fertility in Europe*. Princeton: Princeton University Press, pp. 261–292.

Levi, Edward H. 1948. *An Introduction to Legal Reasoning*. Chicago: University of Chicago Press.

Levine, David. 1977. *Family Formation in an Age of Nascent Capitalism*. New York: Academic Press.

1986. "Review. Review symposium: The decline of fertility in Europe, Ansley J. Coale, and Susan Cotts Watkins (eds.)," *Population and Development Review* 12, no. 2: 335–340.

Levine, Nancy E. 1981. "The theory of rü kinship: Descent and status in a Tibetan society," in Christoph von Fürer-Haimendorf (ed.), *Asian Highland Societies in Anthropological Perspective*. New Delhi: Sterling Publishers, pp. 52–78.

1987. "Differential child care in three Tibetan communities: Beyond son preferences," *Population and Development Review* 13, no. 2: 281–304.

1988. *The Dynamics of Polyandry: Kinship, Domesticity, and Population on the Tibetan Border*. Chicago: University of Chicago Press.

LeVine, Robert. 1959. "Gusii sex offenses: A study in social control," *American Anthropologist* 61: 965–990.

LeVine, Robert and Susan C. M. Scrimshaw. 1983. "Effects of culture on fertility: Anthropological contributions," in R. A. Bulatao and R. D. Lee (eds.), *Determinants of Fertility in Developing Countries*, Vol. II, New York: Academic Press, pp. 666–695.

LeVine, Sarah and Robert LeVine. 1981. "Child abuse and neglect in sub-Saharan Africa," in Jill E. Korbin (ed.), *Child Abuse and Neglect: Cross-Cultural Perspectives*. Berkeley: University of California Press, pp. 35–55.

Lightcap, J. L., J. A. Kurland, and R. L. Burgess. 1982. "Child abuse: A test of some predictions from evolutionary theory," *Ethology and Sociobiology* 3: 61–67.

Lindert, Peter H. 1983. "The changing economic costs and benefits of having children," in R. A. Bulatao and R. D. Lee (eds.), *Determinants of Fertility in Developing Countries*, Vol. I, New York: Academic Press, pp. 494–516.

Livi-Bacci, Massimo. 1977. *A History of Italian Fertility During the Last Two Centuries*. Princeton: Princeton University Press.

Lloyd, Christopher. 1986. *Explanation in Social History*. London: Basil Blackwell.

Locoh, Thérèse. 1994. "Social change and marriage arrangements: New types of union in Lomé, Togo," in Caroline Bledsoe and Gilles Pison (eds.), *Nuptiality in Sub-Saharan Africa: Contemporary Anthropological and Demographic Perspectives*. Oxford: Clarendon Press, pp. 215–230.

Lorenzoni, Giovanni. 1910. *Inchiesta Parlamentare sulle Condizioni dei Contadini nelle Provincie Meridionali e nella Sicilia*, Vol. VI. Roma: Tipografia Nazionale di Giovanni Bertero.

Lorimer, Frank. 1954. *Culture and Human Fertility*. Paris: UNESCO.

Lovretić, Josip and Bartolj Jurić. 1897. *Otok: narodni život i običaji*. (Otok: national life and customs). Zbornik za narodni život i običaje u južnih slavena. Vol. II. Zagreb: Jugoslavenska Akademija Znanosti i Umjetnosti, pp. 91–459.

Luker, Kristen. 1975. *Taking Chances: Abortion and the Decision Not to Contracept*. Berkeley: University of California Press.

Lukić, Luka. 1921. *Varoš*. Zbornik za narodni život i običaje u južnih slavena (Anthology of national life and customs among the southern Slavs), 25: 105–176.

1926. *Varoš*. Zbornik za narodni život i običaje u južnih slavena (Anthology of national life and customs among the southern Slavs), 26: 102–138.

Lulek, Dr. Ante. 1914. Kako se narod liječi i kako živi (How the people cure and how they live), *Liječnički vjesnik* 36, 2: 67–68.

Lupo, Salvatore. 1981. *Blocco Agrario e Crisi in Sicilia tra le Due Guerre*. Napoli: Guida.

McBride, Theresa. 1976. *The Domestic Revolution: The Modernization of Household Service in England and France, 1820–1920*. New York: Holmes and Meier.

1978. "A woman's world: Department stores and the evolution of women's employment, 1870–1920," *French Historical Studies* 10: 664–683.

Macfarlane, Alan. 1976. *Resources and Population: A Study of the Gurungs of Nepal*. Cambridge: Cambridge University Press.

1979. *The Origins of English Individualism*. New York: Cambridge University Press.

1980. "Illegitimacy and illegitimates in English history," in P. Laslett, K. Oosterveen, and R. Smith (eds.), *Bastardy and its Comparative History*. London: Edward Arnold, pp. 71–85.

1986. *Marriage and Love in England, 1300–1840*. London: Basil Blackwell.

Mack Smith, Denis. 1968. *A History of Sicily: Modern Sicily After 1713*. London: Chatto and Windus.

Maclachlan, M. 1983. *Why They Did Not Starve: Biocultural Adaptation in a South Indian Village*. Philadelphia: Institute for the Study of Human Issues.

McLaren, Angus. 1978. "Abortion in France: Women and the regulation of family size, 1800–1914," *French Historical Studies* 10: 461–485.

1983. *Sexuality and the Social Order: The Debate over the Fertility of Women and Workers in France, 1770–1920*. New York: Holmes and Meier.

McNicoll, Geoffrey. 1975. "Community-level population policy: An exploration," *Population and Development Review* 1, no. 1: 1–21.

1980. "Institutional determinants of fertility change," *Population and Development Review* 6, no. 3: 441–462.

1984. "Notes on the local context of demographic change," in *Fertility and Family: Proceedings of the Expert Group on Fertility and Family, New Delhi*. New York: United Nations.

1992. "The agenda of population studies: A commentary and complaint," *Population and Development Review* 18, no. 3: 399–420.

1994. "Institutional analysis of fertility," in Kerstin Lindahl-Kiessling and Hans Landberg (eds.), *Population, Development, and the Environment*. Oxford: Oxford University Press.

McQuillan, Kevin. 1989. "Economic structure, religion, and age at marriage: Some evidence from Alsace," *Journal of Family History* 14: 331–346.

Malinowski, Bronislaw. 1987 [1929]. *The Sexual Life of Savages in North-Western Melanesia*. Boston: Beacon.

Mamdani, Mahmood. 1972. *The Myth of Population Control: Family, Caste, and Class in an Indian Village*. New York: Monthly Review Press.

Mann, Kristin. 1985. *Marrying Well: Marriage, Status and Social Change among the Educated Elite in Colonial Lagos*. Cambridge: Cambridge University Press.

March, Kathryn S. 1984. "Weaving, writing, and gender," *Man (N.S.)* 18, no. 4: 729–744.

Marshall, John F. and Steven Polgar (eds.). 1976. *Culture, Natality, and Family Planning*. Chapel Hill, NC: Carolina Population Center, University of North Carolina.

Marthe. A Woman and a Family: A Fin-de-siècle Correspondence. 1984. Trans. Donald Frame. New York: Harcourt Brace Jovanovich.

Martin, Emily. 1987. *The Woman in the Body: A Cultural Analysis of Reproduction*. Boston: Beacon.

1991. "The egg and the sperm: How science has constructed a romance based on stereotypical male–female roles," *Signs* 16, no. 3: 485–501.

Mason, Karen Oppenheim. 1984. *The Status of Women: A Review of its Relationships to Fertility and Mortality*. New York: Rockefeller.

1986. "The status of women: Conceptual and methodological issues in demographic studies," *Sociological Forum* 1, no. 2: 284–300.

1987. "The impact of women's social position on fertility in developing countries," *Sociological Forum* 2, no. 4: 718–745.

1992. "Culture and the fertility transition: Thoughts on theories of fertility decline," *Genus* 48, no. 3–4: 1–13.

Masulli, Ignazio. 1980. *Crisi e trasformazione: Strutture economiche, rapporti sociali e lotte politiche nel bolognese (1880–1914)*. Bologna: Istituto per la Storia di Bologna.

Matić, Tomo. 1970. "Slavonsko selo u djelima hrvatskih pisaca potkraj osamnaestoga vijeka" (The Slavonian village in the works of Croatian authors at the end of the 18th century). Iz hrvatske književne baštine. *Matica hrvatska*, pp. 293–375.

Mauss, Marcel. 1979 [1935]. "Body techniques," in *Sociology and Psychology: Essays by Marcel Mauss*, trans. Ben Brewster. London: Routledge and Kegan Paul.

Mažuran, Ive. 1988. *Popis naselja i stanovništva u Slavoniji 1698. godine*. (Census settlements and population in Slavonia in 1698.) Jugoslavenska Akademija Znanosti i Umjetnosti. Radovi Zavoda za Znanstveni Rad u Osijeku 2. Osijek.

Meekers, Dominique. 1994. "Consequences of marriage and premarital childbearing in Côte d'Ivoire," in Caroline Bledsoe and Gilles Pison (eds.), *Nuptiality in Sub-Saharan Africa: Contemporary Anthropological and Demographic Perspectives*. Oxford: Clarendon Press, pp. 296–312.

Messerschmidt, Donald. 1976. *The Gurungs of Nepal: Conflict and Change in a Village Society*. Warminster: Aris and Phillips.

Miller, Barbara D. 1981. *The Endangered Sex: Neglect of Female Children in Rural North India*. Ithaca, NY: Cornell University Press.

Ministry of Planning and National Development. 1989. *Kakamega District Development Plan 1989–1993*. Nairobi.

Mirkovič, S. 1903. "Sudbeno liječnička razudba novoredjenčeta zbog čedomorstva odnosno zbog zločina zlonamjernog prijevremenog porodjaja" (Medico-legal harm to a neonate namely on account of infanticide because of the crime of malevolent premature birth), *Liječnički viestnik* 25, 8:269–271.

Mitchison, Rosalind and Leah Leneman. 1989. *Sexuality & Social Control: Scotland 1660–1780*. Oxford: Blackwell.

Moačanin, Fedor. 1984. "Vojna krajina do kantonskog uredjenja 1787" (The military border until the canton system reform of 1787), in Dragutin Pavličević (ed.), *Vojna krajina* (The military border). Zagreb, pp. 23–56.

Moačanin, Fedor and Mirko Valentić. 1981. *Vojna krajina u Hrvatskoj* (The military border in Croatia). Zagreb.

Moch, Leslie Page. 1992. *Moving Europeans: Migration in Western Europe since 1650*. Bloomington, IN: Indiana University Press.

Moock, Joyce. 1976. "The migration process and differential economic behavior in South Maragoli, Western Kenya." Doctoral Dissertation: Columbia University.

Moodie, A. 1961. "Kwashiorkor in Cape Town: The background of patients and their progress after discharge," *Journal of Pediatrics* 58, no. 3: 392–403.

Moore, Henrietta L. 1988. *Feminism and Anthropology*. Minneapolis: University of Minnesota Press.

Mornet, Jacques. 1909. "La protection de la maternité en France." Thèse pour le doctorat en médecine, Faculté de Médecine de Paris. Paris: Rivière et Cie.

Mouillon, Marthe-Juliette. 1970. "Un exemple de migration rurale: De la Somme dans la capitale: Domestique de la Belle Epoque à Paris, 1904–1912," *Etudes de la région parisienne* 44: 1–9.

Mukhopadyay, Carol C. and Patricia J. Higgins. 1988. "Anthropological studies of women's status revisited, 1977–1987," *Annual Review of Anthropology* 17: 461–495.

Munn, Nancy D. 1992. "The cultural anthropology of time: A critical essay," *Annual Review of Anthropology* 21: 93–123.

Munroe, Robert, and Ruth Munroe. 1990. *Logoli Time Allocation. Cross-Cultural Studies in Time Allocation*, Vol. 5. New Haven: Human Relations Area Files.

Nag, Moni. 1962. *Factors Affecting Human Fertility in Nonindustrial Societies: A Cross-Cultural Study*. New Haven, CT: Human Relations Area Files Press.

1973. "Population anthropology: Problems and perspectives," in Morton H. Fried (ed.), *Explorations in Anthropology: Readings in Culture, Man, Nature*. New York: Thomas Y. Crowell, pp. 254–273.

ed. 1975. *Population and Social Organization*. The Hague: Mouton.

Nardi, Bonnie Anna. 1981. "Modes of explanation in anthropological population theory: Biological determinism vs. self-regulation in studies of population growth in third world countries," *American Anthropologist* 83, no. 1: 28–56.

National Council for Population and Development (NCPD). 1989. *Kenya Demographic and Health Survey*. Nairobi: Central Bureau of Statistics.

1993. *Kenya Demographic and Health Survey. Preliminary Report*. Nairobi: Central Bureau of Statistics.

National Research Council. 1993. *The Social Dynamics of Adolescent Fertility in Sub-Saharan Africa*. Working Group on the Social Dynamics of Adolescent Fertility in sub-Saharan Africa, Committee on Population. Washington: National Academy of Sciences Press.

Ndege, James Onyango. 1991. "Correlations and determinants of interspousal communication about family planning in Kenya: A case study of Sabatia Division, Kakamega District." M.A. Thesis, University of Nairobi.

Nelson, Nici. 1988. "Marital options in Mathare Valley (Nairobi)." Paper presented at the Seminar on Nuptiality in Sub-Saharan Africa: Current Changes and Impact on Fertility, Paris.

Nerlove, M. 1974. "Household and economy: Toward a new theory of population and economic growth," *Journal of Political Economy* 82: S200–S218.

Ness, Gayl D. and Hirofumi Ando. 1984. *The Land is Shrinking: Population Planning in Asia*. Baltimore: Johns Hopkins University Press.

Netting, Robert McC. 1981. *Balancing on an Alp: Ecological Change and Continuity in a Swiss Mountain Community*. New York: Cambridge University Press.

New York Times. 1991. "The evil men do to women in Kenya." Sunday, 4 August. Section 4, p. 4.

New York Times International. 1989. "Birth control making inroads in populous Kenya." Sunday, 10 September.

Ngin, Chor-Swang. 1985. "Indigenous fertility regulating methods among two Chinese communities in Malaysia," in Lucile F. Newman (ed.), *Women's*

Medicine: A Cross-Cultural Study of Indigenous Fertility Regulation. New Brunswick, NJ: Rutgers University Press, pp. 25–41.

Ngondo a Pitshandenge, Iman. 1994. "Les législations sur le mariage en Afrique au sud du Sahara," in Caroline Bledsoe and Gilles Pison (eds.), *Nuptiality in Sub-Saharan Africa: Contemporary Anthropological and Demographic Perspectives.* Oxford: Clarendon Press, pp. 117–129.

Nichols, Sandra. 1978. "The making of Maragoli," *Populi* 5, no. 1: 28–31.

Notestein, Frank W. 1945. "Population – The Long View," in Theodore Schultz (ed.), *Food for the World.* Chicago: University of Chicago Press, pp. 36–57.

O'Neill, Brian Juan. 1987. *Social Inequality in a Portuguese Hamlet.* Cambridge: Cambridge University Press.

Ohadike, P. 1977. "Socio-economic, cultural and behavioral factors in natural fertility variations," in H. Leridon and J. Menken (eds.), *Natural Fertility.* Liège: Ordina, pp. 285–313.

Olujić, Marija. 1991. "People on the move: the migration history of a Croatian peasant community." Unpublished doctoral dissertation. Department of Anthropology, University of California, Berkeley.

Omurundo, John Kwendo. 1989. "Infant/child mortality and fertility differentials in Western Province: A Divisional Level Analysis." MSc thesis, Population Studies and Research Institute, University of Nairobi.

Oppong, Christine. 1983. "Women's roles, opportunity costs, and fertility," in R. A. Bulatao and R. D. Lee (eds.), *Determinants of Fertility in Developing Countries,* Vol. I, New York: Academic Press, pp. 547–589.

Ortiz, S. 1973. *Uncertainties in Peasant Farming.* London: The Athlone Press.

Ortner, Sherry B. 1984. "Theory in anthropology since the sixties," *Comparative Studies in Society and History* 26, no. 1: 126–166.

1989. *High Religion: A Cultural and Political History of Sherpa Buddhism.* Princeton: Princeton University Press.

Oucho, John. 1988. "Spacial population changes in Kenya," in Simeon Ominde (ed.), *Kenya's Population Growth and Development to the Year 2000 AD.* Nairobi: Heinemann Kenya, pp. 131–139.

Page, Hilary. 1989. "Child-rearing versus child-bearing: Co-residence of mother and children in sub-Saharan Africa," in Ron Lesthaeghe (ed.), *African Reproduction and Social Organization.* Berkeley: University of California, pp. 401–441.

Parsons, Talcott (ed.). 1947. *Max Weber: The Theory of Social and Economic Organization.* Glencoe, IL: The Free Press.

Parsons, Talcott and Robert F. Bales. 1955. *Family, Socialization and Interaction Process.* New York: Free Press.

Pasternak, B. 1978. "Seasons of birth and marriage in two Chinese localities," *Human Ecology* 6: 299–323.

Pavičić, Stjepan. 1953. *Podrijetlo hrvatskih i srpskih naselja i govora u Slavoniji.* Djela, No. 47. Zagreb: Jugoslavenska akademija znanosti i umjetnosti.

Pavlinović, Mihovil. 1875. Od Posavine (From the Posavina). Kopanica. *Glasnik biskupije Djakovo-srijemske* 3, 21: 191–192.

Pelletier, Madeleine. 1913. *Le droit à l'avortement.* Paris: Editions du Malthusien.

Perrot, Michelle. 1979. "Femmes et espace parisien au XIX siècle. Brèves remarques sur une étude en course." Presented at the Colloquium on Women, Work and City Environment, Fondation Internationale des Sciences Humaines, Paris: 2–9.

1988. "Manières d'habiter," in Philippe Ariès, and Georges Duby (eds.), *Histoire de la vie privée*, Vol. 4. *De la Révolution à la Grande Guerre*. Paris: Seuil.

Petchesky, Rosalind Pollack. 1984. *Abortion and Woman's Choice: The State, Sexuality, and Reproductive Freedom*. Boston: Northeastern University Press.

Pirc, Bojan. 1931. *Opadanje stanovništva u Slavoniji. Socijalno-medicinska studija o prilikama radjanja i smrtnosti u pet slavonskih srezova* (The decline of population in Slavonia: Socio-medical study on the conditions of birth and death in 5 Slavonian counties). Biblioteka Centralnog Higijenskog Zavoda, 5. Beograd: Štamparija Centralnog Higijenskog Zavoda.

Plakans, Andrejs. 1983. "The familial contexts of early childhood in Baltic serf society," in R. Wall, J. Robin, and P. Laslett (eds.), *Family Forms in Historic Europe*. Cambridge: Cambridge University Press, pp. 167–206.

1984. "Serf emancipation and the changing structure of rural domestic groups in the Russian Baltic provinces: Linden Estate, 1797–1858," in R. M. Netting, R. Wilk, and E. Arnould (eds.), *Households: Comparative and Historical Studies of the Domestic Group*. Berkeley: University of California Press, pp. 245–275.

Polgar, Steven, ed. 1971. *Culture and Population: A Collection of Current Studies*. Cambridge: Schenkman.

1972. "Population history and population policies from an anthropological perspective," *Current Anthropology* 13, no. 2: 203–211.

(ed). 1975. *Population, Ecology, and Social Evolution*. The Hague: Mouton.

Potter, Joseph E. 1983. "Effects of societal and community institutions on fertility," in R. A Bulatao and R. D. Lee (eds.), *Determinants of Fertility in Developing Countries*, Vol. II. New York: Academic Press, pp. 627–665.

Prakash, Gyan. 1990. "Writing post-orientalist histories of the third world: Perspectives from Indian historiography," *Comparative Studies in Society and History* 32, no. 2: 383–408.

Pretorius, P. J., J. A. G. Davel, and H. N. Coetzee. 1956. "Some observations on the development of kwashiorkor: A study of 205 cases," *South African Medical Journal* 30, no. 17: 396–399.

Pribram, A.F. 1938. *Materialen zur Geschichte der Preise und Löhne in Oesterreich*. Vol. 1. Wien: Ueberreuters.

Radcliffe-Brown, A. R. 1950. "Introduction," in A.R. Radcliffe-Brown and D. Forde (eds.), *African Systems of Kinship and Marriage*. London: Oxford University Press, pp. 1–85.

Raheja, Gloria. 1988. *The Poison in the Gift*. Chicago: University of Chicago Press.

Rapp, Rayna. 1990. "Constructing amniocentesis: Maternal and medical discourses," in F. Ginsburg and A. L. Tsing (eds.), *Uncertain Terms: Negotiating Gender in American Culture*. Boston: Beacon, pp. 28–42.

1991. "Moral pioneers: Women, men, and fetuses on a frontier of reproductive technology," in Micaela di Leonardo (ed.), *Gender at the Crossroads of*

Knowledge: Feminist Anthropology in the Postmodern Era. Berkeley: University of California Press, pp. 383–395.

1993. "Reproduction and gender hierarchy: Amniocentesis in America," in Barbara Diane Miller (ed.), *Sex and Gender Hierarchies.* Cambridge: Cambridge University Press, pp. 108–126.

Reddy, William. 1984. *Rise of Market Culture: The Textile Trade and French Society, 1750-1900.* New York: Cambridge University Press.

Regmi, Mahesh C. 1971. *A Study in Nepali Economic History, 1768–1846.* New Delhi: Mañjuśrī Publishing House.

1978. *Thatched Huts and Stucco Palaces: Peasants and Landlords in Nineteenth Century Nepal.* New Delhi: Vikas Publishing House.

1986. "Copper and iron mining ijaras, A.D. 1901–02," *Regmi Research Series* 18, no. 11: 172.

1989. "Sulphur mining in Jharlang Khola," *Regmi Research Series* 21, no. 5: 63.

Reher, David Sven. 1988. "Household and family on the Castilian Meseta: The province of Cuenca from 1750 to 1970," *Journal of Family History* 13: 59–74.

Reljković, Matija Antun. 1973. *Satir, ili divji čovik.* (Satyr, or the wild man). Zagreb: Zbornik stihova i proze XVIII stoljéa. Zagreb: Matica hrvatska.

Renda, Francesco. 1977. *I Fasci Siciliani, 1892–94.* Torino: G. Einaudi.

1979. *Movimenti di Massa e Democrazia nella Sicilia del Dopoguerra.* Bari: De Donato.

Renne, Elisha P. 1993. "History in the making: An anthropological approach to the demographic analysis of child fosterage in southwestern Nigeria," in *International Population Conference, Montreal 1993,* Vol. 4. Liège: International Union for the Scientific Study of Population, pp. 327–342.

Retherford, Robert D. and James A. Palmore. 1983. "Diffusion processes affecting fertility regulation," in R. A. Bulatao and R. D. Lee, (eds.), *Determinants of Fertility in Developing Countries,* Vol. II, New York: Academic Press, pp. 761–796.

Richards, Audrey I. 1932. *Hunger and Work in a Savage Tribe: A Functional Study of Nutrition among the Southern Bantu.* London: Routledge & Sons.

Riley, Nancy. 1993. "Challenging demography: Contributions from feminist theory." Unpublished manuscript.

Robertson, A. F. 1991. *Beyond the Family: The Social Organization of Human Reproduction.* Berkeley: University of California Press.

Rochefort, Renée. 1961. *Le travail en Sicile; étude de gèographie sociale.* Paris: Presses Universitaires de France.

Rogers, Susan Carol. 1991. *Shaping Modern Times in Rural France.* Princeton: Princeton University Press.

Rollet, Henri. 1958. *L'Action sociale des catholiques en France 1871–1914.* 2 vols. Paris and Bruges: Desclée de Brouwer.

Rollet-Echalier, Catherine. 1991. *La politique à l'égard de la petite enfance sous la IIIe République.* Paris: INED.

Rosaldo, Renato. 1989. *Culture and Truth: The Remaking of Social Analysis.* Boston: Beacon.

Roseberry, William. 1988. "Political economy," *Annual Review of Anthropology* 17: 161–185.

1989. *Anthropologies and Histories: Essays in Culture, History, and Political Economy*. New Brunswick: Rutgers University Press.

Roseberry, William and Jay O'Brien. 1991. "Introduction," in Jay O'Brien and William Roseberry (eds.), *Golden Ages, Dark Ages: Imagining the Past in Anthropology and History*. Berkeley: University of California Press, pp. 1–18.

Ross, Ellen. 1983. "Survival networks: Women's neighbourhood sharing in London before W.W.I," *History Workshop* 15 (Spring): 5–19.

Ross, Eric. 1986. "Potatoes, population, and the Irish famine: The political economy of demographic change," in W. Penn Handwerker (ed.), *Culture and Reproduction: An Anthropological Critique of Demographic Transition Theory*. Boulder, Westview, pp. 196–220.

Rothenberg, Gunther Erich. 1960. *The Austrian Military Border in Croatia, 1522–1747*. Illinois Studies in the Social Sciences, Vol. 48. Urbana: University of Illinois Press.

1966. *The Austrian Military Border in Croatia, 1740–1881*. Chicago: University of Chicago Press.

Ruggles, Steven. 1987. *Prolonged Connections: The Rise of the Extended Family in Nineteenth-century England and America*. Madison: University of Wisconsin Press.

Sachs, S. B. 1953. *South African Medical Journal* 27, no. 20: 430–432.

Safilios-Rothschild, Constantina. 1980. "A class and sex stratification theoretical model and its relevance for fertility trends in the developing world," in C. Holn and R. Machensen (eds.), *Determinants of Fertility Trends*. Liège: Ordina Editions, pp. 189–202.

1982. "Female power, autonomy and demographic change in the Third World," in Richard Anker, Mayra Buvinic, and Nadia Youssef (eds.), *Women's Roles and Population Trends in the Third World*. London: Croom Helm, pp. 117–132.

Sahlins, M. 1976. *Culture and Practical Reason*. Chicago: University of Chicago Press.

Said, Edward W. 1978. *Orientalism*. New York: Random House.

Sanday, Peggy. 1981. *Female Power and Male Dominance*. Cambridge: Cambridge University Press.

Santow, Gigi. 1993. "Coitus interruptus in the twentieth century," *Population and Development Review* 19, no. 4: 767–793.

Saunders, George R. 1981. "Men and women in southern Europe: A review of some aspects of cultural complexity," *Journal of Psychoanalytic Anthropology* 4: 435–466.

Schacht, Robert M. 1981. "Estimating past population trends," *Annual Review of Anthropology* 10: 119–140.

Schelling, T. 1963. *The Strategy of Conflict*. New York: Oxford University Press.

Scheper-Hughes, Nancy. 1985. "Culture, scarcity, and maternal thinking: Maternal detachment and infant survival in a Brazilian shantytown," *Ethos* 13: 291–319.

1987. "Introduction," in N. Scheper-Hughes (ed.), *Child Survival: Anthropological Perspectives on the Treatment and Maltreatment of Children*. Dordrecht: D. Reidel, pp. 1–29.

Schneider, Jane. 1980. "Trousseau as treasure: Some contradictions of late nineteenth century change in Sicily," in Eric Ross (ed.), *Behind the Myth of*

Culture. New York: Academic Press, pp. 323–356.

Schneider, Jane and Peter Schneider. 1976. *Culture and Political Economy in Western Sicily*. New York: Academic Press.

———. 1984. "Demographic transitions in a Sicilian rural town," *Journal of Family History* 9, no. 3: 245–273.

———. 1992. "Going forward in reverse gear: Culture, economy, and political economy in the demographic transition of a rural Sicilian town," in J. Gillis, L. Tilly, and D. Levine (eds.), *The European Experience of Declining Fertility, 1850–1970: The Quiet Revolution*. Cambridge: Blackwell, pp. 146–174.

———. In press. *Other People's Children: Fertility Decline and the Ideology of Class in Sicily*. Tucson: University of Arizona Press.

Schultz T. Paul. 1983. "Review of John C. Caldwell, *Theory of Fertility Decline*," *Population and Development Review* 9, no. 1: 161–168.

Scott, Joan W. 1986. "Gender: A useful category of historical analysis," *American Historical Review* 91, no. 5: 1053–1075.

———. 1988a. *Gender and the Politics of History*. New York: Columbia University Press.

———. 1988b. "Work identities for men and women: The politics of work and family in the Parisian garment trades in 1848," in J. W. Scott, *Gender and the Politics of History*. New York: Columbia University Press, pp. 93–112.

Scragg, J. and C. Rubidge. 1960. "Kwashiorkor in African children in Durban," *British Medical Journal* 17 December: 1759–1766.

Scrimshaw, Susan. 1978. "Infant mortality and behavior in the regulation of family size," *Population and Development Review* 4, no. 3: 383–403.

———. 1983. "Infanticide as deliberate fertility control," in R. A. Bulatao and R. D. Lee (eds.), *Determinants of Fertility in Developing Countries*, Vol. II. New York: Academic Press, pp. 245–266.

Scrofani, Serafino. 1962. *Sicilia: Utilizzazione del Suolo nella Storia, nei Redditi, e nelle Prospettive*. Palermo: Editori Stampatori Associati.

Seccombe, Wally. 1993. *Weathering the Storm: Working-Class Families from the Industrial Revolution to the Fertility Decline*. London: Verso.

Sella, Domenico. 1987. "Household, land tenure, and occupation in northern Italy in the late 16th century," *Journal of European Economic History* 16: 487–509.

Sen, Amartya. 1981. *Poverty and Famines: An Essay on Entitlement and Deprivation*. London: Oxford University Press.

Sereni, Emilio. 1968. *Il capitalismo nelle campagne (1860–1900)*. Turin: Einaudi.

Sewell, William H. 1985. *Structure and Mobility: The Men and Women of Marseille, 1820–1870*. Cambridge: Cambridge University Press.

Shaffer, John. 1982. *Family and Farm: Agrarian Change and Household Organization in the Loire Valley, 1500–1900*. Albany: State University of New York Press.

Sharlin, Allan N. 1986. "Urban-rural differences in fertility in Europe during the demographic transition," in A. J. Coale and S. C. Watkins (eds.), *The Decline of Fertility in Europe*. Princeton: Princeton University Press, pp. 234–260.

Shorter, Edward. 1975. *The Making of the Modern Family*. New York: Basic Books.

Simmons, Ozzie G. 1988. *Perspectives on Development and Population Growth in the Third World*. New York: Plenum Press.

Simon, Herbert. 1958. "The role of expectation in an adaptive or behavioristic model," in M. J. Bowman (ed.), *Expectations, Uncertainty and Business Behavior*. New York: Social Science Research Council.

1976. *Administrative Behavior*. Third Edition. New York: The Free Press.

Simon, Jules. 1861. *L'Ouvrière*. Paris: Hachette.

Simonelli, Jeanne M. 1986. *Two Boys, a Girl, and Enough: Reproductive and Economic Decision-making on the Mexican Periphery*. Boulder: Westview Press.

Sklar, Kathryn Kish. 1990. "A call for comparisons," *American Historical Review* 95: 1109–1114.

Smith, Bonnie. 1985. *Confessions of a Concierge: Madame Lucie's History of Twentieth-Century France*. New Haven, CT: Yale University Press.

Smith, Herbert L. 1989. "Integrating theory and research on the institutional determinants of fertility," *Demography* 26, no. 2: 171–184.

Smith, Michael G. 1962. *West Indian Family Structure*. Seattle: University of Washington Press.

Smith, Peter C. (Xenos). 1983. "The impact of age at marriage and proportions marrying on fertility," in R. A. Bulatao and R. D. Lee (eds.), *Determinants of Fertility in Developing Countries*, Vol. II. New York: Academic Press, pp. 473–531.

Smith, Raymond T. 1956. *The Negro Family in British Guiana*. London: Routledge and Kegan Paul.

1988. *Kinship and Class in the West Indies*. Cambridge: Cambridge University Press.

Smith, Richard M. 1981. "Fertility, economy, and household formation in England over three centuries," *Population and Development Review* 7, no. 4: 595–622.

Smith, Thomas C. 1977. *Nakahara: Family Farming and Population in a Japanese Village, 1717–1830*. Stanford: Stanford University Press.

So, Alvin Y. 1990. *Social Change and Development: Modernization, Dependency, and World-System Theories*. Newbury Park: Sage.

Somogyi, Stefano. 1974. "La Dinamica Demografica delle Provincie Siciliane, 1861–1971," *Collani di Studi Demografici*, Vol. 5. University of Palermo: Istituto di Scienze Demografiche.

Sremec, Nada. 1940. *Nismo mi krive (Slavonska žena)* (We are not guilty [the Slavonian woman]). Kako živi narod, III knjiga. Zagreb: Gospodarska Sloga.

Ssennyonga, Joseph. 1978. "Population growth and cultural inventory: The Maragoli case." Doctoral dissertation, University of Sussex.

Stacey, Judith and Barrie Thorne. 1985. "The missing feminist revolution in sociology," *Social Problems* 32, no. 4: 301–316.

Stack, Carol B. 1974. *All our Kin: Strategies for Survival in a Black Community*. New York: Harper and Row.

Stannard, D.E. 1977. "Death and the Puritan child," in A. T. Vaughan and R. J. Bremer (eds.), *Puritan New England: Essays on Religion, Society, and Culture*. New York: St. Martin's Press, pp. 232–249.

Standard. 1992. "49,000 to miss university places." 16 July, pp. 1–2.

Stewart, Mary Lynn. 1989. *Women, Work, and the French State: Labour Protection and Social Patriarchy, 1879–1919*. Montreal: McGill–Queens University Press.

Stojanović, Mijat. 1852. *Odgovor na pitanja* (Answer to questions). Arhiv za povestnicu jugoslavensku II: 344–403. Zagreb: Jugoslavenska Akademija Znanosti i Umjetnosti.

Stone, L. 1977. *The Family, Sex and Marriage in England, 1500–1800*. New York: Harper & Row.

Swedlund, Alan C. 1978. "Historical demography as population ecology," *Annual Review of Anthropology* 7: 1137–1173.

Taylor, Charles. 1985. "What is human agency?" in *Human Agency and Language*. Cambridge: Cambridge University Press.

Thadani, Veena N. 1978. "The logic of sentiment: The family and social change," *Population and Development Review* 4, no. 3: 457–499.

Thomas, G. C. 1981. "The social background of childhood nutrition in the Ciskei," *Social Science and Medicine* 15A, no. 5: 551–555.

Thompson, E.P. 1963. *The Making of the English Working Class*. New York: Pantheon.

——— 1978. *The Poverty of Theory and Other Essays*. New York: Monthly Review Press.

Thornton, Arland and Hui-Sheng Lin. 1994. *Social Change and the Family in Taiwan*. Chicago: University of Chicago Press.

Tilly, Charles. 1986. "Review. Review symposium: *The decline of fertility in Europe*, Ansley J. Coale and Susan Cotts Watkins (eds.)," *Population and Development Review* 12, no. 2: 323–328.

Tilly, Louise. 1983. "Food entitlement, famine, and conflict," in Robert I. Rotberg and Theodore K. Rabb (eds.), *Hunger and History: The Impact of Changing Food Production and Consumption Patterns on Society*. Cambridge: Cambridge University Press, pp. 135–151.

Todd, Alexandra Dundas. 1989. *Intimate Adversaries: Cultural Conflict Between Doctors and Women Patients*. Philadelphia: University of Pennsylvania Press.

Tomasevich, Jozo. 1955. *Peasants, Politics and Economic Change in Yugoslavia*. Stanford: Stanford University Press.

Triolo, Nancy. 1989. "The angel-makers: Fascist pro-natalism and the normalization of midwives in Sicily," Ph.D dissertation, Department of Anthropology, University of California, Berkeley.

Turner, B. 1984. *The Body and Society*. Oxford: Blackwell.

Valentić, Mirko. 1981. *Vojna krajina i pitanje njezina sjedinjenja s Hrvatskom 1849–1881*. (The military border and the question of its unification with Croatia 1849–1881.) Zagreb.

——— 1984. "Hrvatsko-slavonska vojna krajina 1790–1881" (The Croato-Slavonian military border 1790–1881), in Dragutin Pavličević (ed.), *Vojna krajina* (The military border). Zagreb, pp. 57–94.

Valjevec, I. 1901. "Čedomorstvo ugušenjem ili izloženjem zimi?" (Infanticide by smothering or exposure in winter?) *Liječnički viestnik* 23, 7: 263–266.

van de Walle, Etienne. 1992. "Fertility transition, conscious choice, and numeracy," *Demography* 29, no. 4: 487–502.

——— 1993. "Recent trends in marriage ages," in Karen A. Foote, Kenneth H. Hill, and Linda G. Martin (eds.), *Population Dynamics of Sub-Saharan Africa: Overview Report*. Panel on Population Dynamics of Sub-Saharan Africa, Committee on Population, National Research Council. Washington, DC: National Academy Press.

van de Walle, Etienne and Andrew Foster. 1990. *Fertility Decline in Africa:*

Assessments and Prospects. World Bank Technical Paper Number 125. African Technical Department Series. Washington DC: The World Bank.

van de Walle, Etienne and John Knodel. 1980. "Europe's fertility transition: New evidence and lessons for today's developing world," *Population Bulletin* 34: 6. Washington, DC: Population Reference Bureau.

van de Walle and Dominique Meekers. 1994. "Marriage drinks and kola nuts," in Caroline Bledsoe and Gilles Pison (eds.), *Nuptiality in Sub-Saharan Africa: Contemporary Anthropological and Demographic Perspectives.* Oxford: Clarendon Press, pp. 57–73.

Vassary, Ildiko. 1989. "The sin of Transdanubia," *Continuity and Change* 4: 429–468.

Vološinov, V. N. 1986 [1973]. *Marxism and the Philosophy of Language,* trans. Ladislav Matejka and I. R. Titunik. Cambridge, MA: Harvard University Press.

Wachter, Kenneth W., Eugene A. Hammel, and Peter Laslett. 1978. *Statistical Studies of Historical Social Structure.* New York: Academic Press.

Wagner, Gunter. 1949. *The Bantu of Western Kenya, with special reference to the Vugusu and Logoli,* Vol. I. London: Oxford University Press.

1956. *The Bantu of Western Kenya. Economic Life,* Vol. II. London: Oxford University Press.

Wall, Richard. 1983. "Introduction," in R. Wall, J. Robin, and P. Laslett (eds.), *Family Forms in Historic Europe.* Cambridge: Cambridge University Press, pp. 1–63.

Wamalma, Elizabeth Nafuna. 1989. "Violence against wives in Kenya," in Mary Adhiambo Mbeo and Oki Ooko-Ombaka (eds.), *Women and the Law in Kenya.* Nairobi: Public Law Institute, pp. 71–78.

Warwick, Donald P. 1982. *Population Policies and Their Implementation in Eight Developing Countries.* New York: Cambridge University Press.

1986. "The Indonesian family planning program: Government influence and client choice," *Population and Development Review* 12, no. 3: 453–490.

Watkins, Susan Cotts. 1986. "Conclusions," in A. J. Coale and S. C. Watkins (eds.), *The Decline of Fertility in Europe.* Princeton: Princeton University Press, pp. 420–449.

1987. "The fertility transition: Europe and the third world compared," *Sociological Forum* 2, no. 4: 645–673.

1990. "From local to national communities: The transformation of demographic regimes in western Europe, 1870–1960," *Population and Development Review* 16: 241–272.

1991. *From Provinces into Nations: Demographic Integration in Western Europe, 1870–1960.* Princeton: Princeton University Press.

1993. "If all we knew about women was what we read in *Demography,* what would we know?" *Demography* 30, no. 4: 551–577.

Weekly Review (Kenya). 1991. "The Meru Tragedy." July 19, pp. 5–12.

Wellman, Barry and Scot Wortley. 1990. "Different strokes from different folks: Community ties and social support," *American Journal of Sociology* 96: 558–588.

Were, Gideon. 1967. *A History of The Abaluyia of Western Kenya.* Nairobi.

Wertsch, James. 1991. *Voices of the Mind: A Sociocultural Approach to Mediated Action.* Cambridge, MA: Harvard University Press.

White, Benjamin. 1973. "Demand for labor and population growth in colonial Java," *Human Ecology* 1: 217–236.

1982. "Demand for labor and population growth in Rural Asia," *Development and Change* 13: 587–610.

White, Luise. 1990. *The Comforts of Home*. Chicago: University of Chicago Press.

Whyte, Martin King. 1978. *The Status of Women in Preindustrial Societies*. Princeton: Princeton University Press.

Williams, Cicely. 1933. "A nutritional disease of childhood associated with a maize diet," *Archives of the Diseases of Childhood* 8: 423–433.

Wilson, M., M. Daly, and S. Weghorst. 1980. "Household composition and the risk of child abuse and neglect," *Journal of Biosocial Science* 12: 333–340.

Wolf, Eric R. 1982. *Europe and the People Without History*. Berkeley: University of California Press.

Wood, James W. 1990. "Fertility in anthropological populations," *Annual Review of Anthropology* 19: 211–242.

1994. *Dynamics of Human Reproduction: Biology, Biometry, Demography*. Hawthorne, NY: Aldine de Gruyter.

World Bank. 1984. *Population Change and Economic Development*. New York: Oxford University Press.

Wrigley, E. 1978. "Fertility strategy for the individual and the group," in Charles Tilly (ed.), *Historical Studies of Changing Fertility*. Princeton: Princeton University Press, pp. 135–154.

Wrigley, E. and Roger Schofield. 1981. *The Population History of England 1541–1871*. Cambridge: Harvard University Press.

Wyon, John E. and John B. Gordon. 1971. *The Khanna Study: Population Problems in the Rural Punjab*. Cambridge, MA: Harvard University Press.

Zola, Emile. 1979 [1872–73]. *Le Ventre de Paris*. Paris: Gallimard/Folio.

Zurick, David N. 1989. "Historical links between settlement, ecology, and politics in the mountains of West Nepal," *Human Ecology* 17, no. 2: 229–255.

Index